Media, Crime, and Criminal Justice

Media, Crime, and Criminal Justice

Images, Realities, and Policies

FIFTH EDITION

RAY SURETTE
University of Central Florida

Australia • Brazil • Mexico • Singapore • United Kingdom • United States

CENGAGE
Learning®

Media, Crime, and Criminal Justice: Images, Realities, and Policies, Fifth Edition

Ray Surette

Product Director: Marta Lee-Perriard

Product Manager: Carolyn Henderson Meier

Content Developer: Wendy Langerud

Product Assistant: Catherine Ryan

Media Developer: Ting Jian Yap

Marketing Manager: Michelle Williams

Art and Cover Direction, Production Management, and Composition: Integra Software Services, Pvt. Ltd.

Manufacturing Planner: Judy Inouye

Photo and Text Researcher: PreMediaGlobal

Cover Image Credit: George Doyle/Stockbyte/Getty Images

For product information and technology assistance, contact us at **Cengage Learning Customer & Sales Support, 1-800-354-9706**.
For permission to use material from this text or product, submit all requests online at **www.cengage.com/permissions**.
Further permissions questions can be e-mailed to **permissionrequest@cengage.com**.

Library of Congress Control Number: 2013958177

ISBN-13: 978-1-285-45905-9
ISBN-10: 1-285-45905-9

Cengage Learning
200 First Stamford Place, 4th Floor
Stamford, CT 06902
USA

Cengage Learning is a leading provider of customized learning solutions with office locations around the globe, including Singapore, the United Kingdom, Australia, Mexico, Brazil, and Japan. Locate your local office at: **www.cengage.com/global**.

Cengage Learning products are represented in Canada by Nelson Education, Ltd.

To learn more about Cengage Learning Solutions, visit **www.cengage.com**.
Purchase any of our products at your local college store or at our preferred online store Purchase any of our products at your local college store or at our preferred online store **www.cengagebrain.com**.

To my wife Susan and my children Jennifer, Paul, and Tim

About the Author

Ray Surette has a doctorate in criminology from Florida State University and is a Professor of Criminal Justice at the University of Central Florida. His crime and media research interests revolve around the media's effects on perceptions of crime and justice, criminogenic media, and criminal justice policies. He has published numerous articles and books on media, crime, and criminal justice topics and is internationally recognized as a scholar in the area. He has published research on the development of public information officers in criminal justice agencies, crime and justice infotainment programming, copycat crime, the effects of news coverage of celebrity trials on similarly charged non-publicized trials and on police recruits, the effects of news coverage of corrections on municipal jail population trends, media oriented terrorism, and the use of computer-aided camera surveillance systems in law enforcement. He is currently working on a book on copycat crime as well as studying the use of camera surveillance systems by law enforcement in neighborhoods and other public areas and the relationship between media and criminal justice policy support.

Brief Contents

Contents

Foreword

Everyone who studies crime and justice shares a sense of frustration about the way media depictions dominate the common viewpoint on crime and criminal justice, often in ways that distort reality. The television show *CSI*, for example, is great entertainment but hardly fits the way 99 percent of crimes are solved. So-called real police stories follow some officers as they go about their duties, but even though the film is real, the portrait of police work that results is distorted by the focus on chase scenes and angry encounters. *Judge Judy* bears little resemblance to actual judges in demeanor or behavior. Law and order SVU always presents cases with some sort of twist, but such cases are the exception rather than the rule. The nightly news covers crime with an eye to generating high ratings, not great insight. American culture has an affinity for crime as a source of stimulation and even entertainment, but the result is that what we think we know about crime and justice from the way our media portray it often corresponds poorly to the everyday reality of crime and justice.

For those who are professionals in the business of criminal justice—those who wish to reform or improve justice practices and crime prevention effectiveness— the media portrayals are often an impediment. It is not so much that the media get it wrong as that they focus on aspects of crime and justice that are, in the scheme of things, not so important. Of course we all want to apprehend serial killers and stop predatory sex offenders, but they are uncommon in the life of the justice system. The more pressing themes of improving the effectiveness of treatment programs, youth prevention systems, crime control strategies, and so forth can get lost in the way the media focus on images of crime that are much more engrossing to the everyday citizen.

It is, therefore, with extraordinary pleasure that I welcome the fifth edition of Ray Surette's *Media, Crime, and Criminal Justice* to the Wadsworth Contemporary Issues in Crime and Justice Series. Created to provide detailed and effective exposure of important or emerging issues and problems that ordinarily receive insufficient attention in traditional textbooks, the series also provokes thought and changes perceptions by challenging us to become more sophisticated consumers of crime-and-justice knowledge. Its titles seek to expose myths about crime and justice, deepen understandings of the nature of crime and the processes of justice, and inspire new perspectives on these topics.

If you seek a book that will make you an informed student of crime-and-justice policy and practice, you could not do better than the one you are now holding. Professor Surette is an astute student of popular culture, the social power of symbols, and the effect of media on public imagination. In this book, he provides a detailed examination of the ways that media coverage affects our popular understanding of justice. The results are sometimes subtle and sometimes blatant. For example, the way the nightly news covers crime creates a subtle bias on the part of the public that our cities are dangerous and that the justice system is incapable of protecting innocents. By contrast, the way punishment is covered creates a much less subtle bias that our system of justice is lenient. Both of these biases are partly right, but mostly wrong. And the reality—much more complex than the public perception—is often not widely understood.

Surette writes about every aspect of crime and justice. The book opens with a thorough and authoritative description of the way our "realities" about crime and justice are constructed from social sources of knowledge. It is this fact that makes the media portrayal of crime and justice so important, because media are among the most powerful sources of social information. The book then considers in turn the three main agencies of criminal justice: the police, the courts, and corrections, with a chapter devoted to each topic. The final chapters consider the broader problem of crime prevention and criminal justice policy in the context of a media-dominated social construction of crime.

In the end, this is a book that helps us to rethink crime by offering a critical perspective on how we go about understanding it. Crime is not popular culture, and criminal justice is not entertainment. On the contrary, crime is a crucial social problem rooted in related social problems such as inequality and poverty. Criminal justice is a key function of the state that is less powerful with regard to our safety than we might like but more important to our everyday rights than we would ordinarily think.

This is an important book, a book that carves out new areas for thinking and challenges the popular mind-set about crime and justice. I commend it to you.

Todd R. Clear
Series Editor

Preface

The fifth edition of *Media, Crime, and Criminal Justice* is designed for undergraduate criminal justice students. It is my belief that to understand contemporary crime and justice, students have to understand the role the media play in the life of criminal justice issues and policies. Living in a culture where crime and justice media content is pervasive, students are attracted to a course that helps them understand the media content they are immersed in. Having lived the subject, they bring enthusiasm and interest to its study. This revised fifth edition taps into that enthusiasm and employs an expanded number of recent examples to connect the book's coverage to the students' lives. In doing so, this book helps students to become critical media consumers and insightful observers of the ongoing relationship between media, crime, and justice. After finishing this book, students who previously had not considered the linkages between media, crime, and justice will be unable to sit through a crime show, podcast, or posted video without a thoughtful reaction and recognition of the underlying processes that generate the crime and justice media they receive and the criminal justice policies they experience.

The knowledge covered in this text is drawn from criminal justice, criminology, sociology, political science, law, public administration, journalism, medicine, psychology, and communication research. Sources include traditional academic and professional journals as well as numerous popular culture media including magazines, newspapers, music, video games, films, and Internet sites wherever there is a special focus on social media, crime, and justice. As an undergraduate introductory text, the fifth edition serves as an entrée to the research questions and social concerns without the weight of extensive graduate level coverage of statistics and research designs. The book discusses the vast and disparate research but does not go into methodological, measurement, or statistical issues in great depth. Instead, the discussions provide basic understandings of the theoretical ideas and concepts that frame the research, the major findings that have been generally accepted by researchers in the field, the issues that are still under debate, and the questions that remain unaddressed.

Massively covered criminal trials, advances in media technology, new types of media content, and new ways of delivering the content are especially important in the construction of crime-and-justice reality and continually increase the impact of media on crime and justice. Historically, most people interacted with the media as passive consumers. They were conditioned to receive knowledge from the media without considering where this information comes from, what effect it had on their attitudes and perceptions, or how it affected society. Today people are encouraged to be active participants in the creation of crime-and-justice media content but they remain unaware of the relationship of their content to social attitudes, behaviors, and policies. This book therefore encourages readers to ask questions about the media, such as why certain images of crime are linked together, why some crimes will be sensationalized and others given scant attention, and why some explanations of crime and some criminal justice policies are forwarded over others.

The fifth edition is offered as a main text in a media, crime, and justice course and as a supplementary work in courses where the instructor wishes to feature connections between media, crime, and justice. It is a particularly useful supplementary text for "introduction to criminal justice," "introduction to law enforcement," "criminal justice policy," "victimization," and "crime prevention" courses. The text can be enjoyed by students with and without substantial backgrounds in communications, journalism, criminal justice, law, and the additional disciplines that make up this inherently interdisciplinary subject.

ORGANIZATION

Newly organized into eleven chapters, the book follows the content and influence of the media from the committing of crime through the sequential components of the criminal justice system as typically covered in undergraduate criminal justice courses. Within this organization, the connection between media and criminal justice policy and the impact of new media are running themes. The book makes the point that pervasive media images of predatory criminals work as steering currents on our criminal justice policy. Each chapter includes discussions of how media renditions affect a particular area of criminal justice policy. Recognition of this policy linkage is vital because the media determine in important ways what behaviors we criminalize, how we approach crime control, how we handle criminal cases, how we sentence convicted offenders, and what correctional conditions and programs we create. In addition, the media's portraits of crime and justice sway the public's beliefs and expectations, as well as the demands placed upon the system. The World Wide Web and social media have changed the media–public policy dynamic. Contemporary media consumers are co-creators of much content and active participants in the development of criminal justice policy. In a new way the media and their consumer partners construct our crime-and-justice reality and subsequent derived criminal justice policy.

Below is a summary of each chapter:

- **Chapter 1, Crime, Justice, and Media** The first chapter provides an introduction to the media, crime, and justice relationship and provides historical and conceptual overviews. The argument for the importance of studying the relationship between media crime and justice is made. Differing types of media, including new media, and the different types of media content are introduced, defined, and exemplified. The idea of crime and justice as a mediated experience is introduced and discussed.

- **Chapter 2, New Media and Social Constructionism** To help students understand how the media relate to crime and justice, the book applies the theoretical perspective of social constructionism. Chapter 2 is devoted to introducing and explaining the basic processes and concepts of social constructionism with accompanying demonstrations of how social constructionism works in the crime and justice new media realm. Employing socially constructed concepts such as claims makers, frames, narratives, and symbolic crimes, and the examples of "road rage," "killer drunks," and the "Rodney King arrest," Chapter 2 demonstrates the social construction of contemporary crime and justice.

- **Chapter 3, Images of Crime and Criminality** This chapter covers the "criminological theory" that one finds in media content. It discusses how crime, criminals, and victims are portrayed in the media. The result is an emphasis on violent crime and predator criminals and a de-emphasis on crime victims and white-collar crime. The associated criminological theories of crime and explanations of criminality that are forwarded by the images are discussed.

- **Chapter 4, Criminogenic Media** New to the fifth edition, Chapter 4 is dedicated to how the media portraits described in the prior chapter can be criminogenic and related to real-world criminal behavior. The ongoing debates regarding the effects of video games on player aggression and the impact of the Internet and social media on criminality are reviewed. Copycat crime and media-orientated terrorism are discussed in detail.

- **Chapter 5, Crime Fighters** This chapter focuses on the media portrait of crime fighting. Describing the professional sworn law enforcement officers and the civilian crime fighters found in the media, the chapter contrasts the images of crime fighters in their media-constructed worlds to the real world of law enforcement. Material on the unique nature of the portrait of policing found in the infotainment media and a "CSI" effect is also included.

- **Chapter 6, The Courts** This chapter covers the judicial system as portrayed in the media, focusing on the media co-optation of the courts as infotainment vehicles within massively covered "media trials." In addition to discussions of long-standing issues like pre-trial publicity, courtroom control of news media, and reporter access to proceedings and offenders, discussions on new media and the public image of courtrooms and male and female attorneys are included.

- **Chapter 7, Corrections** Chapter 7 covers the media portrait of correctional institutions, correctional officers, and prisoners. A discussion that reviews the limited sources of knowledge the public has regarding corrections and the implications of this limitation on the social construction of corrections and correctional policy is provided. The stereotypes of prisoners, correctional officers, and correctional institutions found in the media are discussed. In addition, material on the interactions between terrorism, corrections, and the media is included.

- **Chapter 8, Crime Control** In this chapter, how criminal justice practitioners increasingly use media venues and new media technology to reduce crime, gather information, patrol communities, deter offenders, and process cases is discussed. The recent explosive expansion of camera-based public surveillance systems (CCTV surveillance systems is discussed in depth) is discussed in depth. Sections on Madison Avenue-style anticrime advertisements and the judicial use of cameras and video images in court proceedings are also included.

- **Chapter 9, The Media and Criminal Justice Policy** Chapter 9 provides an overview of the media content of crime and justice and details the connections the content has to criminal justice policy. The chapter explores the two main tenets of crime-and-justice media that have direct implications for criminal justice policy: the backwards law and the operation of immanent justice in crime-and-justice media content. Discussions of the research on media effects on the public's beliefs and attitudes about crime and justice, the rank of crime and justice on the public agenda, and direct and indirect media effects on the social construction of criminal justice policy are included.

- **Chapter 10, New Media, Crime, and Justice** Also new to this edition, Chapter 10 provides a dedicated review of the interactions between contemporary new media and crime and justice. Discussions of cybercrime and the evolution of "performance" and copycat crime driven by social media and the World Wide Web, the utilization of new and social media by law enforcement agencies to investigate crimes, the concern over new media's effects on the courts by altering the behavior of jurors and attorneys and biasing trials and case processing, and the emerging but still limited impact on corrections are all provided.

- **Chapter 11, Media, Crime, and Justice in the Twenty-First Century** The final chapter distills the main points of the book and offers projections about the future of the media, crime, and justice relationship as the impact of new communication media makes itself fully felt. Designed and offered not as serious prophecies but as platforms to launch discussion, forecasts are developed of what readers might find over the next decades using two opposing worst-case scenarios. In scenario 1, "Participatory Spectacles," freewheeling, interactive, infotainment driven media dominates in a society where the audience is actively engaged in how a parade of socially constructed criminal justice spectacles play out. In scenario 2, "Self-Surveillance," rigid restrictions on media coverage of formal crime-and-justice content co-exists with extensive media-based anticrime and public-supported self-surveillance. In this scenario, agencies, businesses, and other social organizations track much of what people do and the general public voluntarily contributes large amounts of personal surveillance information. The lessons of each scenario and the new media age of "criminal justice pixel policy" are discussed.

The primary difference between the fourth and fifth editions of *Media, Crime, and Criminal Justice* is that in the fifth edition recent examples are plentiful and material covering new and social media and crime issues is emphasized. Reflecting the revised focus, a new chapter devoted entirely to crime, justice, and new media is included. In addition, entire sections of chapters are devoted to new topics, including the production of crime news; the dynamics of performance crime; the effect of video games; celebrity crime news; terrorism and the media; the impact of social media, self-surveillance, and memorial criminal justice policies; and mediated criminal justice. Every chapter has been updated and has new photos and examples and an end of chapter set of class discussions are provided.

- New material in Chapter 1 includes new discussions of the creation of crime news and new media and the contemporary crime-and-justice-mediated experience in the new media age. Also new are updated supplemental boxes on memorial criminal justice policy, types of media content, the history of media, crime, and justice, and the Jodi Arias murder trial. Updated images related to video game play, reality TV, and comic book images are provided and updated tables and figures on crime news gatekeeping can be found.

- New to Chapter 2 are boxes on common crime claims, the Sandy Hook Elementary school shooting as a symbolic crime, and the historical development of new media. Revised and new passages on the concepts of social constructionism are expanded to incorporate ideas related to new and social media. New visuals and updated box discussions have been added throughout.

- Chapter 3 has revised discussions of how crime victims and white-collar crime are portrayed in the media, with new material on Bernie Madoff and the Boston Marathon bombers added. Accompanying photos have also been updated.

- As a new addition, Chapter 4 has new discussions of criminogenic media; discussions of copycat crime have been substantially expanded with new examples and figures. Boxes on the video game *Grand Theft Auto*, a copycat crime spree linked to the commercial movie *Project X*, and individual- and aggregate-level copycat crime models can be found. A new figure highlighting the characteristics of media-oriented terrorism as well as updated photo examples are included.

- New to Chapter 5 are a revised box and expanded in-text discussion on the CSI effect. In addition, revised material on the differences between media-portrayed police and real-world police officers and a new box on crime fighting and terrorism in contemporary media appear.

- Additions to Chapter 6 include new material on media trials. One is a revised box on the seminal media trial of O. J. Simpson and its recent off-spring, the Casey Anthony media trial. Boxes on the Amanda Knox murder trial in Italy and the legacy of CourtTV network are updated as well. New and updated images for all boxes are added. A revised updated table of media trial examples now includes the surviving Boston Marathon bomber, Dzhokhar Tsarnaev. A new box on WikiLeaks, Bradley Manning, and Edward Snowden can also be found. Updated images have been added throughout.

- Chapter 7 has a revised box on the growth of incarceration rates in the United States and media developments and new boxes on Lindsay Lohan's encounters with corrections and the recent emergence of the phenomenon of Facebook fugitives. Images of Guantanamo Bay prison and recent correctional entertainment media provide contemporary examples. Revised and new passages on infotainment and corrections; prison films and correctional news; and the media portraits of female inmates, correctional institutions, and officers are included.

- New material in Chapter 8 includes a new, expanded discussion of surveillance of public spaces. A box on new media, privacy, and content and an additional box on profiling and camera surveillance have been added. New visual examples are included throughout and all figures have been updated.

- New to Chapter 9 is a box on celebrity crime and media attention. Revised boxes discuss memorial criminal justice policy and "three strikes and you're out" legislation; a revised figure details the media role in the social construction of criminal justice policy. An extensively revised discussion of the tenets of crime and justice found in the media and their connection to criminal justice policies is included.

- Chapter 10 is a completely new chapter for the fifth edition. Accompanying the text, a set of new boxes and photos are included. Specifically, supplemental boxes providing overviews of cybercrime and the dark web are offered. Two additional boxes cover how new media provide means to commit new types of crimes (based on a discussion of the New York cannibal police officer) and the growth of performance crime (highlighting Smack Cams). Additional boxes on how social media have been used to further victimize crime victims using a Steubenville, Ohio rape case and have helped law enforcement solve crimes utilizing iPhones, Facebook, and YouTube are found. Lastly, a box describing how judges have been encouraged to adjust their juror instructions to reflect the dangers social media hold for trial fairness is included.

- Chapter 11 has a new consideration of competing models of the media's relationship to criminal justice and a new discussion of the evolving mediated crime-and-justice reality that reflects new and social media. New speculative discussions of possible crime-and-justice futures are couched in two new scenarios of "participatory spectacles" and "self-surveillance," with new visuals reflecting the current social media era. There is a new box covering the Boston Marathon bombing that demonstrates how crimes, investigations, and judicial proceedings events will be multi-mediated audience participation events in the future.

LEARNING TOOLS

Each chapter is supplemented with a number of learning tools. Chapters begin with a listing of chapter objectives that target the themes running through each chapter. Each chapter ends with a set of learning tools:

- A bulleted chapter summary which restates and re-emphasizes the main points of each chapter.
- A set of class discussions related to each chapter's content for students to apply the lessons of each chapter.
- A list of suggested additional readings that explore the main themes of the chapter in additional depth and can be used as entrées into the literature for paper assignments.

Additional imbedded chapter learning features are:

- Boxes containing supplemental media-based examples to demonstrate concepts and points from each chapter and to highlight connections between what students are reading in the text and what they are seeing, hearing, and reading in their daily lives.
- Photos to link chapter concepts and themes to visual imagery.
- Bold-faced in-text key terms which link to an end-of-book glossary.

Lastly, the fifth edition includes:

- An extensively updated bibliography and end-of-book footnotes.
- A separate Instructor's Manual with chapter overviews, question pools with objective, short-answer and essay items, and lists of Internet sites and popular music for each chapter.

ANCILLARIES

Instructor's Resource Manual with Test Bank.   The manual includes learning objectives, key terms, a detailed chapter outline, media activities, and a test bank. Each chapter's test bank contains questions in multiple-choice and true–false formats, with a full answer key. The test bank is coded to the learning objectives that appear in the main text, and includes the page numbers in the main text where the answers can be found.

Acknowledgments

I would first like to thank the individuals at Cengage who contributed to the development and production of this book. Carolyn Henderson-Meier provided encouragement and convinced me that enough had changed in the subject to justify a fifth edition. Wendy Langerud provided ongoing support and was especially helpful and patient in transiting from the fourth to the fifth edition. I would also like to thank our Project Manager, Gordon Hammy Matchado for his help and extensive patience. Sofia Priya Dharshini diligently acquired the photographs and assisted in obtaining permissions. PreMediaGlobal created the artwork and graphics. I am also grateful to Kimberly Kampe, University of Central Florida Doctoral candidate in Public Affairs who prepared the Instructor's Manual. I thank all of them for their patience and professionalism.

Also deserving thanks are the reviewers who offered suggestions in response to the fourth edition. I extend my sincere appreciation, for the fifth edition is much improved and strengthened due to their suggestions.

Finally, my family deserves special thanks. My wife Susan and my three children Jennifer, Paul, and Tim provide continual love and understanding. My new granddaughter, Nora, simply makes me smile.

Ray Surette
Orlando, Florida

Crime, Justice, and Media

CHAPTER OBJECTIVES

After reading Chapter 1, you will

- Understand the importance of the relationship between media, crime, and criminal justice
- Appreciate how criminal justice policy is impacted by the media
- Know the history of crime-and-justice media
- Understand the basic differences between the types of media
- Understand how different media content is related to media crime-and-justice portraits

THE MEDIATED WORLD OF CRIME AND JUSTICE

Why should one study crime, justice, and the media in the age of mobile digital communications? There is one good reason and many secondary ones. Before we explore those reasons, try a quick experiment. Log on to a streaming video site and look at the available programming. Note the number of programs and films that deal with committing, solving, or fighting crime. Check out an Internet news site and note the number of crime-and-justice stories. Do the same with the day's news. If you subscribe to any online or print magazines, check their contents for articles that are crime or justice related. If you are reading a novel, is a crime or a criminal an important element of the story? Count how many of your e-mails, mobile communications, or postings refer to crime or criminal trials. If you have a Facebook account, how much of the content you shared with others was crime related? What did you discuss in your social media conversations? In addition, write down the names of five people that you have heard or read a lot about over the past two years. How many of the five were connected to a criminal investigation or trial in some way? Finally, what did people you directly talked face-to-face with yesterday and today talk about? How often were crimes and criminal justice issues discussed?

I'm betting that much of your electronic media, your news, your reading, your social media content, and your direct personal conversations involve crime-and-justice issues. In fiction and fact, crimes, criminals, investigations, and trials course through our media lives.[1] Crime, justice, and the media have to be studied together because they are inseparable, wedded to each other in a forced marriage where they cohabitate in a fascinating, if raucous, relationship.

How did the marriage come about? Crime and justice has always provided a substantial portion of the media's raw material.[2] Criminal trials and infamous crimes, along with their associated victims, investigators, judges, attorneys, and citizens, provide popular crime-and-justice stories, which are packaged and mass-marketed. The images, ideas, and narratives that dominate the media influence how people think about crime and justice. The behaviors we think should be criminalized; who we feel should be punished; what the punishments should be; and how we think the police, judges, attorneys, correctional officers, criminals, and victims should act are all influenced by the media portraits of crime and justice.[3] Compounding these influences, the technological ability of media to gather, recycle, and disseminate information has never been faster or more pervasive. More crime-and-justice media content is available to more people via more avenues and in more formats today than ever before. A flood of new media technologies—originating with personal digital assistant devices (PDAs), and progressing to cable television and satellite networks, to videocassette recorder (VCR), to the Internet, to electronic games, to virtual reality and mobile communications devices and social media platforms—has created a hyperactive media environment. This new, high-speed media world dominated by entertainment value and visual images has a powerful impact on crime and justice.[4]

However, the fact that an interesting contentious relationship exists between media and criminal justice is not the most important reason to study crime and the media. The most important effect of this marriage is on criminal justice policy (discussed in Chapter 9). The media have had significant effects on criminal justice policy in America for a long time. For example, the early-nineteenth-century book *Uncle Tom's Cabin* had an effect on slave laws, the depression era film *I Am a Fugitive from a Chain Gang* affected U.S. correctional practices, and 1980s movies and books like the *Silence of the Lambs* influenced policies aimed at a perceived serial killer threat. That influence has risen to new heights. Today we live in a criminal justice policy era where media-rendered portraits frequently drive crime-and-justice practices at blinding speed.[5] The media and criminal justice policy link is easily seen in **memorial criminal justice policies,** which are named for individuals, usually victims (see Box 1.1). We have Megan's Law and Amber Alerts due to massive publicity of heinous crimes and their innocent victims.[6] The "Three Strikes and You're Out" legislation that followed the co-optation of the kidnapping and murder of twelve-year-old Polly Klaas in California in the late 1990s is a classic example of this media-driven policy process.[7] Even when not named after an individual, much of our criminal justice policy exists because of the impact of high-profile crimes being co-opted as symbols for policy campaigns.[8]

Box 1.1   Memorial Criminal Justice Policy

Nine-year-old Amber Hagerman was abducted while riding a bike near her home in Arlington, Texas. Her body was found four days later in a ditch with her throat slashed. The Amber Hagerman Child Protection Act was signed into law in 1999, creating America's Missing Broadcast Emergency Response (AMBER) Alert system to solicit citizen tips and interrupt in-progress child kidnappings (Miller, Griffin, Clinkinbeard & Thomas 2009). Other memorial crime control–targeted legislation includes "Megan's Law," requiring community notification of sex offenders residing locally; "Jessica's Law," requiring long prison terms and lifetime monitoring for sexual crimes against children; "Carlie's Law" for quicker revocation of federal probationers; and the "Adam Walsh Child Protection and Safety Act," which authorized the creation of a nationwide sex offender database (Griffin & Miller 2008 pp. 161–162). The effectiveness of these efforts remains to be established (Griffin 2010). The most recent effort to memorialize child victims of violent crime involves the gun control legislation being pursued in relation to the 2013 Sandy Hook Elementary school shootings in Newtown, Connecticut, in which 20 children and 6 adults were murdered.

ZUMA Press, Inc. / Alamy

Today, the fact that local criminal justice issues tend to spawn broad-based policy responses is due to the character of the media–criminal justice marriage. Contemporary media often cover local crime through a national lens; a neighborhood crime is portrayed as an example of a society-wide failure and a national crisis. In addition to raising some newsworthy local crimes to national prominence, local crime is portrayed in the media as being beyond the ability and resources of local criminal justice agents, as an out-of-control plague that cannot be handled locally. The solutions to crime painted as sensible are given a punitive federal orientation. "What must the nation do about crime?" is the question of the day, rather than "What does my community need to do about crime and other connected neighborhood social problems?" Hence, the most important reason for examining the media–criminal justice marriage is that it ultimately determines how we react to crime and how we spend our tax dollars as a nation. Criminal justice policy has become a national political issue; crime another media commodity. Both are determined by what is visual, newsworthy, entertaining, and salable.[9]

Although most important in terms of actual social impact, the media–criminal justice policy connection is not seen by the public as the most significant media effect on crime and justice. The public worries most about a set of more visible concerns. These concerns—media-orientated terrorist events, copycat crime, coverage of media trials, and media-linked social violence—provide secondary reasons for studying the media, crime, and justice. The criminal justice policies we support and pursue due to the media ultimately affect these worrisome but secondary issues as well. These are all significant issues, which will be discussed in depth, but it is important to remember that the media's most significant impact is on how we spend our taxes, what and who we criminalize, and how we deal with offenders.

THE BLURRING OF FACT, FICTION, AND THE MEDIA

What is the state of the media–criminal justice marriage today? First, everyone appears to be wedded to media in some fashion. Whether through the Internet, television, movies, music, video games, or multi-purpose new media devices that provide access to all of the other media forms, exposure to media content is ubiquitous. Today, virtually everyone is an audience member of some form of media. In a basic way, media provide the broadly shared, common knowledge in our society that exists independent of occupation, education, and social status. The knowledge acquired via mass media is generally perceived as less important and more transient, but also as more entertaining and enjoyable. When compared to religious information or institutional histories, which can extend for centuries, media-generated knowledge has a shorter life span, usually not exceeding a generation. Indeed, generations are often defined and—particularly true for popular music—can be distinguished by the media that is current during their youth.

With technological progress broadening media's reach, concerns have grown. In addition to worries about direct criminogenic media effects on copycat crime and media-oriented terrorism, there is concern that the reality the media create unduly influences the public's view of reality.[10] The reason for concern is that the snapshots of reality the media present provide the public a dramatic, but reshaped, marketed, and narrow slice of the world.[11] Although most of media crime-and-justice content is recognized by the public as unrealistic and heavily edited, continued exposure to the content influences one's view of reality, and this influence increases in areas where alternate sources of information are less available. Such is the case for crime and justice; like candy to cavities, a diet heavy on media will eventually corrode your perception of reality. Within this media–generated perception of crime-and-justice reality, a core set of images, headed by the image of a predatory violent stranger, is exploited by both the media and criminal justice policy makers.[12]

An important development is the looping of media content. **Looping** results when events and information are repeatedly cycled and recycled through the media into the culture to reemerge in new contexts.[13] For example, a police car chase video cycles from courtroom evidence to local news footage, to info-tainment program content, to a clip inserted in a comedy movie, to sundry Internet Web sites and social media sharing platforms. This continuous looping and reformatting of content results in the blurring of fact and fiction.[14] People come to believe that fictional events are real, that real events didn't happen, and that hybrid—part real, part fiction—events are common. Such effects are perva-sive in the crime-and-justice arena.[15] Many believe, for example, that Hannibal Lecter is a real serial killer and Jack the Ripper is fictional. Real events such as the World Trade Center terrorist attacks become hopelessly confounded in a blur of factual and fictional claims. In an odd way, people no longer trust the news (which is supposed to be true) but seem to be more willing to believe entertainment and infotainment media (which do not even purport to be accurate). Thus, many did not believe the news reports regarding the September 11, 2001, terrorist attacks, instead they believed unsubstantiated claims that the attacks were a CIA/Hollywood special effects stunt.[16]

In the end, the direction of influence between crime and justice on one side and media on the other is a two–way street—the mass media influence crime and justice, and crime-and-justice events become grist for the media.[17] In addition to the myriad entertainment products that deal in crime and justice, the media and media technology are simultaneously perceived as both a major cause of crime and violence and a powerful potential solution to crime. While blaming the media for many social ills, we also look to them to help reduce violence and drug use, deter crime and terrorism, and bolster the image of the criminal justice system. In law enforcement, we look to the media to aid in criminal investiga-tions, manhunts, and street and vehicle patrols. In the courts, we look for assis-tance in processing criminal cases, reducing case backlogs, conducting trials, presenting testimony and evidence, and deciding guilt, all while portraying the courts and trials in infotainment style productions. In corrections, we look to media images for our perception of correctional institutions, programs and per-sonnel, and to enhance security and surveillance. The media–criminal justice marriage is a love-hate relationship. The media are blamed for many of the beha-viors the criminal justice system has to contend with, even as the media are simultaneously looked to for solutions to the problems found in the criminal jus-tice system and society. As far as criminal justice policy is concerned, the media–criminal justice relationship is the most important one that exists. To understand both the historical development and the future of crime and justice in America, one must take into account the influences of the media and understand how crime-and-justice events become popular media products. Gaining that under-standing is the basic goal of this book.

A BRIEF HISTORY OF CRIME-AND-JUSTICE MEDIA

A necessary step in exploring the relationship between the media and crime and justice is to first look at the structure of the media in America. Until recently, the media could be thought of as roughly cleaved along two dimensions: types of media and types of content. Three types of media based on content format differences have been historically found: print, sound, and visual, collectively called "legacy media.". A fourth type of media, ambiguously called "new media," has hastened the blurring of the types of content by providing simultaneous access within one device to all types of content. As shown in Table 1.1, each media type has enjoyed dominance during a historic period. Of course, all types are still found today, and new media often combine print, sound, and visuals in new ways. Table 1.1 also reflects the historic trend in the evolution of media to include more information, which is more easily accessed in a more realistic setting, so that today a mediated experience is in many ways similar to actual experience.[18] Each media type's relationship to crime and justice can be understood through a brief history.

Print Media

Print was the first medium to generate a mass market; in the United States, it is usually dated as proliferating in the 1830s with the emergence of the "penny press" daily newspapers. One of the first such newspapers, the *New York Sun*, began to include a daily police-court news column in 1833 and experienced a notable circulation boost.[19] Other penny dailies followed suit, and human-interest crime stories quickly became a staple of these inexpensive, popular newspapers. These early papers portrayed crime as the result of class inequities and often discussed justice as a process manipulated by the rich and prominent. They frequently contained due process arguments and advocated due process reforms, while presenting individual crimes as examples of larger social and political failings.[20] Helped by the success of the penny press, a market for weekly crime magazines followed.[21] By the twentieth century, magazines focusing on crime, sex scandals, corruption, sports, glamour, and show business all flourished.[22] Providing an early model for contemporary news and modern television programs, mass marketing, and the consumption of crime infotainment was born.

Detective and Crime Thrillers.   The two most popular print-based crime genres to emerge in nineteenth-century print media were detective and crime thriller magazines and "dime" novels. Significant social concerns with the popular media also originated with these products. Both were escapist literature, and by the latter half of the nineteenth century, they described crime as originating in individual personality or moral weakness rather than being due to broader social forces. By downplaying wider social and structural explanations of crime found in the earlier penny press newspapers, these novels helped reinforce the existing social order— the status quo. In addition, the "heroic" detectives in these works closely resembled the criminals they apprehended—calculating and often odd loners.[23] The portraits of crime and justice produced during this time are

T A B L E   1.1   Crime-and-Justice Media History

Sound Media Dominate

Antiquity	Theater, folktales, and myths	Limited access and distribution to local audiences so that content effects are not extensive and media experience is clearly different from real life. Urban legends are a contemporary example.
1200–1500s	Ballads	Popular songs present the criminal as celebrity and aid in the development of a pop culture focus on criminality. Hip-hop music provides contemporary examples.

Print Media Dominate

1400–1700s	Pamphlets and broadsheets	The historical roots of today's crime-and-justice infotainment programming. Crime news reach is wider, though still limited to comparatively small audiences. Gallows sermons were a popular criminal justice example.
1830s	Penny press	Crime news begins to reach large markets and become a central feature of news. First mass-marketed media.
1880s	Dime novels	Detective and crime novels marketed to divergent audiences. The profit in entertainment crime media is recognized and exploited.
1890s	Yellow journalism	News media makes significant shift to become mass Infotainment media. Dramatization of crimes and criminals in infotainment formats is encouraged.

Visual Media Dominate

1910s	Commercial film introduced	Beginning of media audience homogenization via shared content that is consumed regardless of gender, race, religion, or social status. The beginning of everyone having access to similar information about the world.
1920s	Commercial radio networks	Modern programming and economic structure of for-profit media established as an unchallenged assumption. First in-home electronic delivery of media content, which eases access for children and allows media for the first time to circumvent traditional socialization efforts of parents, schools, and religion. Children can now learn about the world directly from the media without having to leave their living room or learn to read.

(continued)

T A B L E   1.1   Crime-and-Justice Media History (Continued)

1930s	Film dominates	U.S. commercial film industry is the dominant media and its crime-and-justice content comes under criticism. Social concerns arise about the glorification of crime and criminals and copycat effects of movies. First serious research of media effects and censorship efforts by government.
1930–1940s	Comic books peak	Comic books fill a reality-defining niche for crime and justice and are read by both adults and children. Violent and graphic content generates public crusades against comics as corruptors of youth and establishes the structure of the argument that subsequent attacks on other media such as pop music and video games will take.
1950s	Television	In-home, electronic live visual media quickly dominate and force other media forms to change. Everyone can now easily see and access the same information about the world. Crime programming becomes a major portion of total content.
1970s	Cable television	Content choices expand enormously. Movement from broadcasting aimed at large audiences to narrowcasting aimed at small audiences. Graphic content becomes easily available for home consumption.
New Media Arrive		
1970s–1980s	Arcade video games and first computer games	Video games introduce interactivity to media experience.
1980s	Videocassette recorders	Decision of where to consume content begins to move from producers to consumers with unrestricted home access to films.
1980s	Gaming Computers	First interactive media where consumer has a role in content development. Consumers begin process of becoming collaborative content authors, such as deciding which crime-and-justice role to assume—criminal or crime fighter—and determining final story outcome.
1990s	Mobile computer games and Internet	Electronic access to information goes global and the development of a digital reality begins to take form.
2000–present	New Media dominates, virtual reality, smart phones, and multi-function media devices	Media and computer-augmented experiences begin to supplant real world experiences for consumers. Much of the world is experienced solely through media devices and content. Fast-paced media-driven crime-and-justice policy era emerges.

surprisingly similar to those found today; both present images that reinforce the status quo; promote the impression that competent, often heroic individuals are pursuing and capturing criminals, and encourage the belief that criminals can be readily recognized and crime ultimately curtailed through aggressive law enforcement efforts. These print media icons would later be repeatedly replicated in radio, film, and television programming.

Comic Books.   Marketed to both children and adults, one of the more socially influential print media to develop in the twentieth century was the comic book. From their beginning, comic books featured crime-fighting policemen, private detectives, and costumed superheroes. Combining pop art with printed texts, comic books have constructed some of the more sophisticated images and analyses of crime and justice found in the media.[24] Evolving out of the newspaper-based comic strips of the 1890s and marketed within the twentieth-century pulp magazine market, comic books first appeared in the 1930s. In addition to fictional comic stories, reality-crime comics appeared in 1942, featuring stories about actual criminals and their crimes (the page from the "Laughing Sadist" in Chapter 3 is an example). These criminal point-of-view comics became the most popular comic book genre between 1947 and 1954.[25] Similar to contemporary popular music and video games, comic books regularly underwent periods of public concern and attack, the strongest coming in the late 1940s and early 1950s. The outcry and criticisms resulted in a self-adopted industry code that banned torture, sadism, and detailed descriptions of crimes. Overshadowed in the 1950s by film and television, comic books still enjoyed great popularity, particularly with young males, into the 1980s because they filled a media void. Comics could present criminals, heroes, and crime-fighting action beyond the technical and censored limits of radio, film and television.[26] Today comic books have declined in popularity as electronic video games have gained in popularity but remain important generators of crime-and-justice icons.[27] Comic books persist as part of the **multimedia Web,** and their crime-and-justice portrayals still prosper via licensing deals that span films, video games, toys, food, cartoons, and television shows.

Contemporary print media flourishes within new media venues. Text in the form of chat rooms, blogs, tweets, and postings have been compressed in length but multiplied in form. Much communication today is via the "printed" word but does not involve an actual printed page. Regarding crime and justice, the primary difference between contemporary print media and contemporary digital media is not found in their portraits of crime or justice but in the access to their content. From the late-nineteenth-century media dominated by print to the contemporary media dominated by electronically delivered visual images, the constructed messages of crime and justice have remained relatively constant. To access print media, the consumer needs to be literate, gain access to the materials, and make a clear decision to use or not use them. Exposure to their content has therefore always been less "mass" and more selective. Exposure to the modern, electronically dominated mass media images and messages, on the other hand, is difficult to avoid. The first medium to have an omnipresent capability was audio, and it was distributed via radio broadcast networks.

© EC Comics, 1954

As this 1954 comic book cover illustrates, a morbid interest in heinous crime and violent victimization of females can be found in many time periods and types of media.

Sound Media

First delivered and mass-marketed via radio networks, pure audio media have evolved from vinyl records to 8-track tapes, to compact discs, to MP3 files and other digital forms. Sound media are obviously neither print nor visual, but they bridge the two by delivering information in a linear fashion akin to print while evoking mental images and emotions analogous to visuals. In the 1920s, radio networks dominated as the home entertainment and news medium.[28] Despite coexisting with film, radio portrayals of criminality were different. The primary difference being, of course, that violence could only be heard, not seen. Their impact should not be underestimated, however, as hearing the sounds of a crime can be an emotionally gripping event. For many, "hearing is believing."

Radio.   Together with films, radio also established the business framework that television would subsequently exploit. Exemplified by coverage of the *Hindenburg* disaster in 1937, the 1925 Scopes "monkey" evolution trial, and the Lindbergh baby kidnapping trial in 1935, radio established itself as the first live, on-the-scene news reporting medium. The television news format of 30- to 60-second news spots presented within established categories (the world, the nation, sports, weather, economics, crime, and so forth) originated with radio programming. Within these news categories, the industry use of "news themes" was created, in which coverage of a particular type of crime would prevail for a time period. Radio news would give a type of crime saturation coverage for a short time and then turn to something new. Together with the producers of the film industry's newsreels, which brought weekly visual coverage of news to the public, radio producers created the reporting style that television would embellish: short-term, visceral, emotional news coverage of discrete "crime events."

On the entertainment side, radio drama, particularly at its height during the 1930s and 1940s, included a substantial and popular—though never a dominant— proportion of crime-fighting, detective, and suspense programming.[29] During this time, a number of classic programs such as *The Shadow*, *Sherlock Holmes*, and *True Detective* could be heard. Other "Radio Noir" programs, as they came to be termed, gave the culture a set of popular fictional citizen crime fighters and private detectives such as Nick Carter and Philip Marlowe, wise-cracking tough guys who disdained the police (discussed in Chapter 5). Radio crime programming also included hardened federal agents and reality crime programs. One popular early show, *Gang Busters*, which began in 1935, was the forerunner of current crime stoppers and *Most Wanted*–style programming (covered in Chapter 8). The best known of the early radio crime shows was *Dragnet*, which made a successful transition to television in the 1950s and established the format for the 1950s television police procedural based on police investigations.

The suspense programming found in radio also foretold the more graphic visual effects found in today's media. Unrestrained by concerns about offensive pictures, radio was able to conjure up gruesome mental images via sound effects that could not be shown in films of the time. These grisly sound effects preceded today's graphic visual special effects—sizzling bacon for an electric chair execution, hard candies crushed between teeth for bones being snapped, chopped cabbages for heads being severed, and wet noodles squished with a bathroom plunger for the eating of human flesh. Collectively, radio crime-and-justice programming provided the models for modern day crime-and-justice reality programming, the contemporary stereotypes of criminals and criminal justice, the heavy emphasis on law enforcement activities over other segments of the criminal justice system, and the exploitation of sensational, heinous crimes. All aspects of contemporary crime–and–justice media that are berated today are traceable to early radio. Not surprisingly, television programmers borrowed heavily from this tested and popular set of narratives in developing their visual crime programming in the 1950s.

Visual Media

Film.   In the early twentieth century, film was the tool that first provided the media with the ability to blanket all of society. The movie industry nationalized media content by making its content available to every social, economic, and intellectual stratum. Initially silent and inexpensive, the crime–and–justice stories in movies could still be followed without understanding English as radio programming required. The images were universally available and widely consumed, and film rapidly came to reflect and shape American culture.[30] By 1917, the U.S. motion picture industry was established as the premier commercial entertainment form in the world. By the 1930s, two of every three Americans attended a movie weekly.[31] With their immense popularity, movies were the first modern mass media, and their emergence heralded the creation of a twentieth-century mass culture that crossed geographic, economic, and ethnic lines. As both a social event and a source of social information, movies were the first medium able to bypass the traditional socializing agents of church, school, family, and community and directly reach individuals with information and images.

Though not every movie, television show, or radio program produced during a particular time frame portrayed the same crime-and-justice theme, dominant themes have been identified with certain periods.[32] Beginning with films and carried on in radio dramas, the first media criminals were descendants of Western outlaws, but unlike the "bandit heroes" and other gang members of Western dime novels, early film criminals were usually portrayed as urban citizens. Most of these early-twentieth-century portraits depicted ruthless crooks engaged in corrupt business practices in the pursuit of wealth, a motif that has remained popular to this day. Also common in film plots between 1910 and 1920 were nostalgic portrayals of a simple youthful criminality, reflecting street gang experiences among working-class immigrants. Such films reflected the social impact of large immigrations into the United States during the early part of the twentieth century. From the 1920s to the 1950s, the media criminal slowly evolved from an early-twentieth-century immigrant into a sullen returning World War I veteran, again transformed in the 1930s into a high-rolling bootlegger and Depression-era gunman, and finally into a modern corporate or syndicate executive-gangster. In the 1940s, depictions of violence, terrorism, and murder also became more graphic as gangsters, policemen, and detectives (many now with weapon fetishes) became more violent and less distinguishable from one another.[33] Following World War II, the new visual medium of television burst onto the scene and combined characteristics of both film and radio to quickly become the dominant media.

Television.   Introduced in the United States between 1948 and 1951, television soon replaced radio as the primary home entertainment medium, forcing the movie industry to restructure and driving radio dramas into history.[34] Television was not just radio and newspapers with pictures, it was an entirely new medium that fundamentally influenced the shape and content of all media and in doing so helped create a new and different society.[35] Television's growth and public acceptance was phenomenal, and the existing business models for commercial radio facilitated television's emergence. Because the nature and needs of the market dominated programming decisions from the beginning, television programming aimed at attracting and holding large audiences. Borrowing its basic themes and programming ideas from film, radio, and stage, and reformatting them in broadly palatable, noncontroversial products, television quickly came to be described as a vast wasteland of recycled, mediocre content. Ignoring the critics, Americans embraced television. In 1977, the number of television sets to Americans reached a 1-to-1 ratio and has never declined.[36] Although other screens besides those in television sets now compete for viewer attention, television viewing remains an important activity for many Americans.[37]

When creating content about crime and justice, television executives found a gold mine in crime programming. Although television was modeled after radio, crime was never a dominant part of radio programming, but crime and justice was a substantial portion of programming and the amount devoted to these topics was a social concern from television's inception.[38] Crime shows became a staple of prime time television entertainment in the late 1950s. Prompted by the success of adult Westerns and later by a program called *The Untouchables*, crime shows accounted for around one-third of all prime time shows from 1959 to 1961.[39] This trend leveled off during the 1960s but began to increase again during the early 1970s until it reached a peak in 1975, when almost 40 percent of the three then dominant networks' prime time schedules contained shows focusing on crime and law enforcement.[40]

While the major television networks periodically de-emphasize crime programming, the total amount of crime-and-justice programming available via television is greater than ever, with crime stories found within all types of programming. Special programming such as movies shown on television, miniseries, program promotions, syndicated programs, and local, satellite, and cable network programming all distribute significant proportions of crime-related content.[41] Collectively, these varied sources of new and recycled programming make crime and violence a significant, continuous element of television content.

New Media

In addition to the traditional print, sound, and visual media, we have today new digital interactive media exemplified by the Internet, electronic games, and smart phones. This set of media delivery platforms and digital content has acquired the umbrella label of "**new media**." (The role of new media in social construction is discussed in detail in Chapter 2 and their effect on crime and justice in Chapter 10.) There are competing definitions of what comprises "new media" and the boundary between old **"legacy media"** and "new media" is blurry. At their core, "new media" are made up of devices and capabilities encompassing digital and Internet technology that are characterized by interactive social media and multimedia content. New media employ digital information that is quickly and easily shared among large audiences and can take the form of print, sound, moving or still images and all of their combinations. Content in new media is highly fluid and allows for faster and broader communication between linked consumers and encourages the merging and looping of content across media forms.[42] The globalization of information has resulted, and the social construction of crime has followed suit.[43] The experience when immersed in new media is significantly different from the older legacy media experience. Most important, new media's unique characteristics of narrowcasting, on-demand access to content, and interactivity shift the audience experience from passive consumers to active participants. A user of legacy media was termed an audience member, a viewer, a listener, or a reader. New media users are often players or surfers and role-playing and content authorship is a common natural part of new media activities.[44] The social significance of these characteristics is that new media moves their audience from passive media customers to active co-producers of media content.[45] Combined with computers to generate virtual realities, new media experiences are the closest to actual experienced reality available.

A recent addition to crime and media concerns is the interactive nature of realistic virtual reality video games. In some games, players participate in violent acts and are rewarded for them within the game.

TYPES OF CONTENT

In addition to the different types of media, four basic types of content appear throughout the media. Figure 1.1 portrays the basic media content areas: advertising, news, entertainment, and infotainment. Traditionally, news, entertainment, and advertising were sufficient to define the media content landscape, but today infotainment is a significant addition. As shown, today advertising content overlays and infiltrates all other content, and infotainment has emerged to create a niche between news and entertainment. With content looping, the movement of information and images into and between the four media content areas today can be rapid and multidirectional. Encouraged by the development of new media, the boundaries between media content areas are porous and increasingly blurred. The result means that one can be hard pressed to decide which of the four content categories some recent media products fit into.

Advertising

Advertising is media at work. It is the lifeblood of the mass media. Advertising can be conceived as all of the media content purposely geared to persuade monetary decisions. Traditionally distinct from other content, the boundary between advertising and the rest of mass media has significantly dissolved. One now commonly sees product placements in films, news stories produced by corporate public relations offices, infomercials disguised as talk and news shows, and product endorsements embedded in Facebook pages. The sole media realm found to be comparatively low on crime and violence; advertising has become a pervasive, multi-venue, continuous media campaign interwoven into and throughout other media content.

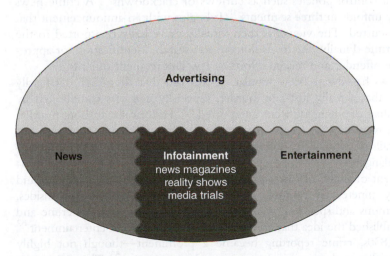

F I G U R E   1.1 Types of Media Content.

Entertainment

Entertainment is escapism. It involves all of the media content that is not for-warded as reflecting any specific reality or real event. Entertainment content is popular because it provides a pleasurable escape from reality. Its narratives engage and transport. Entertainment provides views of realities that cannot be otherwise seen and describes experiences that will not be personally experienced via medi-ated events that did not happen. In the entertainment world of crime and justice, you will see impossible crimes, fights, and adventures by people with abilities that no humans possess, surviving experiences that are not survivable. The enter-tainment products of the media are best thought of as play, and crime-and-justice stories have been estimated to account for about one-fourth of all entertainment output.[46]

News

News is typically marketed as true, current, and objective information about sig-nificant world events. As such, it plays a strong role in one's perception of reality and deserves an extended discussion. Contemporary news is essentially voyeur-ism. In crime-and-justice news, you are usually informed about real events and real people, but these events are often rare and distant. They display the lives of people caught up in extreme circumstances, involving bizarre crimes, spectacular trials, and extraordinary situations. News provides filtered, molded snippets of the abnormal criminal events of the world. Crime-and-justice news today is an escape from the normal via a social construction of the unusual. The amount of contemporary news has markedly expanded due to the increased number of media outlets. For its part, crime news usually is "social control" news, and is often reported with accompanying information about law enforcement efforts and new social control policies such as curfews or crackdowns.[47] A crime news story normally unfolds in three segments.[48] It begins with an announcement that a crime has occurred. The viewer is then visually or verbally transported to the scene of the crime. Finally, the focus shifts to the search, identification, or appre-hension of the offender and related efforts of law enforcement officials.[49]

Crime news has always been popular. It was said that after 1575, "it hardly seems possible that a really first-rate murder, especially if it was complicated by an illicit love affair or a hanging went unreported."[50] Historically, treason, murder, and witchcraft were the most popular story lines. This early crime coverage was laden with details of criminal acts intertwined with moral exhortations to the read-ers about the dangers of sin within reports that are surprisingly similar to the info-tainment content of much of today's crime news.[51] Through the eighteenth and into the early nineteenth century, crime-related street literature (broadsides, pamphlets, sermons and speeches) were the main vehicles for news of crime and justice and established the idea that crime news was for profit and entertainment.[52] In the mid 1830s, crime reporting became a prominent—though not highly regarded—specialty in the previously mentioned penny press.[53] The emergence of specialized reporters marks the beginning of aggressive marketing of crime news to the public. The evolution since has been for news to be produced more and more as a salable commodity.[54] By the late 1800s, newspapers came to be produced by modern corporations with large advertising revenues, staffs, and circulations. Crime coverage increased further with the introduction of a new type of mass entertainment newspaper reporting, collectively known as **yellow journalism.**[55] This new journalism emphasized the details of individual crimes; with this shift, police officers replaced court personnel and witnesses as the primary news source for crime information.[56] This trend has persisted to this day.

An examination of the process by which news is created helps to understand the content of crime news. Two models for the process of news creation—the market model and the manipulative model—compete.[57] The key for both models is **newsworthiness**—the criteria by which news producers choose which of all known events are selected to be news. In the **market model,** newsworthiness is determined largely by public interest, and journalists simply and objectively report and reproduce the world in the news. Under this model, reporters are regarded as reactive news collection agents who meet public interest needs. In the **manipulative model,** news is selected not according to public interest but according to the interests of the news agencies' owners. Under this model, the media purposefully distort reality and proactively use the news as a means of shaping public opinion in support of large social institutions and the status quo.[58]

Both models are inadequate because they ignore the organizational realities of news production, which by its nature makes rendering an objective, unbiased, mirror image of reality impossible.[59] Crime news displays characteristics that can be interpreted as indicative of both the manipulative and market models but that can best be understood within an **organizational model** of news production.[60] Factors related to the organizational needs of news agencies steer the process.[61] Because of the organizational nature of its birth, crime news is inherently subjective, though not necessarily ideologically biased.[62] What the public receives as news is capsulized, stylized, and commodified information.[63]

The bulk of news, then, is less discovered than formed by journalists working under organizational pressures. One organizational pressure on news agencies is that as organizations they need to routinize their work to plan and schedule the use of resources. But news organizations are in the unique organizational position of dealing with a commodity, news, that by definition is supposed to be unique and unpredictable. Their core organizational task, then, is to routinize the processing of non-routine events. To do so, news media personnel must become active co-creators of the news. They cannot be totally reactive, nor can they be totally proactive. In practice, they are somewhere in between—reactive to truly unexpected events, proactive and part of the creation process for the rest of the news.

The construction of crime news can be best understood as the coupling of two information-processing systems—one being news agencies, the other being the government.[64] The reporter *beat system*—under which reporters cover specific subject areas (for example, state politics or downtown crime)—restricts a journalist's sources and perspectives so that, in general, news journalists report on those at or near the top of the social hierarchy and those who threaten them—particularly those at the bottom—to an audience mostly located in the middle.[65] In addition, as profits have fallen, contemporary traditional journalism has become more characterized by the processing of news releases and press conferences than as a news gathering endeavor.[66] This means that in news of crime and justice we normally hear criminal justice system and government officials talking about individual criminals and street crimes or receive non-journalistic accounts directly distributed through new media avenues.[67] Contemporary traditional news agencies often find themselves using unedited images and accounts produced at a crime scene by new media–equipped bystanders. Today one is as likely to see images from a smart phone on the news as see footage produced by a news agency crime reporter.

Regarding which crimes get selected to be crime news, when possible, news agencies prefer unexpected or unusual events, but they present them in terms of previously established stories and explanations.[68] The better an event fits established themes, the more likely it is to be selected. Other, more specific criteria for crime news selection include the seriousness of the event, whimsical circumstances, sentimental or dramatic elements, and the involvement of high-status persons, and, of course, engaging images.[69] In the case of crime news, seriousness is the primary factor. In that crimes occur in the opposite proportion to their seriousness and that the news criterion for seriousness is harm to individuals rather than overall social harm, the media report those crimes that are least common and thus construct a crime reality at odds with the social reality of crime.[70] The result is that to the extent that reporters are encouraged to report the unique crime, it is more difficult for the public to estimate the typical crime.[71]

Within the news production process, historically there were checkpoints through which crime news was processed and passed along, with those processed to the final gate becoming crime news. First coined in 1950, the term for a person controlling the processing checkpoints is **gatekeeper**.[72] As shown in Figure 1.2,

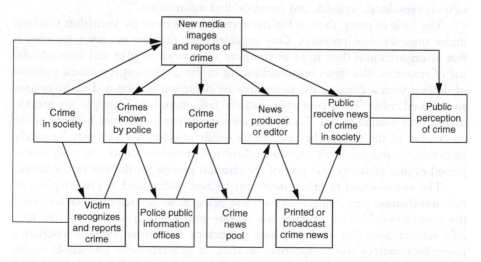

FIGURE 1.2

The Internet and Social Media Have Altered the Crime News Gatekeeping Process by Allowing News of Crime to Bypass Victims, Police, and News Agencies and Flow Directly to the Public.

the gatekeepers in the bottom two rows represent how crime news historically was created. A key gatekeeper in the crime news process was the crime reporter. To provide a steady stream of crime stories, a crime reporter developed reliable police sources and maintained their trust.[73] Although sometimes critical of law enforcement, successful crime reporters developed a working relationship with the police that benefited both.[74] Over time, the two sides developed similar work experiences and outlooks. As traditional news production has lost resources and the specialized crime reporter has become an endangered species, another key gatekeeper has evolved on the law enforcement side—the public information or media relations officer (PIO). Prior to the development of PIOs, interaction with the media was an ad hoc, idiosyncratic process. As the marketing of crime news has heightened, the competition among sources of crime-and-justice information for news media attention has sharpened. While law enforcement agencies still hold the central position in the construction and defining of the crime problem, other public agencies and private lobby and pressure groups have joined the competition. In addition, as reflected in the top row in Figure 1.2, new media content such as cell phone videos have allowed private individuals to influence the crime news gatekeeping process. The gatekeeping process has become more multi-directional, fluid, and rapid with new media, which allows the skirting of the entire traditional news industry so that raw footage of crime scenes sometimes is distributed to the public before it appears in formal news reports.[75]

New media notwithstanding, crime news, particularly statistics, statements about trends, and explanations and policy recommendations, still comes largely from information supplied by the police. Because it can be prepackaged and gathered at little cost[76], crime news helps news organizations in their scheduling and resource allocation and so remains popular with news agencies.[77] And because it is popular with the public, it continues to make up a large part of the total news. Despite its dilution through social media, the gatekeeping process will continue to filter out the vast majority of crime from becoming crime news and make any correspondence between crime news and actual crime unlikely.[78] News, entertainment, and advertising are still what most people think of when they consider the broad categories of mass media content, but a fourth content type, infotainment, which crosses all of the traditional media boundary lines, has emerged as a significant area for contemporary crime and justice.

Infotainment

An important change in contemporary crime-and-justice media is the explosion of infotainment products. **Infotainment** can be defined as the marketing of edited, highly formatted information about the world in entertainment media vehicles. The reality in infotainment is more about the reality we wish for than the reality that exists. The feel with infotainment media is that you are learning the real facts about the world; the reality is that you are getting a highly stylized rendition of a narrow, edited slice of the world. In that infotainment combines aspects of news, entertainment, and advertising under a single umbrella, its emergence makes it less sensible to discuss the three traditional media components separately. News, entertainment, and advertising are no longer unique media spheres due to infotainment's influences.[79]

Crime perfectly fits infotainment demands for content about real events that can be delivered in an entertaining fashion, and infotainment content based on crime and justice has existed for centuries. Crime pamphlets and gallows sermons are two early examples, and infotainment has always played a minor role in the media's crime-and-justice content. Why did the amount of infotainment content take off in the late twentieth century? The basic answer is that as the media, led first by television, became more visual, intrusive, and technologically capable, the viewing audience simultaneously became more voyeuristic and entertainment-conscious.[80] The ability of satellites to instantaneously beam information around the world allowed the public to watch riots, wars, and other events as they happen, heightening the dramatic entertainment value of what previously would have been reported as after-the-fact news stories, or not reported at all. For example, with the use of news helicopters, it became common to follow high-speed car chases and broadcast them live on social media. Irrespective of its social importance, a visual event that might not have been mentioned in the news a decade ago can be a contemporary lead news story as a result of simply being highly photogenic and entertaining. Along the same lines, ubiquitous surveillance cameras provide footage for media that rely on dramatizing "real" crimes. By providing a large inexpensive pool of visual events to market, such technological improvements have allowed for much of the infotainment programming that exists today. While improved technology increased the potential amount of infotainment content, its popularity is due to another factor.

The popularity of infotainment programming is tied to what caused news and entertainment to blur. With expanded hours, more networks, and new media competing for audience attention, more content was needed.[81] The addition of entertainment elements to news content was embraced as a solution.[82] Beginning in the late 1980s, modern crime-related infotainment programs began to appear on television, and the line between crime-and-justice news and entertainment dissolved.[83] Today a clear demarcation between news and entertainment no longer exists, and media consumers are hard pressed to differentiate crime-and-justice news from crime-and-justice entertainment. The news is still looked to for a reliable record of what's real, but today's stew of infotainment and unedited content makes establishing what is accurate a haphazard process.

Led by television, print and radio followed suit, and today substantial amounts of infotainment content can be found across a broad spectrum of media. Some of the more long-lived infotainment programs are crime-and-justice infotainment vehicles. Such programs have never been hugely popular in terms of ratings (*Cops* enjoying the highest numbers), but they continue to attract substantial audiences and are extremely profitable. As a result, the crime-and-justice media landscape is populated with varied infotainment products and venues. Within this media crime-and-justice infotainment world, the crime control model dominates.[84] Employing real crimes, re-enactments, and documentary-like formatting, the realism in which infotainment cloaks itself encourages the acceptance of their portrayals as accurate pictures of the world by audiences.[85] However, contrary to their image of reality, their content is clearly structured along entertainment lines while focusing upon the oldest entertainment crime story structure known: "*A crime followed by a chase ending with a capture.*" Like most media content, crime-and-justice infotainment emphasizes the committing of crime, the investigation and identification of criminals, and the pursuit and arrest of offenders.[86] Three types of crime-and-justice infotainment entities are common: news magazines and Web sites, reality-based crime shows, and media trials. Collectively, they dominate the contemporary mass media crime-and-justice infotainment market.

Newsmagazines and Web Sites. News magazines and Internet Web sites and blogs dedicated to crime extend the application of the entertainment values found in lesser degrees in much of the daily news content. Because of their time and format constraints, daily newscasts and new media–delivered summary

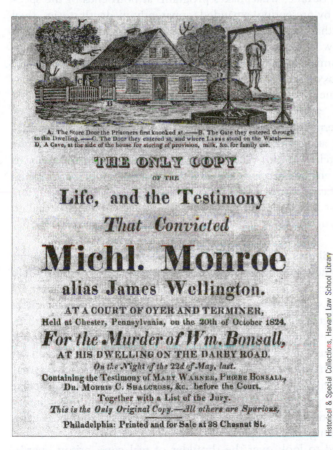

Similar to much of what is found in contemporary media, the focus in this nineteenth-century crime news pamphlet is on a violent, predatory crime and criminal. The symbolic hanging and the drawing of the crime scene with the promise of one-of-a-kind details were harbingers of today's crime-and-justice infotainment media.

accounts do not spend much time on any single story. They therefore cannot fully develop an infotainment context. However, newsmagazines and Internet sites can devote more content to the most interesting (that is, the most sensational, violent, dramatic, visual, or scandalous) crime stories. They provide audiences access to large amounts of information, especially images, and opportunities to share opinions about crimes. Within these avenues, a crime can be fully constructed as an entertainment vehicle along stereotypic story lines, complete with plots, characters, victims, villains, and dramatic endings.[87] At one end of the genre are the electronic versions of the supermarket tabloid newspapers—the trash-TV talk shows emphasizing confrontation and sexual deviance, the tabloid news shows emphasizing bizarre, violent crimes, and the Web sites and online blogs advocating bizarre content and crime theories. At the higher end are the weekly newsmagazine shows such as *60 Minutes* and Web sites associated with mainstream news agencies.

Other than matters of taste, what makes programs at both ends of the spectrum worrisome is that by presenting expanded, apparently in-depth stories, they convey the impression that crime is being discussed from multiple sides and that a full contextual review is being provided. However, as in regular news, in newsmagazine programming high-profile, sensationalist crimes and criminals are emphasized, with a focus on individual, random, stranger-on-stranger acts of violence. They continue the broader popular media's painting of crimes and criminals within simplistic portraits. As found in these other media outlets, newsmagazines and Internet crime news sites reflect the process of **commodification,** the packaging and marketing of crime information for popular consumption and commercial profit.[88] The impact that the economic goals of commodification have on media crime-and-justice content cannot be overemphasized. When a significant source of public knowledge about crime and criminality is steered by what is popular and profitable, the public's ability to evaluate criminal justice policies unavoidably suffers.

Reality-Based Crime Shows.   As news drifted more toward entertainment, entertainment programmers looked to traditional news formats to design talk shows and documentaries that would be accepted as credible and realistic by their audiences. In doing so, they have produced some of the more commercially successful television programming thus far in the twenty-first century. Virtually all aspects of life have been presented as a reality program at one time or another and a connection between the production of reality shows in general and an increase in local crime has been speculated.[89] Reality-based crime shows that entertain by sensationalizing real stories about crime and justice are of particular interest. These shows typically employ dramatizations of actual crimes interspersed with police narratives and interviews or actual video footage that features police officers investigating crimes, questioning suspects, and making arrests.[90] The audience is allowed to look over the shoulder of real cops, prison guards, probations officers, and sometimes offenders.

Concerns with these programs arise directly from their claim to be presenting reality—that they are objective purveyors of true stories about crime and justice. Despite their use of the trappings of traditional news and journalism, crime reality shows are thinly disguised entertainment, and the reality that they construct is not accurate. They mix reconstructions, actors, and interviews and employ camera angles, music, lighting, and sets to enhance their dramatic and entertainment elements. Viewers are encouraged to accept the content as straight-forward through the use of self-labeled "correspondents" and "reporters." Law and order, social control, and the point of view of law enforcement officials dominate within stereotyped portraits of crimes, criminals, and victims.[91] The crime-and-justice world found in reality-based crime shows appears as a violent, crime-prone underclass held in check by the police.

Media Trials.   Society has long been intrigued by the inner workings of the judicial system. Prior to cameras being allowed into America's courtrooms in the late 1970s, the most realistic-looking views of judicial proceedings came from courtroom television dramas and classic films like *To Kill a Mockingbird*. Today the drama is often "real," or at least not based on fictional cases (see Box 1.2). Cameras have moved into courtrooms to cover deliberations, to record the emotional responses of participants, and to conduct interviews with partici-pants. Some made-for-TV courtroom shows are more akin to game shows than to judicial proceedings. The media hijacking and dramatization of actual criminal cases has invigorated the **media trial**—the co-optation of a regional or national crime or justice event by the media, which is developed and marketed along entertainment-style storylines as a source of drama, entertainment, and profit.[92]

   Media trials are distinguished from typical news coverage by the massive and intensive coverage that begins either with the discovery of the crime or the arrest of the accused. In a media trial, the media cover all aspects of a case, often highlighting extralegal aspects. Judges, lawyers, police, witnesses, jurors, and defendants are interviewed, photographed, and frequently raised to celebrity sta-tus. Personalities, personal relationships, physical appearances, and idiosyncrasies are commented on without regard for legal relevance. Coverage is live whenever possible, pictures are preferred over text, and text is characterized by conjecture and sensationalism. Discussed in full in Chapter 6, a media trial is, in effect, a dramatic miniseries developed around a real criminal case. The history of these media trials reveals that they occur with regularity. In the twentieth century, more than two dozen trials were declared the "trial of the century" in the press.[93] Early media trials began to appear in the late nineteenth century with the 1893 Lizzie Borden murder trial for the killing of her parents with an ax one of the best known due to a resulting popular schoolyard poem and song.[94] Over the course of the twentieth century, interest in these trials by the media, the public, and the marketplace grew steadily. Following their period of intense public and media scrutiny, the trials pass into popular folklore and relative obscu-rity. Recognition of names such as Fatty Arbuckle, Sacco and Vanzetti, Bruno Hauptmann, the Rosenbergs, Patty Hearst, Scott Peterson, and Drew Peterson, have faded after once commanding public interest and media attention.

   In their coverage and marketing, these trials become palettes for the social construction of the entire criminal justice system.[95] They provide simplistic

B o x 1.2   Jodi Arias

The salacious trial of Jodi Arias in 2013 was another heavily covered trial in a long parade of media trials that stretches back centuries. Jodi Arias was tried for the murder of her boyfriend, who was found in his shower with nearly 30 knife wounds, a bullet wound to his head, and a slit throat. After initially denying involvement, she eventually admitted to the killing, claiming self-defense, but was found guilty of first-degree murder. In the tradition of the social construction of these media trials, coverage included details and photos of the nature of the couple's sexual relationship, YouTube videos, an appearance by Arias on the television show *48 Hours* (in which Arias claimed that the murder was committed during a home invasion), and daily commentary and coverage by various infotainment media personalities such as Nancy Grace.

POOL/Reuters /Landov

explanations of crime within the authoritative and dramatic vehicle of a "real" trial. In practice, crime in these productions is nearly universally attributed to individual characteristics and failings rather than to social conditions. Media trials represent the final step in a long process of merging news and entertainment—a process that now often results in extensive multimedia and commercial exploitation. That the source of media trials is the judicial system eases the merger, for media trials allow the media industry to attract and entertain a large general audience while maintaining its public image as an objective and neutral reporter of news. The end result is that in media trials, the merging of information and entertainment is fully achieved.

CRIME AND JUSTICE AS A MEDIATED EXPERIENCE

Each step in the evolution of types of media and their content brings the **mediated experience**—the experience that an individual has when he or she experiences an event via the media a bit closer to what it is like to actually personally experience an event.[96] More than ever before, an individual today can experience crime and criminal justice through the media and come away with the sensation of actual experience. Media presentations are evolving toward a media reality that is ever closer to an actual real-world experience and, thus, is more popular and more profitable. Radio provided sound, live coverage, and home delivery. Films provided continuous action and eventually sound and were therefore closer to actual experience than either print or radio. Television provided a combination of image, sound, live coverage, and home delivery—a mediated experience that was both similar to actual experience and easy to access. Recent new media technological developments have evolved to create delivery vehicles that increase access and choice in media consumption and further move media-created realities closer to experienced reality. Lastly, the introduction of electronic interactive games and computer-generated images have moved the mediated experience via virtual and augmented reality to be physically competitive to a real-world experience while simultaneously shifting the audience from passive observers of events to digital participants.

This evolution of the media has had a significant impact on the criminal justice system; today mediated crime-and-justice experience and knowledge dominates real-world crime-and-justice experience and knowledge. Despite media impressions to the contrary, most Americans have limited direct experience with crime and the criminal justice system. Receiving a traffic ticket remains the most common form of contact between citizens and law enforcement. Of those victimized by crime, having something stolen is far more common than violent victimization. Violent victimization also tends to be concentrated in lower-class social groups. Thus, for most Americans, the mediated experience is the main source of their crime-and-justice experience and knowledge. In addition, for most of us, experiencing crime and justice via the media is preferable to experiencing crime-and-justice events directly. Few seek out the experience of being a crime victim, but many enjoy seeing crimes committed in the media. The mediated experience—where one is warm, dry, safe, and able to see and hear from multiple points of view with the capacity to pause and replay the experience—is also preferable to actual experience for many other criminal justice events such as working a street patrol, attending a criminal trial, or serving a prison sentence.

The cumulative result of this ongoing media evolution is that today we live in a multimedia environment where content, particularly images, appears ubiquitously throughout the media landscape in a vast unavoidable morass of mediated information, events, personalities, and products.[97] Caught up in the mutations, the nature of contemporary crime and justice has evolved. In some instances the mediated event blots out the actual event, so that what people believe happened (based on widespread media renditions) supplants what actually happened. The facts of an event become irrelevant in the face of the mediated rendition of the event. This trend toward media portrayal over reality is particularly powerful in crime and justice, where news, entertainment, and advertising combine with infotainment content and new media to construct our mediated crime-and-justice reality. From this mediated reality we create our crime-and-justice policies.

Today, we live in a new media culture with media driven crime-and-justice policies. What we believe about crime and justice and what we think ought to be done about crime and justice is based on a view of reality that has been parsed, filtered, recast, and refiltered through the electronic, visually dominated, multimedia Web. Some crimes will have their images and reports shared in real time in social media and will appear as crime news. Their images and re-enactments will appear in entertainment films and television programming and audience-produced content such as YouTube videos. They will have their 911 dispatch tapes used as background in pop songs and will have the experiences of their victims, offenders, investigators, and attorneys chronicled in books and dissected in blogs, chat rooms, and talk shows. In such ways, mediated crime-and-justice experiences become more socially significant and influential then actual experiences.

In sum, five realities of twenty-first-century media are important for crime and justice.

1. Contemporary mass media is an electronic, digital, visual-dominated media. Print and sound are secondary in social impact. Content is fluid and moves quickly from medium to medium. Images have more value than other media content, and multimedia renditions of events are the norm. The evolution of the media has been toward making mediated experience indistinguishable from actual experience. Within this evolution, new media is altering the manner in which crime-and-justice information is collected, disseminated, and interpreted.

2. The current marketing structure of the media is geared toward narrowcasting, or targeting smaller, more homogenous audiences; however, content is constantly reformatted, reused, and looped to ultimately reach multiple and varied audiences. New media have decentralized the creation and distribution of content. Audiences have moved from passive consumers to active participants.

3. The media are a collection of for-profit businesses. Each media business must make money to survive, and the primary purpose of media is not to entertain or inform an audience but to deliver a consumer to an advertiser. From a media business perspective, advertising is the most important content. From the consumer and social impact side, the most important content is infotainment. New media has begun to drastically change the profitability of legacy media, especially print-based ones.

4. Media businesses exist within a highly competitive environment. Most new media ventures fail, and the expected life spans of media outlets, content, and products are brief. Content must be marketable and must quickly attract an audience and make a profit. Crime content remains a high-profit area.

5. The U.S. media resides in a non-paternalistic relationship with the government. The government is not prone to directly involve itself in determining content (though government officials do enjoy holding periodic hearings about content). The government role in the mass media is largely as a hands-off regulator, issuing licenses and controlling access to broadcast frequencies. Profitable content that may have negative social effects remains popular and common.

What these media realities collectively mean is that the U.S. media is driven by market considerations. The media environment is best understood as a multi-media commodity Web competing in a freewheeling marketplace. Within this market, content appears and reappears in varied and dispersed contexts, and images have the greatest value. Crime and criminal justice content has become a particularly valuable media commodity. The real world of criminal justice has reacted to this media commodification process, and the two sides have entered a twenty-first-century ballet in which each leads the other, spinning off criminal justice policies and programs. In this dance, two views of the media's impact on justice coexist. In one popular perspective, the media are criticized as criminogenic and as undermining the values of law and order. In the second perspective, popular among academics, the media are criticized as purveyors of fear, moral panics, factual distortions, and supporters of the status quo.[98] Being many things with diverse content, but not monolithic as sometimes described, contemporary media in reality do both.

In that the criminal justice system is a process that runs from criminality through law enforcement, courts, and corrections to criminal justice policies, the balance of this book explores this media–criminal justice relationship within a systems perspective. Media constructions of crime, law enforcement, the judicial system, and corrections as currently portrayed in the mass media are presented first, followed by chapters dedicated to media's relationship to crime control and policy formation. Lastly, the impact of new media on crime and justice is discussed.

SUMMARY

- Much of our knowledge about crime and justice come from the media, and media and crime and justice are intertwined.

- The knowledge we gain about crime and justice from the media influence our criminal justice policies.

- New media has accelerated the flow of crime-and-justice knowledge and content.

- Crime-and-justice content has been historically popular in all types of media.

- Print media was the first media to generate a mass market. Print also allowed stricter control of access to information.

- Sound media established the business model of today's media and was the first broad-based home media. Radio also popularized crime infotainment programs and live coverage of criminal justice events.

- Visual media were the first media to blanket society and with the introduction of television brought crime images directly into the home.

- New media has changed the nature of the media–consumer relationship via narrowcasting, on-demand access, and interactivity. New media audiences expect to be entertained and to participate in the creation and distribution of the content they experience.

- Crime news remains a profitable commodity, which due to the nature of its creation unavoidably provides an inaccurate picture of crime. Gatekeepers filter the crimes of the day and pass along the most unique newsworthy ones.

- Infotainment is the most important recent media development, with newsmagazines and Web sites, reality-based crime shows, and media trials dominating contemporary crime-and-justice content.

- Crime and justice are mediated experiences for most Americans.

CLASS DISCUSSIONS

1. Discuss the changes that you have observed since your childhood in the way crime and justice is portrayed in the media. Which changes do you think are positive and which ones do you think are negative? Discuss whether the media today more often promote crime control or due process goals.

2. Discuss recent criminal-justice-related events that have been looped in the media. Talk over how many were originally real versus fictional events and how the original events have been altered and used in new media contexts.

3. Compile a list of criminal justice memorial policies and discuss the characteristics of the persons and events they memorialize and the policies they established. Discuss what the characteristics of the crimes and victims say about criminality and crime in America and what the resulting policies suggest as a general philosophy of criminal justice.

4. Discuss why many common social experiences, such as attending concerts, football games, or meeting new people, are today preferred to be experienced via new interactive media. Discuss the advantages and disadvantages mediated experiences have over real-world experiences.

SUGGESTED READINGS

Carrabine, E. (2008). *Crime, culture and the media.* Cambridge, UK: Polity Press.

Flanders, J. (2011). *The invention of murder.* London, UK: HarperCollins.

Greer, C. (2009). *Crime and media: A reader.* London, UK: Routledge.

Jewkes, Y. (2011). *Media and crime*. London, UK: Sage.

Mason, P. (2002). *Criminal visions: Media representation of crime and justice*. Devon, UK: Willan.

March, I. and Melville, G. (2009). *Crime, justice and the media*. London: Routledge.

Phillips, N. and Strobi, S. (2013). *Comic book crime: Truth, justice, and the American way*. NY: New York University Press.

Robinson, M. (2011). *Media coverage of crime and criminal justice*. Durham, NC: Carolina Academic Press.

Jewkes, Y. (2011). *Media and crime* (2nd ed.). Los Angeles, CA: Sage.

Mason, P. (2003). *Criminal visions: Media representations of crime and justice*. Devon, UK: Willan.

Marsh, I., and Melville, G. (2009). *Crime, justice and the media*. London: Routledge.

Phillips, N. D., and Strobl, S. (2013). *Comic book crime*. New York, NY: New York University Press.

Robinson, M. (2011). *Media, crime, and justice* (2nd ed.). Durham, NC: Carolina Academic Press.

CHAPTER 2

New Media and Social Constructionism

CHAPTER OBJECTIVES

After reading Chapter 2, you will

- Have a theoretical foundation for exploring media, crime, and justice
- Understand the primary concepts of social constructionism
- Know how to use social constructionism to follow developments in criminal justice policy

THE SOCIAL CONSTRUCTION OF CRIME AND JUSTICE

When neighborhood watch volunteer George Zimmerman and Florida teenager Trayvon Martin encountered each other in 2012 they socially constructed the other as threats. Mr. Zimmerman perceived African-American teenager Martin as a criminal prowling his community; Mr. Martin perceived Hispanic American Mr. Zimmerman as a strange man who was following him as he returned to his condominium apartment from a nearby convenience store. Stereotypes and cultural narratives escalated the evening meeting between teenager and community watchman, with the two ultimately fighting on the ground and Trayvon Martin being shot and killed by George Zimmerman. The social construction of this crime-and-justice event continued with Mr. Zimmerman being tried for the killing of Trayvon Martin.[1] The capability for social constructions to drive social behavior for good or ill has been long recognized. In his 1922 book, *Public Opinion*, Walter Lippmann remarked: "For the most part we do not first see, and then define. We define first and then see.... We pick out what our culture has already defined for us, and we tend to perceive that which we have picked out in the form stereotyped for us by our culture."[2] By pointing out that society sees reality largely as society has constructed and agreed to see it, Lippmann insightfully described the core idea of social constructionism.[3] By detailing the consequences of the process in one instance, the shooting of Trayvon Martin points out its real world importance. Under social constructionism, people create reality—the world they believe exists—based on their personal experiences and from knowledge gained through social interactions.[4] Sometimes the process is rapid, as was the case in the Martin shooting, other times it reflects a slow, lifetime-long construction effort. The process is the same for everyone, although the end result, your personal idea of reality, can contain highly individualistic elements. Understanding the social construction of reality process and the concepts of social constructionism helps to understand the impact of the media on crime and justice.[5]

The traditional Western viewpoint is that reality and knowledge of the world are independent of human processes and grounded totally in autonomous, freestanding events. **Social constructionism** sees reality in a different light and views knowledge as something that is socially created by people. Beginning from the premise that accepted knowledge about the world need not mirror an objective reality, social constructionism focuses on human relationships and the way relationships affect how people perceive reality. Social constructionism emphasizes the shared meanings that people hold—the ideas, interpretations, and knowledge that groups of people agree to hold in common.[6] In the social constructionist view, shared meanings are invariably the result of active, cooperative social relationships and may or may not be tethered to objectively measured conditions in the world.[7] In social constructionism people tacitly agree to see the world in a specific way.

It follows that in social constructionism, the degree to which a given constructed reality prevails is not directly dependent on its objective empirical validity but is instead strongly influenced by shifting cultural trends and social forces. The world may be in one state, but people can believe it is in another state and act accordingly. In fact, social conditions may be seen as major social problems at one time and largely ignored at a different time, without the actual conditions having undergone any real change. Regarding crime, for example, not only can social behaviors be criminalized or decriminalized independent of changes in victimization or offense rates; in social constructionism such mismatches are expected.

THE SOURCES OF SOCIAL KNOWLEDGE

Social constructionists seek to understand the process through which agreement is constructed and the forces and conditions that influence when an accepted construction changes—that is, when a society's agreement about its reality shifts. Within the social construction perspective, perceptions of social conditions change as social knowledge about those conditions change. People acquire social knowledge from four sources: personal experiences, significant others (peers, family, and friends—also called conversational reality), other social groups and institutions (schools, unions, churches, government agencies), and the media.

Therefore, in addition to personal experience, which is the most impactful source, we also learn about and define reality from the experiences of others, and to a considerable extent, from the portrayals found in the media. Social constructionists recognize three kinds of reality: experienced reality, symbolic reality, and socially constructed reality.

Experienced Reality

The first source of knowledge, **experienced reality,** is one's directly experienced world—all the events that have happened to you. Knowledge gained from experienced reality is relatively limited but has a powerful influence on an individual's constructed reality. For example, in a survey of citizens in Los Angeles, California, researchers found that nearly twice as many citizens credited direct and conversational reality sources of knowledge as more important than media sources in forming their views of the police.[8] Along the same lines, personal victimization is the most powerful source for defining one's view of how serious a particular crime is. However, even in the fixated-with-crime society found in the United States, personal victimization remains comparatively rare. Irrespective of the impression one might get in the media, crime-and-justice experienced reality is not widespread. What is widespread is access to symbolic reality.

Symbolic Reality

The next three sources of knowledge—other people, institutions, and the media—share their knowledge symbolically and collectively form one's symbolic reality. All the events you did not witness but believe occurred, all the facts about the world you did not personally collect but believe to be true, all the things you believe to exist but have not seen, make up your **symbolic reality.** The difference between experienced and symbolic reality can be illustrated with a few questions: Do you believe the moon exists? Why? Because you can see it directly. You have experienced reality knowledge of its existence. Do you believe the moon has an atmosphere? Why not? Because you have been told it has no air, you've read it has no air, and you have seen pictures of men in space suits on the moon.[9] You have based your belief about the moon's atmosphere on symbolic reality knowledge. Both experienced and symbolic knowledge can shape our view of reality. Now let's apply these ideas to crime. How many serial killers have you personally met? For most of us the answer is none. Yet if asked to list some common characteristics of serial killers, you would likely be able to offer an answer you believe to be correct. Your response would be based totally on symbolic reality knowledge. In fact, most of what we believe about the world comes from symbolic reality. In large, advanced, industrialized societies like the United States, media dominate our formation of symbolic reality, overwhelming our limited experienced reality knowledge and symbolic reality information we receive from other people and institutions. It is because so much of our social knowledge is gained symbolically from the media that there is concern over media's content. Media are centrally situated in the distribution of knowledge, and what we see as crime and justice is largely defined, described, and framed by media content.

Socially Constructed Reality

The knowledge individuals gain from their experienced and symbolic reality is ultimately mixed together, and from this mix we each construct our own "world." The resulting **socially constructed reality** is perceived as the "real" world by each individual—what we individually believe the world to be like. This subjective reality differs to some degree between individuals because their experienced realities differ and what they incorporate from their symbolic realities varies. However, individuals with access to similar knowledge and who frequently interact with one another tend to negotiate and construct similar social realities. The pun "Reality is a collective hunch" is an apt summary of this social construction process. The end result is a socially constructed subjective reality that directs social behavior. People behave according to how they believe the world is. Significant for crime and justice, the media comprise the most important element in defining crime-and-justice reality for most people.[10]

The Social Construction Process and the Media

The role of the media in the social construction process is diagrammed in Figure 2.1, which presents four stages of social constructionism. In Stage 1, we have the actual physical world we live in. In this stage, events such as crimes or terrorist acts occur and are noted by individuals and organizations. The physical world and its properties and conditions provide the boundaries

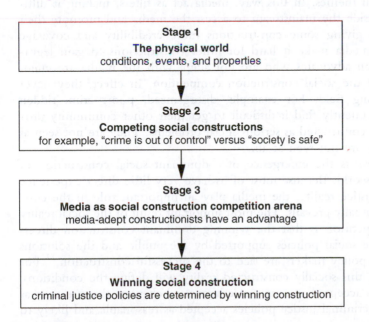

Stage 1
The physical world
conditions, events, and properties

Stage 2
Competing social constructions
for example, "crime is out of control" versus "society is safe"

Stage 3
Media as social construction competition arena
media-adept constructionists have an advantage

Stage 4
Winning social construction
criminal justice policies are determined by winning construction

FIGURE 2.1 The Stages of Social Construction.

that the following stages normally work within. Competing constructions cannot maintain credibility if they obviously run counter to the physical reality of the world. For example, a mayor of a city might wish to forward a social construction of her community as peaceful and safe. However, if there is rioting in the streets, her social construction would not be competitive for long.

In Stage 2, competing constructions first offer differing descriptions of what the physical world is like—what the physical conditions and facts of the world are. Frequently these descriptions are of social conditions that have been identified as social problems, such as drugs or crime. Hence, a social construction of the crime issue might include statistics and stories to support the construction that crime is out of control. Second, constructions usually offer differing explanations of why the physical world is as it is purported to be. The constructions will forward various histories and theories to map out how and why their description of the physical world happened. Therefore, statements like "crime is out of control because the criminal justice system is too lenient" might be part of a construction. Finally, based on their descriptions of the world and their explanations of why it so exists, these competing constructions often argue for a set of public and individual policies that should be supported and pursued. "In order to get crime under control, we must impose longer prison sentences" is an example of one such policy argument.

In Stage 3, the media help filter out competing constructions. This is where the media play their most powerful role. Persons forwarding constructions compete for media attention, and the media tend to favor positions that are dramatic, are sponsored by powerful groups, and are related to preestablished cultural themes. In this way, media act as filters, making it difficult for those outside the mainstream to access the media and promote their constructions. By giving some constructions more credibility and coverage than others, the media make it hard for other constructions to gain legitimacy. Construction advocates who are not adept with the media are effectively shut out of the social construction competition. In effect, they never get on the playing field. For example, disorganized, poor, crime-ridden neighborhoods frequently find it difficult to get their other community problems successfully constructed as serious social problems. They are not seen as unimportant; they are not seen at all.

Stage 4 represents the emergence of a dominant social construction of some part of the world. Because most of us have very little direct experience with crime-and-justice reality, the media play an important role in the construction that eventually prevails. The most important result of the social reality construction competition is that the winning dominant construction directs public policy. The social policies supported by the public and the solutions forwarded by the policy makers are tied to the successful construction.[11] For crime and justice, this socially constructed reality will define the conditions, trends, and factors accepted as causes of crime; the behaviors that are seen as criminal; and the criminal justice policies accepted as reasonable and likely to be successful.

THE CONCEPTS OF SOCIAL CONSTRUCTIONISM

The perspective of social constructionism involves a set of concepts that further detail how the social construction competition works. Basic to the social construction process are claims makers, who compete with one another and argue for the social acceptance of their specific constructions of reality.

Claims Makers and Claims

Claims makers are the promoters, activists, professional experts, and spokespersons involved in forwarding specific claims about a social condition.[12] A century ago, Ivy L. Lee, a founding member of the American public relations movement, noted:

> It is not the facts alone that strike the public mind, but the way in which they take place and in which they are published that kindle imaginations. The effort to state an absolute fact is simply an attempt to give you my interpretation.[13]

Hence, claims makers do more than just draw attention to particular social conditions; they shape our sense of what the conditions mean and what the social problem is. Every social condition can be constructed in many different ways. For example, crime can be constructed as a social, individual, racial, sexual, economic, criminal justice, or technological problem, and each construction implies different policy courses and solutions. These solutions are imbedded in the claims made by the competing claims makers.

Claims can be thought of as coming in two basic flavors: factual and interpretative (see Figure 2.2).[14] **Factual claims** are statements that purport to

---

B o x 2.1   Common Crime-and-Justice Claims Found in the Media

1. Crime fighters must use any means to catch criminals.
2. Corruption runs rampant throughout criminal justice agencies.
3. Bureaucratic red tape and due process protections hinder the honest crime fighters and make it difficult to successfully conclude investigations.
4. Crime fighters need more training and resources because they are not capable of solving crimes legally.
5. Crime is a result of individual characteristics and is not related to social structure, racism, or poverty.
6. Criminals cannot be rehabilitated and, if given a chance, will recidivate.
7. Specific deterrence combined with incapacitation is the only policy approach that will stop criminals from recidivating.
8. The courts allow dangerous offenders to avoid guilt.
9. Probation and parole allow dangerous offenders to go free.
10. Prisons make dangerous offenders more dangerous while brutalizing and criminalizing wrongfully incarcerated ones.

Crime is out of control...	because of the lax sentencing of criminal judges.
Factual claim	*Interpretative claim that offers an explanation of why crime is out of control*

Cocaine is a dangerous drug...	whose use and sale must be criminalized.
Factual claim	*Interpretative claim with associated policy*

FIGURE 2.2   Examples of Factual and Interpretative Claims.

describe the world. These are statements about what happened and are promoted as objective "facts" about the world. For example, "crime is out of control" is a claim about the physical condition of crime in society. Factual claims are also made to categorize or type an event. A statement along the lines of "This murder is an example of the rage that is common on our highways" would be a factual claim forwarded to categorize a murder as fitting into a specific type of killing—in this case, road rage. Factual claims are the descriptions, typifications, and assertions regarding the extent and nature of conditions in the physical world.

Interpretative claims are statements that focus on the meanings of events. They do one of two things: either they offer an explanation of why a set of factual claims is as described, or they offer a course of action—a public policy —that needs to be followed to address the conditions or events described in the factual claims. Together, factual and interpretative claims target the beliefs and attitudes that people hold about the world: what they think the conditions of the world are, what they feel are the causes of those conditions, and what they think the solutions are.

One strategy involving claims often used to get a social construction accepted by the public is called linkage. **Linkage** involves the association of the subject of the social construction effort with other previously constructed issues (see Box 2.2). For example, drugs are often linked to other social problems such as crime. The strategy of linkage would be to argue that a drug must be criminalized or other types of crime will increase. The linkage of crime to danger and calamity is also employed in the social construction process, and crime-and-justice issues are often linked to the endangerment of health, welfare, families, and communities.[15] The acceptance of a claim of linkage between one social phenomenon and another issue that is already seen as harmful raises the concern and public importance of the linked social phenomenon.[16] Hence, the social importance of drug abuse is heightened when drugs are linked to crime, and the same linkage makes other correlates of crime, such as poverty, appear less important.

Claims makers hope to have their claims accepted as the dominant social construction of reality. For a construction to be successful, its claims must be

---

B o x   2.2   Linking Satanic Cults to Serial Homicide and Bullying to Terrorism

Phillip Jenkins provides an example of an attempt to link satanic cults to serial murder:

> Estimates about the numbers of victims varied greatly, but one commonly cited figure suggested that some fifty thousand ritualistic sacrifices occurred each year. In 1988, for example, the American Focus on Satanic Crime (a work especially targeted at law enforcement professionals) suggested that Satanists are connected with "the murders of unbaptized infants, child sexual abuse in day-care, rape, ritual abuse of children, drug trafficking, arson, pornography, kidnapping, vandalism, church desecration, corpse theft, sexual trafficking of children and the heinous mutilation, dismemberment and sacrifices of humans and animals. [They are] responsible for the deaths of more than 60,000 Americans each year, including missing and runaway youth."

In another example of linkage, the lyrics from a public service announcement song by Ian Victorian strive to link bullying to terrorism.

Choose Freedom from Bullies

> *Let me tell ya something about bullies*
> *They can show up anywhere, anytime, and any place*
> *It ain't always about size, looks, or race necessarily*
> *Bullies use intimidation and threats to terrorize others*
> *They don't give a damn about you or your momma*
> *Terrorists use the same tactics too*
> *Always tryin' to steal the freedom from you, you, and you*

SOURCES: Phillip Jenkins, *Using Murder* (New York: Aldine de Gruyter, 1994, 197) quoting Alan Peterson, "The American Focus on Satanic Crime," foreword. http://www.metacafe.com/watch/1077521/choose_freedom_from _bullies_ian_victorian_psa_anti_hatecrime_ad/

---

accepted. If the dominant social construction becomes "crime is out of control," then those who have made that claim have been successful. When President Obama stated that mass shootings by individuals who should not have access to guns is out of control, he was forwarding a claim about the world that also suggested a response to the claimed condition of the world. Passage of new laws and policies directed against the "easy access to guns in America" would indicate the success of the president's social construction effort of a social problem, an effort that had previously failed to gain traction. To further enhance their likelihood of success, claims makers also frequently make use of pre-established constructions, or frames, to advance their claims.

Frames

In the social construction of the crime–and–justice arena, prepackaged constructions, or **frames,** include factual and interpretative claims and associated policies. A frame is a fully developed social construction template that allows its users to categorize, label, and deal with a wide range of world events. Frames simplify one's dealing with the world by organizing experiences and events into groups and guiding what are seen as the appropriate policies and actions. Regarding crime and justice, pre-existing frames make the processing, labeling, and understanding of crimes easier for the person holding that frame's view of reality. If a crime can be quickly placed into a pre-established frame, it will be seen as another example of a particular type of crime needing a particular type of response. A senseless murder, for example, might become "another predator killing that resulted from a lenient criminal justice system." Such crimes can be quickly cognitively dealt with and tied to a policy position. You do not have to spend a lot of time understanding a crime that has been fitted into a crime-and-justice frame. The cause of the crime, explanations for why it occurred, and what needs to be done are already built into the frame. Certain U.S. crime-and-justice frames have deep historical roots; criminologist Theodore Sasson describes five long-standing crime-and-justice frames that compete today in the United States.[17] All five frames offer explanations of crime, point to specific causes, and come with accompanying policies. These frames are summarized in Table 2.1.

Faulty Criminal Justice System Frame.   The first frame holds that crime results from a lack of "law and order." People commit crimes knowing they can get away with them because the police are handcuffed by liberal judges and the prisons are revolving doors. The only way to ensure public safety is to increase the swiftness, certainty, and severity of punishment. Loopholes and technicalities that impede the

T A B L E 2.1   Crime-and-Justice Frames

Frame	Cause	Policy	Symbols
Faulty system	Crime stems from criminal justice leniency and inefficiency	The criminal justice system needs to "get tough."	Aurora Colorado "Dark Knight" shooting, "handcuffed police," "revolving door justice"
Blocked opportunities	Crime stems from poverty and inequality	The government must address the "root causes" of crime by creating jobs and reducing poverty.	Stealing sneakers, black-on-black crime, dead-end, low-paying jobs
Social breakdown	Crime stems from family and community breakdown	Citizens should band together to re-create traditional communities.	Urban riots, Steubenville Rape case, "family values"
Racist system	The criminal justice system operates in a racist fashion	African Americans should band together to demand justice.	Driving while Black, shooting of Trayvon Martin, "profiling"
Violent media	Crime stems from violence in the mass media	The government should regulate violent imagery in the media.	"Life imitates art," copycat crimes, violent video games, Grand Theft Auto, Aurora Colorado "Dark Knight" shooting

SOURCE: Adapted from Sasson, T. 1995. Crime Talk. pgs. 13-17. Hawthorne, N.Y.: Aldine de Gruyter

apprehension and imprisonment of offenders must be eliminated, and funding for police, courts, and prisons must be increased. The faulty system frame is symbolically represented by the previously convicted, repeat rapist or by the image of inmates passing through a revolving door on a prison.

Blocked Opportunities Frame.   This frame depicts crime as a consequence of inequality and discrimination, especially in unemployment, poverty, and education. People commit crimes when they discover that the legitimate means for attaining material success are blocked. Unemployment, ignorance, disease, filth, poor housing, congestion, and discrimination all contribute to crime waves that are seen as sweeping the nation.[18] "If you're going to create a sink-or-swim society, you have to expect people to thrash before they go down" is an example of a claim associated with the blocked opportunity frame.[19] To reduce crime, government must ameliorate the social conditions that cause it. Blocked opportunities are symbolically portrayed through references to dead-end jobs held by inner-city youth, such as flipping burgers at McDonald's.

Social Breakdown Frame.   This frame depicts crime as a consequence of family and community disintegration, skyrocketing rates of divorce, and out-of-wedlock births. Social breakdown has both conservative and liberal versions. The conservative version attributes family and community breakdown to "permissiveness," which is exemplified by protest movements and government-sponsored welfare. The liberal version attributes family and community breakdown to unemployment, racial discrimination, and the loss of jobs and income. An example of a social breakdown claim was made by then President Bill Clinton: "In America's toughest neighborhoods, meanest streets, and poorest rural areas, we have seen a stunning breakdown of community, family and work at the heart and soul of civilized society. This has created a vast vacuum into which violence, drugs, and gangs have moved."[20]

Racist System Frame.   The racist system frame focuses on the criminal justice system rather than on crime. This frame depicts the courts and police as racist agents of oppression. In this frame, police resources are seen as dedicated more to the protection of white neighborhoods than to reducing crime in minority communities. Minority offenders are seen as more likely than whites who commit comparable offenses to be arrested, convicted, and sentenced to prison, and the death penalty is administered in a racist fashion. In radical versions of this frame, the basic purpose of the criminal justice system is to suppress a potentially rebellious underclass. An example of this claim was offered by then Undersecretary of State Nicholas B. Katzenbach: "We have in these United States lived under a dual system of justice, one for the white, one for the black."[21] The racist system frame has been symbolized by the beating of motorist Rodney King, the trial of O. J. Simpson, and the Trayvon Martin shooting.

Violent Media Frame.   It is not surprising in a culture swamped in media that a frame reflecting concerns about the media exists. The media violence frame depicts crime and social violence as a consequence of violence on television, in the movies, in popular music and in video games. It is argued that violence in the mass media undermines respect for life. To reduce violence in society, this frame directs us to first reduce it in the mass media. It is forwarded by claims such as the following: "By the time the average child reaches age 18, he will have witnessed some 18,000 murders and countless highly detailed incidents of robbery, arson, bombings, shooting, beatings, forgery, smuggling, and torture."[22] The media violence frame is symbolically referenced by allusions to violent visual media, video games, and musical lyrics. Theodore Sasson notes that despite being perceived as the least important general explanation of crime and violence, media violence is seen as at least a partial explanation of violent crime by nearly all Americans. Violent media is not seen as the most important source of our cultural violence, but there is a broad consensus that the media substantially contribute to violent crime.

How Frames Influence Crime-and-Justice Policy. All five frames are supported by some portion of the public, and the frames are not mutually exclusive. People often simultaneously support more than one frame, applying one frame to one set of crimes and criminals and another frame to other events. Crime-and-justice claims makers can guarantee a level of support if they can fit their social construction within one of these frames. Analogous to a political candidate running as a Republican or a Democrat, and thereby being assured of the votes of loyal party members, these five established frames are resources that can be tapped by criminal justice claims makers to forward individual claims and policies. By fitting their claims and desired policies within one of these pre-existing frames, they tap into a pool of public support. Many crime-and-justice events can be differently constructed using different frames. For example, O. J. Simpson's murder trial was symbolic for two frames: Those who thought him guilty of murder saw his acquittal as evidence that the criminal justice system is faulty and must be tougher; those who saw him as innocent saw his arrest and prosecution as an example of a racist criminal justice system. Similarly, the 2012 Sandy Hook Elementary School shooting was used as support for the social breakdown frame, with the shooter portrayed as coming from a dysfunctional family; the media violence frame, with the shooter portrayed as under the spell of violent video games; and the faulty system frame, with the system blamed for not recognizing a dangerous youth and preventing his acquisition of weapons.

The five frames jockey with one another for influence over how criminality is understood in society, which criminal justice policies enjoy public support, and how new crimes and criminals are perceived. The process through which crime-and-justice frames fall in and out of favor is closely tied to the social construction competition that is constantly being conducted in the media. In addition to being part of their own frame, by focusing on certain types of crimes or giving access to specific frame promoting claims makers, the media can boost frames ahead of one another.[23] As will be discussed in later chapters, although all five frames get some media play, recent crime-and-justice content and portraits tend to favor the faulty system and social breakdown frames over the other three. In addition to these fully constructed frames, less comprehensive social construction tools, known as narratives, are also available to claims makers.

Narratives

Central to entertainment media but also common in news and infotainment, narratives are popular and useful in the social construction of crime-and-justice reality. Not to be confused with genres or standard story lines, and unlike frames, which are fully developed crime-and-justice constructions, **narratives** are less encompassing, pre-established mini-social constructions found throughout crime-and-justice media.[24] Narratives are crime-and-justice portraits that the public already recognizes and has embraced. Narratives are not broad explanations of crime and do not include wide-scale public policy directions like frames; instead narratives outline the recurring crime-and-justice types and situations that regularly appear in the media.[25] The "naïve innocent" who stumbles into victimization is one recurring crime narrative. The "masculine, heroic crime-fighter" who cannot be swayed by corruption or hardship is another. The most popular, longest-running criminal narrative is the "innately evil predatory criminal" highlighted in serial killer movies. Additional common criminal justice narratives such as the "rogue cop," the "sadistic guard," and the "corrupt lawyer" are found across the media. Narratives can be utilized to quickly establish the characteristics of a criminal, a victim, or a crime-fighter and as supportive examples for larger crime-and-justice frames. In practice, narratives are frequently linked to the faulty system frame by inferring a simplified single-cause explanation of crime and shared elements of random, predatory violence and innocent victims.[26]

The cultural stock of narratives that can be drawn upon also influence what is said and not said about crime. They provide ready-made story lines to apply to current crime-and-justice events and thereby give a sense of predictability and understanding to even the most senseless criminality. As socially shared symbols of crime and justice, their use reduces the need to explain cause and effect, and accompanying crime-and-justice interpretive claims can remain unstated yet implicitly accepted. The evil predatory criminal narrative, for example, offers an explanation of the most heinous crimes. In the same way that a wolf by its nature preys on others, a violent crime needs no further explanation than to evoke the descriptor "evil predator." In the same vein that you don't need an explanation for why a wolf attacks sheep, but would need one to explain a wolf that did not, the predatory criminal narrative supplies an explanation for why criminals attack the law-abiding. Without having to expressly spell it out, the predator criminal narrative explains that it is just the innate nature of criminals; it's what they do and what they are. In the crime-and-justice social construction competitive process, narratives are often applied to specific criminal events, which are then attached to larger constructions and forwarded as examples of what is wrong in society.[27] In crime-and-justice social constructionism, these special focus events are called symbolic crimes, and they play an important social construction role.

Symbolic Crimes

Symbolic crimes are crimes and other criminal justice events that are selected and highlighted by claims makers as the perfect example of why their crime-and-justice construction should be accepted.[28] The beating of Rodney King, the kidnapping and murder of Polly Klaas, the O. J. Simpson murder trial, the

Columbine school shooting, the September 11, 2001, terrorist attacks, the Aurora Colorado theater shooting, the Sandy Hook Elementary school shooting, the Boston Marathon bombing (see Box 2.3), are well-known symbolic crimes. Symbolic crimes are trumpeted to convince people of the existence of a pressing crime-and-justice problem and a desperately needed criminal justice policy. They are taken up by claims makers and forwarded as either "the types of crimes we can expect to happen more often because we have allowed a set of conditions to fester" or as "an example of what a new criminal justice policy will correct if we implement it." Frequently, a symbolic crime is used for both—to show what happens because of, in their view, obviously erroneous past practices and conditions, and as evidence to argue for specific policy changes.

To fulfill their persuasive social construction function, symbolic crimes are often the worst, most grievous examples that can be found. The formula for using symbolic crimes in crime-and-justice social construction is simple:

Step 1. Find the worst crime you can—the most innocent victim (child victims are often used) or most heinous criminal (animalistic, predatory serial killers are popular).

Step 2. Link your construction to your symbolic crime (for example, to raise the issue of pornography, after a child murder claim that "this child would be alive today if the suspect did not have access to pornography."

Step 3. Success equals an increased importance of your issue and public acceptance of your construction (social acceptance of media with sexual content declines as more people see this sort of media as having serious, sometimes deadly consequences).

Thus, if you wish to forward capital punishment as a necessary social policy, as a claims maker you would seek out a symbolic crime committed by someone who had murdered previously, avoided execution, was released into society, and killed again. If you are opposed to capital punishment, you would look for a case where an innocent individual was wrongly executed as your symbol of the wrong that results from a policy of capital punishment.

As the social construction process is distilled into a single, concrete, emotion-laden dramatic event that can be easily portrayed by the media, quickly interpreted by the public, and difficult for opponents to argue against, an effective symbolic crime can be the difference between winning and losing a social construction competition. When claims makers win a social construction competition, they gain another benefit—they gain **ownership** of social problems and issues.

Ownership

Ownership is the identification of a particular social condition with a particular set of claims makers who come to dominate the social construction of that issue. Claims makers own an issue when they are sought out by the media and others for information regarding the problem and for opinions regarding the reasonableness of competing social constructions and policies associated with the issue. Some groups, by virtue of their superior power, finances, status, organization, technology, or media access,

B o x   2.3   Symbolic Crimes: September 11, 2001, Terrorist Attacks; December 14, 2012, Sandy Hook Elementary School Shooting

The September 11, 2001, terrorist attacks on the World Trade Center buildings in New York remain the symbolic crimes for the ongoing U.S. war on terror. In these attacks the Islamic terrorist group al-Qaeda hijacked four commercial aircraft in mid-flight and flew two of them into the World Trade Center Towers in New York City, and one into the Pentagon in Washington, D.C. The fourth crashed in Pennsylvania due to passenger heroics. The Trade Center Towers in New York were selected by al-Qaeda because of their symbolism of the United State' economic power, with the terrorist goal of socially reconstructing them to be a "new symbol of U.S. vulnerability" (Tuman, 2003, p. 65). In a similar fashion, the murder of 20 children and 6 adults in Newtown, Connecticut has become the symbolic crime for gun control. In the words of President Obama: "an unbalanced man shouldn't be able to get his hands on a military-style assault rifle so easily; that in this age of technology, we should be able to check someone's criminal records before he or she can check out at a gun show; that if we work harder to keep guns out of the hands of dangerous people, there would be fewer atrocities like the one in Newtown—or any of the lesser-known tragedies that visit small towns and big cities all across America every day."

Sean Adair/Reuters/Landov

SOURCE: https://petitions.whitehouse.gov/response/message-president-obama-about-your-petition-reducing-gun-violence

B o x 2.4   Ownership, the Media, and Criminal Justice

Phillip Jenkins relates how ownership of "serial murder" by the FBI resulted in substantial tangible benefits for the agency: "The dominance of the FBI's experts can be observed throughout the process of construction. They successfully presented themselves as the best (or only) authorities on the topic, and they assisted journalists and writers who reciprocated with favorable depictions of the agency. The federal officials stood to gain substantially … because establishing the reality of a problem provided added justification for their Behavioral Science Unit (BSU), a new and unorthodox unit seeking to validate its skills in areas such as profiling and crime scene analysis. Once it was established that the FBI could and should have jurisdiction over this type of crime, it was not difficult to seek similar involvement in other offenses that could plausibly be mapped together with serial homicide."

have more ability to make their constructions appear legitimate—to make their version of reality stick—and to take effective ownership of an issue. Because of their media access and control of crime data, law enforcement agencies have proprietary ownership of crime. When a new type of crime is constructed, law enforcement usually has the first call regarding how that crime will be constructed and related policy choices debated. Box 2.4 describes the application of the social constructionism concept of ownership to the relationship of the media and criminal justice and provides a specific example of the FBI and serial murder. While the concepts and elements of social construction have remained stable, the dynamics of the social construction process have been altered by the development of new forms of media. These new media are inherently different from traditional legacy media in how they relate to their audiences and by extension how social construction occurs under their influence.

NEW MEDIA AND SOCIAL CONSTRUCTION

The simplest way to perceive new media and to understand their effects on social construction process is to describe how they differ from old media. As stated in Chapter 1, old or "legacy media" are composed of the dominant-twentieth-century traditional media forms of news broadcasts, newspapers, magazines, television, film, radio, and music. New media incorporates all of these older forms and their content into new high speed, digital, personalized delivery platforms. The key difference between old and new media, therefore, is not in terms of content, but lies in access to content, distribution of content, and creation of content.

Legacy and New Media Differences.   The single most important change between old and new media lies in the relationship found between the creators of media content and the consumers of the content, between legacy and new media. In the legacy media world, media content was created and distributed by distant others, the media industry, to be delivered to distant isolated

Box 2.5   The Development of New Media

A brief history of new media shows the change from passive consumer to active consumer which accompanied the shift. New media began in the 1990s when Internet Web pages (1993) and Yahoo (1994) came into existence. However, the initial "World Wide Web," sometimes referred to as Web 1.0, was not structured for the sharing of information as much as for the retrieval of information. You could extract a document but not easily talk with others about it. For the first time, though, media provided information that could be both quickly accessed and simultaneously tailored through search engines by consumers to fit specific narrow interests. The development of "Web 2.0" in the late 1990s eliminated the isolation of users from other users. Thereafter, users were not only provided access to large amounts of content but put in contact with other users who had an interest in that content and wanted to share content, pictures, and other information. The development of Internet-based networking sites gave users the ability to build online profiles and personalities, self-constructed online identities for anyone who wanted to participate. The rise of social media—highly interactive, multimedia Web sites, devices, and programs that allow individuals to form into virtual communities and share information, knowledge, and experiences—has had immense social effects. After Web 2.0, the audience/consumer moved to the forefront of media-society dynamics. This reformulated relationship between users and their media has been enhanced with the addition of each new media component. Chronicled below, blogging (1997) and Google (1998) followed by iPods and Wikipedia in 2001, Facebook and podcasting in 2004, and YouTube and Twitter in 2005 and 2006 round out most of the current new media.

SOURCES: Batchelor, "Social Media and Youth Culture." *New Media and the Courts;* Hunter, Lobato, Richardson, and Thomas, *Amateur Media: Social, Cultural and Legal Perspectives;* Surette, "21st Century Crime and Justice."

New Media Component	Origin Date	Description
World Wide Web	Aug. 1991	The World Wide Web, not to be mistaken for the Internet, is a "system of Internet servers that support specially formatted documents".
Smartphones	1992	Prototypes of today's devices originated in the combination of cellular phones and "personal digital assistants" (PDAs). Contemporary smartphones are mobile multi-function communication devices that combine phone communication capabilities with Internet access, video viewing, and music storage and playback capabilities. Smartphones outsold older style phones beginning in 2013.
Yahoo	Jan. 1994	Yahoo was created by David Filo and Jerry Yang of Stanford University. They originally wanted to keep tabs on their own personal interests on the Internet. Since then, Yahoo has become a company that focuses on helping users find information across multiple topics.

(continued)

B o x 2.5	**The Development of New Media (Continued)**	

New Media Component	Origin Date	Description
Wiki	Mar. 1995	A content management system, a wiki is "a piece of server software that allows users to freely create and edit Web page content using any Web browser. "
Blogging	Dec. 1997	Periodically updated online journals, blogs are structured in the form of posts or individual entries of news or commentary in reverse chronological order that represent a rolling record of the author's thoughts.
Google	Sept. 1998	Google is a search engine that allows people to perform keyword searches. Aside from being a search engine, Google also provides services that enable users to send e-mails, publish Web pages, and create blogs. Google is currently the most popular and the largest Web-based search engine in the world.
Wikipedia	Jan. 2001	Wikipedia is a Web site that offers free online content and allows individuals to edit and contribute to the information presented on the site.
iPod	Oct. 2001	Initially served as a portable media player that stored songs in an mp3 format and allowed for listening to music on the go. Later versions allow users to access applications such as Facebook and Twitter.
MySpace	Aug. 2003	MySpace was founded in 2003 for persons interested in bands and music. The attraction was the ability to control access and interactivity to "friends".
Facebook	Feb. 2004	Facebook was founded in 2004, rooted in linking college students. Today, it is a general public social networking site that connects colleagues, friends, and family. Users first create a profile and then add friends and strangers. Members have the ability to upload photos, write statuses on their "wall", instant message their friends, and send private messages to other users. In 2013, there were more than 500 million Facebook users.
YouTube	Feb. 2005	A Web site that allows users to upload original videos while also allowing individuals to watch videos uploaded by others. This Web site also allows individuals to connect with one another by commenting, "subscribing" and "liking" videos.
Twitter	Mar. 2006	Twitter answers the question: "What are you doing?" in a short 140-character posts that are distributed to people who have signed on to "follow" an individual.
Instagram	Oct. 2010	This photo sharing social media app allows users to "follow" their friends or complete strangers and "like" others pictures as well as leave comments. As of 2013, there were 90 million people who use Instagram at least once a month.

(cont'nued)

consumers, to have whatever social impact it was destined to have. One side created legacy media content, the other side was affected by it. Feedback loops between audience and creators were weak, slow, and haphazard; there were clear, obvious distinctions between writers and readers, speakers and listeners, performers and audiences, and producers and consumers. The content creation process flowed nearly exclusively in a top-down direction. New media, in contrast, have an inherently different creator/consumer relationship. With new media, consumers can also be producers of self-generated mediated content and assume the role of distributors of content.[29] With new media the "top down" flow for media content and effects has been replaced with audience creative participation, peer-to-peer distribution, and the proliferation of user-generated content.[30] The isolated act of "turning on the television" has been replaced by the collective experience of "going viral". Within this shift, four differences between new media and traditional media are notable.

First, with new media there is less emphasis on attracting large, passive, heterogeneous audiences. Instead, small homogenous audiences that have a special interest in a narrow type of content are targeted. This characteristic was first developed in the traditional media of radio, where you find jazz, classical, and classic rock stations, and in specialized magazines like *True Detective*. Described as **narrowcasting** and opposite to broadcasting, the effect of this difference is readily apparent on the Internet, where one can find a large number of highly focused, narrow content dedicated Web sites. For example, people with a special interest in criminal forensics or serial killers can surf for Web sites that focus solely on forensics or serial killers. Related special interest entertainment programming can be automatically recorded for later consumption and new media devices can be set to automatically send alerts when news of user selected topics appears. Myopic content consumption that ignores most of the available media content while over-sampling narrow topics is today within easy reach of the so inclined.

The archiving of content that frequently accompanies narrowcasting is related to the second unique characteristic of new media—their **on-demand** nature. With new media, the delivery of content is controlled and determined by the consumer. Except for live events that someone wants to experience physically and in real time, little media content must be consumed at a particular time and place and few social events must be directly attended. Unless one actually want to "be" there, one can still have the experience of "being" there while fitting their "being there" mediated experience into a convenient schedule. In addition to attendance in new media being easier to achieve, the sharing of experiences is also eased. The third important difference with new social media is the easy widespread sharing of content. Today media content distribution is no longer a centralized process but instead is a diffused decentralized experience.[31]

The decentralization of the creation and distribution process when combined with the fourth differentiating characteristic, **interactivity**, leads to powerful social effects.[32] A new media consumer can be an active participant in the development, distribution, social assessment, and ultimate social impact of their content. With traditional media consumption, the consumer's only decision was whether to consume the offered content or not. In contrast, in new media the audience moves from passive receptor of pre-determined content to an active participant role in the creation of content. Interactivity is most apparent in the realm of video games, where content is determined live by the actions of game players.[33] For crime-related games, whether a crime victim is killed or spared, a crime solved or not, a criminal caught or escaped is not predetermined by a pre-set story author but is determined after the game has been distributed by each game-playing consumer.[34] Online games that combine role-playing, competition, interactive story creation, and online interactive chats provide multiple game players real-time virtual worlds to interact in. Via these platforms, new-media-based consumer participation is maximized, allowing consumers to create and influence the content they and others consume.[35] Due to the increasingly active role of audiences as co-producers of content, the traditionally separate domains of "media" (where content and information are made) and "society" (where content and information are consumed) are less separated in the new media age.[36] What happens in society frequently becomes media content as it happens and a large portion of society has become authors, directors, and publishers of media content. The traditional research question about the effect of media on society is becoming less relevant than the study of how a "mediated society" functions. Within this new media landscape faster and broader communications and the merging, sharing, and looping of content between mediums and individuals has become the norm.[37] Four general effects on society are important.

The first common social effect from new media is a result of the flow of content and the globalization of information.[38] Because the audience is not isolated as it was with legacy media, individuals communicate anonymously but intimately. The Internet has emerged as a particularly powerful social factor due to it having both mass and interpersonal elements. The Internet provides a unique one-to-many communication avenue.[39] It is word-of-mouth (or mouse) communication with global reach.[40] Consumers often have multiple online pseudonyms and complex social networks.[41] For example, online video games are frequently played collectively by physically separated gamers and many individuals present themselves online through multiple false identities, as when middle-aged males create online identities as teenage females. The rise of mediated over directly experienced reality means that many children today spend more time in a media-constructed world than in a directly experienced one. Starting with home computers and Internet access and enhanced by mobile phones, new media have encouraged and allowed people to live together separately—to be within the family space but to be psychologically elsewhere.[42] For the social construction process this has meant that although the knowledge and claims are obtained from distant media-based symbolic reality sources, they feel like they are coming from your conversational reality, from personal significant others. This social process has resulted in high levels of socialization into virtual peer groups and reduced socialization into physical near groups (and is a significant effect tapped by terrorists for recruitment).

A second significant general new media societal effect is on the news. New media age "news" has reduced timely interpretation of content. The legacy media method of fact-based rendering of events—what a crime means, its genesis, and placement in a broader social context—is too slow of a process in the new media distribution pace. In its place are images and emotional reactions which are often delivered live, on-demand, and before events have concluded.[43] While crime-related content appears to be as ubiquitous in new media as it was in legacy media–based news, exposure to discussions of crime has become more narrow.[44] Because new media users can tightly control their content choices, those interested in crime can watch more crime news and those not interested can avoid crime news. One social effect from new media therefore is a large knowledge gap, where self-selected consumers know a lot about narrow subjects but little about much else.[45] What interpretations and social contextualization they receive tends to be narrowed to fit tight ideological viewpoints where pre-set support for a particular crime-and-justice frame determines what content one is self-exposed to. Described as an "echo chamber" where opposing perspectives are drowned out by the focused recycling of particular sets of frames and narratives, people know more and more about less and less.[46] For example, a recent study of cable talk shows found that discussions of justice issues tended to promote hardline positions and distorted racial and gender portraits of criminality.[47] Online blogs have also been found to not provide broad-based discussions or coverage of crime and justice.[48] As a group, new media have enormously increased access to large amounts of information and multiple worldviews, but strangely, this seems to have had the social effect of decreasing the diversity of the content being accessed and the viewpoints considered. Given a larger menu with new media, users appear to narrow their diets.

There are general effects from new media on the social construction of reality process. First off, the social construction of reality process has become more dominated by media-provided information and the directly experienced world has a reduced effect and influence. The blurring of experienced and symbolic reality also has increased. In addition, as the arena where competing social constructions vie for dominance shifted from legacy to new media platforms, the speed of the competition has increased along with the speed of the distribution of social knowledge. Furthermore, success in the social construction competition has been affected. Successful claims makers are more often those who are sophisticated users of new media and claims that fit the new media formats of brief and visual are the ones that go viral. New communication technologies have affected the claims-making process. On one hand, blogs have made the process more efficient and provided outsider claims makers with greater opportunities to have a voice in the debate. On the other hand, there is no evidence that dialogue about crime-and-justice has expanded.[49]

Social construction strategy is also affected. The linking of events and claims to larger social problems, policies, and frames is pursued more aggressively and with more reliance on visually supported factual claims and with less reliance on well-grounded interpretative claims. The established crime–and–justice frames all simultaneously attract supporters who tend to narrowly expose themselves to frame-supportive arguments and examples and avoid exposure to information that forwards competing frames. The tendency of new media exposure to be myopic and ideologically driven has led to each of Sasson's five crime-and-justice frames (faulty system, blocked opportunities, social breakdown, racist system, and violent media) generating an audience of "true believers" who ridicule other frame supporters and ignore counter-frame evidence. Along similar lines, narratives and symbolic crimes have become points of competition where claims makers and frames advocates seek to gain monopolistic ownership of high visibility, high-value new media crime-and-justice content to which claims and policies can be attached.

A last important change is the decreased ability of traditional criminal justice agencies to maintain ownership of crime issues and events. This is more difficult as new media have broadened access to information. In sum, the social construction of crime and justice in new media is a more fluid, multi-directional process where clear winners and losers are less apparent. With deep changes in social interactions and processes, multiple social constructions emerge and compete, each adopted by different devoted audience segments. Because polarization drives society away from arriving at a consensus view of reality and instead onto ideologically isolated reality islands, the social world that has resulted is far different from the one found a generation ago.

THE SOCIAL CONSTRUCTION PROCESS IN ACTION

"Victim rights,"[50] "cyber stalking," [51] and "juveniles armed with assault rifles"[52] are a few crime-and-justice social constructions described in recent research. Three well-documented criminal justice social constructions are reviewed here to demonstrate the social construction process applied to crime and justice.[53]

Social Construction of Road Rage

In this example, a new crime was constructed by the media. The media do not usually take on this role as much as they act as a filter and playing field among various claims makers, but an example of a media-created crime can be seen in the construction of road rage. Joel Best analyzed the imagery concerning highway violence from several major newspapers and television stations. He found that after an initial story dealing with highway violence appeared, the media began linking a number of different types of highway incidents together as a new type of crime today known as "road rage." Best summarizes:

> In short, the media described freeway shootings as a growing problem,
> characterized by random violence and widespread fear. Without official
> statistics or public opinion polls bearing on the topic, reporters relied on
> interviews with their sources to support these claims. Thus, the eleven
> network news stories used thirty-eight clips from interviews: eleven
> with law enforcement officials promising to take action or advising
> caution; thirteen victims describing their experiences; ten person-in the-
> street interviews revealing public concern; and four experts offering
> explanations.[54]

Socially constructed by the news media, today "road rage" is widely recognized as a type of crime.

Best found that the media sought not only to describe but to explain and interpret the problem. The media would say, for example, that highway congestion coupled with the anonymity of the car could trigger these violent outrages in people. The media also offered competing interpretative claims for the problem of highway violence. Some interpreted it as a faulty system frame problem and that more law enforcement was the solution to the problem. Others saw it as a traffic problem. Freeway violence would be lessened if the roads were not so congested. Other claims were that freeway violence was a gun access problem, or a lack of courtesy problem (fitting the social breakdown frame). Best concludes that in this case the media was the primary claims maker in the construction of road rage, taking on this role in part because of a slow news period. Needing crime news and a new crime, the news media went out and constructed one.

Reconstruction of Driving Under the Influence

Media can also influence the crime construction process by raising the perception of a crime's seriousness. An example of this type of influence can be seen in the public's evolving beliefs about drinking and driving. Driving under the influence (DUI) has been legally defined as a crime for a long time. However, there was not broad, consistent public support for its prosecution. Not surprisingly, enforcement was lax and haphazard. Prior to the 1980s, DUI was socially constructed primarily as an individual rehabilitation problem. News accounts told of how lawmakers wanted to lessen the penalties for DUI. During this period, lawmakers rationalized that the current penalties were too harsh and that the imposition of stiff penalties such as license revocation would interfere with the offender's ability to work. The media used nonpejorative words like *errant* to describe the actions of those convicted of DUI.

Beginning in the 1980s, new claims makers such as Mothers Against Drunk Driving (MADD) attacked this dominant social construction of the drunk driver.[55] Whereas drunk drivers had been seen as troubled individuals, when socially reconstructed, they became individuals who cause trouble. MADD could not have done this without waging a successful media-based social construction campaign that, in turn, affected how this crime was seen by the public.

Since the 1980s, DUI has been socially constructed as a much more serious crime. The drunk driver is now characterized as a "killer drunk" and one of society's crime problems. There was a clear shift in the media's construction of drinking and driving and subsequently how society reacted to drinking and driving. No longer viewed as an individual problem needing treatment, DUI offenders were now constructed as a menace to society, and support grew for much stricter DUI laws and their enforcement and prosecution. DUI was successfully reconstructed and is now seen by most people as a serious crime deserving harsh punishment.

Competing Constructions of the Arrest of Rodney King

One infamous example of social constructionism in crime and justice is the arrest and beating of Rodney King, caught on videotape on the night of March 3, 1991. After a high-speed car chase, Mr. King was arrested and violently subdued by members of the Los Angeles Police Department. This event provides an example of the social construction competition process in which different constructed realities strove to become the dominant view. Even though the arrest was videotaped and many factual claims about the event were unquestioned, such as how many times Mr. King was struck, a competition regarding cause and interpretation of the beating—the constructed interpretation of the event—developed.

Three different constructions of the cause and meaning of the event competed, with each construction suggesting widely different policies. In Construction A, King resisted arrest and the beating was justified by King's prior actions. The law enforcement policy implications from this construction are minimal. The police were justified; therefore, the police officers were not acting inappropriately, and no changes are required.

In Construction B, the beating was unjustified but was an isolated incident of unwarranted police violence carried out by a few rogue police officers. The officers were not acting appropriately but were also not typical or representative of L.A. police officers. This version implies the policy response of firing the bad apples and reprimanding the officers involved in misrepresenting the incident. Targeted internal individual discipline and prosecution of a few officers was all that was needed.

In Construction C, the beating was unjustified and seen as an example of an endemic problem of unwarranted and consistent police violence toward minorities. Fitted within the racist system frame, the officers were seen as acting as many L.A. officers would have acted, and the beating reflected an organizational tolerance of excessive violence toward minorities. The policy changes required from this construction involved drastic change in the L.A. police culture. It indicated the need to revamp the administration and training of the department and make extensive organizational changes.

In the end, Construction B was pursued and a number of responding officers were tried and convicted of civil rights violations, but Construction C eventually won the construction competition. The L.A. police chief eventually resigned, and a new, African-American chief was hired. The Rodney King beating displays how even for events in which factual claims are not disputed, vigorous competition among interpretative claims related to those facts can still occur.

SOCIAL CONSTRUCTIONISM AND CRIME AND JUSTICE

The ultimate social importance of social constructionism is found in its implication for criminal justice public policy.[56] As discussed in Chapter 9, the media and their crime-and-justice content influences the social construction of crime-and-justice reality by supplying the narratives, symbolic crimes, and information needed to create factual and interpretative claims. The media further provide the arena for the crime-and-justice social construction competition to be held. Today the process favors new media-savvy claims makers. This in turn encourages a particular set of social attitudes and perceptions about crime and justice and changes how seriously some crimes are viewed by the public.[57] Predatory criminality, victim rights, terrorism, white-collar crime, gun violence, and an overly lenient justice system are examples of criminal justice social construction efforts.

Media emerge as one of a group of social construction engines. As diagrammed in Figure 2.3, our most influential social construction engine is composed of personal experience and information received directly from people close to us, our **conversational reality**. Together these two components provide the foundation of our personal socially constructed reality. When we have applicable experiences or direct access to people we personally know who have had applicable experiences, we trust that knowledge above all other. Engine 2, legacy media, comprised of news, entertainment, advertising, and increasingly infotainment, creates a pervasive, broadly distributed body of information in the social construction process. The third social construction engine is knowledge supplied by the various institutions, organizations, and agencies that collect and disseminate statistics, information, and claims about the world. Annual FBI and Department of Justice reports about crime in America are crime-and-justice examples. To effectively distribute their claims, the institutions of the third engine have a dependent relationship with both legacy and new media. Little knowledge can be disseminated directly from these institutions and organizations to individuals, so agencies and institutions of the third engine must utilize the media for effective distribution of their factual and interpretative claims. The media, in turn, tap these organizations for credible, newsworthy, and interesting claims makers, claims, and marketable infotainment. As shown, engine 4, new media, today occupies a central position. They sit as a high-speed central clearinghouse that has two-way

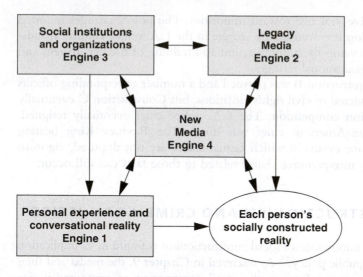

FIGURE 2.3   The Engines of Social Construction.

connections to the other three engines and much of the content of the socially shared knowledge at any particular time is largely determined by the gyrations of new media.

The single most important personal insight to be gained from a social constructionism perspective is recognition of the social construction competition that is being waged. Social construction of crime-and-justice reality is constant, and recognizing the claims makers, claims, and strategies involved helps in following the competition. All views of reality are constructed, and being aware of this aids in deciding which of the competing crime-and-justice constructions you will embrace. The social construction process is not inherently pernicious or evil, but we must recognize the process to thoughtfully evaluate the criminal justice policies that result.[58] The adage "where policy makers stand is determined by where they sit" (or policy choices are determined by the social, political, or organizational position one holds) directs us to consider the positions of claims makers—who they represent and what they stand to gain or lose by having their claims accepted or rejected. Ultimately, the prize from social construction is not the construction of any particular crime-and-justice issue but influence over the social construction process. Access to the media and the social reality media construct are the grand goal. If you can influence a reality-defining engine in a society, you can create the social reality of that society for many people. Therefore, winning one social construction contest puts you on the inside track for winning future contests in the same manner that successfully constructing a new type of crime in the present makes it easier to construct new ones in the future. If one set of claims makers gain control of the media social construction engine, other claims makers and constructions will no longer be competitive. If punitive criminal justice policy and predatory criminality totally dominate media content, entire frames and alternate ideas about crime and justice will disappear from serious public consideration. With these concepts and concerns in mind, we turn to the social construction of criminals, crime, and justice in the media, beginning in Chapter 3 with the images of crimes and criminals found in the media.

SUMMARY

- Social constructionism views knowledge as the result of people interacting and coming to agreement on facts and ideas about the world.

- People socially construct their view of reality from their direct experiences and from information they pick up symbolically via language and images from other people and the media.

- Followed by information received directly from significant others (our conversational reality), personal direct experience is the most influential in the social construction of reality process. The media and other social and government institutions rank next in influence, but because fewer people have direct experience or conversational reality access, the media are more important in the construction of crime-and-justice reality than in other social areas.

- New media mimics conversational reality in how many people interact with it.

- The social construction process involves competing constructions forwarded by claims makers who argue that their claims about reality be adopted by other people. Claims can be either factual (describing the world) or interpretative (explaining the world).

- Five common crime-and-justice frames exist and allow for the rapid social construction of new crimes. These frames are faulty criminal justice system, blocked opportunity, social breakdown, racist system, and media violence. Each frame encourages different policy approaches to deal with crime.

- In the construction of crime and justice, linking a crime to an already accepted social problem is a common strategy.

- Led by the "evil criminal predator," narratives are small, pre-established, commonly recognized mini-portraits found in crime-and-justice media.

- Symbolic crimes are high-profile crime-and-justice events that are used to champion specific crime-and-justice constructions.

- An important goal in the social construction competition is "ownership" of a crime-and-justice issue. Social construction ownership gives a claims maker greater access to resources, the media, and policy development.

- New media have changed the social construction process by changing the relationship between consumers and media from passive to active participants.

- While offering access to more information and competing social constructions of the world, new media appears to have encouraged a narrowing of consumption and exposure to competing ideas.

- The ultimate prizes in the crime-and-justice social construction of reality process are the criminal justice policies society adopts.

CLASS DISCUSSIONS

1. Discuss how the constructed reality you had of college while in high school differed from the reality you found and what your sources of information about college life were. Was information the media supplied important for your initial expectations?

2. Deconstruct recent news media coverage of an ongoing criminal case, listing the claims makers, their factual and interpretative claims, and any use of narratives, symbolic crimes, linkage, and ownership. Discuss which of the five common crime frames the news stories best support.

3. Discuss crime films that fit each of Sasson's five frames.

4. Discuss a recent high-profile crime in terms of how the social construction process was utilized to construct the event as a symbolic crime and any social and policy impacts that resulted.

SUGGESTED READINGS

Barak, G. (1995). *Media, process, and the social construction of crime.* New York: Garland.

Best, J. (1995). *Images of issues.* New York: Aldine de Gruyter.

Gergen, K. (1999). *An invitation to social construction.* Thousand Oaks: Sage.

Jenkins, P. (1994). *Using murder: The social construction of serial murder.* Hawthorne: Aldine de Gruyter.

Potter, G. and Kappeler, V. (2006). *Constructing crime.* Prospects Heights: Waveland.

Malcolm Spector, M. and Kitsuse, J. (1987). *Constructing social problems.* New York: Aldine de Gruyter.

CHAPTER 3

Images of Crime and Criminality

CHAPTER OBJECTIVES

After reading Chapter 3, you will

- Comprehend the common media portraits of criminality
- Understand why the media gives special attention to predatory criminality
- See the link between media portraits of criminality and criminological theories

CRIMINALS, CRIMES, AND CRIMINALITY

A mainstay since ancient Greek theater, portraits of crime and justice are a media staple. From its classical beginnings, Western literature continued to reflect public interest in crime and justice, with romantic and heroic criminals appearing as common figures in the ballads, plays, and folktales of medieval Europe. Parallel with and often entwined within the portraits of crime and justice is the history of violence as entertainment. In Western culture, real-world violence as entertainment has been documented since the Roman gladiator contests. Over the last two millennia, executions as public spectacles have been common, as has violence against and between animals in the form of bull fighting, bear-baiting, dog fighting, and cockfights. While real-world violence has declined as acceptable entertainment, it remains an element in many sports and sports fans themselves sometimes become violent.[1] Fictional violence as entertainment has an equally long history; the earliest fairy tales and folk stories are full of violent acts. Stage plays filled with violent images were common and over time migrated the violence from unseen, off-stage acts to on-stage enactments.[2] As media evolved, the inclusion of violence increased and the earliest films contained violent images, including the killings in the first narrative film, *The Great Train Robbery*, in 1903. Subsequent gangster and horror films cemented the acceptance of visual violence as acceptable mass entertainment content. Entertainment violence is also part of today's music lyrics and music videos as well as contemporary electronic games which present violent scenarios in more sophisticated, realistic, and graphic fashion.[3] The overall history of violence in entertainment media displays a steady trend to include more violent acts in more graphic portrayals.[4]

Furthering exposure to the media's content, modern media technologies enabled violence portraits to be looped over and over so that violence today seems to be everywhere in society and the media.[5] Ironically, because society is media-saturated, there many be less real-world violence in comparison to past historic periods, (as suggested by falling crime rates) but a pervasive media makes it seem like there is more violence. Social constructionists point out that this perception of rampaging violence is important for how society is socially constructed. Connected to the growth of entertainment violence, violent and non violent crimes and criminals have been ubiquitous elements in American media. With large-scale industrialization, urbanization, and ethnic immigration in the nineteenth century, crime became one of the nation's principal social concerns.[6] By the second half of that century, the dominant image of the criminal in popular culture had shifted from a romantic, heroic portrait to feared, negative, violent images. This caricature shift was spurred by growing public concern about crime. The newspapers, dime novels, and magazines of the late 1800s created the stereotypical portraits and themes of crime and justice that would later

Picture Post/Moviepix/Getty Images

A 12-minute "Western" filmed in New Jersey, the 1903 film The Great Train Robbery *was one of the first "narrative" movies (produced to tell a story). The film introduced many features still common in today's crime media—gun-wielding criminals, brazen crimes, brutal murders, dramatic chase scenes, and violent fatal apprehension of the criminals.*

dominate movies and television—portraits and themes still common in today's media. What does this portrait of criminality look like?

Criminals

Since the beginning of the twentieth century, in addition to being the central theme of police, detective, heist, and gangster stories, criminals and their crimes have been popular secondary plot elements in love stories, Westerns, comedies, and dramas. In the pre-television era, media criminals in films, radio, and print enjoyed full lives and were often decisive, intelligent, and attractive individuals. Whether basically good or bad, criminals were shown as active decision makers who went after what they wanted, be it money, sex, or power. They controlled their lives, lived well, and decided their own fates. These early media portraits of criminals allowed audiences to identify with the criminals until the end, at which point the criminal was usually shot and killed.[7] Early media criminals allowed audiences to savor the danger and sin of crime yet still see it ultimately punished.

This portrait began to change with the decline of film and radio as the primary mass media in the late 1940s. The introduction of commercial television, an even more pervasive, direct, and influential medium, began the shift to more one-dimensional heroes and villains. Criminality in the cinema and in radio, however, had provided a fifty-year pool of criminal narratives for television to tap. Not surprisingly, television programming at first constructed images of crime and justice similar to the ones found in film and radio, but in much greater quantity, filling as much as 40 percent of prime time programming during the 1970s.

The resulting portrait of criminals found in today's media has almost no correspondence with official statistics of persons arrested for crimes. The tendency of the media to portray crime and justice opposite that of crime–and–justice reality is termed the "**backwards law**" of media, crime, and justice. In every subject category—crimes, criminals, crime fighters, attorneys, correctional officers, and inmates; the investigation of crimes and making of arrests; the processing and disposition of cases; and the experience of incarceration—the media construct and present a crime-and-justice world that is the opposite of the real world. Thus the typical criminal portrayed in the entertainment media is mature, white, and of high social status, whereas statistically the typical arrestee is young, black, and poor—what they have in common is that both are male.[8] Female offenders are primarily shown linked to male offenders and as white, violent, and deserving of punishment. They are paradoxically portrayed as driven by greed, revenge, and often love.[9] In general, the image of the criminal that the news media propagate is similar to that found in the entertainment media. Criminals tend to be of two types in the news media: violent predators or professional businessmen and bureaucrats. As in entertainment programming, they tend to be slightly older than reflected in official arrest statistics. Overall, the news media underplay criminals' youth and poverty while overplaying their violence.[10] Although other types of criminals are periodically shown, the violent and predatory street criminal is what the public takes away from the media's constructed image of criminality.[11] If there is a single media crime icon, it is predatory criminality—a construction that frames and dominates the media crime-and-justice world.

Predatory Criminality

If one was to randomly sample a media portrait of criminality, a predator criminal would most often be found. In their entertainment, news, and infotainment components, the media construct **predatory criminality**—criminals who are animalistic, irrational, and innately evil and who commit violent, sensational, and senseless crimes—as the dominant crime problem in the nation. History reveals that the image of the predator criminal has dominated in the media for more than a century and is common to all forms of media. Comparable to the hunting down of witches by the medieval church, modern mass media have given massive and disproportionate attention to pursuing predatory criminals as the prime crime-and-justice goal.[12] Found throughout this media portrait are repeated claims that crime is largely perpetrated by predatory individuals who are basically different from the rest of us and that criminality stems from individual deficiencies. Minorities are frequently portrayed as the criminal predators in news reports and racial violence has been an entertainment media theme dating back (conservatively) to Harriet Beecher Stowe's novel *Uncle Tom's Cabin* in the 1850s.[13] And while females are less often portrayed as criminals than males, when females who commit serious crimes are portrayed they are painted in analogous predatory images woven within narratives of aberrant sexuality and broken gender-based social roles.[14] The emergence of new media forms has opened new avenues for real-world predators and new means for moral panics to spread about them.[15] The lurking sexual predator hiding behind the anonymity of the Internet and social media who preys on children has become the twenty-first-century image of criminality.[16] Across the media, criminality is constructed as caused by greedy or evil individuals who know right from wrong but choose to commit crime. Criminals are portrayed in the media as inherently different from the law-abiding.[17] Over the past hundred years, media portraits have increasingly shown criminals as more animalistic, irrational, and predatory and their crimes as more violent, senseless, and sensational. Exemplified by the coverage of the Boston Marathon bombings (see Box 3.1), the media have successfully raised the violent predator criminal from a rare offender in the real world to a common, ever-present image in the media–constructed one. The public is led by the media to see violence and predation between strangers as an expected fact of life. While terrorists are currently also popular predatory villains and have appeared in all types of media including video games,[18] nowhere is the predatory image stronger than in the recent media social construction of the ultimate social predator, the serial killer.

The social construction of the serial killer as a significant new type of criminal began in the 1980s and took off in the 1990s.[19] The commodification, public embrace, and effects on criminal justice policy from the media portrait of serial killers demonstrate the media's crucial role in the social construction of criminality. With the construction of serial killers, the prior generic portrait of predators as dangerous but still human was supplanted by the portrait of animalistic killing machines more akin to gothic monsters than human offenders.[20] The media portrait also implied that these serial killers were everywhere and were the perpetrators of most violent crime. Historian Philip Jenkins, however, reports that although there is evidence of a small increase in the number of active serial killers, in reality serial killers account for no more than 300 to 400 victims each year, or 2 to 3 percent of all

Box 3.1 The Boston Marathon Bombers

Epitomizing the popular predator criminal icon that dominates media content, real-world examples are provided by the Tsarnaev brothers, Dzhokhar and Tamerlan, and the 2013 Boston Marathon bombings. The bombings resulted in three deaths and more than 260 people wounded. A few days after the bombings, the two brothers were involved in a shooting of a MIT university police officer, a car hijacking, and a street shootout with law enforcement which left Tamerlan Tsarnaev dead. Dzhokhar Tsarnaev was captured alive the next day following another shootout. Images of the bombings were repeatedly broadcast globally and the investigation, pursuit, and capture of the two brothers were heavily reported and discussed on social media and both aided (generating a number of useful leads) and hindered (wrongly accusing innocent individuals) by social media.

SOURCES: http://www.cnn.com/2013/05/01/justice/boston-marathon-timeline/index.html?iref=allsearch; http://www.cbsnews.com/8301-504083_162-57580402-504083/boston-marathon-bombings-timeline-of-events-in-the-manhunt-for-bombing-suspects/; http://theweek.com/article/index/243028/4-innocent-people-wrongly-accused-of-being-boston-marathon-bombing-suspects

Aaron Tang/Boston Globe/Getty Images

U.S. homicides, whereas domestic violence accounts for about one-third of all U.S. murders.[21] However, media coverage of serial murderers and the success of fictional books and films about serial killers have swamped the picture of criminality the public receives. The result is that serial killers are commonly perceived as the dominant homicide problem in the United States and as symbols of a society overwhelmed by rampant, violent, incorrigible predatory criminality.[22]

The media focus and immense public interest in violent predatory criminality is ironically tied to a socially palatable explanation of crime. While constructing crime as a frightening (and hence entertaining) phenomenon, predator criminality also presents crime as largely caused by individual deficiencies. This individual-level explanation frees mainstream society from any causal responsibility for crime. Such a perspective puts forth part of the crime problem (the individual offender) as the main problem and any social factors given causal credence such as devil worship or cult membership tend to be on the social fringe rather than conventional social conditions. Predatory criminals are portrayed as springing into existence unconnected to any larger social, political, or economic forces. As constructed, the predatory killer is divorced from humanity and society.[23] Created by bizarre circumstances and individual flaws, irreparably separated from society, and driven by alien needs, the predator criminal is both enjoyably evil and guiltlessly destroyed. In contrast, while criminals are often portrayed in depth in the media, their victims frequently are not. Counterparts to the criminals—victims of crime—occupy a surprisingly low profile in the media.

Crime Victims

Crime victims, although sometimes important for determining a crime's newsworthiness, are more often ignored in the media. A typical crime victim is not a newsworthy or entertaining one. When described in the news media, victims tend to be portrayed as female, very young or old, or a celebrity.[24] News coverage also routinely depicts criminal violence against females differently from that against males and underplays the victimization of minorities.[25] The ideal crime victim from a news perspective is a child or pregnant woman.[26] News coverage of some crime victims may be increasing, however. Since the 1990s, the news' construction of child murder victims has shifted from an emphasis on the stories of their killers to stories about the impact of the murders on the victims' families and communities.[27] Within this new infotainment-formatted coverage of crime victims, victims' rights have been advocated as a needed reform. [28] In this victim-focused news the families of crime victims are shown as doubly victimized, once by the offender and again by the justice system. For example, the recent spate of mass shootings in the United States, Norway, and other countries have been forwarded as symbolic crimes in efforts to emphasize victims in the coverage of crime as well as gun control measures.

In the entertainment media, victims normally play one of two extreme roles. Victims are portrayed either as helpless fodder or as wronged heroic avengers. Murder victims in particular are marginalized, and homicide frequently happens to characters who mean little to the other characters or to the audience.[29] The audience is encouraged to react to murders in entertainment not with a "My God, how horrible" response but with a "How curious, I wonder how it was done" reaction. When the bodies are counted, most entertainment crime victims are found to be white and male—but the entertainment media also over-represents young women in comparison to their real-world victimization rates. Recent entertainment trends in female portrayals are for fewer female villains, more female assistant heroes, and many more female victims. Females victims of crime are fewer in number than male victims but they appear far more often in the media than they do in reality and female victimization is more likely to be dwelled upon and graphically shown.[30] Other common entertainment victim narratives abound. One is the "Undeserving Victim," usually one of the first killed to establish the evilness of the villains and justify their violent death at the end. Another is the "Stupid Victim," often a police officer, who is never

This 1947 comic book story is an early example of the media portrait of predatory killers.

smarter than the criminal or crime-fighting hero and ends up stumbling into their death. A good example is the police officer killed while trying to single-handedly capture the criminals. A final victim narrative is the "Lazy Victim." This is one who is killed while doing something wrong or improperly—the security or correctional officer watching television instead of their surroundings, for example.

Overall, the victimization rates of persons in the media correlate more with fear of crime than with the public's actual victimization risk. In addition to media victim portraits being demographically mismatched with official victim statistics on age and gender, greater proportions of both news and entertainment media victims are portrayed as randomly selected and as having no prior associations with their assailants. Crime victims in the media are often shown as innocent and as noncontributory to their victimization.[31]

Aside from these misleading constructions of victimization, which help paint crime as a random, unavoidable event, victims are of secondary importance in the media. Only if they transform into crime fighters in the entertainment media or have a pre-existing newsworthiness (are already famous or a vulnerable child or pregnant woman) are they focused on by the news media.[32] Unlike the real world of crime, where pre-established relationships between victims and criminals are the most significant factor in the generation of most violence, in the media–constructed world the more important relationship is between the crime fighter and the criminal. This holds true even in police reality programming, where the interactions between the police and suspects dominate the shows. Overall, most victims in the media exist only to be victimized; once that function is fulfilled, if still alive, they are shunted aside to allow the central contest between the heroic crime fighter and the evil criminal to be played out.

Crimes

With predator criminals as the common grist for the media mill, it is not difficult to predict what crimes consumers are likely to find in the media. Not surprisingly, crimes that are most likely to be found are those that are least likely to occur in real life. Property crime is underrepresented, and violent crime is over-represented. Murder, robbery, kidnapping, and aggravated assault made up 90 percent of all prime time television crimes, with murder accounting for nearly one-fourth.[33] In contrast, murders account for only one-sixth of 1 percent of the FBI Crime Index. At the other extreme, thefts account for nearly two-thirds of the FBI Crime Index, but only 6 percent of television crime. Due to the multimedia Web and the constant recycling of content, entertainment media content greatly overemphasizes individual acts of violence, even during periods when new content is less violent.[34]

The content of crime news reveals a similarly distorted, inverted image. Violent crime's relative infrequency in the real world heightens its newsworthiness and leads to its frequent appearance in crime news. Thus, crime news focuses on violent personal street crime such as murder, rape, and assault, with more common offenses like burglary and theft often ignored. According to one study, murder and robbery account for approximately 45 percent of newspaper crime news and 80 percent of television crime news.[35] With regularity, the news media take the rare crime event and turn it into the common crime image. Furthermore, trends that do occur over time in the amount of crime reported in the news have little relationship to trends in societal crime. Neither the content nor the total amount of crime news reflects changes in the crime rate. Crime news also focuses heavily on the details of specific individual crimes, whereas only a minuscule percentage of stories deal with the motivations of the criminal or the circumstances of victims. Even in the news, the focus is on entertaining crimes with dramatic recitations of details about individual offenders and crime scenes. By and large, crime is cast in the media within constructions where large differences exist between what the public is likely to experience in reality and what they are likely to gather from the media. An area of crime that has large social impact but small media attention has been white-collar crime.

White-Collar Crime

Despite encompassing a broad range of acts that cause significant social harm,[36] **white-collar crime** has not been a media focus[37] and exemplifies the adage that a crime's social impact does not always equal its news value. White-collar crime is ignored because it is not visually interesting, and furthermore, there is difficulty in generating and maintaining moral panics about white-collar crimes and criminals.[38] Subsequently, media portraits of economic crimes are rare, and when produced, are framed in celebrity-focused stories or formatted as infotainment and differentiated from "real crime."[39] While extensive coverage of a specific white-collar crime will occur—provided there is some newsworthy link such as a significant fine, prosecution, or company liquidation[40]—and periodic films dealing with white-collar crime are produced,[41] white-collar crime remains a small part of total crime news and entertainment media content. Rooted in the traditions of muckraking and yellow journalism,[42] media portraits of white-collar crimes date back to the 1800s. Historic symbolic white-collar crimes include Ponzi[43] schemes and the Teapot Dome scandal, and more recent examples are Enron, Martha Stewart, Bernie Madoff (see Box 3.2), and the 2008 banking industry collapse. The amount of coverage did increase following Watergate in the 1970s, but news reports continued to avoid attributing criminal wrongdoing to corporations, instead focusing on harm, charges, and probes, not on corporate criminal liability.[44] Coverage has continued to shift attention onto specific individuals[45] and has remained sparse and haphazard into this century.[46] However, a cycle of massive accounting scandals and economic crisis resulted in a recent increase in coverage and a parade of dramatized arrests of white-collar executives.[47] It remains to be seen whether the increase reflects a permanent change in how corporate crime is socially constructed or simply reflects a spate of sensational corporate crimes during a period of economic turmoil to be followed by a return to the low levels of media attention normally found.[48]

Why has media attention to white-collar crime been historically low? While public disinterest is a major factor, additional reasons include that these crimes involve indirect harm to victims and provide few striking visual images, are highly complex and boring, frequently cover years before resolution, and require specialized knowledge on the part of journalists.[49] In gist, white-collar crime stories are hard to make telegenic and are often killed in the news selection filtering process because they are not "news" in the traditional sense.[50] White-collar crimes typically are punished by civil penalties, placing them outside of the criminal justice system and outside of traditional crime news that originates in police reports. News media organizations also likely fear litigation and withdrawal of advertising from the negative portrayal of powerful economic entities.[51] Counterbalancing these coverage-reducing factors are recent increases in investigative reporting as a journalism practice, the availability of Internet sources for information, and the efforts of various advocacy groups to serve as spokespersons.

B o x 3.2   Bernie Madoff and Martha Stewart: White-Collar Crimes

On March 3, 2009, Bernie Madoff pled guilty to 11 Ponzi scheme-related criminal charges and was sentenced to 150 years in prison. Madoff ran his Ponzi scheme by claiming to have signature equipment and programs which could monitor for prime trading opportunities globally. As a result of this Ponzi scheme Madoff's victims were defrauded of 65 billion dollars. This bankrupted many of the investors. The Martha Stewart case is an example of a white-collar crime's social impact not equaling its media impact, the reverse of most white-collar crimes where social impact outweighs comparatively meager news coverage and value. Businesswoman, television host, and magazine publisher Martha Stewart was indicted on charges of securities fraud and obstruction of justice connected to her sale of about 4,000 shares of stock in 2001. Her 2004 trial resulted in convictions for conspiracy, obstruction, and false statements and a five-month prison sentence and a 30,000 dollar fine. Other lesser-known male CEOs who stole millions received far less coverage than Ms. Stewart and often avoided jail time. In comparison to other white-collar crimes such as Madoff's Ponzi scheme, which cost billions, her crime was of lesser magnitude but received more news media coverage.

SOURCES: Pontell, H. and G. Geis, 2010, "How to Effectively Get Crooks like Bernie Madoff in Dutch," *Am. Society of Criminology 9*(3): 475–481; Self, R. 2007, "Stewart, Martha. In *Encyclopedia of White-Collar Crime*, eds. J. Gerver and E. Jenson, pp. 270–271. Westport: Greenwood Press.

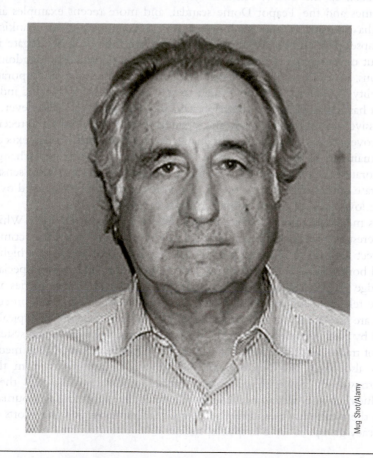

Mug Shot/Alamy

Irrespective of recent trends, similar to other crime news, white-collar crime, when currently covered, is more often treated in infotainment renditions. Corporate celebrities in trouble, normal people committing fraud, identity theft, and long-term concealment of and failure of government entities to discover fraudulent enterprises make up the majority of white-collar crime stories.[52] Analogous to how corrections are covered, predatory individuals, the failure to detect and punish them, and failure to protect the public dominate the news media construction of white-collar crime. The adjudication of individual crimes and the punishment of individual offenders receive the bulk of media attention.[53] However, dissimilar to how other crime is constructed, corporate offenders are rarely cast as pathological, and white-collar crime is sanitized and "decriminalized" as technical law violations rather than as real crimes.[54] Reflecting this construction, white-collar criminals, upon arrest, often attempt to socially reconstruct their crime as noncriminal activity.[55] For example, criminal dumping and chemical pollution cases are often described as accidents.[56] White-collar crimes that are reported are likely to be cast as caused by criminal individuals—a bad apple explanation—rather than as common corporate practices. The harm of such events and the criminogenic nature of certain industries are downplayed.[57]

In the entertainment media, white-collar crime is also infrequently examined, despite a long history traceable back to Upton Sinclair's 1906 book *The Jungle*.[58] There have been more white-collar crime films since 1970, but such films remain a small percentage of the total number of films, with few commercial successes.[59] In the entertainment story lines, businessmen are often portrayed as criminals, but they are usually shown committing crimes of violence such as murder or running businesses as fronts for drug smuggling, terrorism, or violence-based extortions.[60] The white-collar criminals in the entertainment media are more often street criminals dressed up as executives than businesspeople engaged in criminal business practices.[61]

Overall, white-collar crimes are treated by the mass media as infotainment, as individual and corporate celebrities in trouble or as violent predators disguised as executives.[62] Corporate scandals and corporate predators are constructed to fit a predatory criminal icon and thus to better match the wider construction of crime and criminality found in the media.[63] But the social reality of white-collar crime may be undergoing a social reconstruction similar to that of drunk driving in the 1980s. There is evidence that the general public began to see white-collar crime more seriously in the early 2000s and there followed more attention to white-collar criminality.[64] A counterforce, though, is the decline in reporting resources available to news agencies as new media has sapped their audience size. However, the decentralization of content creation and distribution from news corporations to individuals that is also characteristic of new media further encouraged a more diverse media portrait of corporate crime. How these competing effects play out remains to be determined. If the heightened public interest and diverse portraits are maintained, a significant deterrent effect on white-collar crime is possible. Media coverage has been described as more of a deterrent to white-collar criminals than formal sanctions.[65] In these cases and for these offenders public shaming in the media can have an effective crime-reducing impact.

Criminological Theories and Media Explanations of Crime

Has the portrait of crime, white-collar, street, and other, changed over time? The portrait of criminals and crimes in the media does display a number of evolutionary trends. Criminals have become more evil, heroes have become more violent, victims have become more innocent, violence has become more graphic, and crimes have become more irrational.[66] Perhaps this would not be a concern if the portraits of crime and justice in the media were balanced in other aspects and presented various competing explanations of crime. That, however, is not the case. As constructed, the most common and popular media crime narratives forward a particular explanation of crime. They encourage support for certain criminological theories and disparagement of others. The **popular criminology** found in the media does not pretend to be empirically accurate or theoretically valid, but its audience far exceeds that of academic criminology.[67] Surveying the media for the ideas and explanations of crime that reside there is a useful exercise.[68] What criminological theories do well in the media-constructed world of popular criminology is an important question in terms of what criminal justice policies are supported or undermined.

Before answering the question just posed, a brief overview of criminological theories is needed. Criminological theories can be grouped along a number of dimensions, one being where a theory locates the primary cause of crime. Applying that criterion, crime theories fall into five groups. The first group includes the **rational choice theories,** which state that there is no cause of crime and no difference between the law-abiding and the criminal. Crime is seen simply as a rational, freewill decision that individuals will make when the gains from committing a crime outweigh the likely punishment from committing it. Criminals are essentially normal people making bad but reasonable decisions given their circumstances and morals. To control crime, these theories argue that society must deter crime by ensuring that punishments outweigh the rewards of crime and that punishments are known beforehand, are certain to be implemented, and are quickly administered.

The second group is comprised of the **biological theories,** which place the cause of crime in the innate genetic or constitutional nature of criminals. The more primitive theories looked for external physical traits (physical features or "atavisms" such as a sloping forehead first described by the nineteenth-century criminologist Cesare Lombroso as indicators of criminal predispositions); more recent ones look to genetic traits or biological trauma. Criminal justice policies associated with biological theories of crime focus on medical interventions and control of procreation. The appellation "natural-born killers" is often applied by the media as a code phrase for these theories.

Group three are the **psychological theories,** which view crime as caused by defective personality development. Based on the work of various psychoanalytic and personality development theorists, Sigmund Freud being the best known, these theories explain criminality as the result of deviant personalities. In these theories, people commit crime because their "personality" is ill formed. Associated policies are based around counseling and therapy. In the media, these

Warner Bros/Everett Collection/Glow Images

As the character, the Joker, from the Batman films shows, the psychotic murderous criminal continues to be a popular image of criminality in the twenty-first century.

theories come in "twisted psyche" and "sexual deviant" portraits, best shown in Alfred Hitchcock films like *Psycho*.

Group four, **sociological theories,** look at social groups as the loci of the basic causes of crime. Criminals are criminals because of the people they associate with, or share a neighborhood or culture with. Whereas the psychological theories argue criminal personalities, the sociological ones argue criminal environments. These theories, and media renditions of them, argue that essentially normal people are forced or steered into crime by their social circumstances. Found most often in films that can profitably express society as part of the cause of crime, media portraits supporting sociological theories are found less often in other media. Strain, blocked opportunity, and culture conflict are the sociological theories that receive the most media play. Although there are hints of the need to change the social structure in these theories, their basic orientation is usually conservative. The means of fixing the individual criminals generated by the bad environments is to better fit and adjust the criminals to law-abiding society, changing their socialization and only secondarily changing their social environment.

Finally, there are **political theories,** which emphasize the political and economic structure of a society as the root cause of crime. The distribution of political power; unequal access to influence and material goods; and racism, oppression, sexism, and elitism are all central to these theories. Unlike the other theory groups that tend to focus on the need for individual offenders to change, these explanations are more likely to argue for social changes, restructuring society relationships, and revamping the criminal justice system.

Which of these five theoretical perspectives do well in the media and which are disparaged? A historical assessment suggests that different theories have been popular at different times. Nicole Rafter notes:

> The media tend to reflect the criminological theories popular at the time. During the 1930s, crime films tended to portray a [sociological] perspective which painted the urban ethnic inner city as the basic cause of criminality. The 1940 and 1950s films were Freudian based [psychological theories] with deviant personalities the root cause. The 1960s and 70s brought labeling and critical criminology [political theories] to the fore. The 1980s saw films indicting drugs and family violence [a mix of theoretical perspectives].[69]

These criminological theories are usually not explicitly laid out in the media and crime-and-justice media content searches will not find many explicit criminological theory discussions. Support is more often set inside the portraits of criminals and is transmitted via the portrayed characteristics of offenders and their crimes inferring one theoretical explanation of crime as more credible over another. It is in the media construction of criminality where the hidden support for differing criminological theories of crime is found.

Criminality in the Media

Embedded throughout the media, the most common narrative of criminality is the psychopathic criminal, sometimes given super-villain traits to create seemingly indestructible murderous super-criminals popular in slasher, serial killer, and super hero films.

Psychotic super-male criminals generally possess an evil, cunning intelligence and superior strength, endurance, and stealth. Crime is an act of twisted, lustful revenge or a random act of irrational violence. A historical trend has been to present psychotic criminals as more and more violent and bloodthirsty and to show their crimes more and more graphically. Hence, murderous violence that once typically took place completely off screen came to be represented in scenes that were violent but not graphic (such as the shower murder in Alfred Hitchcock's film *Psycho*). However, since the 1980s, violence has been shown in graphic hyperviolent close-ups. As the most popular construction of criminality, the psychopathic criminal clearly supports the individually focused biological and psychological theories to the exclusion of other criminological perspectives.[70] Crime in the media is usually innate, an act of nature gone bad, and not society's fault.

Less common but still popular narratives are those of **business and professional criminals.** Best known through the many media portrayals of organized crime, these portraits are characterized as shrewd, ruthless, often violent ladies' men. Predators disguised as white-collar executives are more directly dangerous than the typical white-collar offender. If psychopathic criminals are mad dogs, these criminals are cunning wolves. The core message is that crime is simply another form of work or business, essentially similar to other careers but often more exciting and rewarding, if more violent. The business and professional criminal portraits also forward individually based psychological theories of criminal personality and psychopathic explanations. However, the classical school of crime garners support in these constructions, and elements of political and economic causes also can be found. Thus these media portraits of criminality tend to be more complex and multi-theoretical, spreading the responsibility for crime over both the criminal and society. It is likely that this very complexity and society having a share of the blame for crime makes these narratives less popular than the more simplistic and consumer guilt-free psychopathic criminal portrait.

A third group of popular criminality narratives are **victims and heroic criminals.** These portraits are the least common and present an alternative perspective that supports sociological and political explanations. Although the criminal as hero and the criminal as victim appeared early and have been presented regularly throughout the history of the media, such narratives have always been less frequent in number than those of the criminal as a psychopath or professional. Depending on how the portrait is structured, this "Robin Hood" criminality narrative supports strain, blocked opportunity, labeling, and critical criminology theories.

Everett Collection

Taking up the modern mantle of heroic "Robin Hoods" are action criminals who less often give to the poor but still battle evil from the wrong side of the law as reluctant heroes forced into criminality by a corrupt criminal justice system.

If you look closely, you will find that the media have attributed a wide range of factors as plausible causes of criminality and provided some support for every criminological theory.[71] However, the dominant and loudest messages in terms of their frequency and popular appeal point to individually based theories of crime and away from social ones. In addition, while criminological theories come into and go out of fashion with criminologists, the criminological ideas imbedded in the media do not. Criminologists drop discredited theories, but the media recycle them.[72] Therefore, even primitive theories of crime such as demonic possession continue to be presented as credible explanations of crime in the media. "The devil made me do it" still carries weight in the media as a valid cause of crime.

In sum, the criminological theories that focus on individual characteristics as the cause of crime clearly fare the best. Of these, the psychological ones, often combined with political or biological elements, are the most popular. The single most common portrait of a criminal features an upper-middle-class person gone berserk with greed.[73] Indeed, greed, revenge, and mental illness are the basic motivations for criminality in the vast majority of crimes shown in the media. In addition, the psychotic criminals portrayed in the media frequently hold positions of political or economic power. The repeated message is that crime is perpetrated by individuals who are different in substantially basic ways from the law-abiding, that criminality stems from individual problems, and that, when not inborn, criminal conduct is more often than not freely chosen behavior.

The dominant media construction of criminals, crimes, and criminality is thus simultaneously both unsettling and conservative. It is unsettling in its emphasis on violent predatory criminality, which is portrayed as random and largely unavoidable. It is conservative in that the explanations of criminality emphasize individual traits as causes and minimize social and structural ones. Social changes are called for far less frequently in the media world of crime and justice than is elimination of evil individuals. Not surprisingly, such a construction, with its emphasis on predatory criminality, has raised accompanying issues concerning its social effects. Specifically, what is the relationship of the media to crime and violence in society? Do we copy what the media constructs and we consume? This question is addressed in the following chapter.

SUMMARY

- Portraits of crime and justice appear throughout the history of media and have continued to be a staple of all types of media content.

- The portrait of criminals found in the media has almost no correspondence with official statistics. The typical media criminal is mature, white, and of high social status, whereas statistically the typical arrestee is young, a minority, and poor. The media does get the gender of criminality correct—most criminals are male in both the media and real world.

- Media female offenders are primarily shown as white, violent, and driven by greed, revenge, and sometimes love. When they offend, females are usually shown as deserving of punishment.

- The media construct criminals who are animalistic, irrational, and innately predatory and who commit violent, sensational, and senseless crimes as the dominant crime problem in the nation.

- Victimization rates in the media correlate more with fear of crime than with actual victimization risk. Victims are frequently portrayed as randomly selected, having no prior associations with their assailants, as innocent, and as noncontributory to their victimization.

- Crimes that are most likely to be found in the media are least likely to occur in real life. Property crime is underrepresented and violent crime is overrepresented.

- Criminological theories that focus on individual characteristics as the cause of crime fare the best in the media. Greed, revenge, or mental illness are the basic motivations for criminality in the vast majority of crimes shown in the media.

- The repeated media message is that crime is perpetrated by individuals who are substantially different from the law-abiding, that criminality stems from individual problems, and that, when not innate, criminality is freely chosen behavior.

CLASS DISCUSSIONS

1. Discuss your views about how much crime and violence in society would disappear if there were no crime-and-justice media.
2. Discuss the character Hannibal Lector as a construction of predatory criminality and why the predator criminal image enjoys lasting popularity.
3. Discuss a commercial film's portrayal of a real serial killer in comparison with the historical facts.

SUGGESTED READINGS

Bing, R. (2010). *Race, crime, and the media.* New York: McGraw Hill.

Boyle, K. (2005). *Media and violence: Gendering the debates.* Thousand Oaks: Sage.

Nichols-Pethick, J. (2012). *TV cops: The contemporary American television police drama.* New York: Routledge.

Oliver, W. and Marion, N. (2013). *Crime, history, and hollywood.* Durham: Carolina Academic Press.

Rafter, N. (2006). *Shots in the mirror: Crime films and society.* Oxford: Oxford University Press.

Rome, D. (2004). *Black demons: The media's depiction of the African-American male criminal stereotype.* Westport: Praeger.

Simpson, P. (2000). *Psycho paths: Tracking the serial killer through contemporary American film and fiction.* Carbondale: Southern Illinois University Press.

CHAPTER 4

Criminogenic Media

CHAPTER OBJECTIVES

After reading Chapter 4, you will

- Identify the issues and concepts associated with criminogenic media
- Understand violent media as a cause of social aggression
- Recognize the nature of copycat crime
- Appreciate the relationship between terrorism and the media

THE MEDIA AS A CAUSE OF CRIME

Criminogenic media refers to media content that is hypothesized to be a direct cause of crime. A continually debated issue is the causal position of the media. Does exposure to media precede or parallel aggressive or criminal behavior? In other words, do the media cause changes in subjects or do predisposed individuals selectively seek out and attend to media content that supports their already preordained behaviors? The public long ago came to its conclusion. As early as 1908, worries appeared that the media (then newspapers and books) were creating an atmosphere of tolerance for criminality and causing juvenile delinquency, and ever since public opinion polls have consistently reported the public's belief in a causal role for the media in crime and violence in society.[1] More than two out of three Americans feel that television violence is a critical or very important cause of crime in the United States, and one-fourth feel that movies, television, and the Internet combined are a primary cause of gun violence in the country.[2] The media violence frame, as described in Chapter 2, continues to find substantial public support.[3]

Three criminogenic media issues are discussed with an extended discussion of video games included. The first area addressed is whether violent media generates aggressive behavior. There has been a great deal of research and public interest regarding this question and the final answer is still being debated. However, most researchers today conclude that the media is a significant contributor to social aggression and as good a predictor of violence as other social factors. Most crime is nonviolent, though, and one can be aggressive without breaking the law (by being rude for example), so even if the media are an important cause of social aggression, media still may not be an important cause of crime. Therefore, the next, more directly relevant discussion for crime and justice looks at the media as a cause of crime, focusing on the generation of copycat crime. The basic question is this: Does the presentation of crimes in the media result in people copying those crimes? The final issue looks at the relationship between the mass media and terrorism. Media–oriented terrorist events have emerged as one of the most worrisome problems of the twenty-first century, and the relationship of the media to terrorism and the use of the media by terrorists is a critical contemporary issue.

Violent Media and Aggression

Driven by the folk logic of "monkey see, monkey do," establishing whether "child see, child do" holds true in terms of the media and aggression has proved more difficult than first expected. Research on the link between media depictions of violence and social aggression initially revolved around two competing hypotheses: one conjecturing a cathartic effect and the other a stimulating effect. In brief, the cathartic effect hypothesizes that exposure to media violence acts as a therapeutic release for anger and self-hatred. In contrast, the stimulation effect hypothesizes that a diet of media violence stimulates violent behavior and fosters supportive values about violence.[4]

Researchers positing a stimulating effect have explored a number of causal mechanisms through which the media could cause aggression. The most commonly advanced mechanism involves imitation, in which viewers learn values and norms supportive of aggression and violence, learn techniques to be aggressive and violent, or learn acceptable social situations and targets for aggression. Advocates of a stimulating effect feel that children, in particular, learn aggression the same way they learn other cognitive and social skills—by watching parents, siblings, peers, teachers, and others. Accordingly, the more violence children see, the more accepting they become of aggressive behavior, and the more likely they are to act aggressively.

Some researchers have argued that the media are not established as a cause of aggression or violence.[5] They assert that to conclude that the media cause negative social behaviors such as violence is unjustified and premature. In their view, exposure to violent content and violent behavior is linked—but not causally. Rather, both stem from the predispositions of some media consumers who seek out violent content and act violently because of their predisposition to aggression. If this position is correct, eliminating portrayals of violence in the media will not reduce the level of violence in society because the number of individuals predisposed to violence will remain the same. Advocates of this model argue that the evidence of a causal link between violent content and social aggression has not been shown. At this point, one side asserts that a clear and consistent pattern of empirical results from decades of research prove that media violence has negative effects and is one of the causes of aggression in society,[6] the other side states that the results do not demonstrate that exposure to media violence causes aggression and queries: If violence in the media cause aggression, how can real-life violence and crime be dropping at a time when movies and television shows are as violent as ever?[7]

Why can't the media's effect on aggression be definitely measured? For one, it is difficult to separate the effects of media on society or individuals from all the other forces that contribute to violent behavior. Media influences are so intertwined with other social forces that finding strong, direct causal effects should not be expected. However, after 100 years of concern and 70 years of research, a small to modest (but genuine) causal role for media violence regarding viewer aggression has been established for most beyond a reasonable doubt.[8] Violent media does cause social aggression; violent media is not the sole cause, or the most important cause, and its causal impact is frequently overstated and overestimated, but it is a cause.[9]

Another undeniable finding is that the cathartic-effect hypothesis has been discredited: people do not become less violent due to media violence. Contrary to what the catharsis theory predicts, when viewing is combined with frustration or arousal, viewers are more rather than less likely to behave aggressively. Current research is exploring the magnitude, mechanism, and significance of a stimulating effect. It is not yet clear whether media portrayals of violence increase the proportion of persons who behave aggressively, encourage already-aggressive persons to use aggression more often, encourage aggression-prone persons to use greater levels of aggression, desensitize people to aggression, or some combination of these outcomes.[10] There is certainly a correlation between exposure to violent media and social aggression, but the strength, configuration, and most importantly, the causal nature of the relationship is simply not understood.[11] Adding to the long-term concern over violent media content, new media have invigorated the debate and its urgency. The new media that have generated the greatest concerns due to their interactive and immersive nature have been electronic video games, particularly those that portray crime and violence. With video games presenting movie-like storylines, an on-going debate about the effect of playing video games on video game players continues to boil.[12] As with prior research, results have yet to produce a consensus.

What Is the Effect of Video Games on Aggression?

The above question is often forwarded as a simple research question when presented to the public, but turns out to be a complex research issue. Video games vary considerably in content and game players vary regarding why they play and what they bring to a game; therefore, effects of any particular game on any specific player are not monolithic. The primary reasons video gamers play video games are "achievement and competition" (to win the game); "mastering the game" (advance through game levels, improve their skill in a game's mechanics); "social connections" (form relationships and teams with other players); and "escapism and relaxation" (immersion in virtual worlds and role-playing).[13] The reasons for playing a video game are not mutually exclusive and game players often simultaneously play for some

Box 4.1   Grand Theft Auto and Copycat Crimes

A number of crimes each year are linked to movies, books, music, YouTube videos, television programs, and other media products. Video games have been especially targeted as crime generators and one series of games, *Grand Theft Auto* (GTA), has undergone great public scrutiny due to the game story lines and a number of crimes that have been described as resulting from the playing of the games. Released for sale on October 22, 2001, *Grand Theft Auto III* had a game story line which revolved around an unnamed protagonist (the player) who has been betrayed by his girlfriend during a bank robbery and is sent to jail. While the player is being transferred to jail, an attack on the police convoy sets him free. Freed, the game player begins to work his way up in the virtual criminal world and undertakes various missions, such as bank robberies, assassinations, stabbings, street racing, carjacking and prostitution.

On June 7, 2003 in the real world, a police officer found eighteen-year-old Devin Moore sleeping in a stolen car, arrested Moore and took him to the Fayette, Alabama, police station. During questioning, Moore grabbed the officer's gun and shot him twice, once in the head. Another officer heard the shots and came rushing, Moore fired several shots, hitting the second officer several times, once in the head. Moore then shot the dispatcher several times; once in the head. Moore picked up keys to a police cruiser, which became his getaway car. All of his criminal acts had counterparts in the GTA game. After Moore was captured he was quoted as saying to police, "Life is like a video game. Everybody's got to die sometime." At trial, it was revealed that Moore, who had no prior criminal history, had purchased *Grand Theft Auto* as a minor and played the game for several hours a day over a number of months. On the day he was arrested he had played *Grand Theft Auto* for hours before stealing the car he was found and arrested in. Describing Moore as a compulsive violent video game player, his attorneys argued a "GTA defense"—that he had lost touch with reality and was acting out the virtual violence scenarios he had experienced in *GTA*. The GTA defense was unsuccessful; Moore was convicted and sentenced to death. Relatives of the three victims filed a multimillion-dollar lawsuit against Sony Computer Entertainment America, Take-Two/Rockstar, GameStop, and Wal-Mart, claiming that Moore committed the 2003 murders after continuously playing the video game *Grand Theft Auto III*.

At least two other subsequent crimes have been described as *Grand Theft Auto* copycats. The first occurred in Thailand in August 2008, when a nineteen-year-old high school student wanted to act out the *Grand Theft Auto* carjacking scene. He carjacked a taxi and murdered the taxi driver. Upon arrest, he stated that he wanted to know if it was as easy in real life to rob a taxi as it was in the game. A police spokesman described the youth as an obsessive player of *Grand Theft Auto* who confessed to committing the crime because of the game. Thai authorities banned the game after this incident. The second GTA copycat crime occurred in June 2008 in Long Island, New York. Police arrested six teenagers following a crime spree in which they mugged and beat a man, attempted a carjacking, and vandalized a vehicle. The teens stated that they were imitating acts seen in *Grand Theft Auto IV* and emulating the popular player/character "Niko Bellic" found in the game. (A video of the story can be found on YouTube.)

The linkage of the 1999 Columbine High School, the 2007 Virginia Tech, the 2011 Netherlands Mall, the 2011 Norway summer camp, the 2012 Aurora, Colorado theater, and the 2012 Sandy Hook Elementary shootings to video game play has become a common part of the social construction of mass shootings. The causal role of video game play is undetermined. In some cases, there is evidence of the shooter's immersion in a game prior to the killings, in others, there is little or no evidence that the shooter owned or played the games mentioned.

SOURCES: Can a video game lead to murder?, *CBS News*, March 6, 2005; Crowley, K.2008. "Video Villains Come to Life,"*New York Post*, Friday, June 26; "Grand Theft Auto pulled from sale after Bangkok teen murders taxi driver to see if it was as easy as in the game," *Daily Mail Online*, Aug. 4, 2008. www.dailymail.co.uk/new/worldnews/; Hourigan, B. 2008, July. "The moral code of Grand Theft Auto IV." IPA Review, pp. 21-22. For a general review of research on violent video games see Anderson, Gentile and Buckley. 2007. *Violent Video Game Effects on Children: Theory, Research and Public Policy*. Oxford University Press.

combination of all four reasons. In that video games can fulfill multiple functions for a game player from individual psychological goals to broad social ones, the immense popularity of video games can be understood. Playing video games can be highly satisfying in both the real and virtual world.

Video games' unique, intensive, interactive, and, for some, addictive nature, their linkage to worrisome social behaviors, and their sometimes graphic portraits of violence have combined to form a groundswell of social concern (see Box 4.1). In response, an ever-growing set of research efforts to determine the effects of video games has reported both negative and positive effects. Evidence of positive effects from playing pro-social video games include increases in helping behaviors, cooperation, problem solving, sharing, and empathy by game players.[14] However, social concern about possible negative effects from playing video games, especially violent and misogynistic games, far outweighs belief in positive effects. [15] The theoretical mechanisms by which violent video games might lead to social aggression have been hypothesized to include social learning (where game players imitate observed aggression), excitation transfer (where the physiological arousal from game playing lingers and transfers to future encounters, which then become aggressive in nature), cognitive neoassociation (where the activation of aggression-associated memories and thoughts in players increase aggression) and a general aggression model (where exposure to video game violence promotes aggressive beliefs and attitudes, the recalling of behavioral scripts and expectations, and the development of a personality biased toward aggression).[16] At this time which of these mechanisms might operate and in what strength and circumstances has not been resolved. Currently, two sets of research compete over defining the effect of violent video games. One camp champions the conclusion of significant negative effects, the other argues for insignificant, largely neutral effects.

Representing the negative effects side, two recent studies exemplify this body of research and additionally incorporate criminogenic effects. In the first report, Julia Fischer and her colleagues reported the results from two small sample laboratory studies conducted in Germany in 2012. In their first study, 25 Munich University students played a video game that positively reinforced illegal street racing or a neutral game for 20 minutes. Afterwards, each student was asked what they would recommend as a punishment for a severe traffic offense. Those that had played the illegal street racing game were significantly more tolerant of similar criminal behavior.[17] In their second study, 28 university students either played as a criminal character in a game or played a neutral game. Afterwards, they were brought into a setting where it was easy to steal pencils and chocolate bars.[18] Fischer and her colleagues reported that delinquency-reinforcing video game players showed more tolerance for a severe road traffic offense and were more likely to steal inexpensive items from a laboratory. They concluded with a strong statement of negative effects: "Video games that positively reinforce crime and delinquency increase the likelihood that players will model these behaviors in real life."[19]

A second example of a negative effects study reported evidence that supported the general aggression model as a mechanism. In this 2011 study, Brad Bushman and Bryan Gibson had 126 U.S. college students play either a violent or a nonviolent video game for 20 minutes. Half of each group was instructed to "ruminate" about the game via the instruction: In the next 24 hours, think about your play of the game, and try to identify ways your game play could improve when you play again".[20] Post play aggression was measured by placing participants in a setting where they could blast another competitor with painful noises and control the noise level and duration. Bushman and Gibson found that playing a violent video game significantly increased player aggression 24 hours after game play for males who had ruminated about a violent game.[21] These and similar studies have begun the slow unpacking of the relationship between video game play and player aggression with other research supporting a socialization process over game selection (game choice predicted aggression more than aggression predicted game choice)[22] and for longer negative effect time periods.[23] In general, this set of research confidently concludes that game players who play violent video games, particularly adolescents, will show significant increases in aggression over time.[24]

Contrasting research argues that violent video games have insubstantial effects on behavior. These researchers conclude that other factors beyond violent content may be responsible for elevated player aggression, for example, that game competitiveness may be more important than game violence in generating player aggression.[25] Additional research has reported insignificant associations for specific categories of game players. For example, a survey of mostly Hispanic youth found that levels of depression symptoms in game players were stronger predictors of serious aggression and violence than either exposure to video game or television violence.[26] Critics of the aggression effects conclusion also point out that increased gaming in the United States ran parallel with significant declines in society-wide crime and homicide rates, a relationship that belies a strong society-wide video game effect. [27]

The unsettled nature of this research is shown by the fact that examples of strong statements supporting opposite conclusions about video game effects are readily available. Supporting the "significant effects are proven" side:

> "The correlation between playing violent video games and delinquency has been described as robust and extending to serious juvenile offenders, even after controlling various factors such as gender, race, offense history, and personality traits. [28]

Supporting the "significant effects not proven" side:

> Studies that have found positive correlations between playing violent video games and violent and antisocial attitudes have been described as typically not controlling for other covariates, particularly gender, that are known to be associated with both video gameplay and aggression. As more demographic covariates are introduced, the video game effects are described as progressively weaker and the overall link between video games and aggression becomes modest and not statistically significant. The remaining positive association appears only for individuals who play 4 or more hours per day.[29]

What should one make of this debate? Based on the research to this point, it first can be concluded that the relationship between violent game content and aggressive player behavior is not universal. Not every player is affected in the same fashion. Second, a set of additional factors appear to interact with the presence of violent content to increase or decrease the likelihood of post play aggression.[30] For example, in addition to violent content, game characteristics such as competition and pace of action have been forwarded as significant.[31] Player characteristics such as depression, ability to delay gratification, peer deviance, academic performance, parental involvement, and school culture also appear to play a role in the effect of game play on game players.[32] The depth of the relationship between the player and game also appears to be important. Hence, a game player who designs a personalized game avatar is more likely to display enhanced game play effects that are separate from exposure to violent game content.[33] Along these lines, the research suggests a significant role for media immersion; the more the games bring the player into the game's world, and the more the gamer player lives in that world, the greater the effect. Thus, the experience of playing a violent character in a video game and of immersing one's self in that role was related to more acceptable attitudes toward crimes and criminals. [34] The research to date and the critiques of the research suggest an interaction between video game characteristics, with violent content as one important characteristic among many regarding electronic games.

In sum, while each of these research studies have individual methodological flaws (small samples, indirect measures, contrived settings, subject mortality, noncausal designs), so that no one study should be overly weighted, a substantial set of research findings suggest that violent video game players show increases in aggression over those who do not play violent video games, and that the effect of violent game play is different from that of nonviolent game play. Replicating the history of research on violent television programming and viewer aggression, research on video gaming has been concentrated on small samples of college-student subjects in laboratory experiments with artificial measures of aggression (noise blasts, hot sauce administration) that show short term effects related to violent video games and large sample self-report surveys of varied populations that suggest the presence of persistent long term effects. Research results are not consistent though, and evidence of a substantial society level effect or the mechanism through which effects on individuals operate has not been produced.

What is most clear at this point is that a consensus does not exist. An assessment offered nearly half a century ago remains valid: For some children under some conditions some media is harmful. For other children under the same conditions, or for the same children under other conditions, it may be beneficial. For most children under most conditions, most media is probably neither particularly harmful nor particularly beneficial.[35] Although experimental studies confirm that visual and interactive media violence can lead to short-term imitation, researchers do not know exactly how and to what extent the media cause long-term changes in aggressive behavior. At this time, a multi-factor approach where exposure to violent media is one of a set of factors that facilitate or inhibit aggression is reasonable.[36] The more risk factors an individual carries, the more likely they are to behave aggressively; the more protective factors they have, the less likely aggressive behavior is. In this perspective, exposure to media violence is equivalent in effect to other factors and deserves neither special attention nor dismissal as a cause of social aggression.[37]

We therefore appear to be a more aggressive society because of our media, and in combination with other factors, violent media help create a more violent social reality. Although research does show a link, social aggression is not necessarily criminal, nor is most crime violent. In addition to the stated unknowns concerning violent media and social aggression, the greatest problem in applying the "violent media causes social aggression" research to the "media causes crime" question is that the validity of extrapolating from the aggression research to a conclusion about media and crime is highly questionable.[38] Consequently, even if the media does significantly foster aggressive behavior, it is a separate question whether media influence extends beyond aggressiveness to cause criminal behavior. Looking at prior video game articles, consistent evidence of a strong, direct, causal video game role in the generation of criminality is limited, but video games, like the media in general, do not escape as benign or bereft of influence. Gaming appears to interact with other prior risk factors to heighten pre-disposed criminogenic effects and impulses. Video games appear capable of playing the role of catalytic rudders in the formation of crime: not directly causing it, but in the right social and individual chemistry, shaping its appearance. Other social and individual factors play a greater role in whether crime occurs or not, but once criminogenic forces are in play, exposure to crime saturated video games can provide powerful models to follow.

Media and Criminal Behavior

There are inherent difficulties in researching the possible relationship between the media and criminal behavior. First, experiments are even more difficult to conduct in this area than in the area of social aggression, so that most of the available evidence consists of anecdotal reports rather than empirical studies. Second, the ways in which media may be affecting crime are numerous. The media could be increasing the number of criminals by turning previously law-abiding persons into criminals. Media portrayals may be helping already active criminals successfully commit more crimes by teaching them better crime techniques. Media may be increasing the seriousness or harmfulness of the crimes that are committed by making criminals more selective or violent. They may be fostering theft and other property crimes by cultivating desires for unaffordable things. They may be making crime seem more exciting, satisfying, and socially acceptable. Any of these processes would result in more crime, or more criminals, or more costly crime. Third, research is also difficult because an aggregate, society-wide media criminogenic effect is likely to be small and intermixed with many other crime-generating factors. In addition, the pool of at-risk individuals who are likely to be criminally influenced by the media is probably small. All of these factors make identifying media criminogenic effects a difficult research question to pursue.

Because of these difficulties, few empirical studies have uncovered large-scale criminogenic effects of the media on the populace. In the best-designed study, Karen Hennigan and her colleagues examined aggregate crime rates in the United States prior to and following the introduction of television in the 1950s.

Hennigan's study examined the idea that television, at least initially, influenced property (rather than violent) crime. They explained their empirical findings thusly:

> Lower classes and modest life-styles were rarely portrayed in a positive light on TV, yet the heaviest viewers have been and are poorer, less educated people. It is possible that in the 1950s television caused younger and poorer persons (the major perpetrators of theft) to compare their life-styles and possessions with (a) those of the wealthy television characters and (b) those portrayed in advertisements. Many of these viewers may have felt resentment and frustration over lacking the goods they could not afford, and some may have turned to crime as a way of obtaining the coveted goods and reducing any relative deprivation.[39]

Because contemporary mass media's influences on society cannot be separated from other social processes, the impact of media on current crime levels is unknown. Hennigan and her colleagues speculated that television still contributes to an increase in property crime rates to some unknown degree, although other research has failed to tie the media to aggregate crime levels. Recent reviews have concluded that any link between exposure to violent media and general levels of violent criminal behavior is weak at best and moderated by consumer predisposition and age, media content, and social factors.[40] A significant relationship between swings in media content and general criminality in society has not been shown; if it exists is more likely to influence property crime than violent crime. But what about influence of media portrayals of crime on at-risk individuals at a level too low to appear in aggregate crime rates?

Copycat Crime

A behavioral process that is widely accepted is the ability of the media to generate copycat crime.[41] Waves of fads and fashions have established the fact that people lift behavior models from the media, and this connection has been extrapolated to include the mimicking of media-portrayed criminal acts.[42] Public interest in the relation of mass media to copycat crime emerged with the entertainment media of the late nineteenth century.[43] The growing concern that media messages could influence people to commit crime sparked investigations and censorship drives against the media in the early 1920s. In 1929, partly in response to these concerns, the Payne Foundation underwrote the first large-scale studies of the social impact of media—at that time, the consequences of movies. Portions of this research examined the effects of movies on deviant, asocial, and violent behavior by juveniles. Combined with public concerns about the influence of the cinema, these research efforts prodded the film industry to create a review board, the Hays Commission, to oversee the content of films and quell the increasing calls for government intervention.[44] The film industry adopted a self-imposed code that forbade crimes shown in film "to teach methods of crime, inspire potential criminals with a desire for imitation, or make criminals seem heroic and justified." A media-generated criminogenic

Box 4.2   Project X: A Film and Its Copycats

The aftermath of a 2012 Warner Brothers movie titled, *Project X* provides a recent example of the interaction of legacy media, social media, and copycat crime. In a typical teenage male's fantasy storyline that involves heavy drinking, topless women, and extensive property damage, the movie plot centers around three high school students arranging an "anything goes" party at one of their homes that spirals out of control. The film has been accused of generating a copycat string of house parties, arrests, and even one fatality. Two Houston, Texas copycat parties attracted between 500 and 1000 people, caused over 100,000 dollars in damage to one house, and trashed another in which nearly every window was broken and sheet-rock was torn from the walls. Thirteen teenagers were arrested in the second case and credited the movie as their idea source. News of the party had spread quickly on Facebook and Twitter. A Florida teen was arrested before his "*Project X* party of a lifetime" took place. The police, alerted by the teen's four-minute YouTube video depicting him spray-painting the home's walls (one with the words *Project X*), arrested him the morning of the scheduled party on charges of burglary and 19,000 dollars worth of vandalism. More than 2,000 people turned up at the home and had to be dispersed by police.

GREEN HAT FILMS/THE KOBAL COLLECTION/Art Resource NY

SOURCES: "Houston Teen Killed at 'Project X'-Inspired Party" abcnews.go.com; "Growing Number of 'Project X' Party Copycat Lead to Arrests Nationwide" abcnews.go.com; "Police foil teen's Project X copycat party after he advertises event on Facebook and Twitter" www.dailymail.co.uk/news/article-2114989; Teens Copycat 'Project X', Destroy $500,000 Home–YouTube www.youtube.com/watch?v=tNL7DNuNjv0

effect was clearly not in doubt. As media technology has evolved so that a mediated experience has come to approach that of a real-world experience, concerns with emulation of media-modeled behaviors have only grown (see Box 4.2).

Irrespective of the long-ago-reached perception that media can be criminogenic, there is no lack of information available in the media on how to commit crimes. Far more than in previous eras, a large body of material detailing how to commit specific crimes is readily available in films, on television, from the Internet, on social media, and in printed form. Texts come complete with diagrams and directions on how to commit robberies, murder, and numerous acts of terrorism, and countless visual examples are accessible. Despite concerns, research, and industry and government responses, specific knowledge about criminogenic media effects is sparse. Why is the research so limited when the questionable content is so available and the concerns span generations?

The reason research is limited is because what seems a simple matter—determining when a media-induced copycat crime has occurred—is complicated by the intrinsic nature of copycat crime. For a crime to be a **copycat crime,** it must have been inspired by an earlier, media-publicized or **generator crime—** that is, there must be a pair of crimes linked through the media. The perpetrator of a copycat crime must have been exposed to the media content of the original crime and must have incorporated major elements of that crime into his or her crime. The choice of victim, the motivation, or the technique in a copycat crime must have been lifted from the earlier, media-detailed generator crime. In broad terms, copycat crime results from the interaction of factors from three sources: media content, persons at risk to be copycats, and the immediate and wider social and cultural setting in which the media content is consumed.

These limits make identifying copycat crimes for study problematic because two independent but similar crimes may be erroneously labeled a copycat pair, and true copycat crimes may go unrecognized and unidentified. As a result, too few copycat crimes or criminals have been identified to allow for generalization or for scientifically adequate research, and although the term *copycat crime* has appeared for many years, a limited amount of empirical research touches upon this phenomenon.[45] Instead, researchers have relied on anecdotal evidence to gauge the extent and nature of copycat crime. The growing file of compiled anecdotal reports does indicate that criminal events that are rare in real life are sometimes committed soon after similar events are depicted in the media.[46] There have been enough real-life incidents that have replicated media portrayals in such detail that they invite a common-sense conclusion that copycat crimes occur regularly at an unknown but significant rate.[47] In addition to anecdotal reports, surveys of offenders have indicated that a substantial proportion—approximately 25 percent—have attempted a copycat crime in their careers.[48] Collectively, the anecdotal examples and offender surveys provide evidence establishing the reality of copycat crime.

By what mechanism do the media generate copycat effects? Here again, knowledge is limited and speculation prevails. In that the concept implies the imitation of an initial crime, the obvious starting point in discussing copycat crime is imitation. Gabriel Tarde was first to offer a theoretical discussion of copycat crime in the late nineteenth century.[49] Focusing on violent crime and observing that sensational violent crime appears to prompt similar incidents, he coined the term *suggesto-imitative assaults* to describe the phenomenon. In a pithy summation, he concluded, "Epidemics of crime follow the line of the telegraph."[50] However, imitation came to have a negative connotation among social scientists, who saw it as a simple, less cognitively demanding activity. Subsequently, Tarde's writings were largely ignored in criminology until the 1970s, when a surge of copycat crimes involving airline hijackings and media interest in them led to renewed attention to the role of imitation in the generation of crime.[51] Picking up directly from Tarde's earlier perspective, initial copycat crime researchers attributed copycat crime to a process of simple and direct imitation based on social learning principles.[52] Over time, imitation came to be criticized as too simplistic an explanation to fully understand copycat crime, failing to explain why most children imitate aggression within socially acceptable limits and only a few imitate aggression with a real gun. Critics also noted that imitation theory focuses on the copycat criminal and tends to downplay other social factors. Today imitation is considered a necessary but insufficient factor in the generation of copycat crime. The primary flaw in imitation theory is that it generally implies that the copied behavior must physically resemble the portrayed behavior and therefore falls short in explaining any generalized effects or innovative applications such as why a media portrayal of a bombing might be a catalyst for arson.[53]

Partly in response, another mechanism, more general than imitation-oriented, by which media portrayals activate similar behaviors has been posited.[54] Through this mechanism, termed **priming,** the portrayals of certain behaviors in the media activate a cluster of associated ideas within the potential copycat offender that increase the likelihood that he or she will behave similarly but not necessarily identically.[55] Priming holds that when people experience an event via the mass media, ideas having a similar meaning to those contained in the media content are activated for a short time, and these thoughts can result in related actions. Thus, after viewing violent media, individuals will be primed to have more hostile thoughts, to see aggression as justified, and to behave more aggressively.[56] Priming can be understood as providing a set of ideas and beliefs that construct a particular social reality—the perception that the nature of the world is such that a particular type of crime is appropriate, justified, and likely to be successful.

A cognitive theory concept of **"scripts"** from the field of communication also has copycat crime applications. Linked to priming, scripts are seen as preestablished behavioral directions that individuals hold in their memory and scroll up to direct their actions as needed. Cognitive scripts serve as guides for behavior by laying out the sequence of events that one believes are likely to happen and the behaviors that one believes are appropriate in particular situations.[57] It is thought that criminal scripts can be acquired by observing criminogenic media during fantasy role-playing, a part of normal child development. Role-playing encourages the generalized acquisition of social role scripts—the role-playing child for example acquires the persona of the social role and subsequently acts like he or she thinks a doctor, athlete, or gangster would in various real-world settings beyond the ones specifically modeled in the observed media content. The more salient the observed criminality, the more the child ruminates upon, fantasizes about, and rehearses it.[58] Cues, such as the presence of a gun, first observed in the media and later encountered in the real world, increase the likelihood of the activation of previously acquired criminal scripts.[59] A study by Allen Mazur offers an example in the area of crime.[60] Mazur reported that bomb threats directed at nuclear energy facilities increased significantly following increases in news coverage of nuclear power issues. Mazur's study is important in that it indicates that media content can initiate crimes even when they don't provide precise models to copy; the bomb threats to nuclear facilities followed news stories that were not bomb-related. In Berkowitz's conceptualization, the news media coverage primed some people to make bomb threats even though the coverage did not provide a specific bomb-threat model to copy. In Huesmann's terms, the coverage activated similar "threatening" scripts.

At this time, copycat crime appears to be concentrated in predisposed, at-risk individuals primed by media characterizations of criminality to activate previously acquired crime scripts and criminal roles.[61] Described and diagramed in Box 4.3, there are multiple paths between the media and criminality that copycat criminals can take. Social cognition theory provides two paths: (1) a systematic central path that requires a copycat offender to evaluate information and is likely related to planned copycat crimes such as a bank robbery; and (2) a heuristic peripheral path that is quickly traveled with little information evaluation and likely leads to emotional, spontaneous copycat crime such as an impulsive assault or hate crime.[62] A third path through **narrative persuasion** is also possible.[63] Most media consumed is narrative or storytelling-based and consumer interaction with narrative media is qualitatively different from the first two paths. The terms "transportation," "engagement," and "absorption" have been used to describe this type of media interaction. As narrative persuasion describes the most common use of media and provides an opportunity to influence individuals who would ordinarily be resistant to media influence due to the "suspension of belief" that is a hallmark of entertainment narrative involvement, this path is speculated to be the most significant copycat crime path.[64] The narrative persuasion path allows for influence-resistant media consumers to be affected by story characters who model both attitude and behavior change.[65] Thus, a consumer who is initially unlikely to copy a particular crime would be persuaded to do so by observing a model who is portrayed as also initially unwilling to commit an offense but who undergoes a transformation in the media-supplied narrative in which the crime comes to be seen in a positive manner.

As shown, the copycat crime model in Box 4.3 is conceptually divided into three blocks. The top portion of the model, from exposure to a media generator crime to acquisition of crime knowledge, is felt to be a common experience for most media consumers in that many persons are expected to learn criminally instructive information from repeated media exposure. Thus, repeated playing of video games will impart the basic knowledge of how to be a sniper to many who will acquire the knowledge and steps necessary to stalk and shoot other humans.

Following crime knowledge acquisition, in block two the model diverges into three possible pathways, determined by the consumer's underlying goal for interacting with the media. From least traveled to most traveled, the paths diverge depending upon whether the consumer is interacting with the media as a source of entertainment or as a source of instruction. As diagrammed, paths 1 and 2 differentiate based upon the cognitive motivation level of an individual and imply different sorts of copycat crime. The first path is related to thoughtful

---

B o x 4.3   An Individual Level Copycat Crime Model

As shown in Figure 4.1, the copycat model focuses on the steps thought to occur between exposure to a copycat-generation crime and copycat attempts. The model conceptually starts with elements of the General Aggression and Social Learning model. Paths are determined by the cognitive motivation (the willingness to invest time gathering and evaluating information) of a copycat offender. When cognitive motivation is high, the first path, *central systematic*, is followed as long as the individual has the capability to understand the information gathered. Instrumental copycat crimes such as the mimicked bank robbery from the film *Set It Off* provide examples of copycat offenders following a systematic central processing path to a copycat crime. The second path, *heuristic peripheral*, is followed when cognitive motivation, or the ability to process available information, is low and its copycat exemplars are spontaneous emotive crimes, such as unplanned opportunity assaults or rapes and some hate crime clusters. In the heuristic process, only a subset of relevant information is retrieved, and that which is retrieved is the most accessible from memory. The third path denotes the psychological involvement people experience when using the media as entertainment and escapism. In this path, factual information is not the goal; being told an interesting story is. After diverging through the three possible paths, the model converges with the communication research concepts of priming and scripts and continues through its final steps. As a research tool, the three path model is both a map of possible individual-level pathways to copycat crime and a diagram of an hypothesized screening process of potential copycat offenders in which only those with a unique combination of media, individual, and social factors come to actually attempt a copycat crime.

---

planned "instrumental" crimes ("Here are instructions on how to successfully commit this crime");[66] the second path involves less rational, emotive copycat crimes ("They are rioting on television and no one's getting arrested! It looks exciting! Let's do the same here").[67]

In the third path, no real-world decision is pending, and instruction is not a goal. In this path, narrative persuasion operates, and deep psychological involvement with media content and storyline develops.[68] This path describes how most people use and interact with most media, seeking entertainment, not explicit instructions. When engagement with criminogenic content is high, transformation or absorption results, and the consumer is transported to a world where criminal behavior is justified, rewarded, and unlikely to be punished.[69] Due to the large quantity of crime-related narratives in the media, media content in general can be thought of as a haphazard entertainment/education effort. Heightening the media's narrative persuasive effect, the higher the level of engagement with the narrative, the less counter-arguing with the content's informational messages will occur.[70] The narrative persuasion path provides a mechanism to influence individuals who would be resistant to following the cognitive persuasion paths.[71] Rather, in the narrative persuasion path, media consumers are "side-participants" in the story line— prepared to play an active role when given the opportunity.[72] In the end, narrative persuasion thereby provides a mechanism for overcoming resistance to imitating

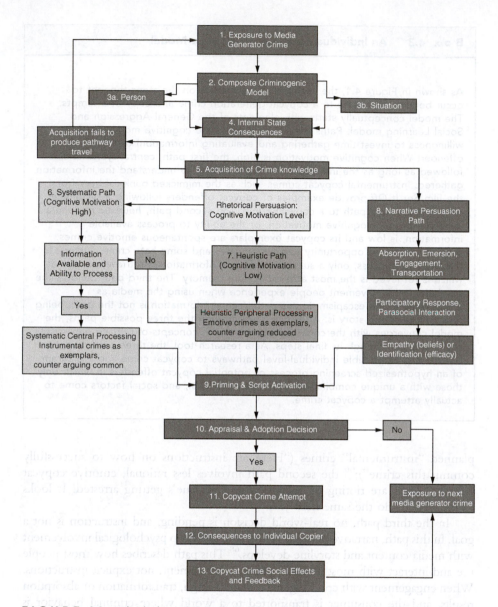

FIGURE 4.1 Individual Level Copycat Crime Pathways.

criminal behavior by decoupling the thoughtful consideration of likely negative reactions to copying a crime.[73] However, it is expected that few transverse the middle block and follow one of the three copycat paths down to the third "appraisal and adoption" block, in which committing a copycat crime is seriously considered. Given the comparative low visibility of copycat crimes, it is speculated that most individuals who have passed through block 2 in the model will decide not to attempt a copycat crime.

The third block is thus the least traveled road even for at-risk copycat offenders. Some individuals, however, come to a positive decision to copy a media-portrayed generator crime and implement the media-modeled crime. These actual copycat crime attempts are hypothesized to be rare as a proportion of all crime, but not rare in terms of criminal life histories.[74] That is, most of the crimes committed by offenders will not be copycat crimes, but many offenders (about one in four if prior surveys are accurate) will have attempted a copycat crime in their lifetimes.[75] Two factors are forwarded as playing central roles in the decision to attempt or not attempt a copycat crime: an individual's criminal history and their associated perception of self-efficacy regarding crime, and the impact of observed and expected punishment for crime on the potential copycat crime offender.

The criminal history of individuals who reach the appraisal and adoption decision is an important factor for copycat crime via its' relationship to a perception of self-efficacy. Via a Skinnerian pattern of rewards and punishments for committing crime, offenders with long criminal records have likely been exposed to a pattern of rewards with some random punishment for their criminality. In such cases, the lesson from a long record of past criminal experience would be that one is able to successfully commit many crimes and the perception of one's criminal self-efficacy would be enhanced. The end result would be the heightened belief in success from copying a media-modeled crime and a correspondent increased likelihood of committing a copycat crime.[76] The traditional counter to this process has been for the producers of media content to portray crime as ultimately punished.

While there is a long-standing belief that the depiction of punishment at the end of a media portrayal of crime will mitigate any pro-crime messages, media-portrayed punishment will not necessarily dissuade copying. Affixing a punishment to the end of a succession of successful crimes or to near-successful ones should not be expected to remove criminogenic learning effects.[77] For one, media-depicted punishments can be seen as instructive lessons on ways to avoiding similar mistakes, and potential copycats may copy a crime on the belief that with slight modification of tactics, they can gain the benefits of crime without suffering the costs. In addition, habitual offenders often overestimate their odds of success and will alter their crime techniques, confident that they have significantly reduced their risk of failure.[78] Criminogenic media content that shows a string of successful crimes or crimes that failed due to perceived correctable mistakes made by a media-portrayed criminal model means that even seeing ultimate punishment will not substantially counteract media criminogenic copycat effects. Although the copycat crime paths are felt to operate universally, it is expected that societies will differ between themselves and over time in their copycat crime rates. Some societies are expected to generate more criminogenic content, more at-risk copycat offenders, and more opportunities and cultural support for applying copycat crime models.

Determinants of Copycat Crime Rates. The individual-level paths are related to the society-level aggregate copycat crime model shown in Figure 4.2. The amount of copycat crime in a society is seen as the result of the interaction of four factors: the generator crime and criminal, subsequent media coverage, the

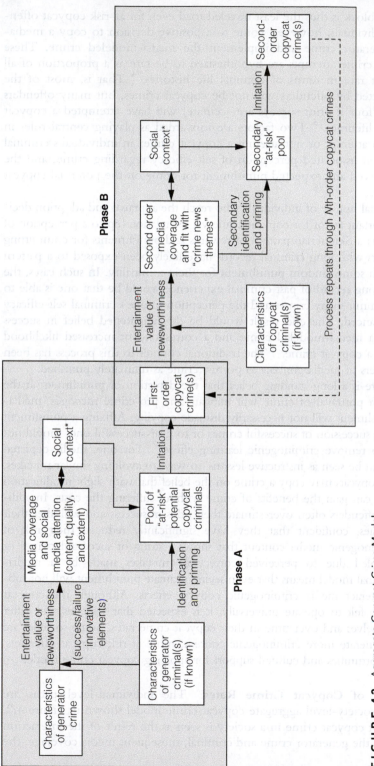

FIGURE 4.2 Aggregate Copycat Crime Model.

*Social context includes social norms regarding performance crime, news and entertainment; quantity of opportunities to commit a generator crime; preexisting social tensions (racism, economic strife, and so forth); and the organization of mass media (state run or private, profit or nonprofit, accessible or restricted, heavily or lightly regulated, large or small audiences, and viewed as credible or suspect by the public).

social context, and the characteristics of the copycat criminal. The model denotes a process in which select, usually successful, highly engaging crimes shown in popular entertainment or news stories emerge as candidates for copying. The media coverage and portrayals first affect individuals by inviting them to identify with the initial crime and criminal and thereby prime a pool of potential copycat criminals. A susceptible at-risk individual—that is, a person who sees other people and the media as profitable crime information sources—is thought to be at special risk for copycat behavior, but cultural factors are seen as more significant for copycat crime rates than individual and media content characteristics.[79] Paraphrasing Bandura (1973, 269):

> Social conditions that increase the permissibility and functional value of [crime] easily override the effects of personal dispositions. For this reason, it is primarily types of social inducements rather than types of people that should be examined in predicting who will put into practice what has been learned from [the media].

Defined as a culture with both pervasive crime and crime media, and social conditions that increase the permissibility of crime and its functional value so that crime is often rewarded, justified, or unchallenged, the United States qualifies as a supportive copycat crime environment.

In sum, social learning theory has assigned greater weight to similarity of expected consequences than to similarity of personal attributes in predicting when imitation will occur.[80] Dissimilar people in similar settings will more often behave more similarly than similar people in different settings will. This acknowledgment does not, however, relieve the media of a significant role. While media are not seen as the dominant cause of copycat crime, they supply criminal role models and crime portraits that create a supportive social atmosphere in which the predisposed few emulate the crimes they see, hear, and read about.[81] In gist, the more forcefully crime is portrayed as rewarding, justified, or unchallenged in the media, the more copycat crime will be generated, and the more a copycat crime culture will exacerbate copycat effects.[82] The size of the copycat crime pool is affected both by the level of media distribution of the criminogenic content and by other social context factors such as social norms regarding deviance and violence; the pre-existence of social conflicts; the number of opportunities available to the potential offender to copy a crime technique (there are more opportunities to copy a car theft technique, for example, than a bank robbery technique); the nature, credibility, and pervasiveness of the mass media; and the size of the pre-existing criminal population. Unfortunately, contemporary U.S. society scores high on all of these criteria; therefore, the generation of copycat crimes should be high in the United States compared to other countries. After the at-risk copycat pool emerges, the first wave of copycat crimes results through a process of generalized primed imitation, limited by and adapted to the copycat criminal's opportunities (Phase A).

Should these first-order copycat crimes receive further media attention, and particularly should they be incorporated into a media crime theme, the likelihood of additional copycat crime increases (Phase B). This extended reiterative process is regarded as much more likely to occur with violent crime because of the high news value of violence.[83] The aggregate model reveals a paradox. The process is more common for property crime and property offenders through first-order copycat crimes (Phase A). But violent copycat crime and offenders are most likely to generate second and higher-order imitations (Phase B) as they are more likely to become the focus of intensive media attention. Once more, the media is likely to take the rare real-world event, the violent copycat crime, and make it the more significant, better-known event in the public's constructed reality. The accepted social construction of a copycat crime is more likely to be of a violent crime such as a bombing, even though in actuality copycat property crimes are probably far more common.

Who is at risk for committing a copycat crime?   Concerning the question of who follows the pathways, commits the copycat crime, and generates the copycat crime rates, a set of five umbrella concepts have emerged as hypothesized flags for at-risk copycat individuals. Immersion in crime-related content appears significant, as well as a set of psychological traits. In addition, a personal belief in criminal efficacy and an individual's personal history of inconsistent punishment for crime are hypothesized as important. Lastly, a number of family, community, and cultural environment factors have been linked to copycat crime behaviors.[84]

Thus, media use that reflects a concentration on a single media source to the exclusion of other media and interpersonal contacts has been forwarded as a copycat crime flag.[85] In particular, offenders who immerse themselves in a criminogenic niche media (for example, watching criminogenic excerpts from a single video repeatedly) and are weakly networked into law-abiding groups and strongly networked into deviant groups are seen to be at greater risk.[86] Regarding the type of copycat crime that generates the most concern, unpredicted bizarre violence by individuals without known violent histories, such as found with the Columbine, Aurora, and Newtown shooters, repetitive viewing, in which the copier watches media content multiple times prior to offending and displays self-editing of content by repetitively watching only the copied sequences (sometimes using freeze-framing to slow down the violent content), delineate the extreme violent media–copycat crime relationship. Additionally, characteristics of delusion, with a history of high interest in guns and law enforcement encounters, and the traits of idleness, isolation, and deterioration in socioeconomic functions accompanied by perceptions of persecution and resentment, have been forwarded as predictors of a propensity to copy violent models.[87]

The likelihood of media immersion increases as peers and family decrease in importance,[88] and by extension, individuals who are deeply immersed in popular culture and media-dependent should also show an increased copycat propensity.[89] Weak social bonding also plays a role, and individuals with less to lose from failed criminality are speculated to more often choose copycat crime, as these individuals will rely more on media for positive social reinforcement.[90] Immersion is also associated with identification with media offenders. Because media-immersed consumers are not necessarily heavy consumers in terms of total hours but appear to form para-social relationships with media personalities, media-immersed individuals who imagine themselves as the media criminals should be more likely to copy their offenses.[91] Finally, even without media immersion, social isolation increases copycat crime risk due to the media increasing in importance as information sources.[92]

Regarding other individual traits, the decision to copy a crime is weighed not only against the expected reward versus punishment from the crime, but also against expected outcomes of alternate law-abiding behaviors. So copycat crime would be more attractive to those who do not see law-abiding behavior as likely to be rewarded.[93] In addition, persons who see media personalities as opinion leaders and as friends are postulated as more likely copycat crime candidates.[94] Other copycat flags are found in individual media preferences and usage motives. Individuals who prefer crime content and who consume high amounts of media content combined with viewing motives of information seeking or learning are hypothesized as more at risk to be copycats.[95] Additional personality traits that have been flagged include low self-control,[96] high criminal innovativeness,[97] and behavior disinhibition tendencies.[98] Regarding consumer intelligence, the hypotheses about copycat crime are mixed, and the role of intelligence levels in copycat crime is likely interactive with other factors.[7]

It is at the family and neighborhood environment levels that the final determinants of copycat crime operate. In these realms, the potential copycat offenders estimate the likelihood of reward versus punishment and the expected social reaction to a copycat offense. Magnifying this environmental mix, the presence of criminogenic parents should produce more copycat offspring.[99] Criminogenic parents can either be offenders themselves or verbally support criminogenic values. Even if they preach law abiding and punish law breaking, if they are offenders, they provide strong criminogenic models that supplement the media-provided ones. The media's criminogenic effects will be further enhanced by racial strife, income disparities, and detrimental social conditions and contribute to an increased number of people at risk for criminogenic media influences.[100] A criminogenic media also supports criminogenic cultures, neighborhood structures, and family environments, which in turn increase the capability of the media to teach crime.[101]

Based on available research, working hypotheses are that copycat criminals are more likely to be career criminals involved in property offenses than first or violent offenders (although a violent copycat episode will usually receive a greater amount of media coverage when identified due to the greater newsworthiness of violent crime). If there is a consensus regarding the nature of copycat crime, it is that a media criminogenic influence will concentrate in pre-existing criminal populations. In the anecdotal case histories, most of the individuals who mimic media crimes have prior criminal records or histories of violence,[102] suggesting that the effect of the media is more likely qualitative (affecting criminal behavior) rather than quantitative (affecting the number of criminals). The limited research also indicates a pragmatic use of the media by offenders, with borrowing media crime techniques as the most common practice. Copycat offenders usually have the criminal intent to commit a particular crime before they copy a media-based technique.[103]

The specific relationship between media coverage and the generation of crime remains unknown, as do the social context factors that are most important. There is no evidence of a strong media criminalizing effect on previously law-abiding individuals and the media influence how people commit a crime to a greater extent than they influence whether people commit a crime. Criminogenic media content is often erroneously described in the media as a crime trigger. In reality, the media are most often a crime rudder, molding crime's form rather than being its engine. [104] Unknown are what factors launch the short-term bursts of high profile criminogenic copying that periodically occur. Understanding the dynamics of copycat crime waves such as have been seen in product tampering, airline hijacking, hostage taking, and suicide bombings awaits further research. [105] Even before the September 11, 2001, terrorist attacks, the copycat crimes that generated the greatest concern were those related to terrorism and the fear that a successful highly publicized terrorist act would produce a global pool of imitators. Today, terrorism's relationship to the media remains a leading source of anxiety in the media, crime, and justice arena.

Media-Oriented Terrorism

Terrorism's relationship with the media epitomizes the dangers of copycat effects. Carlos Marighella, a Communist insurgent terrorist in the 1960s, described the terrorists' aim in their interactions with media:

> These actions, carried out with specific and determined objectives, inevitably become propaganda material for the mass communication system.... The war of nerves or psychological war is an aggressive technique, based on the direct or indirect use of mass means of communication and news in order to demoralize the government. In psychological warfare, the government is always at a disadvantage since it imposes censorship on the mass media and winds up in a defensive position by not allowing anything against it to filter through. At this point it becomes desperate, is involved in great contradictions and loss of prestige, and loses time and energy in an exhausting effort at control which is subject to being broken at any moment. [106]

The strength of the symbiotic media–terrorism relationship is such that in many ways the modern terrorist is the creation of the media. If mass media did not exist, terrorists would have to invent them. [107] Media and terrorists share several needs. Most fundamentally, both are trying to reach the greatest number of people possible. Driven by their mutual goal to maximize audience size, **media-oriented terrorism,** where violence is scripted to earn publicity, has significantly increased. [108] Media-oriented terrorism is "propaganda by deed," a purposely symbolic crime. Today a steady stream of terrorist acts can be identified as media-oriented terrorist events characterized by the selection of high-visibility targets, graphic terrorist acts, pre-event contact with media outlets, and post-event videos, interviews, postings, and other media accommodations. [109] In the research literature on terrorism, no doubts are expressed that the media motivate copycat terrorist acts or that a substantial number of terrorist events are aimed primarily at garnering publicity. [110] Differences between media-oriented terrorism and non-media-oriented terrorism are shown in Figure 4.3.

Media-Oriented Terrorism	Non-Media-Oriented Terrorism
> Terrorists involve journalists or media personalities > Terrorist group announces their association with terrorist act > Terrorist group informs media of act and purpose > Terrorist representative is willing to be interviewed > Terrorist group tapes or photographs event and provides it to the public through the Internet or media > Attacks are in news-worthy countries or on people from news-worthy countries > Terrorism causes fatalities or injuries > Act of terror is purposely unique and dramatic > Most common event hijacking or hostage taking, kidnapping for non monetary reasons, bombing of high profile site or person.	> Events are unclaimed > Tapes and photographs are not made public > Attacks are made in low news-worthy countries > Terror act is standard in tactic and common to prior acts > Low profile victims > Most common event is a random bombing or tactical assault.

FIGURE 4.3 Differences between Media-Oriented and Non-Media-Oriented Terrorism.
SOURCE: Surette, Hansen, and Nobel, "Measuring Media Oriented Terrorism", p. 362

Contemporary media-oriented terrorists are guided by five principles.[111] First, their acts are not tactical in nature but are aimed at distant external audiences. Second, victims are chosen for symbolic meaning to maximize fear and public impact. Third, the media are eager to cover terrorist violence and will devote significant resources to reporting terrorist events. Fourth, the media can be activated, directed, and manipulated for propaganda effects. Fifth, target governments are at a disadvantage because their choice is usually between censorship or allowing terrorists to use the media. The application of these principles has resulted in the spread of media-oriented terrorism around the world.

Like politicians, terrorists have learned to manipulate media coverage to bypass editorial gatekeeping and contextual formatting by journalists and go directly to the public with their message, a process made easier by social media.[112] In the process, terrorism has become a form of infotainment and public theater. On the other side, the media can be thought of as "terrorism oriented" in terms of the commercial value of terrorist events. Due to the huge audience it attracts, media-oriented terrorism is highly valuable to media organizations.

For the media, terrorism is dramatic, often violent, visual, and timely. Unlike wars which are usually protracted and highly complex events … acts of terrorist violence normally have a beginning and an end, can be encompassed in a few minutes of air time, possess a large degree of drama, involve participants who are perceived by the viewing public as unambiguous, and are not so complex as to be unintelligible to those who tune in only briefly.[113]

All of this has transformed terrorism into a profit source for the media. And as the media pursued terrorists, terrorists became media wise. They came to understand the dynamics of newsworthiness and the benefits of media exposure: increased legitimacy and political status; heightened perception of their strength and threat; and an increased ability to attract resources, support, and recruits, particularly via social media and Internet sites.

However, media attention is not guaranteed to a terrorist group. Worldwide, many more acts of terrorism are committed than are reported in the media, and U.S. media give more coverage to terrorism aimed at U.S. citizens or property.[114] Coverage of domestic terrorism, at least prior to the September 11, 2001, terrorist attacks, received little coverage, and coverage today remains focused on events with casualties, with new media raising the value of terrorist acts which are visual for both news agencies and terrorists.[115] The resulting competition for media attention causes terrorists to escalate their violence, because more violent and more dramatic acts are necessary to gain news coverage as the shock value of ordinary terrorism diminishes. Occupation of a building, for example, no longer garners world or even national coverage in many instances. As long as media content is a commercial product whose content is influenced by sensationalism, visually violent terrorist acts will garner disproportionate attention.

In the end, the impact of media attention to terrorism is twofold. First, coverage of a terrorist act encourages copycats.[116] As with general copycat crime, there is much anecdotal evidence that terrorist events such as kidnappings, bank robberies in which hostages are taken, plane hijackings, parachute hijackings, planting altitude bombs on airplanes, suicide bombings, and online beheadings of hostages occur in clusters.[117] These copycat effects are especially strong following a well-publicized, successful terrorist act using a novel approach. Second, although their numbers wax and wane, the pattern of these violent performances suggests that media-oriented terrorism has become a persistent element of the total terrorism picture, starting with the 1972 Olympics, when Palestine Liberation Organization terrorists killed members of the Israeli Olympic team.[118] The World Wide Web has also provided a new avenue for terrorists to disseminate their messages and has reduced their need to attract news media attention in order to reach target audiences.[119] Today terrorism is often a twisted public relations "infotainment" effort. Like other types of crime, terrorism would still exist if the media disappeared, but the media-terrorism relationship exacerbates the prevalence of the terrorist act as a performance. Terrorism performed for both old and new media is a common feature in the twenty-first century.

CRIMINOGENIC INFOTAINMENT

Where does the research about violent, criminogenic, and terrorism-related media lead? The existing research suggests the following propositions. Most people exposed to pernicious media will show no negative effects. Some small proportion of people—the proportion is not clear—will show slight effects, concentrated more in attitudes than in behaviors. Strong behavioral effects are relatively rare and are most likely to appear in at-risk individuals predisposed to crime, but the reality of long-term effects on a large number of people remains a distinct possibility. In addition, the media's ability to generate greater numbers of predisposed at-risk individuals also appears to be real. Therefore, the media's criminogenic effects will be enhanced as their current criminogenic content in combination with racial and ethnic strife, income disparities, and poor social conditions contribute to more people at risk for negative media influences in the future. Violence-prone children and adults are especially at risk for emulating media violence. When sex and violence are linked, hyper-masculine males are most influenced to be sexually aggressive. When the news media sensationalize crime and make celebrities of criminals, the danger of imitation for notoriety increases. When successful crime is detailed, criminals will emulate it. And when a successful terrorist event is shown or a terrorist group is able to gain the attention of the media, media-oriented terrorism will increase.

New media have hypothesized criminogenic effects when they provide avatar-like criminal models to copy and stimulate interpersonal communications about crime.[120] For example, a rap song can generate interpersonal conversations that encourage vandalism or violence within youth gangs, or new media communications such as blogs, Twitter, and e-mails can encourage imitation among geographically separated terrorist groups. The Internet is seen as a particularly powerful criminogenic influence due to it having both mass and interpersonal elements. As part way between mass media and interpersonal communication, the Internet provides a unique one-to-many communication avenue.[121] It provides word-of-mouth communication with global reach. Where real-world criminogenic instructors are not available, the Internet can substitute with interpersonal communications and deliver detailed how-to crime instructions.[122] For crime and justice, this means that media consumers can experience committing a murder rather than just observing one, help to catch an offender rather than just watch over the shoulder of a crime fighter, and determine guilt or innocence of the defendant rather than just follow a trial.[123] A candidate copycat offender can search out like-minded role models and interact with them on a personal level while anonymously learning crime techniques.

Whether criminogenic effects, such as copycat crime, emerge in any particular individual depends on the highly idiosyncratic interactions of the content of a particular media product (its characterizations of crime and criminals), the individual's predispositions (personal criminal history, family, and environmental factors), and the media's social context (preexisting cultural norms, crime opportunities, and pervasiveness of the mass media). A media-generated criminogenic effect ultimately depends on the combined influences of social context, media content, and audience characteristics. The more heavily the consumer relies on the media for information about the world and the greater his or her predisposition to criminal behavior, the greater the likelihood of an effect.

Media effects are real, but it is also apparent that the media alone cannot make someone a criminal. You can get an idea of what society would be like if the media went away by looking at the United States before the mass media existed. What you will find is a violent land with many violent people.[124] That fact is the core reason it does not make sense to blame the media for the bulk of our violence and crime today. Based on our heritage, we would certainly be a violent and crime-burdened society today without the media's influences, but are we more violent and criminal because of them? Yes. Violent media alone does not make a violent person, but violent media can apparently make a violent person more often violent. Criminogenic media won't make a law-abiding person a criminal, but a preexisting criminal may become a greater threat. The media play their role after the biological, economic, and social factors do. To blame only the media is to ignore a host of more significant factors. But while you can argue that the media are not the main engines in our crime rate, media do facilitate the packaging and delivery of a criminogenic boost.

In the end, the media's influence on the behavior of most of us is to cause us *not* to do certain things. The media do not turn law-abiding people into criminals or nonviolent people into assaulters, but they keep people from flying, taking a foreign vacation, going downtown, or opening their door. Media make us wary of each other and in doing so make us more isolated and subsequently more dependent on them for our knowledge about crime and other social conditions. Media cannot be painted as the dominant cause of crime in society, but their portraits of criminality cannot be ignored. By painting crime in a particular hue, the media color the actual world as violent, predatory, and dangerous. They supply criminal role models and techniques; create a conducive social atmosphere for the predisposed few to emulate the crimes they see, hear, and read about; and provide the theoretical ideas that explain it all to the public while largely absolving that public of any social responsibility. With these images of criminality in mind, Chapter 5 looks at the relationship between the media and the first line of response to crime, law enforcement.

SUMMARY

- Criminogenic media refers to media content that is hypothesized as a cause of crime.

- Exposure to violent media has been found to be correlated with aggressive behavior. What remains under debate is how strong the relationship is and whether exposure is a direct cause of aggression.

- An interaction between media content, media consumer, and media exposure characteristics is thought to best describe the relationship between media and aggression.

- Research on the effect of violent video games reports a correlation between game play and player aggression but the substantive importance of the relationship is argued.

- Although many will acquire knowledge on how to commit crime from the media, the current consensus regarding copycat crime is that a criminogenic influence will display most frequently in pre-existing criminal populations.

- Potential copycat criminals can decide to commit or not to commit a copycat crime through various pathways, either thoughtful review of media-provided crime instructions or psychological immersion in crime related narratives.

- Media generated criminogenic effects are most likely to appear in at-risk individuals predisposed to crime.

- How much media-generated crime a society experiences is related to how supportive its culture is of crime. The more crime content in its media, the more supportive its values are of crime, and the more opportunities for crime in a society determine how much its media will influence its crime.

- Terrorism's relationship to the media has resulted in copycat terrorism and media-oriented terrorism being common elements of twenty-first-century acts of terror.

CLASS DISCUSSIONS

1. Discuss whether you feel that some types of media (films, books, electronic video games, for example) are more criminogenic than others or whether some content is more dangerous than other content.

2. Discuss the social and psychological characteristics of individuals who would travel each of the three copycat crime pathways diagrammed in Box 4.3.

3. Discuss the differences between cultures that appear to have large amounts of criminogenic media but small levels of copycat crime, such as Japan, and those that have higher levels of both, such as the United States. What might change in a culture to increase the copying of media portrayed crimes?

SUGGESTED READINGS

Coleman, L. (2004). *The copycat effect*. New York: Paraview.

Fisher, J. (1997). *Killer among us: Public reactions to serial murder*. Westport: Praeger.

Freedman, D. and Thussu, D. K. (Eds.) (2012). *Media & terrorism: Global perspectives*. Thousand Oaks: Sage.

Leitch, T. and Grant, B. (2002). *Crime films*. Cambridge: Cambridge University Press.

Matusitz, J. (2013). *Terrorism & communication*. Thousand Oaks: Sage.

Nacos, B. (2007). *Mass-mediated terrorism*. Lanham: Rowan and Littlefield.

Rogers, E. (2003). *Diffusion of innovations*. New York: Free Press.

Tuman, J. (2010). *Communicating terror: The rhetorical dimensions of terrorism*. Thousand Oaks: Sage.

CHAPTER 5

Crime Fighters

CHAPTER OBJECTIVES

After completing Chapter 5, you will

- Know the major divisions in the media portrait of law enforcement and crime fighting
- Understand the differences between professional and civilian crime fighters
- Recognize the media portraits of lampooned police, G-men and cops
- Appreciate the differences between media-portrayed police work and real-world police work
- Appreciate the differences between the media portraits of private eyes and private citizens with the media portraits of police officers
- Understand the link between media portraits of crime fighting and public support for anticrime policies

LAW ENFORCEMENT: A HOUSE DIVIDED

After criminality, the media pays the most attention to fighting crime. In the United States, law enforcement has high visibility coupled with low public knowledge.[1] That is, the public is exposed to large amounts of crime-fighting content in news, entertainment, and infotainment, most of it terribly distorted if not plain wrong. The public therefore generally holds an erroneous view of what the police actually do and how they do it.

The first problem with the media construction of law enforcement is that it is schizophrenic, persistently presenting two competing law enforcement frames of "good cop" or "bad cop." In the good cop frame, the criminal justice system, particularly the police, are part of a justice machine with dedicated professionals using the latest technology to repeatedly prove that crime does not pay. In the competing bad cop frame, the criminal justice system and its police are so inefficient and bound by regulations, politics, corruption, and incompetence that only the outsider rogue cop or citizen crime fighter can get anything positive accomplished. Within both good cop and bad cop frames two subgroups of crime fighters are found—distinguished by who they work for, one finds professional crime fighters who are employed in some fashion within the criminal justice system or **civilian crime fighters** who work outside of the system.

The professional soldiers in the media war on crime usually occupy law enforcement positions, but lawyers, judges, wardens, spies, and corrections officers also sometimes morph into crime fighters. These are the professional, career soldiers in the media's portrait of the war on crime, and they are often matched up with a competent criminal justice system filled with effective crime scene technicians and experts in criminalistics who help solve crimes. When the professionals of the criminal justice system are the main crime fighters in the media, civilians usually have a minor role, frequently serving solely as hapless victims. The war-on-crime professional soldiers either expertly or incompetently (depending on whether they are within a good cop or bad cop frame) wage a war against predatory violent crime. The terms *war* and *soldier* are not used here simply as colorful adjectives; across the media, crime fighting is depicted as a never-ending battle against evildoers in much media content.[2] The enemy is everywhere, the battlegrounds can be anywhere, and anyone may be caught in the crossfire at any time.

In addition to the good cop/bad cop division, another split exists. In the media, crime is fought by either criminal justice professionals or private citizens. When civilian crime fighters are portrayed as the primary crime fighters, the police and the criminal justice system are downplayed and often disparaged. The effectiveness of civilian crime fighters is enhanced when paired with an incompetent criminal justice system. When civilian crime fighters are on the scene, the traditional criminal justice components and personnel—especially the police—become part of the crime problem either through corruption or ineptitude. The "citizen soldiers" in the war on crime are shown to be successful where the bureaucratic, hampered, and often not so bright, career law enforcers are not. The media portraits of law enforcement reflect basic divisions between bad and good cops, professionals and citizens under an overarching construction of warlike combat as the most effective anticrime policy.

This media house divided subsequently projects conflicting messages about law enforcement. The first is that the expertise to deal with crime can only be found in the criminal justice system. The need to enhance the criminal justice system and unleash the police is a core message in the media's construction of crime fighting. The second and opposite message is that the incompetence of the criminal justice system and its people requires that individuals protect their own homes and communities and solve crime themselves. In the first social construction, we are told to wait for heroes to save us; in the second, we are told we had better save ourselves. What the two messages share is that the solutions will require violence.

Whether a criminal justice or a civilian hero is emphasized is not, for the most part, related to the type of crime being portrayed. Most types of crime stories are comfortable with either official or civilian heroes. Popular mystery and detective tales in which the search for clues is the key story element have employed both private investigators and police as their heroic sleuths. Similarly, crime thrillers that feature endangered victims and heroes; modernized Westerns in which heroic outsiders reluctantly clean up a town; crime, revenge, and vigilante stories in which a victim/hero is injured and retaliates; and action crime stories that feature superhero crime fighters all utilize both criminal justice employees and private citizens as heroes.[3] Within these stories both civilian and professional crime fighters can be either law-abiding role models (good cops) or less straight-and-narrow adventurers, gunfighters, loners, and sometimes criminals themselves (bad cops). The first group represents the incorrupt-ible all-American hero narrative; the more ambiguous individualistic and self-reliant second group represents our cultural admiration of the rebel. The rebels seem to enjoy themselves more and appear to be effective more quickly (not having to wait for search warrants or worry about repercussions from using entrapment or coercion), so it is not surprising that they outnumber the law-abiding crime fighters in the media. As the largely inaccurate legends of Jesse James, Bonnie and Clyde, Wild Bill Hickok, Eliot Ness, and Al Capone exemplify, media reconstructions have habitually made folk heroes out of criminals and heroic crime fighters out of less-than-stellar indivi-duals. By-the-book crime fighters are usually outdistanced by kick-your-butt, recently suspended, or wanted ones. Be it professionals or civilians, good cops or bad cops, it is undeniable that the media supplies a great number of law enforcement depictions. Solving crimes and apprehending criminals is an immensely popular media interest.

MEDIA CONSTRUCTS OF PROFESSIONAL SOLDIERS IN THE WAR ON CRIME

Culturally, we have long been fascinated with the police and their work. We relish and devour media that is front-end-loaded, which concentrates on the origins of crime and crime's investigation and solution. As discussed in Chapter 3, our first crime-and-justice love is media constructions of crime and criminality. Surpassed only by fas-cination with criminals, the people who enforce the laws and pursue the criminals are next in media and public interest. We relish the investigation, pursuit, and capture of criminals by crime fighters.[4] Three stereotypes of formal agents of the law are found in the media: lampooned police, G-men, and cops.[5] Like most media constructions, once created they never totally disappear and all three compete for influence today. Each contributes in its own way to the social construction of law enforcement.

Lampooned Police

Lampooned police appeared soon after the birth of the film industry and initially were introduced by the Keystone Kops and Charlie Chaplin films in the 1920s. The **lampooned police** officer is a popular media narrative that satirizes law enforcement officials as foolish, slapstick characters. These depictions continue to be popular with the public, if not always with real police. Some of these early por-trayals of the police so upset the International Association of the Chiefs of Police, for example, that its members passed a 1913 resolution pledging to change the depic-tions.[6] The Barney Fifes, Inspector Clouseaus, and vaudeville-styled *Police Academy* and *Super Troopers* films all provide escapist entertainment. Like gallows humor, they allow serious issues of police power and crime control to be discussed indirectly and in less threatening portraits. A police force that can be poked fun at is not one that is likely to be perceived as oppressive. Similarly, crime that can be resolved by cartoon

The lampooning of police officers and formal law enforcement is found in some of the earliest silent movies. Shown are the Keystone Kops, a popular early media lampoon of the police first seen in 1912.

violence is less threatening. However, when the satire is felt to reflect a reality of incompetence or when it undermines the public support of police, these images raise an outcry among law enforcement personnel.

G-Men and Police Procedurals

G-men, also historically known as "crime-busters," arose during the Depression and have periodically been invigorated by media attempts to provide more realistic content. **G-men** represent a media law enforcement frame that focuses on effective, professional crime-busters. Tough federal agents emerged in the 1930s media as Hollywood responded to the Payne Fund research on the film industry and its social impact.[7] The resulting Hays Commission heavily criticized the movie industry for glorifying criminals and encouraging copycat crime (see Box 5.1).[8] In response, the movie and radio

---

B o x 5.1   The Hays Code in Hollywood

The Hays Code, adopted by major American movie studios in response to the criticisms voiced by the Hays Commission, imposed severe limitations on celluloid crime and justice:

General Principles: 1. No picture shall be produced that will lower the moral standards of those who see it. Hence the sympathy of the audience should never be thrown to the side of crime, wrongdoing, evil or sin. 2. Correct standards of life, subject only to the requirements of drama and entertainment, shall be presented. 3. Law, natural or human, shall not be ridiculed, nor shall sympathy be created for its violation…

Crimes Against the Law. These shall never be presented in such a way as to throw sympathy with the crime as against law and justice or to inspire others with a desire for imitation. 1. Murder: a. The technique of murder must be presented in a way that will not inspire imitation. b. Brutal killings are not to be presented in detail. c. Revenge in modern times shall not be justified. 2. Methods of crime should not be explicitly presented:

a. Theft, robbery, safe-cracking, and dynamiting of trains, mines, buildings, etc., should not be detailed in method. b. Arson must subject to the same safeguards. c. The use of firearms should be restricted to the essentials. d. Methods of smuggling should not be presented. 3. Illegal drug traffic must never be presented.

SOURCE: Will H.Hays, President's Report to the Motion Picture Producers and Distributors' Association (Washington, DC:U.S. Government Printing Office, 1932).

---

industry shifted to G-man portrayals, in which federal law enforcement agents rather than criminals were the heroes. Stars such as James Cagney, who had previously played criminals, now found themselves cast as heroic crime fighters. These crime fighters were shown as professional, straight-laced, and, Cagney aside, usually boring. This change in the construction of law enforcers marks the media shift from the local neighborhood "officer friendly" portrait of police officers, who were well meaning but largely incompetent against serious crime, to that of professional federal crime-busters. Previously, if police officers were shown at all, more often than not they were just there, walking a beat, personable but largely irrelevant. In contrast, the new crime fighters were aggressive, smart, and proactive. Because they were clearly not local police officers, the shift to G-men crime-busters also marks the beginning of a long-term denigration of local law enforcement. The G, after all, stood for "government" and that government was the one in Washington, D.C. With the exception of local sheriffs in Westerns, local street police would not commonly be presented as capable of dealing with serious crime again until the 1970s. The tradition of professional, crime-busting portraits successfully made the transfer in the 1950s to television and continued as the dominant crime-fighting narrative. *Dragnet* on radio and then television, and *Dick Tracy* in the comics and later films are well-known examples.

Beginning a bit after and then paralleling the G-men portraits, the police procedural originated in the United States in the 1940s. **Police procedurals** attempt to portray the backstage realities of police investigations in dramatic media portraits. They were, in essence, the first infotainment docudramas produced on working in

NBC/Getty Images

Based on the investigation of crimes by two Los Angeles Police Department detectives, Dragnet was one of the first and most successful police procedural style programs. Originating on radio in the late 1940s and running on television from 1952 to 1959 and again from 1967 to 1970, Dragnet emphasized police jargon and the technical aspect of law enforcement. Episodes began with the promise that "the story you are about to see is true; the names have been changed to protect the innocent."

the criminal justice system. The crime fighters in these portraits normally rely heavily on teamwork and criminalistics to solve crimes. Especially well-suited to television's stereotyping, simple story lines, and preference for short-term violent events, the police procedural presents policing in infotainment-based constructions in which a continuous response to an unending series of violent criminal acts is needed. Crime, and the fight against it, is constructed as the province of professional experts. Civilians and other law enforcement personnel should not get involved, and do so at their peril. Analogous to the manner in which real and fictional crimes and criminals coalesced in the 1980s to socially construct serial killers, the G-men and the police procedurals portraits and the ongoing real-world police reform movement of the first half of the twentieth century collectively constructed criminality as a threat to middle-class lifestyles while encouraging a faith in expert police knowledge as the crime solution. The combined effect of the media portraits and the police profession-alism movement was the social construction of aggressive proactive policing as the best policy course to address an apparently burgeoning crime problem.

Cops

The **cops** frame originated in the 1970s with the return of media portraits of pro-fessional, competent, local law enforcement heroes, which had disappeared from the media with the demise of the Western local sheriffs in the 1950s. In a small number of television shows, like *Dragnet*, the professional police hero was kept alive until the 1970s, when the cop narrative emerged. With the release of the film *Dirty Harry* in 1971, the premiere of the television show *Police Story* in 1973, and the publication of the novel *The New Centurions* in 1970, local street police as heroes was once again in vogue. The new cops construction portrayed the local police as aggressive, crime-fighting, take-no-prisoners, frontline soldiers in the war on crime. Far from irrelevant, they were now the combat grunts who fought the crime war battles. Community policing, public service, traffic, and order maintenance duties were nowhere to be found in this new construction of the local police. Police became paramilitary units, citizens became civilians and collateral damage, and crime fighting became urban warfare. Local "cops" emerge in this construction as professional, gristled soldiers engaged in pre-emptive law-and-order battles—combat–hardened street solders in an unpopular war. Within the cop construction, criminality was simultaneously portrayed as the result of evil and weak individuals making bad choices. The criminals were clearly enemies, not citizens who had broken a law, and they had to be defeated, as opposed to being deterred or rehabilitated.

Archive Photos/Moviepix/Getty Images

The continued popularity of the cops frame in the media portrait of law enforcement is displayed in commercial film franchises such as Die Hard.

Within this constructed world of domestic combat, special socialization by a veteran crime fighter was needed to change the naïve civilian police recruit into the professional frontline crime-fighting soldier.[9] Police, like the combat veteran, have to be initiated into the police culture and instilled with the special knowledge and skills needed to survive in combat and deal with rampant criminality. Gaining this special knowledge frequently involved a violent unlearning of prior social conceptions picked up in the civilian world and the police academy. To survive, cops adopted the antibureaucracy attitude of the World War II–era private eye. Middle-class status, liberal attitudes, those college criminology and criminal justice courses, official police department procedures—all must be forgotten. As Dirty Harry says to his new Mexican American partner, "Don't go letting that sociology degree get you killed."[10]

Still highly popular, several different cop narratives are found today.[11] One of the most popular is the "rogues," officers who go off on their own in their pursuit of criminals and justice. Throwing off the restraints of agency approval, due process, and legal procedures, they display single-mindedness in a less than legal but usually moral crusade. Also common are the "corrupt cop" narratives, which have the officers taking the extra step and actually joining the dark-side forces of crime and evil. At the other extreme are "honest cop" narratives, which trace the hardships of cops trying to do the right thing in a corrupt police culture. "Buddy cop" stories work off the conflicts and complications from opposite personalities forced to work together; mismatched racial partners are a standard. A relative to lampooned police "comedy" and "action comedy," cop narratives toss reality to the winds. Comedy portrayals incorporate harmless slapstick violence in which bullets and punches fly but no one gets seriously hurt. Action comedies liberally add in explosions and spectacular stunts in which only the bad guys are seriously injured. Two recent additions to this family are "female cop" stories and "aging cop" stories. Female cop narratives have the positive, if yet unfulfilled, potential to lift women from their stereotypical crime-and-justice portraits as pseudomasculine or hyperfeminine creatures to equal crime-fighting heroes.[12] Aging cop stories are a market response to the aging of the baby boom generation and the need to provide heroes they can identify with. In these stories, a weathered but still virile (mentally, physically, and sexually) police officer manages to be successful on all fronts. Except for the woman cop story lines, hyper-masculinity is the common thread throughout the cop narratives. These portraits collectively reduce the crime issue to a contest between individuals. Not only is a social solution not needed, in the cop narratives, crime is no longer even an agency problem. To solve crime, you don't need a criminal justice system, or even a police department. You don't even need a few good men, just one good cop will do.

On the journalism print side, the combat cop was accompanied and enhanced with the marketing of **true crime** books, many written by newspaper crime reporters. These reporter memoirs are traditionally initiation narratives about a reporter's introduction into the cop world.[13] Similar to the necessity for police recruits to discard misleading knowledge acquired in the police academy and college to become effective combat cops, in these true crime narratives journalists have to be socialized into the ways of the street police. In the process they have to leave behind their journalistic sensibilities and social values and learn that fighting the modern predatory criminal requires a different worldview.

In these true crime books the crime is usually homicide, and the reader looks over the cops' shoulders as they pursue criminals and clean up after violent, messy events. (Of course, the other popular view in the true crime tradition looks over the shoulders of criminals while they violently create messy events. Not surprisingly, an interest in crime fighters is only exceeded by fascination with predator criminals. Tales of serial killer narratives dominate the true crime genre.) The cop-oriented true crime memoirs contribute to the comforting illusion of police expertise, and that crime, while pervasive, is effectively being handled by dogged, heroic police work.[14]

Turning to the news portrait of professional crime fighters: despite great interest in law enforcement, the news media rarely focus on individual crime fighters except in police brutality cases.[15] Instead, they prefer to focus on crimes and criminals. In the news, law enforcement is normally referred to as generic agencies rather than individual police officers. When individuals are interviewed, they are most often administrators or media-relations specialists. Therefore, most individual crime-fighter portraits come not from traditional news, but from either pure entertainment content or infotainment products. Infotainment programming fills in whatever gap exists between the entertainment and news portraits in the public's construction of the modern professional crime fighter. Reality police shows, a subset of infotainment programming, are of special interest because these shows are promoted as delivering a slice of unaltered crime fighting and, unlike the news, focus heavily on individual crime fighters.

Police as Infotainment

First appearing in 1989, **police reality programs** have become a regular part of the crime-and-justice media, with the theme song of one show, *COPS*, becoming a pop music hit.[16] In these productions, viewers are invited to share a real street cop's point of view as a partner officer. Not surprisingly, the demographic that most future police officers will be recruited from—young, white males—are their largest audience component. The attraction of these shows is clearly voyeuristic, with content running the gamut from dealing with ordinary street crime to the unusual violent predation. The cooperating police departments also have editorial input into the end product and routinely eliminate any scenes of police violence, malfeasance, or ineptitude. In her study of these shows, Pamela Donovan found that the final construction invariably shows the police as sensitive, knowledgeable, and competent, never careless, corrupt, foul-mouthed, or overwhelmed.[17] In a companion study, Aaron Doyle points out the highly selective picture of criminal justice found in these programs, which over-represents both violent crime and the proportion of crime solved by police.[18] Violent crime such as murder, rape, aggravated assault, and robbery were found to make up 84 percent of all the crime shown in one season of COPS.[19] Reflecting the backwards law, here again the media presents the opposite of crime-and-justice reality, and the distribution of violent and property crimes on these shows are consistently opposite their real-world proportions.

Crime selection aside, how realistically do these reality shows portray police work? In the view of Paul Kooistra and his colleagues, "Crime [fighting] on these shows is a caricature that is shaped more by the organizational demands of television than by carefully documented representations of reality."[20] Unlike the traditional news, where you can see the commentators and reporters and editing decisions are more apparent, reality programming works from a different process in its format, style, and texture. In these shows, there are no production clues, narrators, actors, scripts, or hosts to suggest editing or formatting. The infotainment audience does not easily realize and are not given hints that they are receiving a heavily reconstructed piece of reality. As shown in Figure 4.1, because the content is presented as if unaltered, the constructed reality found in reality programming is more misleading than the constructed reality portrayed in the news, where editing and production decisions are clearly visible.

For reality shows, production techniques are borrowed from entertainment shows. These programs are formatted to unobtrusively fill in missing facts and scenes to hide the editing and molding of their content. Time gaps are smoothed over, and holes in knowledge or action are filled. It is through their production techniques that these shows can grossly misrepresent police work and still manage to come across as reality programming. As criminologist Gray Cavender points out, realism is achieved in these efforts by mimicking the early entertainment "police procedural" films of the 1940s and 1950s and applying an entertainment style of "gritty realism."[21] Employing low-cost production values establishes an atmosphere of "being there" for the viewer. Ironically, producing reality programs cheaply results in increasing their believability.

The demographics on these shows constructs crime so that nonwhites account for more than half of all suspects shown, about two-thirds of the police are white, and more than half of the victims shown are white. These shows construct a reality in which the most typical police crime-fighting events are white

Police reality show like COPS tend to focus on the action related crime fighting aspects of law enforcement and avoid the less dynamic but more common community service and paperwork elements of policing.

police battling nonwhite criminals while protecting white victims. In addition, almost 75 percent of the crimes portrayed in these infotainment shows are cleared by arrest, compared with the 18 percent clearance rate for property crime and 44 percent clearance rate for violent crime reported in the Uniform Crime Report (UCR) statistics. Because of these factors, reality police programs most closely resemble pure entertainment media portrayals of crime fighting. As found in other media, the media crime-and-justice backwards law is equally applicable to police reality shows.

The backwards law results in these infotainment shows promoting two claims about crime fighting.[22] The carefully chosen and edited footage encourages the claims that:

> The police are in a contest with criminals who are unlike law-abiding citizens. Reality police shows further encourage the construction of criminals as predatory deviant others, people who are unlike the rest of us.

> The police invariably get it right. The people they stop really are criminals. Viewers never get to see the police battering down doors to the wrong apartment or arresting the wrong person. Legal rules invariably hamper the police needlessly and get in the way of effective law enforcement. There appears to be no reason to place legal checks on how the police do their job, and constitutional safeguards make no sense.

In the end, crime control is applauded and due process is disparaged. Individual causes of crime, assumed guilt of suspects, and an "us versus them" portrait dominates these constructions. The police emerge as our best defense, but they need help—in this constructed world, the audience and the police must work together to fight crime. Analogous to videogames, viewers are prodded to become interactive—to be on the lookout, call in tips, and help catch fugitives—to, in effect, enlist in the war on crime.

What is the effect of these shows? Aaron Doyle reports that most viewers see the shows as realistic and think of them as informational rather than entertainment, as more similar to local news than to fictional storytelling.[23] Society is seen to be in decline and in a constant state of crisis because of spiraling crime, particularly violent street crimes committed by lower-class offenders, and aggressive law enforcement is shown as the last hope. Another concern with the portrait of police work found in police reality programming comes from its effect on real police. Doyle reports that, like courtroom cameras influencing trial attorneys, there is anecdotal evidence of police tailoring their behavior for the cameras, behaving not as they actually do but as they believe the audience expects them to. Shows like *COPS* appear as a fantasy come true for police officers raised on the media's fictional police heroics found in entertainment crime dramas.[24] Here is the law enforcement career as they were led to believe it would be, full of crime-busting excitement. Finally, the solution proffered in police infotainment programming is drawn from the faulty system frame: crime is out of control because the criminal justice system is misaligned. Society needs tougher crime control: due process and civil rights are part of the problem, and more unfettered police are needed. The real world must be altered to better match the media-constructed one. Recent media portrayals of forensic science and its capabilities is another area that has been credited with constructing unrealistic expectations in the real world.

The CSI Effect: Forensic Science and Solving Crimes

The most recent iteration (and revival) of the police procedural is found in the spate of forensic science-based shows led by the television program *CSI: Crime Scene Investigation* and its derivatives. The history of a "**CSI effect**" begins in the early twenty-first century.[25] Generated from anecdotal reports from attorneys and judges, a CSI effect first appeared around 2002–2003 as a characterization of the perceived impact of forensic crime programming on juror verdicts.[26] The perception of the effect quickly evolved from a "potential nuisance" in 2002 to a "huge problem" by 2006.[27] By 2007, a mini-moral panic had been generated and a CSI effect had become the subject of numerous news stories in which it was usually described negatively. [28] In these stories, a CSI effect was most often constructed as resulting in juries holding unrealistic expectations regarding case evidence and that these media-generated expectations were altering jury verdicts.[29] The existence of a real-world CSI effect appears logical. As related in Box 5.2, the difference between crime scene investigations and their media portrait is large. These front-end-loaded "howdunnit" rather than "whodunit" shows depict police agencies with limitless resources, small caseloads, unrealistic scientific testing procedures, impossible forensic test time frames, and inaccurate depictions of what crime scene investigators actually do.[30] They present a prosecutorial view of investigation and give the impression that trials are mere formalities.[31] Crimes are solved in the lab, not resolved in the courtroom. The result is that the most prominent law enforcement crime-fighting hero today is a forensic scientist.[32] Concerns about a CSI effect on justice were a natural outgrowth of this popular image of crime fighting, but opposite effects on jurors came to be observed. CSI effects on jurors have been credited with both pro-prosecution and pro-defense impacts.[33] Ironically, while the concerns have focused on effects on jurors, the only research establishing a CSI effect appears to be on the behavior of attorneys and judges.

Based on surveys of trial attorneys and judges,[34] the strong belief of a significant CSI effect exists within most criminal justice system communities. Criminal justice professionals have altered their courtroom behavior accordingly and have changed their voir dire questioning and juror selection practices, the content of their juror instructions, their willingness to include forensic related witnesses, and their presentation of evidence.[35] These steps are taken because a CSI effect is commonly believed to influence juror expectations of what evidence will or should be presented and their assessment of evidence that is presented. Specifically, attorneys believe that jurors deliberating under the CSI effect perceive that lack of forensic evidence is an indication of sloppy police work; furthermore, the power of forensic evidence causes jurors to devalue eyewitness testimony. Police, prosecutors, and judges have reported that they have had to explain the lack of irrelevant forensic evidence or employ unnecessary expert witnesses to accommodate a set of media-driven juror expectations. As a group, they feel compelled

---

B o x 5.2 The CSI Effect

The scene, on TV, is of a dead kid in a high school bathroom (or as pictured, a homeless person in an alleyway). Such images, in themselves, are not funny. What cracks up the senior forensic criminalist at the State Police Crime Laboratory is watching the forensic crew work a case on *"CSI: Crime Scene Investigation."*

[Real] Crime scene investigators don't tackle murder suspects or pack heat. They don't storm into the lab demanding DNA reports. They don't prance around in leather pants and a halter top. It can take days to fingerprint a scene, months to process a single DNA sample. Most of that used to be inside crime scene stuff—shoptalk for cops and forensic scientists. Then CSI and a handful of bloodstained copycats took over prime time.

Real-life investigators are watching this gross new world and bracing for each boob-tube breakthrough. They call it the "CSI effect," a phenomenon in which actual investigations are driven by the expectations of the millions of people who watch fake whodunits on TV. It has contributed to jurors' desires to see more forensic testimony from the stand. Academic programs are springing up to accommodate people who now want to be forensic scientists. And it has spurred a phenomenon that defense lawyers call "junk science," in which high-paid, under qualified consultants are hired to lend a little razzle-dazzle to a case because in prime time we've learned that virtually anything left behind can solve a crime: sofa cushions, a dead insect, lint.

Jurors watch TV shows in which investigators walk onto scenes soaked with forensic evidence. Then they want to know why there's no DNA on the suspect's shirt collar or blood on his hands. Why aren't the hairs at the scene a match for those found inside the accused's cap? Even in the face of eyewitness testimony, juries are starting to say, "If all the possible forensic tests weren't done in a case, maybe somebody else committed the crime."

While the extent and impact of a CSI effect is being studied, one obvious effect has been the growth and popularity of crime shows built around forensic science. In addition to *CSI: Crime Scene Investigation*, there are the direct spinoff shows *CSI Miami* and *CSI New York*, and *CSI* copycat shows include: *Body of Evidence, Bones, Cold Case, Criminal Minds, Crossing Jordan, NCIS,* and *Numbers.* In addition to these fictional programs, a number of forensic documentary-style programs built around the infotainment presentation of the role of forensics in real criminal cases include *Cold Case Files, Forensic Files, The First 48, The New Detectives, Trace Evidence,* and *48 Hours Mystery.*

SOURCE: Excerpted from Carlene Hempel, "TV's Whodunit Effect," The Boston Globe Magazine, February 9, 2003.

---

to explain the differences between *CSI* shows and real–world trial uses of forensic evidence. In gist, they feel that actual trial evidence is held to forensic television standards. [36] In addition to an effect on police, attorney, and judge behavior in cases, anecdotal CSI effects have also been reported for offenders. The extent of such behavior is unknown, but thieves have been reported to dump absconded ashtrays in stolen cars in hopes of generating a pool of alternative suspects and rapists have been reported to use condoms and to force victims to shower to avoid leaving DNA evidence. [37] Belief in a CSI effect is substantial,

Monty Brinton/CBS/Getty Images

but a CSI effect impact on jurors is a different issue. At the core of the concerns is the belief that these shows deify forensic evidence so that when it is presented in a trial its validity and accuracy is unquestioned by jurors.[38] A dual CSI effect on jurors has been hypothesized. If no forensic evidence is presented, an increase in acquittals has been posited. If forensic evidence is available, convictions are speculated to increase. Driven by these dueling expectations, research on a CSI effect on jurors focusing on assessment of evidence has been pursued.

Irrespective of the beliefs of many attorneys, judges, and apparently some criminals, based on a set of survey research that variously queried jurors, registered votes, general community members, and juror-eligible college students in the United States, Canada, and Australia, evidence of a strong consistent CSI effect has not been found.[39] Overall the results have been mixed and ambiguous.[40] For example, in one study that surveyed jurors, evidence was reported that nearly half of them expected scientific evidence in every criminal case. However, in the same study, when an effect on verdicts was explored, the expectation of forensic evidence did not translate into more acquittals when it was absent, and, significantly, viewers of the *CSI* shows were more likely to convict without scientific evidence than nonviewers, except in rape cases.[41] Similarly, viewing forensic crime shows has been reported to affect attitudes toward the value of scientific evidence but not respondent beliefs about their willingness to convict or acquit.[42] Further belying a significant negative effect, the majority of a general community in California were found to be unaware of a possible CSI effect and those who watched *CSI*-type programs shows were more likely to see such an effect as educational rather than negative and biasing.[43]

At this time, while many in the criminal justice field believe that a CSI effect operates, there is no empirical study that has shown a CSI effect on jury decisions. The best overall conclusion at this time is that watching these shows alters viewers' perceptions of the accuracy, reliability, and validity of forensic evidence but there is no evidence of a CSI effect extending to influence jury verdict decisions.[44] Most results indicate a mostly null juror CSI effect.[45] On the other hand, there is a CSI effect on attorneys and judges who prepare and conduct their cases differently because of anticipated juror expectations regarding scientific evidence. Based on a number of studies conducted prior to the *CSI* shows that established the compelling power that scientific evidence has on juror verdicts,[46] this remains a safe if sometimes expensive strategy for criminal justice practitioners. Pending new research, the CSI effects that remains established are the belief by criminal justice professionals that these shows influence jurors and a renewed popularity in the field of criminal forensics.[47]

Police and the Media

In the 1990s, there was a transition to community policing in the real police world and a media fixation on criminal profiling in the media-constructed one. In the resulting mix, the media did not simply lionize police professionalism or technical expertise. Criticisms of the police abound in the media, but as the media drifted into infotainment content, media dependence on police cooperation increased. The police are sought, quoted, and catered to on one hand, but marginalized and criticized on the other. In Table 5.1, the basic differences between media cops and real-world street officers are summarized. From an "endless budget" to their actions, media cops hardly compare to their real-world counterparts. And when the real police do not act like their media portraits, the unrealistic public expectations generate real-world public dissatisfaction with law enforcement.[48]

T A B L E   5.1   Differences between Media Cops and Real Cops

	Media Cops	Real Cops
Action	Never a dull moment. They are doing something, about to do something, or planning to do something.	Tedium and adrenaline are both experienced. Paperwork is the norm. Action is unexpected, not predictable.
Crime	Fighting serious crime is foremost. Felony arrests are common. Each crime is unique and exceptional. Cops are attuned to these nuances and pay attention.	Felony arrests are rare; officers often spend time preventing crime and defusing social situations. The repetitive stories and explanations for breaking the law rapidly dull their impact and the believability of suspects.
Violence	Cops are violent. They menace, fight, shoot, and kill with relative impunity. Physical force, even brutality, is part of solving crimes.	Officers often work in a mean world, but usually one of potential rather than actual violence.
Heroes and villains	Clearly defined good and evil with any ambiguities resolved by program's end.	The good and the bad are mostly gray. Good people do bad things; bad people sometimes perform good acts. Most people have elements of both.
Status	Patrolmen are often dumb background foils; plainclothes detectives are the brilliant problem solvers.	Officers are gatekeepers of the criminal justice system who make the crucial early decisions.
Insight	With an almost psychic awareness of what people are thinking and where clues and evidence are, they uncover the truth. Omniscient qualities allow them to defy procedures and still triumph.	Officers are given almost no advance data for encounters and are under great pressure to obey procedures and policy.
Closure	There are almost no unsolved cases left at the end of the story.	Events have a middle, but no beginning and no end. Cops arrive after trouble has started and rarely see the resolution of cases they confront.
Justice	Cops rarely deal with law, which is often seen as an obstacle to justice and as a source of technicalities used by shyster lawyers. The hero cop directly dispenses justice and avenges wrongs.	Real cops must obey the law. Because of the complexity of the law and the emphasis on due process rights, its glacial pace leaves cops often enforcing rules they do not think work.

(continued)

TABLE 5.1   Differences between Media Cops and Real Cops (Continued)

	Media Cops	Real Cops
Back stage	Sanitized back stage. No matter how crude, the hero cop rarely alienates the audience.	Sex, lies, and stupidity are common themes. Cops often make fun of, complain about, or criticize many of the victims and suspects they encounter.
Budget and Resources	Uncapped budgets with endless forensics, equipment, and reinforcements available.	Hard limits on the amount of evidence gathering and testing, investigation time, and departmental resources that can be devoted to a case.
Chronology	Time compression, months are covered in minutes. Events are edited to render swift progress of the story and rapid resolution.	A glacial war with long periods between steps. Cops understand how long it can take the system to address an issue.
Factual Knowledge	Godlike powers of observation by the audience, who see clues, overhear conversations, see revealing facial close-ups, and hear voiceovers with insider information kept from the cops. The audience ends up knowing more than the cops.	Uniformed police are first on the scene. They see what no one in the public sees except for perpetrators and victims, misery and bloodshed and the aftermath of violence at close quarters.

SOURCE: Adapted from David Perlmutter, Policing the Media (Belmont, CA:Sage, 2000), pp. 41–52.

Factual and fictional cop narratives remain popular and, as shown by the development of women and aging cop portraits, are flexible enough to evolve and to respond to changing politics, demographics, and market needs.[49] In addition to female lead crime fighters, the emergence and acceptance of minority actors as lead heroic cops is another healthy trend.[50] The media–constructed world of professional crime-fighting soldiers is secure. Ironically, this world is largely constructed in the entertainment and infotainment segments of the media. The traditional news media do not normally focus on crime fighters except when they suffer a personal fall from grace or are killed. That is, individual crime fighters become newsworthy when they become criminals or victims. This lack of traditional news media attention is also true for their counterparts, the citizen soldiers in the war on crime.

MEDIA CONSTRUCTS OF CITIZEN SOLDIERS IN THE WAR ON CRIME

The second major brigade of media crime solvers comes not from the official world of criminal justice and government agencies, but from the ranks of citizens. When portrayed, these "citizen soldiers" in the war on crime often save the day for bungling police officers. Other times they battle the corrupt forces of government and official law enforcement.

Private Investigators

One division of these civilian crime fighters occupies the boundary between civilians and police officers. They are the independent contractors of law enforcement, the **private investigators**, or PIs. Private investigators were popularized in film noir movies in the 1940s. Historically male, sexual, debonair, hard-boiled, and smart, the PI lives on the borderline between criminality and the law-abiding, solving crimes with inside knowledge combined with the freedom to act outside the restraints of agency policies and due process rules. In addition to these semiprofessional private eyes, another group of personally motivated private citizens take on solving crimes as a hobby or due to some personal connection with a crime victim.

Private Citizens

Predating the private eyes, private citizens have been successful media crime fighters for at least 600 years, as can be seen in the tales of Robin Hood and other citizen heroes. Although usually adult white males, citizen crime fighters in the media include a diverse group: elderly female novelists (Angela Lansbury in *Murder She Wrote*), teenagers (the *Bobbsey Twins* and *Hardy Boys*), children (*Tom Sawyer*) and cartoon dogs (*Scooby-Doo*).

The citizen crime fighter can be found in a number of entertainment narratives that share the characteristic of being outside of and sometimes in conflict with the traditional criminal justice system. Rooted in the Western, "heroic" outsiders who save the day remain a popular crime-fighting narrative. Unfettered by official red tape and due process considerations, the heroic outsider can cut to the heart of the crime problem and quickly (and usually violently) deal with it, riding or driving off into the sunset, as it were, after his work is done. Avengers and vigilantes are related to the victim crime-fighter narrative. In these portrayals, the citizen crime fighter has a personal interest or has been personally wronged by a criminal. At the extreme are tales where the citizen hero has been unjustly criminalized by the official criminal justice system. These criminal Robin Hood heroes are among the oldest Western citizen crime-fighter narratives available. A more recent citizen crime-fighter narrative is the superhero, which originated in Depression-era comic books and today is found in action films. Still cartoonlike and clearly functioning as an escape from reality for their audiences, these crime fighters are the most "outside" of the outsiders. Mutants, aliens, ninjas, or just "regular" people who apparently are impossible to kill or defeat, these superheroes overcome massive odds to prevail and, as Superman states, defend "truth, justice, and the American way."

The success that private citizens and private investigators have enjoyed when solving crime in the media has been impressive. For example, media researchers Robert and Linda Lichter found that private citizens and private investigators solved many of the crimes shown in prime time television programming.[51]

Crime fighters of every other type failed to capture the criminal more often than they succeeded. Cops, being rule bound, cannot possibly be as effective as private investigators. By contrast, private eyes and private citizens proved almost incapable of failure. This tradition of citizen success coupled to official police failure has deep roots. Penned in the 1840s by Edgar Allan Poe, the very first detective stories had the French police fumble and fail while citizen-hero, outsider American detective Dupin, solved the crimes.[52]

Combined with the media's proclivity to show professional crime fighters as loners and mavericks, as not fitting comfortably into their agencies, the cumulative media message regarding citizen crime fighters clearly is that it is outsiders who save the day and that ordinary law enforcers are unequal to the task of fighting crime. Collectively, the citizen soldier crime fighters reveal the media tendency to present crime not as a social problem but as an individual contest. In these portraits private citizens supplant the entire criminal justice system. Crime fighting becomes a private issue of good versus evil between autonomous individuals. The larger society, and particularly its formal institutions, is little involved if not a direct obstacle to successful crime fighting. The message is that if you have a crime problem the regular police are unlikely to be helpful, and you had best deal with it on your own.

PROFESSIONAL VERSUS CITIZEN CRIME FIGHTERS

The basic distinction between media crime fighters is whether the crime fighter is a member of the established criminal justice system or a citizen. If one combines the citizen crime fighter with the rogue, special-unit, maverick law enforcers, criminal justice system outsiders and marginalized employees are far more common and more successful in the media-constructed world of crime fighting than traditional mainstream criminal justice system personnel. Successful crime fighters are usually portrayed as antisocial, unattached loners even when they are members of an established law enforcement agency—the icon of Clint Eastwood's *Dirty Harry* is a prime example. The media super-cop is accordingly usually not a regular cop at all, but someone from outside the system, or a maverick officer within it. Whether an outsider or not, the successful crime fighter is usually a heroic man of action. Media crime fighters are portrayed as very effective in solving crimes and apprehending criminals but not at all effective in preventing crime. They are better agents of punishment than deterrence. The basic crime-fighting narrative is that early crimes are successful and that a criminal enterprise has been ongoing for years. Only later, after the hero has arrived on the scene, are crimes unsuccessful. Similar to the manner in which crime is covered in the news, media crime fighters are reactive and incident-driven rather than proactive and community problem-oriented.

The main message these crime-fighter constructions convey about crime is that crime is not a social problem to be solved at the community level. Instead it is an invading social evil that must be confronted and destroyed. The social construction of law enforcement repeatedly points out that a crime "war" is being waged, and society needs crime *fighters*, not peace officers or God-help-us, legal due process protections, social services, or community-based rehabilitation programs—all of which come across as blatantly naïve and wrong-headed. Because of crime's insidious nature, the traditional criminal justice system's due process constraints and rehabilitation mandates make it unable to cope with crime. The system needs the assistance of either a rebellious law enforcement insider who is willing to ignore or bend the law or an unencumbered civilian outsider. Justice, which in the media means law enforcement, is achieved by individual stars, not by the criminal justice system. Effective conformist law enforcement officers are rare, and when they are portrayed, they normally have to resort to innovative special tactics, weapons, technology, and support units to successfully deal with crime. More recently, the crime fighter is frequently portrayed battling serial killers and terrorism in military-like actions (see Box 5.3). The media world of crime and terrorism is not a world for standard operating procedures and community-oriented police officers, or for the unarmed, the hesitant, or the faint-hearted. The media message concerning crime fighting is one of "legitimized corruption"; solving crimes and preventing terrorism requires breaking the rules.[53]

Also significant in media portrayals of law enforcement is the use of violence. Violence has been an element in the depiction of crime and justice throughout media history, but in the twentieth century the entertainment media came to portray both crime fighters and criminals as more violent and aggressive and to show this violence more graphically. Since the 1960s, a distinct style known as **ultraviolence**—which entails slow-motion injuries, detonating blood capsules, and multiple camera views—has become common entertainment media content. Indeed, so brutal have media crime fighters become over the course of the last century that they now have more similarities to older gangster portraits than to older crime-fighting heroes. In today's media, the distinction between the crime fighter and the criminal has all but disappeared with regard to who initiates violence and how much force is used.

Finally, the increasing emphasis on graphic violence has resulted in a kind of media weapons cult. Over the years, weapons have become increasingly more technical and sophisticated but less realistic. More important, guns are shown as useful problem solvers and necessary crime-fighting tools in modern America. In the media, the people who get their way, both heroes and villains, are the ones who have the guns. Furthermore, weapons—especially handguns—tend to be portrayed as either ridiculously benign, so that misses are common and wounds minor and painless when the crime fighter is the target, or ridiculously deadly, so that shots from handguns accurately hit moving, distant people, killing them quickly and without extensive suffering when the crime fighter is the shooter. People in crime-and-justice media who use guns seldom suffer psychological, social, or legal repercussions. A street gun battle is played out and everyone is back at work the next day. Adding to the unreality, when a gunshot victim is described, rarely is the victim's pain or that of the victim's family or friends shown.[54] In general, the media play up the violence and play down the pain and suffering associated with criminal violence and gunplay.

B o x 5.3   Crime Fighting and Terrorism

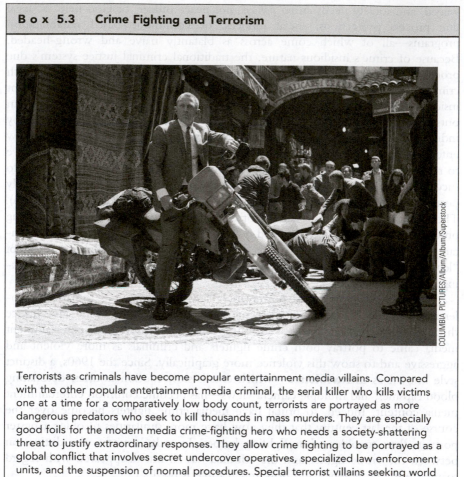

COLUMBIA PICTURES/Album/Album/Superstock

Terrorists as criminals have become popular entertainment media villains. Compared with the other popular entertainment media criminal, the serial killer who kills victims one at a time for a comparatively low body count, terrorists are portrayed as more dangerous predators who seek to kill thousands in mass murders. They are especially good foils for the modern media crime-fighting hero who needs a society-shattering threat to justify extraordinary responses. They allow crime fighting to be portrayed as a global conflict that involves secret undercover operatives, specialized law enforcement units, and the suspension of normal procedures. Special terrorist villains seeking world domination justify special tactics, such as torture unfettered by due process and law suspending operations that cross international boundaries and legal systems. Even more than for serial killers, when fighting terrorists, the ends justify the means.

In conclusion, the construction of law enforcement as a criminal justice endeavor dominates over the courts and corrections and is portrayed as a glamorous, action-filled process of detection and pursuit that glorifies violence. Dealing with crime is a battle of good versus evil. Historically this battle was invariably won by the good guys, but today an increasing number of evil criminals escape; corrupt, brutal police officers are more common; and crime control goals are heavily advanced over due process protections.[55] Civil liberties are ignored and degraded as mushy-headed hindrances that result in a less safe, more violent society. Professional crime fighters compete with citizen crime fighters for attention and effectiveness, but in both groups individual loners tend to be the most successful. Translated to the real world, the need for special undercover police units, vigilantes, and individual armed protection is implied. In the end, the media's social construction of crime fighting shows crime not as a social problem at all but as an individual concern to be solved by force and technology by either a core of beleaguered frontline cops, special tactic federal officers, or well-armed individual civilians.

SUMMARY

- The portrait of crime fighting in the media is split between crime fighters employed by the criminal justice system—police officers and investigators and government agents—and those outside of the system—private investigators and private citizens.

- Dealing with crime is shown as a battle that must be violently fought.

- Criminal justice–employed crime fighters are portrayed as satirized lampooned officers, professional federal agents, or hardened street cops. Rogue police officers willing to break the rules are the most effective. From these portraits, the public draws unrealistic expectations about the capabilities of the police and their activities.

- Private citizens and private investigators are often shown as better at dealing with crime than the police.

- Crime control trumps due process in the media crime fighter world. Due process protections and departmental policies are portrayed as hindrances to effectively dealing with crime.

- Crimes in the media are solved by aggressive investigations backed by science and technology. Crime is not presented as a social problem tied to other social problems.

CLASS DISCUSSIONS

1. Watch a week of crime shows and discuss their portraits of crime fighters.

2. Discuss the connection between the portrayal of guns, violence, and victims in the media and the crime-fighting policies that are implied in these portrayals. Discuss how the portrayal of crime fighting as individual battles between predatory criminals and heroic crime fighters rather than as a social problem encourages punitive criminal justice policies and discourages preventive and rehabilitative policies.

3. Discuss the reasons that civilians are portrayed so often as successful crime fighters while traditional police officers are portrayed as unsuccessful in the media.

4. Discuss any additional differences between media police and real police beyond the ones mentioned in Table 5.1 and differences between real and media crime scene technicians as described in Box 5.2.

5. Watch an episode of the show *COPS* and discuss how editing and formatting are used to frame the portraits of police officers, suspects, and victims in the show.

SUGGESTED READINGS

Doyle, A. (2003). *Arresting images: Crime and policing in front of the television camera.* Toronto: University of Toronto Press.

Fishman, M. and Cavender, G. (Eds.) (1998). *Entertaining crime: Television reality programs.* New York: Aldine de Gruyter.

Lawrence, R. (2000). *The politics of force: Media and the construction of police brutality.* Berkeley: University of California Press.

Leishman, F. and Mason, P. (2003). *Policing and the media.* Devon: Willan.

Perlmutter, D. (2000). *Policing the media.* Thousand Oaks: Sage.

Wilson, C. (2000). *Cop knowledge.* Chicago: University of Chicago Press.

CHAPTER 6

The Courts

CHAPTER OBJECTIVES

After reading Chapter 6, you will

- Recognize the media portraits of the judicial system, judges, and attorneys
- Comprehend the concept of media trials
- Appreciate the love–hate relationship between television and the courts
- Know the judicial mechanisms available to deal with publicity
- Understand the issues associated with media strategies to maximize access to judicial proceedings and minimize government access to media-held information.

MEDIA, INFOTAINMENT, AND THE COURTS

"Law in our time has entered the age of images, legal reality can no longer be properly understood, or assessed, apart from what appears on a screen."[1] For many in today's world, mass media images are their primary source of knowledge about law, lawyers, and the legal system. In addition to being an important source of knowledge about the judicial system, judicial images found in the media are significant in another way. Courtrooms are a society's formal social construction arena, where the significance and meaning of a wide range of social behaviors are determined—for example, the courts have recently defined, or attempted to define, what is or is not insane behavior, proper or improper child-care, marriage, torture, privacy, and acceptable law enforcement policies. Judicial proceedings function, therefore, not only as mechanisms for resolving individual disputes but also as mechanisms for legitimizing the broader society's laws, policies, government agencies, and social structure. Accordingly, anything that influences the public image of the courts invariably influences the courts' ability to be a legitimizing social mechanism and to fulfill their function as definers of what is unacceptable social behavior.

If the media's renditions of court proceedings influence how the public sees the courts, in turn, the public's perception of the courts results in expectations of how judicial proceedings should look and play out. Media–induced public expectations cycle back to affect the real courts. How the judicial system conducts procedures, how attorneys and judges try cases, and how participants behave in courtrooms are all influenced by the media. The mass media portrait of the judicial system constructs a reality that the public comes to expect and the courts subsequently strive to fulfill. The judicial portrait found in the media is examined in three realms: the entertainment media's construction of the courtroom; the development of infotainment style media trials; and the concerns associated with pretrial publicity, government access to media–held information, and media access to government–held information. The impact of new and social media are also discussed. The end result of the collective media portrait of the courts is the modern construction of the judicial system as a source of drama and infotainment.

COURTS, ATTORNEYS, AND EVIDENCE

Directly and indirectly, the media paint a distorted image of the courts. When portrayed indirectly as in the law enforcement-focused media, the courts are often alluded to as soft on crime, easy on criminals, due process-laden institutions that repeatedly release the obviously guilty and dangerous.[2] In law enforcement portraits of crime fighting, most of the criminals being fought are recidivists, which implies that criminals go through the court system and return to the streets undeterred and unrehabilitated. The message is clear: the legal system is an obstacle and a frustration to investigators trying to protect the law–abiding and searching for the truth.[3] When shown directly, court officers are often more engaged in fighting crime than in practicing law.[4] When shown practicing law, they are usually immersed in high–stakes dramatic trials. In accordance with the media's myopic concentration on the rare event such as murder, media–rendered court procedures emphasize the rare-in-reality adversarial criminal trial as the most common judicial proceeding.[5] Less often are preliminary procedures or informal plea-bargaining shown, and post–trial steps are even less common. In contrast to real court systems, in the media most defendants go to trial. The courts and the law are constructed in the media as complicated, arcane contests practiced by expert professionals and beyond the understanding of everyday citizens. The confrontations, oratory, and deliberations in the media courtroom are in stark opposition to the criminal justice system's daily reality of plea bargains, compromises, and assembly-line justice. None of the media judicial images you are likely to be exposed to represent the reality of the judicial system.

As with most components of the criminal justice system, the dominant popular image of courtrooms was initially constructed within Hollywood films.[6] The construction of the judicial system found in the cinema differs in basic ways from the typical constructions of crime and law enforcement found in other media. For one, courtroom films more often locate the obstacles to justice in society and the legal system rather than within individual offenders. And because they also frequently show the impediments to justice being overcome, trial films do not require an incorrigible criminal who must be destroyed. Courtroom films, however, do reflect the operation of the backwards law; that is, they present the opposite of crime-and-justice reality. Films feature the ever-popular crime narratives of murder, abuse of power, and sex, not the more mundane matters of stolen property and broken contracts generally before the courts.

Although movies loosely based on actual events are still popular, recent courtroom portraits have evolved from the fictional and highly unrealistic media courtroom stories where attorneys investigate and solve crimes by eliciting confessions during cross-examination to showing more nontrial, backstage aspects of practicing law. This trend can be traced to Hollywood's need since the 1960s to appeal to audiences that have been raised on television. Television programmers, in turn, have applied a soap opera format to TV courtroom dramas. Scriptwriters and television programmers attempted to add more realism to their shows by revealing more of the backstage behavior and private lives of their crime-fighting lawyers.[7]

The next step for television was to develop courtroom docudramas in which real cases are turned into infotainment, re-enacted, and adjudicated in realistic-looking courtroom scenes. Lastly, spurred by the immense popularity and profits of the first O. J. Simpson trial in the 1990s, the infotainment format has been incorporated into a number of contemporary court-based media productions.

With new media increasing audience perceptions of participation in courtroom proceedings, the social construction of the courts is rendered through a triumvirate of trial and law films, infotainment-style pseudo-judicial programs, and heavily publicized co-opted live cases. All of these media judicial portraits emphasize rare events (trials), uncommon charges (homicide), improbable evidence (criminalistics and CSI laboratory results), and unlikely interactions (dramatic adversarial confrontations) to collectively present a heavily skewed unrealistic picture of the courts and the rendering of law. How are the attorneys, the practitioners of law, portrayed in these renditions?

Crime-fighting Attorneys

Although criminal law is only one area of law and in the real world most attorneys practice other specialties, most lawyers in the media are criminal lawyers and specialize in criminal law.[8] Based on the most prominent media images of courtrooms, most law school graduates apparently wanted to attend the police academy. In the media, the protectors of due process are also frequently advocates of crime control. Thus, although shown less frequently than police officers in the entertainment media, attorneys and judges, when they star, are like their law enforcement counterparts, often expending as much effort solving crimes and pursuing criminals as they do interpreting and practicing law.[9]

The crime-fighting lawyer has not always been a common image. In earlier, generally uncritical portraits of the judicial system such as the film classic *To Kill a Mockingbird*, lawyers were constructed as homespun, simple yet crafty all-American due process practitioners.[10] In contrast, in the contemporary period legal skill and justice are less important and have been replaced by attorneys hunting down predator psychopaths or involved in sundry action scenes. Trial scenes are now more likely to be episodes imbedded within a thriller, and heroic lawyers are as likely to appear in fight and chase scenes as in court proceedings.[11]

When they are not also crime-fighting heroes, attorneys can expect to be portrayed negatively. For example, Robert and Linda Lichter found that in prime time television programming attorneys are more likely than police officers to be shown as greedy and nearly as likely to be shown as corrupt. In sum, in another backwards portrait, attorneys in the media are not shown spending much of their time practicing law, and when they do practice law, it is overwhelmingly criminal law. A group that has particularly suffered in its media constructions is female attorneys.

Female Attorneys

Similar to the portrayals of policewomen, female attorneys—while enjoying a longer history in the media—are frequently defeminized as career women or projected as people dominated by sexual conflicts. The media construction of the female lawyer frequently assumes the incompatibility of the social roles of attorney and woman. Even so, female attorneys in the media appear to fare better than their policewomen counterparts, in that some aspects of their real-world experiences are portrayed.[12] The scarcity of female lawyers, the gender-based attitudes prevalent toward women lawyers, and the social friction generated by the clashing of traditional female social roles and their functioning as effective attorneys can all be found in their media constructions. However, like policewomen, their sexuality and unresolved sexual tensions are likely to dominate their media portrayals. Female attorneys are more often shown as young, white,

Reflecting the media's focus on romance over lawyering for many portraits of female attorneys, in the film, Laws of Attraction, Julianne Moore plays an attorney who falls in love during litigation with a rival attorney.

single, childless, and in lower-echelon positions in their law firms and criminal justice agencies. They share with male attorney portrayals an unrealistic level of involvement in dangerous and sensational criminal law cases.

In total, the courts and attorneys are usually unrealistically constructed in the media. Rare real-world events and activities are common in media judicial portraits; common judicial procedures and attorney duties are rare in the media. Although not as wildly inaccurate as the image of police, the courts and attorneys are still more often shown in crime-fighting narratives than in more realistic story lines. Even when the portrayals are based on real cases, the infotainment criteria that drive the selection of cases culls out the usual and nonviolent case in favor of the abnormal and predatory. Some of these selected cases become multimedia, pop culture bonanzas, generating enormous markets, profits, and spinoffs for news, entertainment, and infotainment media.[13] Termed "**media trials**," these judicial miniseries have become the most important single contributor to the social construction of the courts in America.[14]

MEDIA TRIALS

Media trials involve the social construction of select criminal justice cases that are taken up by the media, commodified, and marketed as mass infotainment products. As legal historian Lawrence Friedman points out (2011, 1243): "The common law trial can be quite a dramatic event. Trials are a kind of stage-play, with a definite story or plot—usually, in fact, two stories or plots, which are in sharp contrast to each other—and a suspenseful and exciting ending, when the jury files into the room and announces its verdict." Learning about the courts from these trials is analogous to learning geology solely from volcano eruptions. You will be impressed and entertained but you will learn little about the common workings of the courts. Mass-mediated trials appeared in the United States soon after the establishment of the first mass media, the daily penny press newspapers.[15] One of the first was the 1859 trial of anarchist John Brown, which attracted daily coverage and widespread dissemination via the nationwide telegraph system. A later example is the 1875 trial of nationally known preacher Henry Ward Beecher, a trial narrative built around an adultery trial. The Lizzie Borden 1893 trial for the ax murders of her parents foreshadowed the lurid murder trials involving celebrities popular today and set the stage for a steady parade of media trials through the twentieth century. Since the 1890s media trials have been a consistent presence in the media, crime, and justice world and were constructed every three to five years over the course of the twentieth century. Increasing in frequency as the century ended, they show no evidence of abating. Indeed, new media have heightened access and interest in media trials.[16]

An important factor behind the recent increase in the number of media trials is that late-twentieth-century news organizations faced with harsh competition increasingly structured the news along entertainment lines. Since the news came to be presented within frames, formats, and explanations originally found solely in entertainment programming, fast-paced, dramatic, superficial crime news with simplistic explanations of crime became the norm. As this trend developed, criminal trials came to be covered more intensely, and news organizations expanded their coverage from hard factual presentations to soft human-interest news, emphasizing extralegal human-interest elements.[17] The process culminated in the 1990s with the total merging of news and entertainment. Today the sensational, titillating, and dramatic judicial elements determine media attention.[18]

Originally these show trials served political or didactic purposes; today such trials receive massive publicity not as object lessons but because they captivate the public as public entertainment. They are the final remnants of the widespread historical phenomenon where justice and punishment were public entertainment spectacles.[19] Accordingly, contemporary media trials are distinguished from typical judicial news by the massive and intensive coverage that begins either with the discovery of a newsworthy crime or the arrest of a noteworthy defendant.[20] In these trials all aspects of a case are covered and extralegal facts are highlighted. Judges, attorneys, law enforcement officers, victims, witnesses, jurors, and particularly defendants are interviewed, photographed, and raised to celebrity status. Heightened by the growth of the twenty-first-century celebrity culture in which people can be famous for being famous, the erosion of the expectation of privacy, and the expansion of who is a "public figure," the media trial has become a regular and profitable feature of the media–criminal justice industry.[21] In these productions, personalities, personal relationships, physical appearances, and idiosyncrasies are

Bettmann/Corbis

In 1927, Charles Lindbergh made the first solo, nonstop New York to Paris flight in the airplane Spirit of St. Louis. He returned an international hero and the most famous man in the world, becoming, in effect, the first mass media celebrity. The kidnapping and murder of his infant son in 1932, and the subsequent trial and execution of Bruno Hauptmann for the crime, foreshadowed today's massive coverage of media trials. Shown are the reporters gathered to cover the 1935 trial of Bruno Hauptmann.

commented on regardless of legal relevance. Coverage is live whenever possible, pictures are preferred over text, and text is characterized by conjecture and sensationalism.[22] These media constructions offer simple and individualistic explanations of crime: lust, greed, immorality, jealousy, revenge, and insanity.

Media Trial Effects

The relationship between the media and the justice system is strained by media trials because different considerations and values govern the means by which each obtains knowledge and evaluates its worth. The criminal justice system is guided by legislative and constitutional mandates, and the courts have the task of separating legally relevant from irrelevant information. Media, however, respond primarily to newsworthiness and entertainment considerations. Each side's considerations dictate what facts are presented as well as when and how they are disclosed. Traditionally, in the courtroom information is imparted in a form and by a process different from that preferred by the media. Courtroom knowledge is extracted point by point in long story lines following legal procedures and rules of evidence. Moreover, the information is specially prepared for a limited audience of a judge or jury.

In contrast, media renditions are outwardly directed and developed in accordance with entertainment values rather than legal relevance. They are brief, time- and space-limited constructions that must make their points quickly, and they are built around whatever film or dramatic elements are available. In sum, the courts have traditionally presented internally controlled, front-stage events to a small, specific audience of judges and jurors, whereas media-produced products tend to present dramatic backstage information to an external, general mass audience. This inherent conflict between media and justice systems crystallizes in the media trial, where the courthouse becomes a production stage. With the ascendance of media trials, the traditional courtroom audience became secondary to the external media audience both inside and outside of the courtroom.[23] The development of new social media has hastened the shift from internal to external audiences; while live trial attendance is down, virtual trial attention is up.[24] Similar to attendance of sporting events, new media technology allow spectators to attend from afar and to watch only the best parts. Trials are reduced to their highlights as a physical audience has given way to a larger virtual audience.[25] The trial of Bruno Hauptmann for the murder of Charles Lindbergh's infant son which attracted huge crowds to its 1930s courthouse, would today attract even larger crowds who would however stay home, follow it via highlighted excerpts, and blog about it to one another.

For these reasons, despite their relatively small numbers, media trials are crucial in the twenty-first-century social construction of crime-and-justice reality.[26] They serve as massive public stages that disseminate crime-and-justice knowledge to vast audiences of ordinary citizens.[27] In a media trial, both the jury and the vicariously attending public can decide between one reality constructed by the state in which the accused is guilty and another constructed by the defense in which the defendant is not guilty. In this way, trials are small-scale examples of the social construction process. As the dominant delivery medium of these trials, visual media direct the facts that are selected, constructed, and presented to the public. Not surprisingly, media trials involve cases that contain the

B o x 6.1   The Casey Anthony Media Trial and the Legacy of O. J. Simpson

The 2011 Florida Casey Anthony murder trial in which a mother was accused of murdering her two-year-old daughter is a recent media trial reflecting the legacy of O. J. Simpson's 1995 murder trial. Following her daughter's disappearance, Casey Anthony (pictured below) provided varied explanations regarding the girl's whereabouts, including that the child had been kidnapped by a nanny. After a heavily covered, nationally televised trial which *Time* magazine described as "the social media trial of the century," Casey Anthony, like O. J. Simpson, was found not guilty. Since the Simpson trial, which demonstrated the immense popularity and profit that is possible from the exploitation of these judicial events, the style in which media trials are covered has become cemented. The history of trial exploitation by media is traceable to the 1800s, but it deviated in a quantum way with the impact of new media in the 1990s. The full effect was first observed and crystalized with the 1995 trial of O. J. Simpson for a double murder.

As these media trials often are, the O. J. trial was frequently described as the "Trial of the Century." Rather than the trial of the century, Simpson's 1995 trial is best understood as the signal television event of the twentieth century. Coverage of the case consumed thousands of hours of media time and uncounted pages of print. A large part of the interest and social impact of his trial stemmed from it becoming a long-running mass media entertainment vehicle—a drama-in-real-life, covered more along the lines of a sports spectacle than a criminal trial. The trial set the style that persists today in how to cover and exploit high profile criminal cases in the media. Regarding the trial's social impact, most commentators focused on its impact on race relations. Other concerns related to the coverage included the prospect of more criminal defendants refusing to plea bargain, a skepticism about police testimony, more judicial gag orders on trial participants, and less camera access to courtrooms, and the general degrading in the public's eye of judges, juries, attorneys, and the judicial system. Coverage of the trial is considered by many as American media and culture at one of its lowest voyeuristic points. Today, the judicial system continues to be exploited regularly in intensely covered criminal cases and trials. Since the O. J. trial's rating and monetary successes, the regular spectacle of a salacious media trial occurs every year or two. In addition to the sex- and violence-related trials exemplified by the Jodi Arias and Amanda Knox trials, recent media trials include the trial of doctor Conrad Murray for the manslaughter of Michael Jackson, a string of terrorist-related trials such as airline shoe-bomber Richard Reid and airline underwear-bomber Umar Abdulmutallab, and the forthcoming trials of 9/11 plotter Khalid Mohammed and Boston Marathon pressure cooker bomber Dzhokhar Tasrnaev.

same elements popular in entertainment programming—human interest laced with mystery, sex, bizarre circumstances, and famous or powerful people (see Box 6.1). Tabloid trials such as public horror movie tabloid trials, celebrity victim and defendant trials where the crimes are secondary to the names of the participants, murder mystery whodunit trials, and soap opera love triangles make up a constant parade of commodified, co-opted judicial events.

Lawrence Friedman points out that media trials collectively forward two contradictory misconceptions about justice. First, that the courts comprise a meticulous system of due process, attention to detail, and the rule of law. Due to the evaporation of normal discretion and negotiation that media attention forces on proceedings, the trials appear as rigid, formal, rule bound judicial conflicts. Paradoxically due to the speculation and discussion of alternate

Red Huber/MCT/Newscom

SOURCES: Bains G., "The Criminal Trial as a Sports Spectacle." *McLean's 108* (February 20, 1995): 55; Barak, G. Ed., *Media, Process, and the Social Construction of Crime.* New York: Garland, 1995; Cloud, J. "How the Casey Anthony Murder Case Became the Social-Media Trial of the Century," *Time* (June 16, 2011); Fox, Sickel and Steiger, *Tabloid Justice*; Gaines, S. "O. J. Simpson, Mark Fuhrman, and the Moral 'Low Ground' of Ethnic/Race Relations in the United States." *Black Scholar 25* (1995): 46–48; Garvey, J., "Race and the Simpson Verdict." *Commonwealth 122* (1995): 6; Gelernter, D., "The Real Story of Orenthal James." *National Review* (October 9, 1995): 45–47; Handy, B., "Our Mutual Houseguest." *Time 146* (October 16, 1995): 108; Pillsbury, S. "Time, TV, and Criminal Justice: Second Thoughts on the Simpson Trial." *Criminal Law Bulletin* 59(3) 1997: 3–28; Reed, T., "Files Untangle Tales from Missing Fla. Girl's Mom", *Associated Press* (August 26, 2008); Rosenblatt, R. "A Nation of Painted Hearts." *Time* (October 16, 1995): 40–46; Schmalleger, F., *Trial of the Century.* Englewood Cliffs: Prentice Hall, 1996; Walsh, J., "Special Report: The Simpson Verdict." *Time 146* (October 16, 1995): 62–64; and Whitaker, M., "Whites v. Blacks." *Newsweek 126* (October 16, 1995): 28–34.

explanations of events, competing legal strategies, and multiple interpretations of evidence that accompanies the coverage of these trials, the courts are also shown as places where tricks, smart lawyering, and procedural quirks can manipulate justice and juries and where money can buy acquittals.[28] As a final point, the media construct these trials in ways that simplify their task of reporting, interpreting, and explaining the proceedings. As in the entertainment media, recurrent themes dominate media trial constructions, and crime is nearly universally attributed to individual failings rather than to social conditions. The three most common types of media trials utilize narratives taken directly from entertainment media: abuse of power, the sinful rich, and evil strangers.[29] These frames provide the news media with powerful pre-established conceptual scaffolding to present and mold the various aspects of a trial's coverage.[30]

Media trials that fit the **abuse of power** theme include those cases in which the defendant occupies a position of trust, prestige, or authority. The general rule is the higher the rank, the more media interest in the case. Cases involving police corruption and justice system personnel in general are especially attractive to the media. **Sinful rich** media trials include cases in which socially prominent defendants are involved in bizarre or sexually related crimes. These trials have a voyeuristic appeal, and the media coverage aims to persuade the public that they are being given a rare glimpse into the backstage sordid world of the upper class and powerful. Love triangles, deviant sex, and inheritance-motivated killings among the rich and famous are primary examples.[31] The category of **evil strangers** is composed of two subgroups: non-Americans and psychotic killers. Non-American evil stranger media trials may involve—depending on the time and political climate—immigrants, blacks, Jews, socialists, union and labor leaders, anarchists, the poor, members of counterculture groups, members of minority religions, or political activists and advocates of unpopular causes. Foreign terrorists provide recent examples. Psychotic killer media trials usually focus on bizarre murder cases in which the defendant is portrayed as a predatory killer—exemplified historically by Lizzie Borden (in spite of her acquittal) and more recently by Jeffery Dahmer, John Wayne Gacy, Aileen Wuornos, Scott Peterson, and Jodi Arias.

All three media trial types have long histories in popular entertainment narratives, and these pre-established entertainment narratives help determine the content of the coverage in the real cases. Entertainment story lines provide the news media with the frames by which to measure, choose, and mold aspects of real trials that will be reported and highlighted. Media trials thereby reinforce the similarity between news and entertainment. They inspire news personnel to structure their coverage along familiar entertainment narratives and provide storylines for fictional entertainment productions.[32] Attorneys rely on these familiar frames to construct infotainment-styled courtroom narratives to steer the interpretation of evidence by juries. The public, in turn, receives the responsibility-diverting messages that the rich are immoral in their use of sex, drugs, and violence; that people in power are evil, greedy, and should not be trusted; and that strangers and those with different lifestyles or values are inherently dangerous. In the process, the pursuit of justice is reduced to the single-minded combating of evil, sinful, predators. Table 6.1 lists some well-known examples of media trials and their outcomes.

Merging Judicial News with Entertainment

Media trials represent the final step in a long process of merging judicial news and entertainment—a process that today results in multimedia products and extensive commercial exploitation. The Internet has extended this process and provides detailed information about these cases to a much greater degree than previously available. The Internet also provides a vehicle for the public to become active trial participants in dedicated trial chat rooms, providing running evidence and testimony assessments complete with votes on guilt or innocence.[33] If prior coverage of media trials resembled a miniseries, today it is more like a

T A B L E   6.1   **Media Trial Examples**

Abuse of Power

Rodney King Beating (1992)	*Trial.* Four Los Angeles police officers were accused of using excessive force in arresting Rodney King following a car chase. The acquittals in the state trial triggered riots in Los Angeles, leaving 53 people dead, more than 7,000 people arrested, and more than $1 billion in property damage.	*Verdict.* In the first state trial, the jury acquitted three of the officers of all charges and was unable to reach a verdict on one charge against the forth. In a subsequent 1993 federal trial on charges of violation of civil rights, a federal jury convicted two of the officers and found the other two not guilty. No disturbances followed the verdict.
Bernard Madoff Ponzi Scheme (2009)	*Trial.* A former chairman of the NASDAQ stock exchange, he was accused of securities, wire, and mail fraud; money laundering; theft; false SEC statement filings; and perjury. His massive Ponzi scheme investment operation was estimated to have cost his clients billions.	*Verdict.* He pled guilty to eleven felonies and was sentenced to 150 years in prison.

Sinful Rich

Sam Sheppard (1954)	*Trial.* An Ohio doctor who was tried for the murder of his wife.	*Verdict.* Found guilty by a jury of murder in the second degree and sentenced to life in prison. Sheppard won a retrial in 1966 after a successful U.S. Supreme Court appeal arguing prejudicial impact from news coverage surrounding his first trial. He was acquitted by jury in second trial and died in 1970 at the age of 46 of liver failure.
Paris Hilton (2007–2010)	*Trial.* American heiress, socialite, and reality television star Paris Hilton described as "being famous for being famous" was first arrested in 2006 for DUI and began a series of persistent, if less than felony-related, judicial proceedings. Hilton pled no contest in 2007 to reckless driving and was placed on 36 months of probation and fined $1,500. She was again arrested in 2010 on suspicion of cocaine possession in Las Vegas.	*Verdict.* Found in violation of her probation in 2007 and sentenced to 45 days in jail. Pled guilty in connection to her 2010 cocaine arrest to two misdemeanors, sentenced to one year of probation, a $2,000 fine, 200 hours of community service, and a drug treatment program.

(continued)

T A B L E   6.1   Media Trial Examples (Continued)

Evil Strangers
Non-Americans

Bruno Hauptmann (1935)	*Trial.* A German immigrant, Hauptmann was accused of the 1932 kidnapping and murder of the infant son of aviator Charles Lindbergh.	*Verdict.* He was found guilty and electrocuted in 1936.
Dzhokhar Tsarnaev (2013)	*Trial.* Pending. With his brother Tamerlan Tsarnaev arrested in connection with the April 15, 2013 pressure cooker bombing at the finish line of the Boston Marathon which killed 3 people and injured 264. Their pursuit resulted in the death of a local campus police officer and the shooting of an MBTA police officer, critically injuring of Chechen brothers Dzhokhar and Tamerlan Tsarnaev. In the associated shootouts, Tamerlan Tsarnaev was killed and Dzhokhar Tsarnaev was injured.	

Psychotic Killers

Jeffery Dahmer (1992)	*Trial.* A cannibalistic serial killer who preyed on Milwaukee's young men from 1987 to 1991, he was accused of killing 17 men.	*Verdict.* Sentenced to 15 consecutive life terms, he was killed in prison by another inmate in 1994.
Dennis Rader BTK Killer (2005)	*Trial.* Known as the BTK (bind, torture, kill) serial murderer, he was accused of killing ten people in the Wichita, Kansas area from 1974 to 1991.	*Verdict.* Pled guilty and received ten consecutive life terms.

game show. Along with extensive interest, the money to be made from a popu-lar long-running media trial is enormous. That the source of media trials is the judicial system eases the merger and heightens the profits, for media trials allow the news media to attract and market to large audiences while maintaining their preferred image as objective and neutral. A trial is also a natural stage for present-ing drama and comes supplied with tax-supported sets, lead and secondary char-acters, extras, and dialogue. Media trials provide the media with ready-made narratives for entertainment vehicles in the form of movie scripts, episodes for weekly crime and law dramas, and content for infotainment talk shows, books, and other spinoffs. They become, in effect, an entire media industry line.

The social impact and importance of media trials is seldom connected to the extent of social harm from their associated crimes. Their significance comes from the attention they receive and the public debate generated from the intense media and public focus on the trial proceedings. These trials are significant because they influence the public's attitudes and views regarding crime, justice, and society for years.[34] A specific concern for a judicial system experiencing a medial trial is the generation of a secondary effect on nonpublicized cases. Fol-lowing a media trial, a coverage effect influences the processing and disposition of similarly charged but unpublicized cases.[35] This coverage echo has been described a number of times in the literature:

> But while the impact of the press is most direct on specific cases covered, there is good reason to believe that [their] sway extends considerably beyond the cases actually appearing.... From the cases that are covered, officials become conditioned to expect demands for stern treatment from the press, and in the unpublicized cases they probably act accordingly.[36]

> This unwillingness [to plea bargain] appears to occur relatively infre-quently. It is most likely to occur when there is strong pressure upon the prosecution to obtain maximum sentences for a particular class of crime: for example, after a notorious case of child rape, the prosecutor may refuse to bargain, for a time, with those charged with sex offenses involving children; after a series of highly publicized drug arrests, for a time, to engage in reduction of charges from sales to possession.[37]

Empirical evidence of a punitive echo was found in a study of a decade of felony case processing in one jurisdiction. Following a heavily covered case involving child abuse at a daycare center a significant jump in similarly charged cases occurred.[38] The implication of a publicity spillover effect is that media attention influences the processing and disposition of a large number of cases, the majority of which receive no coverage. Such effects are, of course, heightened when live television is part of the media trial package.

Live Television in Courtrooms

When trials began to be televised in the 1950s, concern heightened over the social effects. In the Estes case in 1965 (which resulted in banning television cameras in courtrooms), Chief Justice Earl Warren stated: "Should the television industry become an integral part of our system of criminal justice, it would not be unnatural for the public to attribute the shortcomings of the industry to the trial process itself." [39] The passage of time has not reduced this concern. The basic issue is whether attorneys, judges, and other participants react to the presence of cameras by altering their courtroom behavior. The fear is that participants will change the way they testify, argue, and construct their cases to fit the needs of an electronic visual media and that attorneys will audition for a massive external audience rather than litigate to a small courtroom audience. Media-driven changes have been documented in religion, sports, and politics where small live audiences are less important (and sometimes skipped entirely) in preference for large, external media-supplied ones. [40]

Often a component in the construction of media trials, live television coverage of judicial proceedings represents the most intrusive media interaction with the judicial system. The schizophrenic judicial posture toward televised proceedings is shown by its embracement in the first O. J. Simpson criminal trial and its banishment from his civil trial. The judiciary has long been skeptical about visual coverage of trials. Recognition of photography's unique potential for disruption originated with Bruno Hauptmann's trial for the kidnapping and murder of Charles Lindbergh's baby son in the 1930s. [41] In response to problems that arose during this trial, the American Bar Association in 1937 issued a new rule (or canon) regarding the use of photographic equipment at trials:

> Proceedings in court should be conducted with fitting dignity and decorum. The taking of photographs in the courtroom, during sessions of the court or recesses between sessions, and the broadcasting of court proceedings are calculated to detract from the essential dignity of the proceedings, degrade the court and create misconceptions in the mind of the public and should not be permitted. [42]

This recommended ban on photography in the courtroom was widely adopted and was extended in 1952 to include television cameras as well. Despite the extension of the ABA rules (which are unenforced recommended standards of expected conduct), the first trial to receive television coverage took place in 1953 in Oklahoma City, and the first to receive live coverage in 1955 was in Waco, Texas. These cases stand as exceptions to the more broadly upheld aversion to television in the courts that existed into the 1980s.

The U.S. Supreme Court first reviewed the question of television access to courtrooms in *Estes v. Texas* in 1965. [43] Involving a prominent businessman with White House connections, the Estes trial received intense regional television coverage with nightly news reports broadcast from the courthouse. Following his conviction, Estes appealed and the Supreme Court reversed Estes's conviction, ruling that television was unavoidably disruptive and should have been banned: "Television in its present state and by its very nature, reaches into a variety of areas in which it may cause prejudice to an accused.... The televising of criminal trials is inherently a denial of due process." [44] In the Estes aftermath, most states severely limited television's access to their courts, and many simply banned all TV coverage.

However, encouraged by the development of less obtrusive television equipment, various states continued to experiment with televising proceedings. In 1979, the Florida Supreme Court allowed television reporting from trial courts without requiring the permission of defendants. Florida's procedures were reviewed by the U.S. Supreme Court in 1981 in *Chandler v. Florida*.[45] At that time, the Court rejected many of the assumptions about television it had forwarded 16 years earlier. The most significant assumption it rejected was that televising a criminal trial without the defendant's consent is an inherent denial of due process. Emphasizing the modernization of the medium, the lack of evidence of a psychological impact from televised coverage on trial participants, and an increase in the public acceptance of television as a fact of everyday life, the Court upheld the *Chandler* conviction.

Although unstated by the Supreme Court, additional reasons for this reversal had developed in the years between *Estes* and *Chandler*. Backed by surveys of the public, during this period there was growing concern among the judiciary that the public lacked confidence in the courts' ability to confront crime and criminals.[46] The courts were viewed as part of the cause of a steadily increasing crime rate. In this negative atmosphere, televising trials began to look like a possible counterweight to negative public perceptions. As front-stage events constructed for public consumption, trials show the justice system at its best. It was increasingly felt that the cameras would show impartial justice, fair procedure, conviction of the guilty, and imposition of fair sentences. By contrast, the seamy backstage of the criminal justice process—the plea bargaining, the procedural inefficiency, the arbitrary decision making inherent in police and prosecutor discretion—would go unseen. Televising trials, in other words, was seen as unlikely to hurt and possessing the potential to help shore up the judicial system's poor public image. By the 1980s, the courts saw televised trials as a means of presenting controlled, formal front-stage events to the public while protecting their backstage assembly-line processes from exposure.

The basic question of whether or not to allow television cameras in the courtroom was never whether television reporters had the freedom to report courtroom matters—broadcast journalists could attend and report trials on the same basis as other reporters, that is, without their cameras—but concerned the effect of expanding the trial audience to include persons not in the courtroom. In the 1960s—at the time of the *Estes* ruling—the court feared the effects of this expansion on both the trial participants and the expanded electronic audience. By the 1980s the courts felt that a broadly expanded audience of external spectators was a good thing that would have an uplifting impact on the negative image of the courts. In addition, judges came to accept the courtroom presence of news media and became more comfortable with the measures necessary to control media behavior during trials.

In addition, as predatory criminality became the dominant social construction of crime and began to influence criminal justice policy, the constitutional importance given to defendants' rights diminished in favor of general social interests and an accompanying increase in support for electronic media access. As a result, opposition to courtroom television evaporated. The *Chandler* decision marks a remarkable shift in the attitude of the judicial system toward the presence of television in courtrooms. In 1976, all but two states prohibited cameras in courtrooms. Since 2005, all 50 states allow some type of coverage at either the appellate or trial level or both. The *Chandler* decision emerged as a broad victory for the electronic media and the assumption of media access to judicial proceedings. Courtroom cameras are today a growing international phenomenon and are common in a number of regions including the United Kingdom, Europe, and Australia.[47] Their use in the United States continues to expand within states, appellate courts, and the federal court system.[48]

The effects of cameras on courtroom proceedings are no longer seen as a prime concern, but the effect of those cameras on those outside the courtroom is still worrisome.[49] Most worrisome is that public disturbances and full-scale riots have been triggered by court decisions in highly publicized cases.[50] Other unresolved issues include a chilling effect on victims reporting crimes, particularly victims of rape, witnesses seeking to avoid embarrassing coverage being reluctant to testify, heightening the public's fear of crime, distorting the public's beliefs about the workings of the judicial system, encouraging copycat crimes, and publicly pillorying defendants who are eventually found innocent. However, the infotainment value of media trials is too great, public interest too high, and none of the negative effects or speculated concerns severe enough to curtail coverage. In fact, the social and economic pressures to grant media access are so great that even in trials that are obviously about to be flooded by massive coverage, the cameras and intense media scrutiny are usually allowed.

So it is that today intensive, and sometimes intrusive, news coverage is accepted as a fact of life in the judiciary. Future clashes between the two are to be expected as the media seek access to previously backstage judicial proceedings and as media technology makes recording and marketing them easier. The media are aided in this process by the society-wide effects of the electronic and digital media over the last 50 years. The social impacts of television and new social media have undermined public support for closing off social institutions. Country clubs, golf courses, prisons, bars, fraternal organizations, and a host of other institutions, as well as the courts, are less successful in claiming a traditional right to insulate themselves from broad public and media access. Currently the evolution of the media and the judiciary's unsteady relationship has three areas of concern and unresolved conflict—the effect of pretrial publicity, the appropriate judicial mechanisms to be used by the courts when they are faced with intense media attention, and access by both sides to information held by the other.

PRETRIAL PUBLICITY, JUDICIAL CONTROLS, AND ACCESS

Pretrial Publicity

In 1807, Aaron Burr's attorney claimed that jurors could not properly decide his client's case because of prejudicial newspaper articles.[51] From this initial point of contention, the media and courts have continued to joust over pretrial publicity. Ironically, despite their adversarial history and contentious interactions, the media and the judicial system react to criminal events in much the same manner. Both concentrate on constructing a particular version of reality to be presented to a specific audience—jurors, viewers, readers, or Web surfers. The relationship between the media and the judicial system is sometimes cooperative, but more often each jealously guards its information while attempting to discover what the other knows. This is particularly true during the investigative and pretrial period of a case. Publicity before and during a trial may so affect a community and its courts that a fair trial becomes impossible and due process protections such as the presumption of innocence are destroyed. Exposure to negative pretrial publicity has been associated with greater likelihood by jurors to discuss the coverage in deliberations and be influenced in their recollections of case-specific facts, and such publicity may also influence their emotional reactions to evidence and testimony.[52] The media especially create problems when they publish information that is inadmissible in the courtroom and construct a community atmosphere in which finding and impaneling impartial jurors is not possible.

Unfortunately it is not always clear when particular media content is prejudicial (see Box 6.2). **Prejudicial publicity** can take two forms: factual information that bears on the guilt of a defendant and emotional information without evidentiary relevance. Factual information includes allusions to confessions, performances on polygraph or other inadmissible tests, and past criminal records and convictions. Emotional information includes stories that question the credibility of witnesses or present personal feelings, stories about the defendant's character (he hates children and dogs), associates (she hangs around with known syndicate gunmen), or personality (he's a mean-spirited, bad-tempered degenerate), and stories that inflame the general public (someone has to be punished for this!).

Despite the concerns about prejudicial coverage, the U.S. Supreme Court has not operationally defined prejudicial coverage for the lower courts. Faced with ambiguity and forced to render largely subjective determinations, both trial and appellate courts have focused on jurors as the key to determining the fairness of a trial. In practice, the operational definition of an impartial juror is derived from the 1807 Aaron Burr case: "An impartial juror is one free from the dominant influence of knowledge acquired outside the courtroom, free from strong and deep impressions which close the mind."[53] Though not a precise rule, this definition does eliminate ignorance of a case or a total lack of exposure to media coverage as a requirement for impartiality. Jurors can be exposed to extensive media content regarding a case and still be considered impartial. If a jury is deemed impartial and uninfluenced by media coverage, then the proceedings are usually considered fair.

Paralleling this issue is the concern that trial publicity will result in unwarranted harm to a defendant. Appeals courts have thus far not recognized media coverage as a mitigating factor in sentencing decisions. Left unaddressed are cases in which a defendant is found innocent of criminal charges but has his or her reputation permanently ruined by publicity. The consequence of publicity has

B o x 6.2   Amanda Knox's Italian Media Trial

A media trial that generated international media attention and a large amount of prejudicial pretrial publicity was the 2009 trial of American college student Amanda Knox in Italy for the murder of her British roommate, Meredith Kercher. Knox and her Italian boyfriend were accused of killing Ms. Kercher during a violent sex game. The pretrial publicity surrounding the trial of Knox became an issue, as a posting from a "Friends of Amanda" Web site states:

> The mission of the Friends of Amanda is to achieve some measure of balance in the pre-trial publicity. Prejudicial and erroneous public accounts resulted from leaks and false information from the closed-door year-long pre-charging proceedings. As we have stated, turning around the "super tanker" of negative publicity against Amanda Knox has been a slow, difficult, and laborious process. We believe we have now had a significant impact in achieving some balance in what has been reported and have achieved our purpose. Now that a public trial is underway, we will stand back and let the international public see what there is to be seen in the public trial proceedings. We hope only for fairness and justice in the proceedings for all, including for Amanda Knox.

In a convoluted judicial process, Ms. Knox was found guilty in a 2009 trial and sentenced to 26 years in prison. This conviction was initially overturned on appeal in 2011 and Knox was released and returned to the United States. In 2013, the Italian Supreme court overturned the prior overturning of her 2009 conviction. Ms. Knox did not return to Italy for subsequent proceedings and was ultimately convicted in absentia for falsely implicating another person and sentenced to three years (credited with time served) and a monetary fine. However, in a 2014 retrial, an Italian appeals court reinstated the 2009 guilty verdict for murder. This verdict is expected to be also appealed. As with other media trials, a host of civil lawsuits, books, and movies have been generated.

SOURCES: www.annebremner.com/Amanda_Knox.htm; www.cnn.com/2014/01/30/world/europe/italy-amanda-knox-retrial/index.html

AP Images/Antonio Calanni

been described in this way in relation to government officials who have been investigated:

> Once again the tendency to portray public officials accused of criminal or unethical activities as guilty [is displayed].... We find it appalling that long after many of these individuals have been found innocent of the accusations against them, the disproved accusations continue to be repeated as almost a permanent addendum to their name in news stories.[54]

The concern is that media coverage incites such negative feelings against defendants that, even if they are later acquitted, the feelings are irreversible. The modern media have constructed a new case disposition: legally innocent but socially guilty. In the process, media coverage confounds the concepts of legal guilt (is the defendant legally responsible for a crime?) and factual guilt (did the defendant actually commit the criminal behavior?). Factual guilt is not always equivalent to legal guilt, and the general public little understands and is poorly instructed by the media in the differences between the two. If defendants who have been found innocent are subsequently still punished by losing their career or reputation because of publicity, then the criminal justice system loses legitimacy with those who identify with the defendants.

Judicial Mechanisms to Deal with Pretrial Publicity

Faced with a case that will generate significant pretrial publicity, the courts have two strategies they can pursue. One is proactive and seeks to limit the availability of potentially prejudicial material to the media. The second is reactive and seeks to limit the effects of the material on the proceeding after it has been disseminated to the public. Under the first strategy, if a court deems information to be prejudicial, it acts to restrict either media access to the information or, if the material is already in the media's possession, restricts the publication of the information. **Proactive mechanisms** include closure, restrictive, and protective orders (see Box 6.3). This approach directly clashes with the First Amendment protection of freedom of the press and has been vigorously resisted by the media. It has also not been the favored strategy of the appellate courts, as shown in test cases in which the Supreme Court has been more likely to uphold appeals by the media where a proactive strategy had been used.

Appeals by the media have been less successful when the courts employ a reactive strategy, allowing the news media access and publication but attempting to compensate for negative effects from the resulting publicity. In this approach, trial court judges can invoke a number of reactive steps to limit the negative effects of publicity. These **reactive mechanisms** are generally preferred over closure, restrictive orders, and protective orders because they do not directly limit the activities of the media and thus do not directly undermine the First Amendment freedom of the press.[55] They rest on the premise that even if most of the public may be influenced and biased by media information, an unbiased jury can still be assembled and an unbiased trial conducted. Applying a reactive

---

B o x 6.3   Proactive Judicial Mechanisms to Control Prejudicial Publicity

---

Mechanism	Description of Procedure
Closure	Closure involves isolating judicial proceedings from outside (public and press) attendance. Closure is felt to be a very effective means of preventing prejudicial coverage once a proceeding has begun because there can be no prejudice if there is no coverage. In opposing closure, the media argue that they are proxies for the general public and therefore have a right of access to the court proceedings under the open trial provision of the Sixth Amendment.
Restrictive orders	The next most effective step available to control prejudicial materials is the use of restrictive orders (also termed prior restraint or gag orders). Restrictive orders prevent the media from printing or broadcasting information. If information is not published, it cannot cause bias. Not surprisingly, the media have argued vigorously for the right to publish what they have already discovered, and this right has generally been upheld.
Protective orders	The third judicial mechanism used to limit the availability of prejudicial materials is the protective order. Trial participants are a common source of prejudicial information. By issuing a protective order, the trial judge prohibits attorneys and others from making statements outside of the courtroom. These orders are most effective in the early stages of a case. The legal rationale behind protective orders allowing speech to be restricted is that trial participants possess privileged information regarding a criminal case and no longer have the same First Amendment right to freely speak as a member of the general public. As it now stands, it is currently easier for a trial judge to restrict the speech of a trial's participants, excluding the defendant, than to close a proceeding or to restrain the media from publicizing information and statements they have obtained.

---

strategy, judges can expand jury selection (the voir dire), grant trial continuances, grant changes of venue, sequester jurors, and give special instructions to the jury to counteract the effects of publicity (see Box 6.4).

Case law and legislation provide little direction concerning the appropriate use of these reactive mechanisms, and little empirical research is available regarding their relative effectiveness. Therefore, although each mechanism has recognized strengths and weaknesses, its application is based on unproved but commonly accepted assumptions concerning its effectiveness and appropriate use. Given the pervasiveness and intrusiveness of the media, these after-the-fact attempts to compensate are often costly and disruptive, and, most important, of questionable effectiveness in massively covered media trials.[56] Evidence suggests that media influences may persist even when the legal system makes efforts to limit those influences.[57] Proactive mechanisms are more effective, but they tend to close off the judicial system and therefore run counter to the society-wide, media-driven trend to open social

Box 6.4	Reactive Judicial Mechanisms to Control Prejudicial Publicity

Mechanism	Description of Procedure
Voir dire	Voir dire, "to speak the truth," is a process in which prospective jurors are queried regarding prejudice. Attorneys can prevent jurors from serving either through challenges for cause, where they must state a valid reason for eliminating a juror, or through peremptory challenges (normally limited in number) that do not have to be supported by a reason. Voir dire will only identify those jurors who admit knowledge and prejudice about a case, and it is based on the premise that jurors will recognize themselves as biased and truthfully admit it.
Continuance	Continuance is simply a delay in the start of a trial until media coverage and its effects are thought to have subsided enough to allow an unbiased trial. The practice is based on the premise that media interest in the case will wane and that jurors will forget details of past media reports. Disadvantages include that it is inconsistent with the defendant's right to a speedy trial and the possibility that witnesses and evidence may not be available at a later time.
Change of venue	A trial may be moved from a location in which the case has received heavy media coverage to one in which it has received less coverage and is of less interest, and where residents are assumed to be less biased. Although costly and questionable in effectiveness, venue changes are deemed necessary in certain cases—for example, in rural areas where the jury pool is limited and a major crime is likely to be the dominant news story for a long time.
Sequestration	Isolating a jury to control the information that reaches it can be very effective if the jury has not been exposed to prejudicial information prior to being impaneled. However, it is costly and disruptive to jurors and is felt to generate animosity toward the accused.
Jury instructions	The simplest and least expensive judicial mechanism that can be invoked, jury instructions comprise the directions the trial judge gives to the jury. They fundamentally consist of telling jurors to ignore media coverage. Empirical studies that have examined this mechanism suggest, however, that for the most part standard jury warnings do not eliminate publicity-generated bias and that juries commonly discuss prejudicial information despite instructions not to.

institutions. They also preclude any positive social effects that might be generated from media coverage. Although sometimes employed, proactive mechanisms continue to lag in popularity, reserved for the rare and unusual case and usually challenged when used.

Regardless of which strategy they employ, to enforce their decisions, trial judges rely on contempt-of-court rulings to deter and punish those ignoring their orders regarding media publicity. In practice, the threat of a contempt find-ing works better with local criminal justice system personnel, as they have to consider future dealings with a trial court, and less well with jurors, witnesses, reporters (especially those from other jurisdictions), and other temporary partici-pants. As a last resort, a mistrial can be declared and a retrial ordered if jurors are exposed to or admit to being influenced by prejudicial news once a trial has begun. A retrial can be thought of as the ultimate reactive judicial remedy for media publicity—but it also represents an expensive failure of the judicial system and does not prevent the recurrence of renewed massive coverage.

In addition to pretrial publicity and strategies to deal with the media, access to files, records, notes, photos, and databases have raised concerns. Issues here take two forms: those related to the media desiring access to government-collected and -controlled information and those related to government agencies gaining access to media-collected and -controlled information.

Media Access to Government Information

In a significant number of instances, a government agency has possession of information that the media deems newsworthy. Oftentimes the government is reluctant to release such information, and in response the press has worked to increase its access to government-held data and files. The first national response to obtaining information held by the government was the federal Freedom of Information Act, adopted in 1966. This act opened up numerous government files to the media and the public. A later associated law was the Government in Sunshine Act, passed in 1976, which prohibits closed government meetings that concern public policy. Both of these efforts have been duplicated in numerous states but have had mixed results in easing the news media's access to govern-ment files and information. Part of the cause of the mixed impact of the laws targeted at access stems from the competing federal Privacy Act in 1974, which aimed to reduce access. Recently, Internet-based hackers, bloggers, and other online entities such as WikiLeaks (see Box 6.5) have entered the fray and conflict over the distribution of government files and documents has taken a global turn.

Concerns over privacy and misuse of information collected by government regarding individuals led to support for a counterbalance. The goal was to control the misuse of government information and to restrict access to certain information in criminal files and judicial records. Information required to be disclosed under the Freedom of Information Act cannot be withheld under the auspices of the Privacy Act, but the boundary between the two acts has always been blurred. Further mud-dying the water, while expanding government access to privately held information, the effects of the Patriot Act of 2001 and the Homeland Security Act of 2002 on media access to government-held information remain unclear. As in other areas regarding the media, the lower courts, agency personnel, and the media operate without clear rules in determining when privacy supersedes public interests, and decisions are rendered on a case-by-case basis. To date the overall effect of this leg-islation has been more symbolic than significant, and today the media's access to government-held files and information varies significantly by jurisdiction.[58]

B o x 6.5   WikiLeaks and Conflict Over Government Held Information

The Internet has added a new dimension to the conflict over access to and distribution of government-held information. Massive amounts of detailed information can be taken electronically and quickly distributed globally. These capabilities have generated great concern about the security of information held by both governments and businesses about private individuals and the harm that distribution of sensitive information can cause. Two recent cases exemplify the issues.

The first case involves the Internet Web site, WikiLeaks, which specializes in posting for public view files and information deemed secret by governments and other organizations such as the Church of Scientology. The pre-eminent WikiLeaks scandal involved a U.S. Army Intelligence analyst, PFC Bradley Manning, who in 2010 provided U.S. State Department documents to the WikiLeaks Web site that contained information regarding U.S. diplomatic practices, including details on spying on foreign diplomats. Following the documents release, WikiLeaks and its British creator, Julian Assange, came under pressure, with Web sites such as Amazon.com blocking WikiLeaks and credit card companies and PayPal halting payment services. Assange also faced extradition from the United Kingdom when Swedish authorities summoned him in connection to accusations of rape and the U.S. Attorney General authorized a criminal investigation. Released on bail, Assange took refuge in the London Ecuadorian Embassy.

Regarding PFC Manning, he was charged with violating a number of army regulations by placing unauthorized software on a classified computer, transferring information to a personal computer, and violating federal laws for handling government documents. In 2012, he was officially charged with aiding the enemy, transmitting national defense information, stealing public property/records, and causing intelligence information to be posted on the Internet. Manning subsequently pled guilty to 10 of the 22 charges brought against him. In 2013, a military judge sentenced Manning to 35 years in prison.

The second, more recent example involves a U.S. National Security Agency employee, Edward Snowden, who leaked NSA information regarding a domestic electronic surveillance program called "Prism." This secret NSA effort collected records regarding domestic telephone calls and overseas Internet activity by U.S. residents. The release of information about the nature and existence of Prism created a public outcry about government-based surveillance programs of U.S. citizens. Proponents of Prism argue that such programs have prevented attacks against the United States. Opponents argue that they are an unnecessary intrusion and unconstitutional abuse of government power. The debate and the Snowden case remain unresolved.

SOURCES: WashingtonPost.com (Feb 8, 2011). Timeline of the WikiLeaks cable release. Retrieved from: http://www .washingtonpost.com/wp-srv/special/world/wikileaks-julian-assange-timeline/ WashingtonPost.com (Nov 29, 2010); WikiLeaks's unveiling of secret State Department cables exposes U.S. diplomacy. Retrieved from:http://www .washingtonpost.com/wp-dyn/content/article/2010/11/28/AR2010112802395.html CNN.com (Jun 17, 2013); Details on NSA-thwarted plots coming, lawmaker says. Retrieved from:http://www.cnn.com/2013/06/17/politics/nsa-up-to -speed/index.html?iref=allsearch CNN.com (Jun 15, 2013); Holder: Leaks damaged US security. Retrieved from: http://www.cnn.com/2013/06/14/world/europe/nsa-leaks/index.html?iref=allsearch CNN.com (Jun 3, 2013); and Hero or traitor? Bradley Manning's court-martial set to start Monday. Retrieved from: http://www.cnn.com/2013/ 06/02/us/manning-court-martial/index.html?iref=allsearch

Reporters' Privilege and Shield Laws

On the opposite side of the access to knowledge issue, the media sometimes possess information that the courts or law enforcement officials want but that reporters do not want to provide. Controversy generally revolves around journalists' claims to

the right of a **privileged conversation.** Journalists argue that they should be protected from having to divulge information or identify their sources to the same
extent that communications between husbands and wives, attorneys and clients,
priests and penitents, and psychiatrists and patients are protected. In each of the latter
relationships, the courts cannot compel disclosure. Journalists argue that to fulfill
their constitutional function as watchdogs of government activities and to guarantee
their access to information, their news sources must be similarly protected. Opponents to the extension of privileged protection to media sources have argued that
the media should have no more protections or privileges than the average citizen,
whose duty to provide testimony in criminal matters has been regularly affirmed.

Paralleling media efforts for recognition of a constitutional right to privileged
conversation protection, the media have also lobbied for **shield laws**, or legislative protection from forced divulgence. The first reporters' shield law was passed
in Baltimore, Maryland, in 1896. Since then, the media have continued to lobby
successfully for shield laws with 40 states and the District of Columbia having
enacted reporter shield laws.[59] Most qualify the protection afforded reporters
and provide a judicial test to be applied to assess whether the media's information
is relevant and whether it can be obtained from other sources.[60] The effectiveness of shield laws is questionable, though, as the protection they afford the
media is subject to state court interpretations and judicial rulings.[61] Often the
degree to which reporters are shielded depends not on what a state's laws say
but on a judge's attitude toward the press.[62] A second serious deficiency with
state shield laws is that they operate only within each state, and contemporary
news organizations are national and international in scope. Because of these deficiencies, few journalists believe their state's shield laws provide substantial help in
protecting confidential files or preventing forced testimony.

A recent issue regarding journalists and courts concerns how journalists should
be defined by the courts and thus covered by reporter's privileges. The emergence
of online bloggers has raised the question of whether they qualify as journalists and
are entitled to the same legal protections as mainstream media reporters.[63] Who is
a 'journalist' in the new media era, where anyone can publish their opinions,
thoughts, and reports, remains an unanswered question. The courts have begun
to address this question and in initial state appeals court decisions have stated that
simply being a blogger does not qualify an individual for shield law protection. In
a "quack like a duck" requirement, a blogger must look and act like a traditional
journalist to expect to be shielded like a news journalist. First, an affiliation with
traditional news media should exist. Second, a blogger must prove intent to disseminate collected information to the general public. And third, information must
be obtained in the course of professional newsgathering activity.[64] The broad
application of these guidelines would mean that some online bloggers would be
protected by their state shield laws, but most would not.

Currently, the media are seldom asked to provide information. But due to the
absence of new Supreme Court decisions, a narrow interpretation of shield statutes
at the state level has occurred and there has been a subsequent concern over the
erosion of journalist protections.[65] When judges and law enforcement personnel
do request information, reporters can usually be forced to divulge it—especially if

the information can be shown to be central to a case and the information is unavailable from other sources. The media's efforts have made obtaining their information more costly, time consuming, and difficult, and in that sense they have successfully increased control of their knowledge. But like the courts them-selves, the media are now also more open to inspection and more often pressed for access and information from nongovernmental sources such as citizen and lobby groups. Ironically, the very process of access that the media initiated has cycled back to affect their own social reality.

THE COURTS AS TWENTY-FIRST-CENTURY ENTERTAINMENT

Today phrases such as "government in the sunshine" and "freedom of information" reflect a larger, media-driven social trend toward greater openness of public institu-tions. The two social institutions involved in this trend, the media and the criminal justice system, play critical roles. It was inevitable that the courts, as central players in these struggles, would be pressured by the media, especially social media, to open their institutions to scrutiny (see Box 6.6). Simultaneously, the media have also felt the pressure to open their institutions, processes, and files and have suffered through their own exposés of backstage activities. For better or worse, the courts and media are tightly coupled in the twenty-first century, where both internal courthouse and external media audiences dance to an infotainment tune.

The place where the change in the dance is most readily observed is in the courtroom. In the process of defending or prosecuting, lawyers construct reality and reach into the popular culture for images and symbols for their narratives. The popular characters and plot lines serve as the building blocks for courtroom social reality construction by evoking what "everybody knows" about the world. Thus, prosecuting attorneys invoke the mystery narrative to deliver an evidence-based story to jurors; defense attorneys counter with a beleaguered hero narrative to construct their client as the innocent victim of state power.[66] As the dominant media in the United States have moved from print to visuals, so has the style of legal story construction. Today, one is much more likely to see visual represen-tations in courtrooms: videos, computer-based animations, and re-enactments that reflect the influence of the new digital media.[67] The end result is that info-tainment has worked its way into court proceedings.

Commenting on this process regarding a case that involved a babysitter's sexual affair with the baby's father and her shooting the baby's mother, Richard Sherwin states:

> The role of the litigator, unlike that of journalist, is to come up with a narrative truth [or social construction] that can successfully compete against a counter-narrative [a competing social construction] offered by the other side. Consider the case of Amy Fisher. In the sense of the prosecution Amy Fisher represented threats to the established moral order. As a consequence, [she] would have to pay the penalty for her

Box 6.6   The Legacy of CourtTV

CourtTV (today called truTV) was created in 1991 with two goals: it would entertain viewers with real-life legal dramas and would teach them about the judicial system. CourtTV featured continuous live trial coverage as its programming core. Its philosophy regarding content distinguished CourtTV from other then-available crime-and-justice media content. Trial selection employed an infotainment filter and CourtTV producers looked for melodrama, popular issues, and charismatic lawyers. Over its history, CourtTV has broadcast the majority of its cases along the lines of abuse of power, sinful rich, and evil strangers. CourtTV's style of trial coverage created the now common news media use of on-screen crawl lines and subtitles, the use of attorneys as anchorpersons and reporters, and the use of subject area experts to explain scientific tests and to provide background information. It was the date-rape trial of William Kennedy Smith, a member of the Massachusetts Kennedy family, in 1991 that first brought CourtTV national prominence. Ratings continued to increase with the trial of Lorena Bobbitt in 1994, a wife who had severed her husband's penis and argued a defense of spousal rape. After the O. J. Simpson trial in 1995, ratings declined, and CourtTV began to expand to non-court related content.

Both positive and negative effects of CourtTV's style of coverage have been argued. Proponents argued that gavel-to-gavel coverage resulted in an improved public view of justice by examining significant social issues, providing understanding of criminal trial procedures, teaching the public the importance of legal technicalities such as rules of procedure and evidence, and enhancing public monitoring of elected officials. Supporters saw CourtTV as painless legal education and noted that not a single overturned decision resulted from its coverage. It is inarguable that CourtTV provided a more complete picture, at least of one judicial trial, over then-existing news, entertainment, and infotainment content. CourtTV effectively exposed the judiciary and criminal procedures to public scrutiny.

On the other hand, opponents argued that as CourtTV was a commercial venture, an unavoidable profit motive would drive sex and drama cases to be overly selected for broadcast. It was argued that in many ways, CourtTV was as misleading as any prime time legal drama because their cameras broadcast more than the jury ever heard, confusing the viewing public when verdicts differed from the infotainment-formed public consensus. Because juries had access to only legally relevant evidence, while the viewing public had access to both legally relevant and infotainment knowledge, the concern was that coverage increased public mistrust of the system when jury verdicts clashed with public perceptions of guilt, such as in the O. J. Simpson trial. This concern is related to the larger phenomenon of public injection into trials as pseudo-arbiters. CourtTV content bias included portraying trials as common (continuing the backwards law) and the glamorization of litigation by making murder and other violent crime trials the center of the legal universe (ignoring that most cases in the criminal justice system are plea bargained and involve theft). These portrayals of a snippet of justice provided a deep picture of a small but very entertaining part of the entire system.

transgression. On the side of the defense, Fisher would be framed within a counter-narrative. The image of Lolita gives way to "the poor unfortunate," the victim…. In Fisher's case, it is a story of psychological disturbance and parental complacency in the face of her increasingly desperate, and futile, cries for help … [established social] myths and

The impact of CourtTV is difficult to determine. Notwithstanding the concerns, CourtTV represented an improvement over prior trial coverage. CourtTV also laid the foundation for a popular set of entertainment television programs such as *Law and Order* and *The Practice* based on inside backstage views of the criminal justice system. The main social effect was that America changed into a nation of vicarious jurors. The foundation for today's Internet-based viewer participation in criminal cases was established in the trials broadcast by CourtTV. However, studies of a direct relationship between watching CourtTV and perceptions show that viewers thought they had learned something from watching a CourtTV trial but had not learned anything substantial. For example, it was found that a substantial portion of CourtTV's viewing audience did not learn criminal or civil law fundamentals. However, CourtTV viewers did understand that CourtTV trials were the exception, not the norm.

In sum, as a result of CourtTV the criminal justice system as a whole is covered today in greater detail by all media. Following its premiere in 1991, all other networks and news stations have come to follow the CourtTV style of courtroom reporting. In a now-accepted infotainment style, today's media generally focus on stories about the external life of trial participants and work to have viewers emotionally invest in trial outcomes. The final legacy of CourtTV is today's gavel-to-gavel judicial infotainment. Currently, the descendant of CourtTV, truTV, has branched out into more infotainment "caught on video" reality programs, or as truTV calls it, "actuality" television. TruTV also maintains truTV video, a streaming video player, where viewers "can watch footage of car chases, dumb criminals, gun fights, drunk drivers, drug busts, naughty girls, police, things that blow up, taser attacks, naked thieves and more!" Crime and justice as infotainment marches on.

SOURCES: Bennack, F., May 1999. The National Conference on Public Trust and Confidence in the Justice System, Washington, D.C; Brill, S. July, 1994. "Letters: Personal Grudge?" *ABA Journal 80*, p. 10; Courtroom Television Network, 1992. *Viewer's Guide 24* cited by Nasheri, 2002, p. 31 in *Crime and Justice in the Age of Court TV*; Cox, D. and Jan, G. 29, 1996. "Lights, Camera, Justice?" *The National law Journal*, p. A12; Cripe, K. L. 1999. "Empowering the Audience: Television's Role in the Diminishing Respect for the American Judicial System." *UCLA Entertainment Law Review 6* pp. 235–281; Dershowitz, A. May 1994. "At Issue: Court TV." *ABA Journal 80*, p. 46; Doug J. 2002. "Executive Vice President and General Counsel of Court TV", N.Y, interview cited by Hasheri 2002, p. 50 in *Crime and Justice in the Age of Court TV*; Harris, D. 1993. "The Appearance of Justice: Court TV, Conventional Television, and Public Understanding of the Criminal Justice System." *Arizona Law Review 35* p. 785; Keygier, M. K. 1995. "The Thirteenth Juror: Electronic Media's Struggle to Enter State and Federal Courtrooms." *The Catholic University of America CommLaw Conspectus 3*, p. 785; Nasheri, H. 2002. *Crime and Justice in the Age of Court TV*. New York: LFB Scholarly Publishing, LLC; Paul, A. 1997. "Turning the Camera on CourtTV: Does Televising Trials Teach Us Anything About Real Law?" *Ohio State Law Journal 58*, p. 655; Podlas, K. 2001. "Please Adjust Your Signal: How Television's Syndicated Courtrooms Bias Our Juror Citizenry. "*American Businesses Law Journal 39* p. 1; Rapping, E. 2003. *Law and Justice as Seen on TV*. New York: New York University Press; Surette, R. 2012. "21st Century Crime and Justice, New Media, and Maximizing Audience Participation." *Pop Culture Universe: Icons, Idols, Ideas*. ABC-CLIO, 2012. Web. 12 Dec. 2012; Sullivan, T. 1999. "Sullivan Special Project Producer, CourtTV," interview cited by Nasheri 2002, p. 32 in *Crime and Justice in the Age of Court TV*; and Takata, S. 2006. "Review: Crime and Justice in the Age of Court TV." *Criminal Justice Review 31*, pp. 389–391. www.trutv.com downloaded May 12, 2009.

archetypes contribute to this process. When a crime occurs, the media, and in time the lawyers for the parties involved, struggle to come up with the most compelling means [to present their construction] conveying what occurred and what it means. In this way, Amy Fisher comes to be known as "the Long Island Lolita."[68]

In their utilization of narratives, the courts provide a perfect small-scale model of the social construction process. For the internal judicial audience, two constructions of reality are created by competing claims makers who use factual and interpretative claims (evidence and explanations) and submit them to an audience (judges and jurors) that chooses and validates one or the other (guilty or not guilty verdicts). The media have tapped into this internal judicial social construction process and transformed the judicial system into a massive public infotainment machine. Attorneys, judges, defendants, witnesses, and victims sometimes protest, but more often they embrace their celebrity status and the chance to play a leading role. The courts have found their place in the twenty-first-century world of media, crime, and justice. The judiciary functioning as a combination studio and production company is where the most popular and gripping crime-and-justice dramas are today cast and marketed.[69]

The impact of new social media on the judicial system and the media trial production process is multiple. In a positive effect, new media have raised low visibility events and lower appellate courts to higher public visibility. New media has helped to "brighten the shadows" of some elements of the courts and justice. In a negative effect, they have increased the difficulty of insulating jurors, witnesses, and other participants from outside information and influences. Lastly, they have increased the general challenge of conducting high profile trials by increasing the pressure for continuous and live reporting, by more often turning local trials into national judicial events, by creating greater demand for trial access from bloggers, and by generating more demand for wi-fi capable courtrooms.[70]

All these developments can be understood as a broad social reconstruction of the courts by the media simultaneously carried on within entertainment, news, and infotainment media. The notable transformation of attorneys from lawyers to crime fighters in the entertainment media is one indicator of the wider social ideological transition from left to right and the shift of the courts from a closed judicial system to an open source of public entertainment.[71] Today, the courts struggle to construct public images that better align with their traditional social reality—that of the courts as fair, impartial institutions that determine truth and dispense justice based on the rule of law. To what extent new media will further degrade this historical construction remains to be determined, but the current public expectations and media content are clearly steered by infotainment values.[72] For the near future, it appears that the judicial system will be seen more as a source of entertainment than a source of justice. Another set of criminal justice institutions would also like to reconstruct its media portrait. Corrections have fared even worse than the courts and Chapter 7 explores the historically poor media–corrections relationship.

SUMMARY

- The media portrait of the courts is unrealistically constructed as a source of drama and infotainment. Rare real-world events and activities are common; common judicial procedures and attorney activities are rare.

- The courts are alluded to as soft on crime, easy on criminals, due process-laden institutions that repeatedly release the obviously guilty and dangerous.

- When they are not crime fighters, attorneys can expect to be portrayed negatively in the media.

- Female attorneys are frequently defeminized as career women or shown as sexual creatures forwarding the incompatibility of the social roles of attorney and woman.

- Media trials which regularly appear every three to five years involve commodified and mass marketed cases displayed as massive infotainment products. The three most common types utilize narratives taken from entertainment media: abuse of power, sinful rich, and evil strangers.

- New media provide a means for the public to be active media trial participants rather than just trial followers.

- The U.S. Supreme Court reversed its view of courtroom television from the *Estes* to the *Chandler* cases and after being banned for much of the last century, live television coverage has become a common element in newsworthy trials.

- Prejudicial publicity has been the greatest concern regarding court-related news coverage.

- There are two strategies for dealing with pretrial publicity. Proactive mechanisms include closure, restrictive, and protective orders; reactive steps include expanded jury selection, granting trial continuances, granting changes of venue, sequestering jurors, and jury instructions.

- Journalists argue that they should be protected from having to divulge information or identify their sources in order to fulfill their constitutional function as watchdogs of government activities and to guarantee their access to information. The news media has also lobbied for shield laws, or legislative protection from having to divulge information.

- The courts' place in the twenty-first century is as a combination studio and production company where the most popular and gripping crime-and-justice dramas are cast and marketed.

CLASS DISCUSSIONS

1. Discuss how a trial by jury is a small-scale example of social constructionism.
2. View and discuss the portrait of the judicial system found in a commercial courtroom film, discuss if the criminal law is shown in a positive or a negative light.
3. Discuss how case processing in real courtrooms compares with those shown in the media.
4. Discuss how crime shows violate an adherence to due process protections. Also discuss how civil liberties, judges, attorneys, and the judicial system are portrayed positively and negatively.

5. Discuss why, even though the courts determine what happens to offenders, media portraits of the courts are fewer in number than those of law enforcement.

SUGGESTED READINGS

Bailey, F. and Chermak, S. (2007). *Crimes and trials of the century*. Westport: Praeger.

Fox, R., van Sickle, R., and Steiger, T. (2007). *Tabloid justice*. Boulder: Lynne Rienner Pub.

Nasheri, H. (2002). *Crime and justice in the age of Court TV*. New York: LFB Scholarly Publishing LLC.

Sherwin, R. (2000). *When law goes pop*. Chicago: University of Chicago Press.

Bruschke, J. and Loges, W. (2004). *Free press vs. fair trials: Examining publicity's roles in trial outcomes*. Mahwah: Lawrence Erlbaum.

CHAPTER 7

Corrections

CHAPTER OBJECTIVES

After reading Chapter 7, you will

- Comprehend the common entertainment media portrait of corrections
- Understand the news media portrait of corrections
- Know correctional personnel concerns regarding negative news coverage
- Understand why television and infotainment programming give corrections scant attention
- Realize how media portraits of prisoners, correctional officers, and correctional institutions are connected to public support for correctional policies.

HISTORICAL PERSPECTIVE

"What we've got here is failure to communicate" (*Cool Hand Luke*, 1967). The words of the warden in the film *Cool Hand Luke* apply as much to the social construction of corrections as they did to Paul Newman's film character. The last step in the criminal justice system, the field of corrections, is also the last thought. Society has always been more interested in catching criminals and holding media trials than in what happens to convicted offenders in our correctional institutions.

In colonial America, jails and prisons were places to hold offenders until they could be otherwise punished, usually by a corporal method such as branding, flogging, or hanging. Corrections were of little interest as institutions or as symbols of criminal justice policy. Following the enlightenment, when loss of freedom became the punishment rather than just the precursor to punishment, societal interest in prisons, prison programs, and prison conditions increased, but never to the level of interest held by policing or courtroom proceedings. Corrections has always been the stepchild of the criminal justice system. The police get the glory and the courts get the public spectacles, but corrections— both monetarily in the real world and symbolically in the media-constructed one—get the shaft.

Like a plain child who puts his worst face forward for the camera, correctional institutions have contributed to their poor image. Historically, corrections suffers from its own lack of media sophistication. Correctional personnel have been notorious for poor media and public relations, frequently blocking access to inmates and staff, withholding information, and stonewalling in times of crisis. Fortress corrections has been both a mentality and a philosophy in the field.[1]

Despite the correctional field's historic adversarial relationship with the media, the media have played a strong role in corrections' public image. It is a tenet of social constructionism that the more remote the subject, the more the public perception of it will be shaped by media content. Unlike experiences with the police, who are seen in public daily, and the courts, whose institutions are prominently displayed in our cities and can be easily visited, few people have direct knowledge about corrections. Most of the general public has neither experience knowledge (from having visited a jail or served a correctional sentence) nor conversational knowledge (from talking with people who work or have been in prison). Therefore, most people receive very little nonmedia-rendered information about prisons, jails, prisoners, probation and parole, and other correctional programs. Access to direct nonmediated knowledge of corrections is concentrated in the poor. The affluent, who influence correctional policy more, construct their corrections reality largely from media renditions.[2]

Adding to the significance of this lack of direct experienced or conversational knowledge about corrections is the historical distrust between corrections personnel and the news media. The information flow from corrections to the media can be generously described as a trickle.[3] The scarcity of information about corrections from correctional personnel compounds the public's lack of experienced and conversational knowledge. Combined, the public's lack of direct information about corrections and the correctional field's inability to successfully get realistic correctional information into play in the news and infotainment media makes the public dependent on the unrealistic correctional images and stereotypes found in the entertainment media. Driven by profit motives, the entertainment media have not been overly concerned with projecting an accurate image of corrections. Instead, the entertainment media use the institutions as backdrops to construct stories of social power, personal morality, and action that have little connection to correctional issues. Box 7.1 displays the growth in the incarceration rate in the United States along with major developments in the media technology and noteworthy crime-and-justice media events.

Lacking other sources of knowledge, the public constructs its perception of corrections from the source most easily and consistently available. The limited visual images of corrections found in television programming, news, and infotainment shows and the print-based descriptions of corrections contribute to the public perception, but prison films have been by far the most influential sources for determining the social construction of corrections.[4] The importance of the prison film is due to the fact that books and magazines are less widely distributed and lack the visual impact of film. For its part, television has produced only a handful of programs based on corrections that have lasted beyond one season.[5] News stories and documentaries about corrections tend to be few in

B o x 7.1   Incarceration Rates and the Media

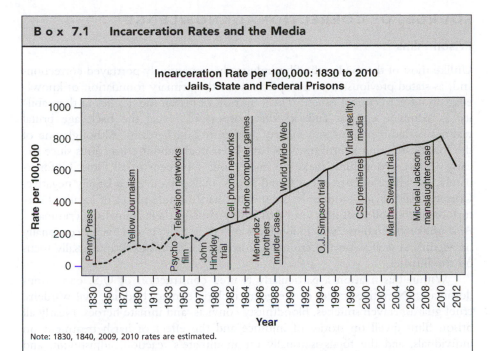

Incarceration Rate per 100,000: 1830 to 2010
Jails, State and Federal Prisons

Note: 1830, 1840, 2009, 2010 rates are estimated.

Noting that the far left side covers the 140 years from 1830 to 1970 and the right side the 40 years from 1970 to 2012. As shown, the incarceration rate in the United States has greatly increased since 1830, the dawn of mass media. The incarceration rate grew slowly for more than a century (covering the print and early visual media eras) before beginning a rapid increase during the electronic visual media era in the 1970s. Incarceration rates then hovered below or near 200 per 100,000 residents until the 1980s. In the 10 years from 1980 to 1990, the incarceration rate more than doubled. The rate continues to climb rapidly into the twenty-first century, exceeding 750 incarcerated persons per 100,000 residents. This rate is among the world's highest. A causal connection between media evolution and correctional incarceration rates, of course, is not proven, but the simultaneous emergence of harsh punitive correctional policies, pervasive infotainment content, and various types of new media in the 1970s is apparent.

SOURCES: Beck, A. and Gilliard, D. 1995. *Prisoners in 1994.* Bureau of Justice Statistics Bulletin, NCJ-151654. Washington, D.C.: U.S. Department of Justice; Beck, A. and Karberg, J. 2001. *Prison and Jail Inmates at Midyear 2000.* Bureau of Justice Statistics Bulletin, NCJ-185989. Washington, D.C.: U.S. Department of Justice; "Bureau of Justice Statistics—Table on number of persons in custody" downloaded April 24, 2009 from http://www.ojp.usdoj .gov/bjs/glance/tables/corr2tab.htm; Cahalan, M. 1986. *Historical Corrections Statistics in the United States, 1850–1984.* Rockville: Westat, Inc.; Harrison, P. and Beck. A. A. 2006. *Prisoners in 2005.* Bureau of Justice Statistics Bulletin, NCJ-215092. Washington, D.C.: U.S. Department of Justice; Sabol, W. and Couture, H. 2008. *Prison Inmates at Midyear 2007.* Bureau of Justice Statistics Bulletin, NCJ-221944. Washington, D.C.: U.S. Department of Justice.

number and negative in content. New media–based infotainment media that touch upon corrections exist but are usually divorced from reality, dominated by violent "escape from prison" video games. This leaves commercial films as the primary medium that creates and supports the dominant social construction of corrections.

SOURCES OF CORRECTIONAL KNOWLEDGE

Prison Films

Unlike most of the media, the film industry has extensively portrayed corrections and, as stated previously, motion pictures are the primary foundation of knowledge about correctional issues.[6] The attraction of prison movies lies in their ability to combine escapist fantasies that purport to reveal the backstage brutal realities of incarceration with tales of adventure and heroism. Although one of the longest-running genres (movies have been made about corrections since the early 1900s), prison films make up only about 1 percent of all films. Unfortunately, the image of corrections found in this small percentage is largely negative. Correctional movies commonly show either harsh, brutal places of legalized torture or uncontrolled human zoos that barely contain their animalistic criminals.[7] And unlike crime films, which also focus on crime fighters and even occasionally on victims as well as on the criminals, correctional films nearly universally focus on the inmates.

Within this fixation a particularly twisted construction of U.S. corrections dominates. Narrative staples of the genre include convict buddies, evil wardens, cruel guards, craven snitches, bloodthirsty convicts, and inmate heroes. Nearly all prison films dwell on stories of injustice and the effect of harsh treatment on individuals, and the focus is usually on an inmate's reaction, adjustment, and triumph over the correctional system. The movie world of corrections is a place where long-suffering virtue is rewarded and where, ironically, one has to look to the prisoners to find moral, trustworthy men.

Cameron Davidson/Alamy

Literally an island and thus a perfect icon for the near but isolated realm of corrections, Alcatraz has served as a popular setting for a number of films.

These correctional archetypes exist within fantasies about sex, violence, and salvation built around cinematic constructions marketed as "insider views" of the realities of prison life. Unique to correctional films are pervasive promotional claims of being based on a true story or actual event. Keenly aware that the public lacks other information sources, film producers' claims of being true and accurate are stressed more with prison films than with films about any other part of the criminal justice system. As criminologist Nicole Rafter observes, "No other genre so loudly proclaims its truthfulness."[8] But despite their claims of verisimilitude, prison films distort their subject more than other criminal justice movies. Except perhaps for the media portrait of superhero crime fighters, the construction of reality found in prison films is more distant from the real world than the entertainment realities constructed for criminality, law enforcement, and the courts. However, due to their validity claims and the lack of other information sources to counter them, prison movies remain the most influential correctional social construction source for the general public.

In an extensive content analysis study, Derral Cheatwood named four different prison film narratives: the nature of confinement, the pursuit of justice, authority and control, and freedom and release.[9] These narratives dominate and guide the stories of correctional life found in the media. Although the themes take differing tacks in portraying prison life, all four invariably focus on inmates and take an inmate's perspective. These narratives are found across the history of prison films, but Cheatwood identifies four eras in which each specific perspective dominates.

Nature of confinement correctional films (1929 to 1942) dominate the first era and are exemplified by classic films such as *The Big House, I Am a Fugitive from a Chain Gang,* and *20,000 Years in Sing Sing.* In this perspective, inmates appear as victims of injustice, either as good men framed or imprisoned by a chance accident or pushed into crime by powerful societal forces. A recurrent message in these films is the corrupt values of the correctional system and its administrators. This first era established and cemented the unique correctional backwards law common to prison films. In prison films the corrections backwards law works through a role reversal derived from the dynamic of the underdog, wrongly jailed inmates pitted against oppressive correctional employees. The inmate-hero was born in this era and has since dominated the portrait of corrections.

Pursuit of justice correctional films (1943 to 1962) dominated the second era, and *The Birdman of Alcatraz* and *Riot in Cell Block 11* are typical examples. Though they mostly featured a more hopeful narrative, these films retained a focus on violence in prison which they share with the nature of confinement films. In this era, however, offenders were portrayed as personally responsible for their actions, less often as victims and more often as criminals. Confinement is therefore justified, and the focus shifted to the flaws of the criminal and away from the flaws in the criminal justice system. Although many of this era's films revolve around violence—riots, escapes, and inmate and guard hostility—individual offender rehabilitation is seen as a possibility.

The third era, **authority and control correctional films** (1963 to 1980), is exemplified by films such as *Cool Hand Luke* and *Escape from Alcatraz*. This era reintroduced a pessimistic view of corrections against a continuing backdrop of riot and escape stories. Offender confinement is still justified, but it occurs for less serious offenses. This era is most significant for immortalizing the "smug hack" portrait of correctional officers as the evil foil of the inmate heroes. In these films correctional officers are borderline crazy, insensitive, and ineffective. Officer corruption is portrayed as universal. The world of corrections is constructed as a free-standing social ecosystem with corrupt correctional officers as just one of the system's species. Like the Galapagos Islands, correctional institutions are painted as isolated primitive islands, long separated from mainland society, where bizarre species have evolved to fill unique local niches. Within this isolated ecosystem, all facets of prison life became subject to exploitation, producing the first, if unrealistic, media portrayals of real prison problems—rape, racism, and drugs.

The fourth and current prison film era, **freedom and release correctional films** (1981 to present), is represented by futuristic science fiction films about prison colonies and prisoner transportation systems, exemplified by the films *Escape from New York*, *The Fortress*, and *Aliens 3* or by throwback renditions of early-era portraits represented by films like *Holes* and *The Shawshank Redemption*. Extreme violence appears for the first time in prison movies, and the "prison action film" appears. The ambiguity and confusion about the function and role of prisons in society is reflected in these films, which finalize the process of humanizing the inmates and dehumanizing the guards. In this era, the keepers are certifiably insane and are sometimes inhuman creatures or simply machines. Images of prison violence, rape, and death remain common.[10] The correctional world as constructed in these films reflects a fantasy comic-book-like world more than any recognizable social reality.

With this sometimes bizarre, always myopic, long-running cinematic base of misinformation, the public is more disadvantaged in constructing an alternate worldview of corrections than it is in constructing other components of the criminal justice system. The true issues and needs of corrections are absent or perversely distorted in these constructions. Prison films remain silent on the fundamental issues of imprisonment, reveling in violence and cruelty instead.[11] In these movies, the kept are the heroes and the keepers are the villains. In film, correctional institutions are as removed from their real-world counterparts as most science fiction films are from the NASA space program. Unfortunately, when the other limited sources of correctional information available to the public are examined and added, their contribution does little to correct the dominant prison film constructions of a world sprinkled with a few good men among a population of violent, crazed, sex-driven individuals. True to form in getting it backwards, in the media, more often than not, the best people are wearing inmate jumpsuits; some of the most crazed, violent, evil ones are wearing correctional officer uniforms.

Correctional Television and Infotainment

In television entertainment programming, corrections is the least-shown component of the criminal justice system—and therefore by implication the least important. Television has had fewer shows focused on corrections and they have been shorter lived than any other aspect of the criminal justice system.[12] The few television programs that have featured jails or prisons have either been slapstick comedy or featured inmates rather than staff. More often, television information about corrections is communicated through indirect negative allusions to correctional alumni, the recidivist offenders found in law enforcement shows. With habitual criminals outnumbering first offenders by more than four to one on television, media indirectly constructs corrections as ill equipped and unable to rehabilitate offenders. Instead, media imply that the corrections system is for criminals simply a temporary way station from which they frequently return to society as worse criminals than when they were sentenced. With the scarcity of programming that looks directly at corrections, perhaps the greatest impact of television on the social construction of corrections is as a means of extending the life and reach of commercial prison films. Television's recycling of the more than one hundred corrections movies made since the 1920s provides a continuous media loop in which corrections is constructed negatively anew for each succeeding generation.

The infotainment genre has slowly discovered corrections. There are now television programs with titles like "Inside American Jail," "Intervention," "Street Time," and "Parole Board" that mirror popular court and police counterparts. The delay in correctional infotainment programming is partly due to the fact that, as noted, prison entertainment films already market themselves as accurate portraits of correctional life. The public was told that it was already getting correctional reality programming in movie theaters. Even when greater media interest to create correctional infotainment products exists, correctional administrators have little incentive to cooperate. Coupled with the historical distrust of the media on the part of correctional officials and their reluctance to provide access, correctional content continues to lag in infotainment media. And due to the entertainment criteria that drive infotainment programming, correctional infotainment is not likely to result in greater public support for corrections. The historical impact of film documentaries that have focused on corrections substantiates this expectation. Correctional documentaries that have received widespread public play have ultimately resulted in negative attention and criticism for their subject institutions. For example, the documentary film *Titticut Follies*, which shows life in an institution for the criminally insane, and *Scared Straight*, which describes a popular shock incarceration program for juveniles, both resulted in criticisms of the correctional administrators and personnel and lawsuits against the institutions. Whether the current spate of correctional infotainment programs will improve the image of corrections, correctional officers, or correctional programs remains to be determined, but is not forecast as likely.

Corrections in the News

Contrary to common impressions, there is not a lack of attention about corrections in the news.[13] In a study of television and newspaper news, Steven Chermak found that 17 percent of crime-and-justice stories involved correctional institutions in some manner.[14] This is still substantively less than the level of attention given to law enforcement or courts, but corrections is not as off-the-radar in the news as it is in television entertainment programming.[15] Most references to corrections, however, are found inside stories focused on a different component of the criminal justice system or are found within stories that trace an individual offender or case as it progresses through the system. Still, about one-fifth of the crime-and-justice news at least acknowledges the existence of corrections.

Exemplified by the coverage of Lindsey Lohan's brushes with corrections (see Box 7.2), the mainstay. The mainstay of correctional news are stories about individual offenders. Chermak's findings reveal how correctional news is usually intermixed with law enforcement and court news and presented as the next installment in an ongoing story that originated as crime or trial coverage. News that focuses exclusively about corrections is usually related to an offender's commitment to prison, behavior on parole, or execution.[16] Looking at the total amount of crime and justice news focused on the separate components of the criminal justice system, the operation of the front-end focus of the news media on law enforcement is clearly reflected. News reports that concentrate on law enforcement activities (discovery of crimes through the formal charging of suspects) comprise more than 50 percent of news stories, court proceedings (pre-trial motions through Supreme Court decisions) about 30 percent, and corrections (probation to execution) less than 5 percent.

As far as the bulk of offenders are concerned, what happens to them in the corrections system is not a newsworthy story. Once they leave the courtroom, offenders usually disappear from the news unless they violate parole or probation, are released from prison, or are executed. News stories that discuss correctional institutions are found either inside stories about other criminal justice topics or within lengthy special reports, usually produced by the print media. In television news coverage of corrections, extraordinary events dominate. The more mundane aspects of prison management, legislation, and litigation are unlikely to appear on national televised news.[17] More developed and contextualized issue-focused news stories that discuss the daily operation of prisons, how inmates adapt to the conditions of incarceration, and institutional programs do exist. Unfortunately, they are rare and can distort correctional policies and practices.[18] In contrast, many news stories incorporate day-to-day police and court operations such as arrests, charging, verdicts, and sentencing. Nonincarceration aspects of corrections, such as probation or community corrections, receive even less media attention.[19]

Why do corrections fare so poorly in the news? A number of factors determine the quantity of correctional news coverage. First, compared to other crime-and-justice stories, corrections has a relative low newsworthiness value. News personnel do not think a defendant's correctional behavior is interesting to the public. Once a newsworthy individual enters a correctional institution and settles into the routines of correctional life, unless he or she does something noteworthy in prison, such as dying, the individual is not often again seen as particularly newsworthy. Second, corrections stories are difficult to produce because news media traditionally have only limited access to corrections sources. There is no corrections newsbeat that matches the police and court beats in journalism, so corrections stories are time consuming to produce because a pre-existing journalism–corrections link does not exist. The information channels and public information officers commonly found in police stations and courthouses, while increasing, remain absent in many correctional institutions. Third, reporters usually have limited prior knowledge of corrections and likely need to be introduced to the discipline during a breaking news story—almost always a negative one involving an escape, assault, or riot. Reporters do not maintain relationships with correctional officials as they often do with police or court officials. The weak news media–correctional personnel relationship is reflected by the fact that correctional personnel are the least likely of all criminal justice sources to be quoted in news stories, accounting for less than 1 percent of the total.[20]

On the corrections side of the news creation process, the closed environment of correctional programs helps to shield officials from external scrutiny. Correctional officials are more able to control information because media access to inmates is limited by law to a much greater extent than in the other components of the criminal justice system.[21] For corrections administrators, controlling information frequently translates into releasing no information. Prison administrators have a large number of justifications and mechanisms available to limit media access. Claims of institutional security needs; ongoing investigations; prisoner confidentiality, privacy, and rehabilitation considerations; and bureaucratic red tape (especially in arranging interviews) are common justifications to deny access. Delaying mechanisms include using uninformed personnel to slow the release of information to the media (corrections are the least likely criminal justice agencies to employ trained public information officers and to seek positive coverage, so the majority of prison news stories are initiated by the media), directing staff to present themselves as apolitical and inappropriate to comment on political decisions such as punishment policies, and simply being geographically isolated.[22] Ironically, the net result of these information blocks and delaying tactics is that newsworthy offenders are often pilloried by the media before trial, when they are still presumed innocent, and shielded from the media afterwards, when they have been declared guilty.[23]

But while they can limit media access using the above-mentioned blocks and delays, prison officials are not able to control the content of news coverage that does occur because alternate sources of information about correctional conditions are available. These include inside leaked information provided by correctional officers (this source is limited, however, by the historic media portrait of correctional officers as "hacks" and the resultant officer distrust of the media, job loss if their identity is revealed, and confidentiality agreements many institutions require correctional officers to sign); inmates (also limited because inmate interviews are usually severely restricted); and inmate families, elected officials, defense attorneys, researchers and academics, and prison support and prisoner rights groups. In addition, due to correctional administrators being less likely to have the media competing for access, they cannot use a need for access to influence the content of coverage. Aaron Doyle and Richard Ericson describe this relationship:

Box 7.2   Lindsay Goes to Jail—Corrections and Infotainment

Corrections receives an infotainment treatment when a celebrity receives a jail sentence, even a short one. When Lindsay Lohan was sentenced to jail, the event received international coverage. An example of the coverage and social construction of her corrections encounter from the ABC News Web site is typical.

Lindsay Lohan's Jail Stint: From 90 Days to Two Weeks

Lindsay Lohan's stint in the slammer could be as short as two weeks.

ABC News affiliate KABC TV in Los Angeles has learned the actress, who began her sentence today at the Century Regional Detention Center in Lynwood, California, has a projected release date of Aug. 2. Earlier this month, she was sentenced to 90 days in prison and 90 days in-patient rehab for violating her 2007 probation. Lohan could spend more time in jail because Beverly Hills Judge Masha Revel ruled out work release or electronic monitoring in her probation violation case.

Ten minutes late, clad in sunglasses that couldn't hide a steely glare, Lohan marched past a throng of photographers and glitter-throwing fans today for a pre-prison court hearing. She sat through a brief courtroom discussion before Revel ordered that all cameras be shut off for Lohan's handcuffing. The actress stood, placed her hands behind her back, and let two deputies cuff her and lead her out of the courtroom without making a scene.

From the courtroom, Lohan went to a courthouse holding facility before shipping off to the Lynwood facility. Before leaving the courthouse, she swapped out her jeans, sleeveless top, cropped jacket and corset belt for her new, albeit temporary, wardrobe: an orange jail jumpsuit. Shawn Chapman Holley, who resigned as Lohan's lawyer after her July 6 sentencing, represented the actress at the hearing. "She's stepped up, she's accepted responsibility," Holley said about Lohan. "She's scared as anyone would be, but she's as resolute and she's doing it." Lohan's surrender came two weeks after her tearful sentencing hearing, in which she sobbed as Judge Revel handed down her sentence.

What Lindsay Lohan's Jail Stint Looks Like

Lohan will serve her time at the same facility that housed Paris Hilton in 2007 and will be segregated from the general jail population. At most, she may only end up serving 23 days of the 90-day sentence. At the July 6 hearing, L.A. County Sheriff's spokesman Steve Whitmore noted that "female, non-violent prisoners will do about 25 percent of their sentence" because L.A. jails suffer from "an overcrowding situation."

At a news conference outside the Lynwood facility today, Whitmore said Lohan "has been extremely cooperative" so far. "As with any inmate, Lohan was treated just like any other," he added, noting that most inmates don't draw throngs of paparazzi. "Inside it's business as usual." Her time in prison won't be posh. Lohan will swap her plush bed for a vinyl mattress and her sprawling home for a 12-by-8 foot cell. She won't be able to smoke in jail or wear makeup.

According to a former inmate, today will be brutal for the 24-year-old starlet. "It is something you will never forget," former inmate Tanya told "Good Morning America" today. "When you get strip searched it takes away a lot of dignity. You are not in a room by yourself." But ABC News legal analyst Dana Cole said that for most of her time behind bars, Lohan will just be bored. "It's not going to be the worst situation imaginable, far from it," Cole said, noting that she'll be separated from other inmates for her own protection. "It's just going to be boring basically." Of course, because Whitmore noted that Lohan "will be kept away from [the] general population" of the jail, they may not meet at all.

Lindsay Lohan's Road to Jail

The days leading up to Lohan's surrender were anything but serene. According to People magazine, she spent a stressful weekend at the Pickford Lofts sober living facility in L.A. "She has not been able to sleep and has barely been eating. All weekend, Lindsay kept crying, chain smoking and chewing her nails," a source told People. "She is a nervous, fidgety mess, and her legal team, family and friends are very concerned about her fragile state." But the night before heading to court and then jail, Lohan seemed at least a little lighthearted. On Twitter, she wrote "the only "bookings" that i'm familiar with are Disney Films, never thought that i'd be "booking" into Jail... eeeks."

This will be Lohan's second time in jail. She spent 84 minutes in prison in 2007 after pleading guilty to two misdemeanor counts of being under the influence of cocaine and no contest to two counts of driving with a blood-alcohol level above 0.08 percent and one count of reckless driving. The year 2007 was also the year of two very public arrests for Lohan. She was sentenced to three years of probation but requested a one-year extension in October after failing to complete her alcohol-education courses on time.

Lohan is scheduled to be released from jail in time for the premiere of her newest movie, "Machete," in which she plays a gun-toting nun. Her legal troubles continued. On February 9, 2011, Lohan was charged with the theft of a necklace from a jewelry store. She was sentenced to 120 days in jail and 480 hours of community service for misdemeanor theft and probation violation. She was ordered to remain under supervised probation until the completion of her community service. Due to jail overcrowding, Lohan served the sentence under house arrest wearing a tracking ankle monitor for 35 days. Lohan violated her probation by failing to perform the required community service and was sentenced to 30 days of jail and 400 hours of community service. Lohan spent less than five hours in jail due to overcrowding.

SOURCE: http://abcnews.go.com/Entertainment/lindsay-lohans-jail-stint-14-days/story?id=11206049; http://en.wikipedia.org/wiki/Lindsay_Lohan

MARK RALSTON/AFP/Getty Images

Lindsay Lohan arrives to begin her 90 day jail sentence at the Beverly Hills Courthouse.

Prison officials are less able to offer "exclusives" or "scoops." Unlike the situations with police, the routine operations of prisons seldom offer news items for which media outlets will compete. As interviews with correctional officials responsible for public relations show, the chief messages they are trying to mobilize consist of "good news" about the system, such as stories about Christmas in prison or prisoners doing woodwork or growing flowers. These represent puny coin in the currency of crime news, compared to accounts featuring more dramatic fare such as official deviance and mayhem within the walls.[24]

Because the media do not have a daily corrections news need, which would give a correctional administrator more influence over correctional news creation and more leverage to influence content, negative coverage of corrections can be produced without much concern. In that there is no media need to maintain ongoing regular access to correctional authorities, the news media need not worry about burning their bridges to corrections; there is no continuous bridge traffic. Negative correctional news can be produced without media concern about subsequent repercussions or access restrictions.

The cumulative effect of these factors is that access to the criminal justice system as well as the resulting media content remains heavily front-end loaded. Compared with the police, who are sometimes eager to interact with the media and who work on the public streets, and the courts, whose main events are usually open to the public and press, the daily lives of prisons are far more shrouded. Normal correctional operations simply are not newsworthy. Therefore, most of the news of corrections that is produced is dominated by riots, escapes, and the release or death of newsworthy individuals—just like in the movies.

In the end, three types of negative stories typify correctional news. The first are stories about correctional failures to protect the public. These include prison escapes, staff negligence in supervising inmates, and failure to control prisoners. Second are stories of corrections pursuing inappropriate goals in which punishment is absent while amenities are highlighted. The description of prison partying by inmates, plush recreation rooms with cable television, and air-conditioned cells are the stock of these stories. Third are stories of **correctional horrors,** which are exemplified by corruption and misconduct exposés. These can be either individual bad-apple stories (the sadistic guard) or systemic corruption stories (the corrupt warden and administration), and they often employ the death of a preyed-upon inmate as the symbol of the correctional system's own criminality. As Box 7.3 highlights, when presented with a story that fills one of these niches, the media are willing to expend considerable effort and resources, at least for a short time, to explore and construct another correctional system gone bad.

In sum, the news construction of corrections is scanty, and when covered, corrections are marketed in a manner that emphasizes predators and criminogenic institutions. The day-to-day administration of punishment as a loss of freedom and attempts to rehabilitate do not fit common media narratives.[25] The prison sentence as a long tedious block of time where nothing changes is absolute anathema to the dramatic event that is necessary to be "hard news" or an engaging entertainment storyline. There are few dramatic rituals or events involved in prison life, and those that do occur are negative and involve death and violence.

Finally, just as in the entertainment media, news of corrections focuses on the inmates and ignores the staff. After a content study of 1,546 newspaper articles, criminologist Robert Freeman reports that negative stories about corrections significantly outnumber positive ones, and the positive ones tend to focus on inmates, not staff.[26] Thus, as also found in news of crime, law enforcement, and the courts, corrections is covered more often as an act connected to an individual than as an issue connected to a system. Even so, corrections news does focus on policy questions more often than do police and court news. Release policies, institutional conditions (usually as follow-up to riot, death, and escape stories), execution coverage (which sometimes incorporates the debate over the death penalty and the issue of the racial composition of death row), and the incarceration of juveniles and mentally deficient offenders, and the imprisonment of terrorists (see Box 7.4) all receive periodic coverage. In addition, news stories periodically appear concerning innovative correctional efforts such as intermediate sanctions, shock incarceration, or electronic home monitoring. A final irony of correctional news coverage emerges. Although corrections is the least covered component of the criminal justice system, it is the most likely to have its policies, missions, and basic functions discussed. Corrections is comparatively ignored by the media, but at least it is ignored in depth.

CORRECTIONS PORTRAITS AND STEREOTYPES

What are the portraits of corrections that are constructed from these information sources? The three most important ones involve the social construction of prisoners, correctional institutions, and correctional officers. The construction of incarcerated prisoners together with the construction of freed offenders discussed in Chapter 3 provide the public with its cumulative picture of criminality, its nature, and, most important, its amenability to rehabilitation. If inmates are constructed as incorrigible and innately evil, this logically leads toward correctional policies of incapacitation and capital punishment. On the other hand, if inmates are shown as victimized—basically good but misled—then policies of rehabilitation and resocialization make more sense. In essence, the more inmates are constructed as similar to the rest of us, the more it makes sense to offer more help and less punishment. The more they are constructed as different, as predatory and inhuman, the more sensible it is to permanently remove, punish, and execute them.

In the same vein, the manner in which correctional institutions are constructed is important for the correctional policies and programs that make sense to society. If the institutions are violent madhouses filled with irrational predators (inmates or staff), money for work, education, or counseling programs will appear to be wasteful. However, if the institutions are constructed as understaffed, underfunded places where humane correctional officers are trying to supervise large numbers of offenders, some of whom are redeemable, then public monies for these institutions and their programs will make more sense. Again, the more inmates are seen as like the rest of us—if there is a "there but for the

---

B o x 7.3   Correctional Bad News

Riots An Atlanta police source called a veteran police reporter of the *Journal and Constitution* with a blockbuster: The Atlanta Federal Penitentiary was under siege. "He said the [Cuban] detainees had taken over part of the prison and they might have hostages." The tip was passed to the day city editor. Within minutes, amid the normal pressure of an early deadline, the newsroom kicked into high gear. During the eleven-day crisis, the assistant managing editor would assign more than a hundred staffers to the story:

> We had constant updates for all seven editions. The Staff produced nine to 12 new stories daily. In 48 hours we did mini-profiles on 65 of the hostages plus nine others who had been released. And a 5,000 word history of the Marielitos and a 2,500 word piece about what life is like inside the prison.

Four extra open pages provided prison news each day. Photographers were stationed in helicopters, in cherry pickers, in trees, and on rooftops around the clock. Reporters worked shifts at the prison, and each shift included one person who was fluent in Spanish. A Spanish-speaking copyeditor was sent with a news team to Oakdale, Louisiana, to cover events at the federal detention center there, where rioting had begun two days before the Atlanta uprising. A Hispanic copy clerk monitored radio transmissions in the newsroom. Suburban reporters maintained a 24-hour vigil at Dobbins Air Force Base near Atlanta to alert editors if federal troops arrived. (They didn't.) The Washington bureau covered angles at the Immigration and Naturalization Service and the Justice Department.

  Escapes On July 30, 2010, three men escaped from the Arizona State Prison in Golden Valley. All three were serving time for murder. The fiancé of one of the escapees aided in the escape by throwing tools over a perimeter fence so that the prisoners could cut their way out of the prison. Following their escape, one became separated and one was soon apprehended. The other two proceeded to force a couple into their trailer at gunpoint. They then set the trailer on fire, killing the couple, in an effort to hide evidence. The second escapee was apprehended on August 9, while the third and his fiancé were caught on August 19. Following the escape, the state of Arizona and Management Training Corp, the company that runs

---

grace of God" reaction to the way they are portrayed—the more palatable improvements to conditions and programs in these institutions will be viewed. The more the portrait generates a "thank God they've locked those animals up" response, the more palatable punishment, long-term incapacitation, and minimum funding will make sense as correctional policies.

  Finally, the social construction of correctional officers is important, particularly if they are villainized. The more violent and predatory the staff is shown to be, the less attractive these positions appear to recruits as possible careers and the more the public is led away from putting money into corrections. Why give money to innately corrupt vile administrations or raise the salary of brutal guards? In contrast, a social construction of a humane staff striving to help salvageable inmates brings an opposite reaction. In that frame of mind, steering public resources into corrections would be sensible. With these implications in mind, the portraits and stereotypes of prisoners, correctional institutions, and correctional officers are described.

the private prison, faced a wrongful death suit regarding the death of one of the individuals killed by the fugitives.

SOURCES: http://www.nbcnews.com/id/38502099/ns/us_news-crime_and_courts/t/one-three-escaped-inmates-captured-colo/#.UecCn9JfExE; http://www.cnn.com/2010/CRIME/08/10/arizona.escapees/index.html?iref=allsearch; http://www.azcentral.com/news/articles/2010/09/03/20100903arizona-prison-escape-lawsuit-brk03-ON.html

Relatives of prisoners clash with Mexican police after 44 prisoners died in a prison riot.

Xinhua/ZUMAPRESS/Newscom

Prisoners

Two popular constructions of inmates are found in the mass media. One is for male prisoners and the other is for females. The dominant construction of male prisoners derives from the role reversal of a heroic offender caught up in a violent correctional system run by predatory criminal justice system workers. Those in authority are portrayed as predators and those caught up in the system are shown as victims. A minor portrait in the total media picture of law enforcement and court personnel, in the social construction of corrections such role reversals are common and result in a portrait that frequently sides with the kept rather than the keepers. Tapping into the American cultural tendency to root for underdogs, the irony of the media construction of male prisoners is that most of the predator criminals who terrorized society in the crime-fighting media content are reconstructed in the correctional media as victims. The predatory offenders who remain and appear in corrections media constructions are there to threaten the **heroic**

B o x 7.4   Terrorism, Corrections, and the Media

The ongoing war on terror has resulted in additional negative media attention on corrections. First off, terrorists as prisoners create new concerns for correctional personnel. Even a small number of ideologically dedicated terrorists in a prison population will generate a unique and significant challenge and raise fears of personnel, public, and institutional safety and security. Inmate terrorists increase the possibility of the radicalization of other inmates, the targeting of correctional institutions and personnel for terror attacks, and the operating of terror cells from within prisons. Correctional personnel need to be aware that they are viewed as soldiers in an opposing army and as legitimate targets by terrorists. Secondly, following the September 11, 2001, terrorist attacks and the Iraq war the number and dangerousness of imprisoned terrorists increased rapidly. Subsequent drives to prevent future terror attacks in the United States resulted in extraordinary correctional practices by the United States throughout the world and brought the previously disparate realms of military prisons, intelligence gathering, the media, and civilian corrections together.

Driven to deter future attacks in the United States and facing pressing counter-intelligence needs generated by the insurgency in Iraq, a subculture tolerant of the torture of prisoners held in U.S. custody developed. The world media eventually focused on three related story lines. The first and the most dominant concerned the abuse of Iraqi prisoners held in the U.S. military prison Abu Ghraib. Triggered by the 2004 release of graphic photos of prisoners being abused by U.S. military personnel and subsequently a picture-driven more newsworthy story, prisoner torture at Abu Ghraib quickly become an international news focus. Adding to concerns about the use of torture in Abu Ghraib was the emergence of the second news story line about secret prisons established and run by the U.S. Central Intelligence Agency in various countries around the globe. As with Abu Ghraib, torture of prisoners under U.S. control was alleged. The third story line followed the creation and operation of the military prison in Guantanamo, Cuba, administered by the U.S. military and set up to house terrorist and Taliban combatants. The status of the inmates generated legal challenges and, in turn, more negative news coverage.

Driven by these parallel streams, through the 2000s a steady flow of news stories demonizing the CIA, military prisons, and their personnel added to the pre-existing tradition of negative news construction of civilian correctional institutions and personnel. Today, the interplay of media, corrections, and terrorism continues with the trial in civilian court of former Guantanamo prison inmates. In early 2013, Guantanamo Bay prisoners began a hunger strike to protest their indefinite detention and treatment. One result has been the force-feeding of about 40 prisoners and a set of unresolved lawsuits aimed at ending the force-feeding. Demonstrating media content looping and the reach of the multimedia Web, a four-minute video was released in July, 2013 in which American rapper Mos Def (Dante Terrell Smith) underwent a similar force-feeding procedure but was not able to complete the process. Collectively, the social construction of these twenty-first-century correctional "symbolic institutions" extends the general pre-existing negative public perception of corrections with media examples of "smug hack" corrections from the real world.

inmates and to create an atmosphere of a constant threat of violence within the institutions. In total number, prisoners are constructed as violent and dangerous.[27] The inmate lead characters, however, are heroic victims.

If the male prisoners appear within narrow stereotypes, female inmates fare even worse. With remarkably few exceptions, female inmates are found in constructions containing high levels of gratuitous sex (primarily lesbianism and rape)

SOURCES: Berger, J. 2009. "Giuliani Criticizes Terror Trials in New York." *The New York Times*, November 16. Downloaded January 26, 2010 from http://www.nytimes.com/; Gerstein, J. 2009. "New York Terrorist Trial Raises Stakes" November 13, Downloaded January 23, 2010 from http://www.politico.com/new/stories/1109/29486.html; Grey, S. and Carvajal, D. 2007. "Secret Prisons in 2 Countries Held Qaeda Suspects, Report Says." *The New York Times*. June 8: A12. Downloaded January 19, 2010 from http://proquest.umi.com/; Hamm, M. 2008. "Prisoner Radicalization: Assessing the Threat in U.S. Correctional Institutions." *NIJ Journal 261*. Washington, D.C.: National Institute of Justice; Hersh, S. 2004. *Chain of Command: The Road from 9/11 to Abu Ghraib*. New York: Harper Collins; Hunter, S. 1988. "Terrorists in Prison: Security Concerns and Management Strategies. "*Corrections Today 50*(4): 30, 32, 34; Latanya, A. C. and Abeles, N. 2009. "Ethics, Prisoner Interrogation, National Security, and the Media." *Psychological Services, 6*(1):11–21; Priest, D. 2005. "CIA Holds Terror Suspects in Secret Prisons." *The Washington Post*, November 2. Downloaded January 20, 2010 from http://www.Washingtonpost.com/; Useem, B. and Clayton, O. 2009. "Radicalization of U.S. Prisoners." *Criminology and Public Policy. 8*(3): 561–592; Vogt, E. 2007. *Terrorists in Prison: The Challenge Facing Corrections*. Inside Homeland Security. Downloaded January 26, 2010 from http://www.nicic.org/Library/022793; Weiser, G. 2009. "Secret C.I.A. Jails an Issue in Terror Case." *The New York Times*, July 2: A20. Downloaded January 25, 2010 from http://proquest.umi.com/; http://security.blogs .cnn.com/2013/07/09/pressure-mounts-on-obama-to-stop-guantanamo-force-feeding/?iref=allsearch; http://www .cnn.com/2013/07/03/us/guantanamo-lawsuit/index.html; http://www.cnn.com/2013/05/15/us/guantanamo-crisis/ index.html; http://ccrjustice.org/files/Final%20Hunger%20Strike%20Report%20Sept%202005.pdf; http://security .blogs.cnn.com/2013/06/17/u-s-releases-names-of-indefinite-detainees-at-guantanamo/?iref=allsearch

Ron Sachs/CNP/Corbis

Prisoners sit in a holding area under the guard of military police in Camp X-Ray in the U.S. naval base at Guantanamo Bay, Cuba.

and correctional officer dominance and sadism.[28] The most common portrait of female prisoners is found in bad-girl, low-budget B movies that have been described as squalid mixtures of sex and violence.[29] The films reinforce stereotypes about female prisoners as violent, worthless, sex-crazed monsters.[30] Not limited to commercial films, this focus on violence and sex in female prisons has also been found in reality-infotainment newsmagazines, talk shows, and documentary programs which frame women's imprisonment in a similar fashion and focus on violence, sex, and failed motherhood.[31] Other issues such as drug, sexual, and physical abuse histories are downplayed. These images provide unchallenged negative and distorted images of female corrections, especially to young males who comprise a large proportion of their audience.[32] Overall, media portraits of female prisoners adhere to the backwards law and focus on atypical female inmates while ignoring the reality facing incarcerated women.[33] The construction of women offenders and female correctional institutions is so juvenile and ridiculous that it could be dismissed if there were alternate information sources to counter them. Unfortunately there are not.

Collectively then, male and female prisoners are often portrayed as victims rather than as offenders. The more normal and similar to law abiding people they appear, the more they are constructed as victims of corrupt correctional systems. Victimization of offenders can come from other predatory, violent, psychotic inmates or predatory, violent, psychotic correctional officers. Both clearly are more dangerous than the struggling inmate heroes. The message is that both the predatory inmates and predatory correctional officers need to be removed from the correctional institutions they are terrorizing. The constructed portrait of these institutions reflects the paradoxical construction of their populations—that reform must begin not with the prisoners but with the institutions and staff. Prisoners are either incorrigible and beyond rehabilitation and need to be separated from the redeemable or are the moral superiors to staff and administration and must not be brought down to their level.

Correctional Institutions

The media-constructed universe of corrections contains a galaxy of institutions in which the most sensational and dramatic correctional stereotypes are emphasized. The complex political, social, and economic realities of correctional facilities are ignored, and a corrections template that is stark and bleak is presented instead. **Smug hack corrections,** described as several interwoven portraits of negative correctional imagery, make up the media-constructed correctional world.[34]

Physical brutality in the name of inmate discipline is common. Control is maintained with corporal punishment and severe infliction of pain, often for trivial rule violations. This physical brutality is often linked with the exploitation of inmates as a cheap source of labor and profit. Staff incompetence, corruption, and cruelty are common, ingrained, and unchallenged. Under the thumb of a despotic staff, the prisoners suffer systemic racial prejudice, homosexual rape, and institutionalized violence. If female, the inmates suffer further degradation, sexual assaults, and harassments. Ironically, although the inmates are often shown sympathetically, the overall construction of corrections does not result in public support for correctional programs. The largely negative portraits of correctional officers and staff and the violent institutions they inhabit promotes a nonsupportive public image of corrections. Not only is this negative media image of correctional institutions the historical portrait found in film, but recent media depictions found in new media and in popular literature show little progress.

Correctional Officers

As pointed out, correctional media usually focus on the inmates, frequently ignoring the staff and administration totally, or, when they are portrayed, showing them negatively. The **smug hack** portrayal of correctional officers—caricatures of brutality, incompetence, low intelligence, and indifference to human suffering—dominates. This negative correctional officer construction creates a perception of modern corrections that remains locked in a pre-1960s frame of punitive human warehousing. The media-promulgated imagery provides the baseline for the public's construction of corrections and correctional officers. Whereas the police are heroic rescuers and the attorneys (at least sometimes) are the preservers of truth and justice, media-constructed correctional officers are, more often than not, oppressive villains. If not oppressive, they are irrelevant. In the media, incarceration turns criminal predators into imprisoned prey and villainous criminals into inmate heroes. These inmate heroes need villains to defeat, and the correctional staff members are enlisted to fill that role. The result is that the hero inmates end up as more sympathetic characters than the correctional officers who, along with stereotypic predator prisoners, appear as cardboard cut-out clichés.[35] The accompanying role reversal makes good theater and escapism, but it paints a particularly onerous portrait of correctional officers.

THE PRIMITIVE "LOST WORLD" OF CORRECTIONS

The prison is present in our society while, at the same time, absent from our lives.[36] In the novel *The Lost World*, by Arthur Doyle, an isolated primitive environment filled with prehistoric beasts is found to secretly exist. The media-constructed portrait of corrections shares similarities with Doyle's fictional lost world: primitive predators, bizarre rituals and tribes, a society ruled by the law of the jungle, hidden but existing near our own—there but invisible. Lacking direct knowledge of corrections, the public believes a number of corrections myths. Described by criminologist Ian Ross, these include myths regarding the quality of living conditions within prisons as either exceptionally harsh or luxurious; the perceptions of convicts' physical appearance as unattractive, their nature as innately violent, their guilt as unquestioned, and their redemption as unlikely; the perceptions of correctional officers as brutal, uncaring, and unintelligent; and the effectiveness of corrections as means to rehabilitation and as a cost effective criminal justice policy as low.[37] Not surprisingly, most of the myths are common in media content. At the same time, the media tends to ignore a number of correctional realities regarding the economic costs of high imprisonment rates, the pains of imprisonment, and the number of mentally ill inmates.[38] Due to their low visibility, the field of corrections is the criminal justice component where myths dominate the public's view more than found for the courts or police. Lastly, unlike the impact that they are having on the operations of law enforcement agencies and the courts, new media have not altered public access to or knowledge of corrections in any

B o x 7.5   New Media and Corrections—Facebook Fugitives

New media has made slow inroads into corrections in the form of GPS systems to monitor home confinement inmates and the use of live video camera links to conduct family and attorney visits. For good or ill, Internet applications have also begun to appear. Thus, a number of live webcams sited in correctional institutions can be found in a Google search. And carrying on the tradition of bad news dominating news about corrections, one jail escapee used Facebook postings to taunt police and merge "being on the run" with the communication capabilities of new media.

Fugitive on the run finds time for Facebook updates

He's on the lam, but Travis A. Nicolaysen still had time to update his Facebook page. The 26-year-old has eluded authorities since two foot chases Wednesday and a dragnet that included a police dog tracking him through a Port Angeles neighborhood. The dog came up only with a blue bandanna he had been wearing.

Travis A. Nicolaysen is shown in this undated photo taken by the Washington state Department of Corrections and provided by the Port Angeles Police Department.

meaningful ways. The impact of new media in corrections has mostly been connected with keeping the new devices and their effects out of institutions. Thus, correctional institutions are concerned with prisoner access to mobile phones and prisoner access to the Internet and social media. New media have not yet opened correctional institutions to public view in the way that the

His first day on the run, one friend posted to his account: "Cops all over you." Nicolaysen responded the next day with: "ya got away thanks bro." A post from another friend told him to be careful. Another urged him to surrender and set a better example for his children. "You're not getting any younger and you're looking at a lot of time," the friend writes. A picture on the Facebook page shows Nicolaysen with two toddlers.

Nicolaysen has been convicted of five felonies, including domestic violence, burglary and theft of a firearm, police said. He is wanted by the Washington state Department of Corrections for failing to check in with his community corrections officer since January. He's also accused of assaulting his girlfriend on March 28, police said. Better make that his ex-girlfriend. In a post Saturday, Nicolaysen changed his relationship status to single, the Peninsula Daily News reported.

Police are among those checking the page. "Absolutely," Deputy Chief Brian Smith told The Associated Press on Monday. "We're used to pinging databases and sources of information," he said. "It's normal for us to look at Facebook accounts." Smith also saw the growing number of comments on Nicolaysen's account—some of them mocking police—as he remained at large Monday. "I don't think it's going to make it any easier for him," Smith said. A lot of people communicate openly and can remain beyond the long arm of the law, at least for a while, he said.

Facebook tells its users that it may share certain information if it gets requests from law enforcement, and that it does have some ability to track people via IP addresses and GPS location. Serving Facebook with a search warrant is a possibility, but there are no immediate plans for that, Smith said. For now, police hope the publicity alone may be enough to flush him out in a city the size of Port Angeles, population 19,000. "In a smaller community, it's harder to disappear and be anonymous," Smith said. "We're hoping people who know him call police." "People are giving him advice" to surrender, Smith said, "and he might want to follow it."

While police find the fugitive Facebook posting a little frustrating, it's a source of glee for Teri Newell of Port Angeles, who says she helped raise Nicolaysen and describes herself as his aunt. "I think it's hilarious," said Newell, who confirmed the Facebook account belonged to Nicolaysen. "That's my boy, Travis," she said. "Every single time he gets out of jail, he doesn't check in," said Newell, who also complains that police are heavy-handed. She said she doesn't know where he is. "If he's smart, he's hidden away, tucked away safe," she said. Port Angeles attorney Robert Vienneau, who says he knows Nicolaysen, says the fugitive does what he has to do to get by. "Travis comes from a rough background, but he's got a good heart," Vienneau said.

An email to Nicolaysen from The Associated Press bounced back. Nicolaysen was discovered hiding in a basement a few days later, arrested and held in the county jail without bond.

SOURCE: http://www.nydailynews.com/news/national/fugitive-run-finds-time-facebook-updates-article -1.1058964 http://www.peninsuladailynews.com/article/20120417/NEWS/120419991/facebook-fugitives-new -status-arrested THE ASSOCIATED PRESS: Monday, April 9, 2012, 11:46 PM

review and critique of police actions have resulted from the ubiquity of digital cameras in the hands of the public has.

The impact of the media on the public's constructed portrait of corrections is due to its primacy effect. That is, like the adage about "making your first impressions count," the first set of information about a person, group, or organization that one receives has greater weight than later information because it creates an initial resilient perception. In constructionist terms, once a construction takes root, it is resistant to change. If the first information is negative, the unflattering initial impression created by that information will tend to dominate and persist even if later information is positive. For corrections, first impressions are usually picked up from prison films and other entertainment media and perhaps today from new media (see Box 7.5). Regardless of the source, the impressions are likely to be negative. They also are likely to be reinforced rather than challenged by information provided in the news and infotainment media. The impact of the initial negative messages is compounded for the public through its repeated exposure to the continually rerun prison films and recycled news footage of past prison riots and escapes. It is highly unlikely for the typical media consumer to have positive perceptions of corrections or to have his or her negative perceptions of corrections challenged in the current media environment.

Prison films, tabloid-style crime reporting, television programming, the focus on prison riots and brutal attacks by paroled assailants, and the less-than-flattering portrait of correctional staff and administrators comprise the foundation for the social construction of corrections. This construction has been blamed for helping to heighten the public's fear of crime; for eroding public confidence in the ability of corrections to deter, rehabilitate, or even retain criminals; and for increasing the public's desire to make the system more punitive for all offenders regardless of their offense history or forecast dangerousness.[39] Although there is no conclusive evidence of how viewers are affected by these works[40] and although there exist examples of prison reforms triggered by media exposure,[41] their media images are felt to normally translate into a lack of public support for real-life correctional institutions while ironically constructing prison as the sole solution to violent crime—in which rising criminality is viewed as proof of their necessity.[42] Like the police who gain public support when crime goes up, corrections, at least in term of more cells, gain public support in times of increasing crime rates, a tendency countered only when economics force institution closures and early prisoner release.

To this point the tour of the media-constructed world of criminal justice has made its way from the crimes and criminals, to the crime fighters, through the courts, and into the correctional system. In general, neither the criminal justice system nor its employees are positively presented in the media, and the further one moves into the system, the less information is available and the worse the constructed image is. How does this portrait of criminality and criminal justice translate into criminal justice policy? What public attitudes about crime and justice are associated with these constructions? Which steps to deal with crime are encouraged and which ones are discouraged? The next two chapters answer these questions. Chapter 8 examines crime control efforts based on media communication campaigns and media technologies. Chapter 9 looks at the media's influence on the public's support for various criminal justice policies.

SUMMARY

- The public is most dependent on the media for information about corrections, but compared to criminals, crime fighters and criminal trials, corrections is given substantially less attention in the media.

- The most prevalent portrait of corrections is found in commercial prison films, which construct prison life as violent and dehumanizing while promoting heroic inmates as protagonists. Correctional officers are often portrayed as villains.

- Prisoners are frequently portrayed as victims rather than as offenders.

- Female prisoners are portrayed within sexually charged sadistic institutions.

- Correctional institutions are portrayed as stark, bleak, violent places staffed by brutal, incompetent guards.

- The field of corrections has historically had an adversarial relationship with the news media and the news usually covers corrections only after a negative event such as an escape, death, or riot.

- Media access to correctional institutions and inmates has been poor and often blocked by correctional administrations.

- Due to the historical adversarial relationship between media and corrections, infotainment media has been slow to exploit corrections for programming.

- Corrections as an issue is seldom addressed in the media and corrections is constructed as a separate primitive world divorced from mainstream society.

- New and social media have not yet had an impact on corrections equivalent to their effect on law enforcement or the courts.

CLASS DISCUSSIONS

1. Discuss why bad news about corrections is more newsworthy than good news and what, if anything, correctional personnel can do to change the public image of corrections. Discuss who is most responsible for the content and nature of news about corrections—correctional personnel, administrators, journalists, news agency administrators, or the public?

2. Similar to the differences pointed out in Chapter 5 between media and street police, discuss the differences between media correctional officers and real world correctional officers.

3. Watch a prison film and discuss its use of correctional stereotypes and what correctional policies are supported or opposed in the film's portrait of corrections and prisoners.

4. Discuss how many criminals are portrayed as ex-prisoners in crime programming. Also discuss how often deterrence and rehabilitation are portrayed as likely outcomes of incarceration in the media.

SUGGESTED READINGS

Bailey, F. and Hale, D. (1998). *Popular culture, crime, and justice*. Belmont: West/ Wadsworth.

Freeman, R. (2000). *Popular culture and corrections*. Lanham: American Correctional Association.

Mason, P. (2006). *Captured by the media: Prison discourse in popular culture*. Cullompton, U.K.: Willan Publishing.

Rafter, N. (2006). *Shots in the mirror: crime films and society*. Oxford: Oxford University Press.

Wilson, D. and O'Sullivan, S. (2004). *Images of incarceration: representations of prison in film and television drama*. Winchester: Waterside Press.

Yousman, B. (2009). *Prime time prisons on U.S. TV: Representation of incarceration*. New York: Peter Lang.

CHAPTER 8

Crime Control

CHAPTER OBJECTIVES

After reading Chapter 8, you will

- Understand how the three types of Madison Avenue-style anticrime ads are employed
- Comprehend the increased use of media technology to process criminal cases
- Appreciate the growth of surveillance of public spaces and associated controversies

MEDIA AND CRIME CONTROL

It's rude to stare. We all have heard this common admonition. Violation of this and other taken-for-granted clauses of the social contract underlie the concerns discussed in this chapter. Much has been written concerning the media as a cause of crime. This chapter examines the increasing use of media and media technology to control crime and to administer justice. These efforts are historically rooted in the success of prosocial entertainment programs and public information campaigns. More recently, media technological advances, which allow easy recording, transmittal, storage, and review of moving images, further spurred criminal justice interest. Beginning in the 1970s these factors resulted in a number of media-based anticrime programs and the widespread adoption of media technology in the criminal justice field. Now common, these programs and applications can be divided into three areas: anticrime advertising, case processing using media technology, and public surveillance systems. This chapter examines how the adoption of media technology has changed the reality of criminal justice.

Public Service Announcements

Media-based anticrime efforts are targeted at three audiences: criminals, victims, and witnesses. Programs targeting criminals are mass media communication campaigns geared to deter offenders from future offending. Programs targeting citizens include media-based campaigns aimed at reducing victimization as well as solving crimes. All three types of programming are designed to reduce crime and are usually driven by crime control values. Conversely, critiques of these programs usually raise due process and civil liberty concerns.

Efforts to use the media to reduce and solve crimes are not new. The "Wanted Dead or Alive" posters on the Western frontier and the FBI's "Most Wanted" list are two long-standing examples of fugitive searches that employed available media. What is new is the rapid increase in the number of media-based anticrime efforts since the 1980s. With broad-based support, these efforts use the media to attempt to construct a social reality with less crime. The history of these projects begins with the ability of propaganda to negatively affect social attitudes established during World War I. Following the propaganda campaigns conducted during the war, projects to positively influence public attitudes using media information campaigns took hold in the 1930s.[1] Social planners and politicians set out to employ the media to generate planned positive changes in public attitudes and perceptions.

In the 1950s, media-based campaigns aimed at changing social practices in health and other areas began to appear. For a time during the 1960s, negative research findings led to widespread pessimism about the media's ability to influence audiences. In the late 1960s, however, bolstered by evaluations of **prosocial television** programming such as *Sesame Street* that found that children display positive social behaviors after watching prosocial television episodes, attempts were again made to use the media to purposely influence the public. Research revealed that programs of various types (animated, adventure, comedy, and fantasy) all had the ability to elicit socially valued behaviors from children and adolescent viewers. In contrast to the bulk of negative assessments of commercial television programming, it was concluded that properly designed television programs could have beneficial effects.[2] Encouraged by these findings, newfound enthusiasm for mass media developed in the 1970s with the expectation that media-generated positive social effects could be gained in a number of social areas—including crime reduction.

From this foundation, media-based anticrime programs proliferated. The current renditions utilize advertisement-like media messages and separate into three groups. The first group—aimed at offenders—employs ads designed to deter people from committing crimes. These anticrime messages are deployed in existing mass media advertising avenues as **public service announcements** (or **PSAs**). A second group of PSAs—these aimed at citizens—are victimization-reduction messages which often rely on the persuasiveness of celebrities with the goal of crime prevention.[3] Similar in form to the deterrence messages, victim-targeted PSAs use existing mass media outlets to distribute crime-reducing information and work to reduce opportunities for crime by inducing citizens to better protect themselves. In the third set, anticrime ads are designed to increase crime clearance and arrest rates by encouraging witness cooperation with law enforcement investigations. Table 8.1 summarizes these three approaches and their basic designs.

Media-based anticrime efforts have a long history as shown by the 1930s U.S. government produced film Reefer Madness.

Both the earliest and some of the most recent mass media efforts to reduce crime involve media campaigns aimed at drug abusers. Antidrug media campaigns have a historical tie to *Reefer Madness* and similar films produced by the Federal Bureau of Narcotics in the 1930s. Laughable and cumbersome, these films and the associated media campaign nevertheless facilitated the criminalization of marijuana in the United States.[4]

T A B L E 8.1   Three Basic Types of Media Anticrime Ad Programs

Program Type	Behavior Change Sought	Mechanism	Example
Targeting Offenders			
Deterrence	Voluntary reduction of criminal behavior by criminals	Deterrence	Anti-media piracy ads
Targeting Citizens			
Victimization-reduction programs	Adoption of self-protective, crime preventive behavior by citizens	Target hardening	Protecting yourself against identity theft ads
Citizen participation programs	Increased public cooperation and involvement with law enforcement efforts	Monetary rewards and anonymity	Crime Stoppers and police investigation requests for citizens cell phone videos

These early campaigns never generated the hoped-for deterrent effect, however. Although they seemed able to influence public opinion, they were not able to influence offender behavior. Evaluations of media–based antidrug projects during the 1970s first offered an explanation for the difficulties in using media to deter. The failure to deter was blamed on the inability to make drug abuse a salient issue for individual drug abusers and the resulting irrelevance of the media campaign messages to an audience of drug users. To be effective, it was found that a media campaign must tailor its content to a specific population, and that population cannot be simultaneously receiving competing conflicting information. The target audience cannot be simultaneously told in PSAs that drugs will ruin your life and that drugs are funny and harmless in movies.[5]

Because the early antidrug campaigns were unfocused and the content of the mass media was rife with prodrug images, the initial media–based antidrug efforts were fatally flawed. In reaction, subsequent successful lobbying efforts have reduced the levels of prodrug information in the media, and more recent media antidrug campaigns are better designed. Their evaluations indicate that well-designed media campaigns can significantly affect attitudes toward drugs among preteens, teenagers, and adults. Whether behavioral changes and reduced drug use follow as a result has not been substantiated.[6] As in other areas where the media are seen to influence perceptions more easily than they do behaviors, antidrug media messages are more likely to affect the attitudes of non–drug users about drugs than the drug using behavior of drug abusers. Available research indicates that the media appear best able to deter offenders involved in victimless crimes such as drug abuse by increasing their fear of health and social consequences rather than through increasing their fear of punishment.[7]

Another problem in using the media to deter crime is that offenders some-times display a type of anticipatory reaction, termed an **announcement effect,** to a media campaign. Evoked in offender populations, this effect occurs when media publicity causes offender behavior changes in anticipation of a new crimi-nal justice policy or program that has been heavily publicized. This media-induced behavior effect will occur with or without an actual criminal justice change. For example, a jurisdiction can reduce DUIs for a short time just by publicizing that they are instituting an aggressive, special anti-DUI enforcement effort. They do not have to actually have an anti-DUI unit to gain the reduc-tion; publicity about a phantom unit will suffice. Such announcement effects decline and dissipate fairly rapidly, however.

Announcement effects generated from the publicity surrounding the imple-mentation of new criminal justice policies and programs interweave with any effects from actual criminal justice changes. This makes separating the media announcement effects from those of the criminal justice programs difficult. New criminal justice policies have been acclaimed as successful by too quickly ascribing the media-induced change in offender behavior to a new criminal jus-tice policy when it is only the announcement effect that has reduced offenses.[8] The entrenchment of an ineffective criminal justice program or policy can result. Because offenders think that enforcement has significantly changed, they are more cautious for a while, and the new policy gets credit and is termed a success. Eventually offenders realize that the new policy or program is not meaningful and resume their offending while an ineffective criminal justice policy has become entrenched.

Victimization-Reduction Ads

Programs aimed at reducing victimization, usually by teaching and encouraging crime prevention techniques, obviously differ from offender-deterrence pro-grams. Victimization-reduction campaigns strive to increase the use of personal crime prevention techniques by citizens. Crime prevention falls under the umbrella of self-protective behaviors, which include avoiding health risks and other social hazards. Identified as key for triggering self-protective behaviors are people's beliefs about their likelihood of being harmed (What are my chances of being robbed?), the likely severity of an injury or illness (Will a robbery be fatal?), the efficacy of recommended precautions (Will doing this prevent a robbery?), and the costs of taking action when compared with inaction (How much time and money is involved?). Persuading people to adopt more self-protective behaviors is difficult because of the complex interactions among these four factors.

Programs advocating the adoption of behaviors to prevent possible unpleas-ant future events, such as crime, tend to be less successful than those that encour-age actions with an immediate recognizable reward, such as an increase in health from exercising or dieting.[9] In general, unless individuals are recent victims of crime, they do not see crime as a likely event, do not feel that they will be injured, see precautions as not particularly useful, and see better uses for their time and money. In addition, perceptions of the importance of crime and the effectiveness of preventive behavior vary considerably among groups. Like campaigns aimed at offenders, messages must be carefully matched to target populations to have any impact. A campaign to reduce elderly victimization by increasing gun ownership among them is likely to be unsuccessful for example. Adding to the difficulty of determining which campaigns actually work, victimization-reduction programs have rarely been adequately evaluated. The McGruff "Crime Dog" campaigns in the United States have received the most extensive study.[10]

Victimization-reduction campaigns are considered useful means of disseminating anticrime information to the public and sometimes influencing related attitudes, but they appear to affect behavior only marginally. More significant effects may be beyond their reach. That is, people will change how they feel about crime prevention and more will see it as a good thing, but few will actually begin to take additional precautions. To be effective, programs must tailor their message to their audience; focus their efforts on visual media, which seems to have the greatest impact; present simple messages; and directly and clearly instruct audiences on crime prevention behavior. Most important, additional local community follow-up and the creation of community support organizations such as citizen crime watch groups are necessary to achieve sustained effects. However, similar to the media's deterrent effect on offenders, based on the available data, media-based victimization-reduction campaigns appear able to affect people's attitudes toward crime prevention more easily than their actual involvement in crime prevention behavior.

Citizen-Cooperation Ads

Citizen-cooperation ads aim to increase the level of crime-related information made available to law enforcement by the public. These programs use re-enactments of crimes to obtain information (tips) through anonymous phone calls, dangling reward money to incentivize tipsters.[11] The logic is the same as the Most Wanted reward posters of the nineteenth century and the FBI's "Ten Most Wanted" list. Getting images and descriptions of wanted suspects and unsolved crimes out to as many people as possible and enticing reluctant citizens with monetary rewards increases the prospects for solving crimes and apprehending suspects. The innovation is using contemporary media to distribute electronic wanted posters, thereby enormously increasing the audience.

Development of these efforts raises a number of questions. The first and most obvious is what is their effectiveness? Do they result in more arrests and solutions of crimes, and are they an efficient means of generating information? Second is the question of the image of criminality that such programs project. Do they perpetuate stereotypes of criminals, victims, and crimes? Third, what is the proper role of the media in law enforcement efforts?

Handout/Reuters/Landov

The widespread distribution of digital images of wanted terrorists has increased as new social media has become a pervasive worldwide phenomena. Shown is U.S. citizen Omar Shafik Hammami (alias Abu Mansour al-Amriki) in an undated FBI photo. Labeled the "rapping jihadist", he was killed in 2013 by rival al-Shabaab militants in Somalia.

First, no one knows if citizen–cooperation programs affect the crime rate. The number of cases cleared is not great enough to expect an effect on the overall crime rate in a community unless one assumes a general deterrent effect from the mass media coverage. No effect has been reported. But anecdotal evidence does suggest that the programs solve felony cases that are unlikely to be solved otherwise.[12] They appear especially effective in solving cases involving fugitives, bank robberies, and narcotics and may be useful in antiterrorist efforts. The visibility of these programs also increases their effectiveness by attracting secondary tips for unadvertised crimes. Indeed, given the large amount of unsolicited information received regarding unadvertised crimes, crime re-enactments shown in the media appear to be more important as vehicles for obtaining tips regarding other crimes than as a means of solving the crimes actually publicized. Bolstered by supportive court rulings and by low operational costs, these programs are generally viewed as cost-effective and their continuance currently assured. Despite their support and successes, critics argue that their gains against crime are outweighed by other negative social effects. Paying for information from anonymous sources is at the crux of the uneasiness felt toward these programs. The fear is that paying rewards and providing anonymity for informants will reduce voluntary citizen cooperation and encourage malicious retributive snitching by citizens on their neighbors, family, and friends.

Second, because citizen–cooperation ads are presented as representative of real crime in a community, the image they portray has great potential to influence the social construction of criminality. Presented in news-like segments akin to reality programming, these anticrime ads focus on unsolved cases in the community committed by dangerous-looking suspects. The image of criminality shown in these ads is similar to that portrayed in the general entertainment media—that of a dangerous, crime-ridden world where violent attacks are common.[13] In addition, these ads are often produced in infotainment programming styles, with mood music, voice-overs, and heightened dramatic elements.[14] Furthermore, by emphasizing predatory violent crimes that appear to be due to greed or irrationality, individual explanations for crime and crime control-based punitive crime-and-justice policies are emphasized while broader structural, social, and economic factors are downplayed.

Finally, what is the proper role of the mass media in law enforcement efforts? Should the media restrict themselves to basic reporting of events or become involved in their resolution? Citizen–cooperation ads shift the media from their traditional roles as watchdog observers and reporters to active infotainment participants in investigating crimes and hunting fugitives. Some argue that the media should cooperate because it is their civic duty. Many news media agencies do not cooperate, however, apparently because they perceive involvement as contrary to the philosophy of separation of press and government.[15] How these concerns are to be resolved is unclear. Unfortunately, we have little independent data to support or lay to rest the expressed fears. We simply do not know at this time if the hypothesized negative consequences of citizen–cooperation programs counteract their positive anticrime effects. For one thing, we don't know how much of an anticrime effect they actually have.

Collectively, PSAs, victimization ads, and citizen–cooperation ads are popular, have demonstrated some positive effects, but have also encountered unanticipated problems. Success has not been as direct or as simple to achieve as first envisioned.[16] Despite their current popularity and transition to new media, their actual impact on crime levels is ambiguous. All of these efforts aim for behavioral changes in the audience to reduce crime, but most are actually designed to influence attitudes and perceptions about the reality of crime under the belief that attitude changes will subsequently lead to changes in behavior. All three of these media campaign types accordingly rest on a questionable premise, and they have not been able to produce hoped-for crime reductions. Regardless of these issues, their successes have encouraged the migration of media technology into the criminal justice system as a tool for case processing in law enforcement and judicial efforts. This is the subject of the next section.

CASE PROCESSING USING MEDIA TECHNOLOGY

In general, the ultimate goal in using media technology in criminal justice case processing is to simulate a traditional, live, face-to-face proceeding.

Unlike face-to-face encounters, however, participants in media technology-rendered proceedings must interact through the equipment, often testifying directly into a camera or participating by watching a monitor screen. In contrast to the use of media equipment in news coverage, here the technology has changed from a tangential, temporary visitor to an unavoidable, permanent judicial tool. New technology has introduced 'wired courtrooms' with eye-tracking cameras, witness stands with smart monitors, and other new media-based capabilities.[17] Media technology has been embraced as a means to efficiently process cases, and cost and speed are the usual factors considered in these applications.

Though the use of media technology has come to be widely accepted in the presentation of physical evidence and testimony, using the technology to create permanent records and conduct live proceedings currently enjoys only limited support. Expanded applications such as prerecording entire trials have been experimented with but generally have been rejected. The acceptability of media technology in the courtroom seems to rest on how much the media-constructed judicial reality is seen as different from the traditional judicial reality. For preliminary and short procedural steps, most participants, including defendants, appear to feel that the integrity of the process is unaffected. With regard to longer, more significant, and more symbolic steps such as trials, concerns and resistance rise.

Judicial System Use

In the judicial system, visual records of arraignments, first appearances, bond hearings, and pleas have proven inexpensive and useful.[18] A single memory device can hold thousands of cases and be stored as a permanent record that can be consulted should the state of mind of a defendant, his or her comprehension of rights or instructions, or the voluntary nature of a plea later be questioned. Once instituted these systems gain support from both crime control and due process advocates. Crime control proponents like the savings of time and money. Due process adherents feel the knowledge that a permanent record is being created makes law enforcement and judicial personnel more conscientious in following due process rules. Visual records of these procedural steps also provide a means not previously available of resolving any subsequent due process concerns. Furthermore, the same technology used in creating visual records and testimony also allows, if desired, the physical separation of the participants, thus allowing a judicial proceeding to be conducted in a new way—in live media-linked sessions. Judges and attorneys can now be in a courtroom, defendants in a jail, and witnesses in another state, all simultaneously participating in a live hearing. In the courtroom, interactions in "facetime" like encounters have become common.

Recent new media technologies have brought new issues to the table, however, including the digital manipulation of visual images. A CSI effect applied to visual evidence is a danger. The same tools that can be used to crop, retouch, and edit images can be used just as easily to distort, alter, and fabricate them.

This ability undermines the previously unquestioned validity that pictures enjoyed as evidence. The use of obviously faked but realistic-looking photos in advertising and entertainment—the creation of alien worlds, for example— repeatedly demonstrates the sophistication of visual deception. The uncertain validity of visual images has implications for the evaluation of visual evidence in the criminal justice system. The public is constantly reminded by entertainment media content that it should not automatically believe what it is seeing.[19] A problem is that photographic evidence in the courtroom will be viewed as less trustworthy. Ironically, new media advances may ultimately result in questioning all media-based information so that eyewitness and human testimony may regain its evidence dominance role in the criminal justice process.

In addition, when the traditional, familiar reality of the judicial system is drastically changed by the use of media technology, resistance to the new reality rises. For the now common applications of media technology, the alteration of the reality of the judicial system is connected to three concerns: the effect of media technology on working relationships among courtroom personnel, concerns about depersonalization of the criminal justice system, and the impact of media technology on the perceived legitimacy of the judicial system.

Comments from attorneys (especially public defenders) and judges indicate that the relationships among courtroom personnel can be upset by the introduction of media equipment between participants.[20] It is significant that in a number of projects public defenders remained largely skeptical of the advantages of processing cases through media technology. Unanswered questions concern whether attorneys deliver equivalent representation if they feel legally and organizationally disadvantaged in media-constructed proceedings, and if morale suffers, do their subsequent efforts on behalf of clients also suffer?

One concern is that expanded use of media technology within the judiciary will lead to further depersonalization of criminal justice proceedings. Adjudication within the criminal justice system has traditionally been based on face-to-face interaction, particularly that the accused are entitled to face their accusers. Extended use of media technology, however, will reduce live, face-to-face encounters between witnesses and defendants, police and the public, attorneys and clients, judges and defendants, and jurors and all the previous groups. These media-processed interactions will seriously alter the nature of the personal relationships within the criminal justice system. Technological advances that make this equipment more economical are likely to speed the process while advances that make the encounters more like live meetings will lessen the depersonalization.

The third unresolved concern is what is lost in legitimacy and the public image of justice when new media technology is employed. In addition to being a means of adjudicating guilt and administering punishment, the judicial system is also a means of legitimizing the whole social system—its rules, laws, and government. Accordingly, the judicial system and its personnel have a symbolic value. Loss of these symbolic qualities may diminish the aura of legitimacy sustaining the entire criminal justice system. From the social construction perspective, how the system is seen as treating individuals is crucial. If people become alienated from the system or if they feel intimidated or dehumanized by it, the benefits from using media technologies in the courtroom will be of little value. If these technologies ultimately result in the further isolation and separation of the police from the policed and the courts from the public, the social costs of such losses would outweigh any administrative benefits that accrue from their use. As crime control values become more popular, there is considerable desire, especially on the part of criminal justice administrators, to make the system more efficient. Nevertheless, the criminal justice system must remain legitimate in the public eye if it is to remain a viable system of justice.

Lastly, the visuals created by this technology are frequently used in news reports, contributing directly to the social construction of the public's image of justice. The criminal justice system will become, for good or ill, a less arcane, more open system as its procedures become more visible. The myriad applications of media in the courts have changed the reality of justice on many levels and have opened previous backstage judicial activities to public scrutiny. Ironically, although the courts are still wary of the news media, the judiciary's adoption of media technology has had many of the same effects that were feared from news coverage. The main concern remains whether this new reality of justice comes to be seen as impersonal, unfair, and unacceptable.

The greatest concerns with the use of media technology are not associated with its use in case processing, however. The greatest concerns revolve around the law enforcement use of media technology and the enhancement of law enforcement surveillance of the public.

Law Enforcement Use

After the development and widespread acceptance of videotaped evidence and testimony in the 1970s, **videotaped interrogations** were the first expanded uses of video technology into law enforcement practices. A videotape record was felt to provide more objective, fuller accounts of interactions between police, witnesses, and suspects, as well as evidence regarding the voluntariness of statements, suspects' understanding of their rights, police coercion and interrogation practices, and the physical and mental condition of suspects. Following pilot projects, most have embraced this law enforcement use of media technology. For example, a two-year evaluation of a Canadian experiment in videotaping police interrogations showed that the expected advantages of protection against unwarranted allegations of misconduct, the introduction of accountability in interrogation procedures, and the reduction in challenges to the admissibility of suspect statements were all realized.[21]

The evaluation further reported that suspects did not appear inhibited by the cameras and that the suspect confession rate remained the same. In fact, police, prosecutors, and defense counsel all came to support continuation and expansion of the project—police because it relieved them of the need to take written notes during interrogations and reduced their court appearances, prosecutors because it usually disposed of all legal questions surrounding the police–suspect interview, and defense counsel because it ensured that police more strictly followed legal procedures and because the defense could use the tapes to demonstrate their client's intent and remorse for sentencing purposes. The interrogation videotapes provided a record of the frame of mind and emotional state of a suspect much nearer in time to the commission of a crime than was previously available.

An increasing number of police departments also use media technology to record the booking of their arrests. These video mug shots provide a pictorial record of arrestees that includes voice, accent, and continuous front-to-profile views. These video records have also allowed changes in two traditional law enforcement practices—identification of a suspect from a traditional lineup and identification of a suspect from a set of photographs (a mug book) of known offenders. In a **media lineup,** a crime witness is shown a series of video bookings selected for their similarity. The witness chooses from this lineup the individual he or she feels is the offender. This process is felt to be fairer than the old practices in that the individuals in video lineups more closely resemble one another than the groups usually assembled for a live lineup, and it provides a permanent record of the lineup for later review should questions of fairness arise. In **media mug books,** a computer program searches a pictorial data file for specific characteristics (for example, tattoo, bald, heavy, white, and male) and displays matching images.

SURVEILLANCE

"You watched TV. Now it watches you"[22] neatly summarizes the past and future of modern surveillance. The police surveillance stakeout has a long history and has been an accepted part of police investigations.[23] Surveillance applications based on media technology have been in use for a number of years— surveillance cameras in banks, subways, and department stores are well-known examples—and have been expanded to include public schools, airports, highway toll booths, and other locales. The police have also traditionally used temporary camera surveillance of specific locations after obtaining a court order. While not a mass media technology in that there is no public audience that receives the images,[24] the increase in surveillance is considered a media effect for two reasons. First, the increase in surveillance is facilitated by advances in media technology, especially advances in visual communications. Second, the use of surveillance images in news and infotainment content contribute to the total portrait of criminal justice that the public holds. Enhanced visual media and communication capabilities and reduced equipment costs, coupled with concerns about terrorism, have created a strong impetus for surveillance systems that enhance the ability of law enforcement agencies to "police-at-a-distance" as well as increased academic interest in the effects of broad-scale surveillance.[25] Contemporary media technology has also changed the nature of surveillance from on-scene, with limited human observers and whatever notes they might produce, to the automated technological interception, recording, and transmittal of immense amounts of information. Drone-based cameras are expanding the surveillance capability to the entire outdoor environment while body worn cameras are extending it to all police–citizen encounters.

In the United States, surveillance camera systems have increased exponentially since the 2001 terrorist attacks.[26] Taking advantage of the **surveillance effect**— the psychological effect of fearing that you might be under observation— surveillance programs have expanded the traditional police use of the stakeout and hidden camera to encompass general public space applications.[27] Media technology has made constant surveillance of broad public areas possible and an expected norm in contemporary U.S. urban areas. Surveillance cameras permanently mounted on street corners, in patrol cars, in the air, and within and without various public and private buildings are common community features. The traditional uses of surveillance in stakeouts and banks differ from newer applications in that in the past, areas surveilled were small and public areas were watched for brief time periods. In contrast, the new surveillance programs use media technology in large public areas such as outdoor malls, downtown centers, parks, arenas, theaters, and residential streets.[28] Traditional surveillance was also aimed at gathering evidence for a specific case or deterring crime at a specific place such as a toll booth, but today the prime justifications for public surveillance systems are couched in broad-scale public safety and antiterrorism goals. The reality of surveillance has shifted from a rare, narrow, activity determined by a need related to a specific criminal case to a common, pervasive, constant presence. As the criminal justice system shifted its temporal attention from postcrime reactions, investigations, and prosecutions to precrime prevention, risk reduction, and target hardening, the historical idea that you have to be under suspicion of having done something to be brought under surveillance has faded and broadly targeted, automatic, continuous surveillance systems became the norm.[29] This potential surveillance of everyone whenever they appear in public and the simultaneous surveillance of all potential criminals and victims lie at the root of unease over pervasive surveillance.[30] Not surprisingly, the use of this powerful and intrusive technology has raised fears concerning its impact on society.

Contemporary surveillance projects aim to provide either retrospective scene analysis following crimes, deterrence of future crimes, facilitation of real-time intervention, or some combination of these goals.[31] Figure 8.1 outlines the three influence paths through which surveillance systems can affect crime. As shown, effects through law enforcement actions and effects on citizens and offenders are both possible. When and how these systems work in specific applications is still under study.[32] It is not clear, for example, to what extent offenders take the presence of cameras into account when deciding whether or not to commit an offense.[33] Irrespective of this and other unanswered research questions, adoption of camera surveillance has continued unabated.[34]

History and Issues

A surveillance effect that has raised concern involves the increase in surveillance based on new media technology and an accompanying loss of privacy.[35] A decline

The 2013 surveillance camera image shows the two suspects in the Boston Marathon bombing walking near the marathon finish line. Similar images combined with social media communications proved invaluable in identifying the suspects.

in privacy is intertwined with an increase in surveillance, so as the capability for surveillance has increased, the negative impact on privacy has become a criminal justice issue. Privacy and surveillance are often thought of as mutually exclusive states, one loses privacy to the level that one is under surveillance. However, beginning with Web 2.0, the direction of social surveillance somewhat reversed, and in today's celebrity culture, surveillance commonly originates from the bottom up, with numerous members of the public watching a famous few.[36] In addition, the phenomenon of self-surveillance, where individuals voluntarily make private information and images available to the public, has changed the expectation of privacy. The new media–based social sphere is a high-visibility, high-surveillance, low-regulation world. Standards for privacy and access are largely determined by businesses such as Google and Apple that provide the communication platforms and market mobile communication devices that frame the social media–based culture.[37] In this translucent new world, individuals do have some expectation of privacy, but it is fragile and fluid (see Box 8.1, Rutgers). The unresolved issue is who owns the digital content that is created and distributed through new media? Once content is posted on the World Wide Web for example, it is difficult to determine who has ownership. At this time, public concerns appear to be focused on protections from unreasonable government collection of the content; while at the same time many people appear willing to disclose much of their personal information to private entities, including businesses and Web-surfing strangers. New media has diminished the historical "reasonable expectation of privacy" standard and has

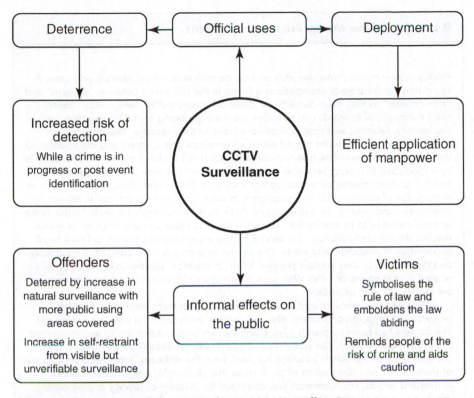

Deterrence ← Official uses → Deployment

Increased risk of detection
While a crime is in progress or post event identification

CCTV Surveillance

Efficient application of manpower

Offenders
Deterred by increase in natural surveillance with more public using areas covered

Increase in self-restraint from visible but unverifiable surveillance

Informal effects on the public

Victims
Symbolises the rule of law and emboldens the law abiding

Reminds people of the risk of crime and aids caution

F I G U R E   8.1   An Illustrated Model of How CCTV May Affect Crime.
SOURCE: Adapted from Williams (2007, p. 99) "Effective CCTV.

replaced it with a "reasonable expectation of distribution". Most users expect privacy while their information is in transit, but are not aware or not concerned with their lack of control of its distribution after its delivery. They expect their pictures and thoughts to be posted undisturbed but to date have worried less about who can access them afterwards.

The use of telephone wiretaps in the 1900s first raised the specter of surveillance abuse. Writing before the era of electronic eavesdropping and visual technology, Justices Earl Warren and William Brandeis predicted that "mechanical devices threaten to make good the prediction that 'what is whispered in the closet shall be proclaimed from the housetops.'"[38] The updated fear would be "whatever is done in the dark will be shown on the news." To understand the social impetus for these new surveillance systems and the likely future of police surveillance in the United States, one must look to the United Kingdom. No Western democracy has embraced police surveillance systems more than the United Kingdom (although the United States appears to be rapidly catching up).[39] The electronic recording of images and pervasive, broad-scale, permanent surveillance systems in use in the United Kingdom have resulted in the English population being described as the most surveilled population on the planet.[40]

B o x 8.1   New Media, Privacy and Content

Privacy in new media terms depends on how content is obtained, shared, and used. A key distinction for privacy expectations is found in the difference between "*content*" and "*non-content*" as they have come to be defined for new media. New media "content" can be thought of as words and speech—the message being sent. Non-content involves the identity, location, and time stamps connected to the message. The difference is analogous to a written letter placed within an envelope (the content) and the address on the outside of the envelope (the non-content). Court rulings have suggested that there is no expectation of privacy with non-content information because that information is needed to direct messages to appropriate locations. The sender does, however, have an expectation of privacy while the message is in transit and can expect that it will not be intercepted and read to the same degree that one does not expect a sealed letter to be opened en route to its destination. As with a physical letter though, once the message reaches its intended recipient, the sender has no expectation of privacy unless a legal expectation of confidentiality exists. The person who receives the content can publicize and distribute it as they could a physical letter. In addition, electronic communications posted in chat rooms or other Web sites where users submit content for others to read are clearly not seen as private.

A recent case that brought a number of privacy concerns involved a Rutgers University undergraduate student who was secretly recorded on a webcam having sex. The camera had been purposely placed and hidden by his roommate to secretly record the romantic encounter. The student's roommate also "tweeted" other students and encouraged them to watch a second live feed from the webcam. After becoming aware of the webcam and distribution of the images, the distraught, embarrassed student committed suicide. His roommate was convicted for invasion of privacy among other crimes and sentenced to 30 days in jail, 3 years' probation, 300 hours of community service, a 10,000 dollar fine, and counseling on cyber bullying and alternate lifestyles.

SOURCE: Karpf, J. 2013. "The Cost of Convenience: The Extent of the Reasonable Expectation of Privacy in the Internet Age." University of Central Florida Honors Thesis, Department of Legal Studies.

The rise of surveillance capabilities increased dramatically with the development of modern camera-based systems in the 1960s.[41] **CCTV, or closed circuit television,** was initially used in both the United States and the United Kingdom sparingly as an in-store means of apprehending and deterring shoplifters. Although the technology became less expensive and increased in its capabilities throughout the 1970s, the Western political environment remained hostile to surveillance of the general public. The Cold War discouraged the use of police surveillance systems that smacked of Communist-style secret police tactics. Western politicians and police chiefs did not want to be viewed as advocates of systems that could be described as "Big Brother" spying.

In the mid-1980s, as the Cold War dissipated, municipal police CCTV surveillance systems appeared across the United Kingdom. By the mid-1990s, a rapid increase in the number of systems was well under way in that country, and today it is the rule rather than the exception for any reasonably sized British community to have police camera surveillance of its public spaces.[42] By the turn of the century, there were more than 500 operating CCTV systems in the United Kingdom, exploding to millions of cameras and estimated at about one camera for every thirty-two people.[43] Beyond the defusing of the Cold War, rising local crime rates, a declining faith in the traditional criminal justice system's ability to deal with crime, and the ubiquity of video cameras have been credited for the increased public support for law enforcement-operated surveillance systems.[44]

Capping the British social construction of police surveillance systems as positive and necessary was a symbolic crime, the 1993 murder of a two-year-old boy who was recorded on a mall security camera being taken away by his two teenage killers. The use of the security camera video resulted in demands for more camera systems following its widespread broadcast on news programs.[45] The images gave an irresistible push for the adoption of CCTV systems, and the British media shifted from questioning whether surveillance is a good thing to asking why cameras are not everywhere. Similarly in the United States, symbolic crimes, usually murders, have periodically supercharged the steady growth of surveillance throughout society in bursts of surveillance surges.[46] Once installed, logic inevitably calls for coverage of larger areas, and every murder or terrorist act intensifies the demand for expanded surveillance.[47]

The result in the United Kingdom has been the normalization of police surveillance systems to the level that CCTV surveillance has been described as a public "fifth utility," along the lines of water, electricity, and telephones.[48] Described as an everyday experience[49] and driven as much by politics as by empirical evidence, CCTV surveillance in the U.K. came to be widely perceived as an affordable and efficient technical fix for crime[50] and described as equal to full-time police officers on the beat 24 hours a day, all taking notes without meal breaks, holidays, or sick leave.[51] In the aftermath of the September 11, 2001, terrorist attacks and passage of the Patriot Act and related legislation, the United States is on track to join the United Kingdom as a massively camera-surveilled society.[52]

In the United States and elsewhere, camera surveillance programs today take one of two basic forms: completely hidden systems that give potential offenders no indication that they are being observed, and clearly marked, open systems. Although the first form functions more as a means of gathering evidence and aiding in apprehensions, both forms take advantage of the surveillance effect, using the psychological impact of the belief that one might be under surveillance to influence people's behaviors.[53]

How effective are surveillance systems in reducing crime? Evidence based largely on interviews with offenders does suggest that offenders take into account the perceived level of surveillance and the likelihood of intervention when deciding whether to commit some types of crimes, especially instrumental street crimes such as car break-ins.[54] Emotional, spontaneous crimes such as assaults are less affected. And the presence of cameras can be an attractor for some criminals and terrorists who desire publicity and the distribution of visual accounts of their crimes. Evaluations suggest that the systems are most effective in reducing crime when combined with other interventions,[55] and evidence of significant crime reduction from public surveillance systems has been reported.[56] Early evaluations reported that camera surveillance generated short-term deterrent effects and reduced property crime more than violent crime.[57]

However, if the threat of police intervention is absent, the impact of surveil-lance fades.[58] That is, unless surveillance results in someone showing up to address the observed problem, a surveillance-generated deterrent effect will eventually wane. Camera placement, site conditions that affect camera views, and pre-existing crime levels have been found to significantly interact and affect the crime reduction impact of these systems.[59] Thus, within a single multi-camera system, some cameras may have substantial impacts on some crimes while other cameras have none or influence different types of crimes. Cameras in crime hot-spots that reside in well-designed and operationally integrated projects are more effective crime deterrents than are widely diffused community blanket deploy-ments.[60] Police surveillance cameras have been shown to be useful in a postcrime investigation, less so in the identification of suspects.[61] Even when a crime is not recorded, knowledge of the movement of individual and vehicles prior to and following an incident has proven crucial in solving a number of crimes. In addi-tion to benefits to investigations, reduced costs, swifter justice, and increases in the public's perception of safety have been reported.[62]

Benefits and Concerns of Increased Surveillance

The concerns raised about police camera surveillance boil down to privacy (the unnecessary exposure of peoples' lives and activities), legitimacy (impact on civil rights and control of power in democracies), and efficiency (crime reduction and increased public safety).[63] The benefits usually cited for police camera surveil-lance systems also incorporate the concerns raised about these systems.[64] Thus, a surveillance benefit is to be able to observe and react to previously unnoticed acts; the concern is that net-widening from police arresting more people—particularly juveniles—for minor offenses will result in more people with formal arrest records.[65] A benefit is to be able to expel actual and potential deviants from specific locations; the concern is that profiling, polarization, and radicaliza-tion will result if certain social groups are targeted for exclusion from public spaces, especially commercial shopping districts.[66] A benefit is to provide evi-dence against offenders; the concern is the development of databases to track and identify specific members of the population based on their already having been labeled as individuals that "need to be watched," rather than being sur-veilled because of their current behavior (see Box 8.2). A benefit is the creation of quiet, public spaces; the concern is over-policing of legal but marginal social behaviors such as loitering as well as the decline of informal neighborhood guardianship activities.[67] Lastly, a benefit is the creation of crime-free surveillance zones; the concern is that displacement effects will push crime into adjacent communities without the money or political clout to obtain surveillance systems. Surveillance would be a privilege and mark communities as "worth watching," simultaneously making crime invisible to most of society without reducing it.[68] Ironically, the rich and powerful (who are not celebrities) are able to accrue the benefits from anticrime surveillance programs while to a large degree avoiding the intrusions of everyday surveillance. The powerful control how and when they are surveilled whereas the powerless do not.[69]

Of the concerns, **displacement of crime** to adjacent areas has been empirically examined along with the additional potential benefit of a diffusion of crime reduction impact.[70] **Diffusion of benefits** is seen as a possible effect from surveillance systems because offenders might not be aware of the boundaries of the surveillance coverage and therefore reduce their offenses in adjacent, nonsurveilled areas. In the reported evaluations, evidence of both displacement and diffusion effects has been reported.[71] For example, in the United Kingdom, evidence of the local diffusion of benefits in reduced car theft and break-ins has been reported as well as evidence of significant crime displacement to outlying distant English towns from a single system.[72] Recent research suggests that crime displacement may not, however, be a universal effect.[73] This suggests that diffusion of benefits may accrue near to these systems while crime displacement can be simultaneously occurring farther away.

The use of video cameras mounted on patrol car windshields in the United States represents another expanded, mobile use of surveillance. The mobility of the patrol car extends the practice of general law enforcement surveillance to virtually the entire society without the need for permanent fixed systems. Challenges to this practice based on privacy concerns have been rejected by the U.S. Supreme Court, which has stated that an invasion of privacy cannot result unless there is a reasonable expectation of privacy. Because there is no expectation of privacy in a traffic stop or on a public street, the use of in-car video cameras by police on patrol or on fixed streetlight mountings monitoring public streets is allowed under almost all circumstances.[74] The next evolutionary step will be cameras worn on the body of officers that will record all officer–citizen encounters.[75]

The extension of surveillance to airborne drones has heightened the debate. Unlike police car-mounted systems which are constrained to streets and street views, and police worn cameras which are limited to officer movements, drones provide law enforcement the ability to surveil any part of society not inside a structure. The public belief that walls and distance equals privacy is destroyed. Who gets watched is also a concern; research has suggested that camera monitors are not particularly accurate in predicting victimization.[76] Those most often focused upon by camera operators are "young, scruffy, loitering males," a profile that has not proven particularly effective in maximizing crime prevention effects from these systems.[77] In addition to public concerns about drones and surveillance, resistance to greater adoption of surveillance cameras is found within law enforcement agencies when officers perceive the cameras as an administrative tool, installed to watch them, more than as a law enforcement tool. In reality the cameras are both: the police on the surveilled street, in front of their patrol cars during a videotaped traffic stop, and when equipped with a body camera are also under surveillance and a number have lost their jobs as a result.

The prime effect of surveillance video is that it transforms the relationships between line police officers, their administration, and the public by providing a reviewable record of officers' street interactions. The benefits of having a visual record are many; administrators and the courts can later review officers' and suspects' actions, and thereby decide liability, voluntary search consent, misconduct claims, and have more credible, objective evidence of behavior and statements for DUI and drug intoxication cases. In addition, the cameras are credited with

---

B o x 8.2   Profiling and Camera Surveillance

Monitors of public space surveillance systems are sometimes accused of inappropriately profiling which persons are watched. Thus, people at a public outdoor mall might be selected to be watched based on who they are (teenagers or minorities) rather than what they are doing. Norris, Moran, and Armstrong (1998, p. 8) summarize this issue:

> [Camera surveillance] is more than just crime prevention. It enables a vast amount of visual data, in the form of images on the screen, to be processed and interpreted. What interpretive schemes guide operator judgments? What forms of behavior or people trigger suspicion and at what point does this result in a deployment? Is this deployment confined to explicitly criminal concerns or is intervention directed at regulating matters of decorum and demeanor in public space and aimed at excluding certain types of people?

Research has indicated that demographic profiling does occur. Williams and Johnstone (2000, p. 193) report that CCTV operators selectively target those social groups they believe are most likely to be deviant, singling out certain people and behaviors as inappropriate and therefore warranting surveillance. They found that young males, especially young black males, were regularly targeted for surveillance as much for their race, posture, and dress as for their behavior. In their study, Norris and Armstrong (1999, p. 110) found that in one British community black people were two and a half times more likely to be the object of surveillance and over one and a half times more likely in another U.K. community. The concept of "otherness" comes into play with the social construction of suspicion resulting in blacks and teenagers being more likely to be watched without cause and ascribed criminal intent on the basis of appearance (Norris and Armstrong, 1999, p. 118). Of the 900 surveilled events reviewed, 45 resulted in police deployments, and 12 resulted in arrests. One-third of surveillance targets were selected based on categorical criteria such as dress, race, or subculture group membership, whereas surveillance based on suspicious behavioral represents only one out of four uses (Norris and Armstrong, 1999, p. 112; see also Goold 2004, chapter 6). Due to this concern, racial and class profiling has been a persistent criticism levied against the utilization of public space surveillance systems.

SOURCES: Goold, B. 2004. *CCTV and Policing*. Oxford, UK: Oxford University Press; Norris, C., and G. Armstrong. 1999. *The Maximum Surveillance Society: The Rise of CCTV*. Oxford, UK: Berg; Norris, C., Moran, J., and Armstrong, G. (1998) (Eds.) *Surveillance, closed circuit television and social control*. London; Ashgate; Williams, K., and C. Johnstone. 2000. "The Politics of the Selective Gaze: Closed Circuit Television and the Policing of Public Space." *Crime, Law and Social Change* 34: 183–210.

---

deterring suspects from resisting arrest and deterring officers from mistreating suspects and engaging in other unprofessional acts.[78] In effect, in a democratic society the technology appears to protect police officers from frivolous charges of abuse and misconduct while protecting the public from actual abuse and misconduct by officers. In addition, the ubiquitous video cameras in citizens' hands mean that a surveillance effect will have an impact on the police as well as on the public. Research has indicated that citizen-videotaped arrests have a significant negative impact on the public's perception of police use of force.[79] In response, the police are advised to operate under the premise that cameras are

The operation of camera equipped aerial drones by governments, businesses, and citizens will dramatically change the scope of surveillance and the nature of privacy.

AP Images/John Giles/PA Wire

everywhere and that any of their actions might be taped.[80] A final, ironic consequence of more surveillance cameras in society is their use by offenders to provide early warnings of police raids on premises being used for illegal practices. This turns the acquisition of surveillance technology into an offender/police arms race that law enforcement is not necessarily favored to win.[81]

Balancing Police Surveillance and Public Safety

All surveillance systems raise issues related to the role of media in the daily policing of our society. Surprisingly, concerns over Big Brother are usually raised by the news media, law enforcement officers, and external observers, not by many citizens under surveillance, who appear quite ready to trade off a measure of personal privacy for a potential reduction in victimization and fear. The public acceptance of surveillance is high and is linked to the new media-based increased exposure of private, backstage behaviors in the news, entertainment, and info-tainment media—if privacy is already rare and voluntary self-surveillance is common, then government surveillance is less offensive. Since the terrorist attacks of September 11, 2001, public support in the United States for surveil-lance systems has been strong, with close to 80 percent in one poll supporting the installation of surveillance cameras in public places to prevent terrorist attacks.[82] The social construction of the need for police camera surveillance depends upon references to dramatic crime risks such as a terrorist attack or the predator pedophile even for applications related to traffic control and school campuses.[83]

Unresolved questions concern effects on the legitimacy and public image of justice when surveillance technology is employed. Public perception of law enforcement significantly determines support for the entire criminal justice system. Accordingly, the police have a symbolic value. On the street, both the presence of a live police officer and the assurance of knowing when one is being observed by the police affirm the values of voluntary consent and public control of law enforcement. Loss of these social attributes can diminish the aura of legitimacy sus-taining the entire criminal justice system. An unresolved concern is "function creep," a process in which surveillance systems are marketed as protections against terrorism but once installed are utilized to address mundane low level offenses such as littering.[84] Misuse or overuse of surveillance will construct a social reality of mistrust and cynicism, where fear of crime is replaced by fear of authority. In addi-tion, police surveillance systems may be ineffective over the long term if their ill-considered deployment and rapid numerical increase cancel benefits.[85]

In addition, their use could result in the neglect of broader approaches to crime control. It is feared that reliance on technological fixes for crime can have negative community effects, working against positive community participa-tion, creating a siege mentality, generating social resistance to the police, and undermining natural community surveillance by residents.[86] For example, the presence of a police surveillance system might result in fewer phone calls to the police if residents assume that the local police surveillance camera will observe incidents and alert the authorities. Police camera surveillance may thereby under-mine natural surveillance by encouraging people to have faith in the disembo-died electronic eye and encourage a "why get involved" attitude. Instead of worrying about Big Brother watching them, the public may expect that "Big Father" will sort everything out.

Cameras unavoidably change the nature of the relationship between those being watched and those doing the watching.[87] Most of the time, the negative social consequences of increased surveillance dominate the debate. However, the latest applications have positive potentials also. When the actions of the law enforcers and the public are both monitored, stored, and subject to later review, surveillance cameras can restrain the actions of authorities as much as offenders. It remains to be seen whether the impact of these projects in democratic societies will be greater on the police than on the public. A significant effect on employees has already been reported in correctional settings where the behavior of both correctional officers and prisoners is monitored.[88] Like other two-edged swords, the dual nature of police camera surveillance is apparent. In the wrong hands, it can invade privacy and make Orwell's *1984* a reality. But it can also, in a different political context, be liberating and protective.[89] Which reality will emerge is yet to be determined.

The basic problem these programs present is how to balance police surveillance and public safety—how much safety is gained at what cost? The equation seems clearly to be that increased fear of crime and terror results in increased tolerance for surveillance. Surveillance is usually marketed to the public with assurances that the focus will be on serious threats and crimes and that law-abiding people need not be concerned.[90] Citizens fearful of crime and terrorism are willing to open more social areas to observation, even when the observers are hidden. Orwell's *1984* society of total surveillance is less frightening than a local mugger or terrorist bomber. The danger is that fear will drive citizens to glibly surrender personal privacy for an unknown measure of personal security. Whether these programs actually reduce crime or protect against terrorist attacks enough to warrant the loss in privacy is an open question.[91] They are capable of producing positive near-term effects for certain types of crime, with vehicle-related offenses appearing to be most effectively deterred. Whether the systems can maintain positive effects over the long term is not known. In addition, how the power to surveil is held accountable and what limits are placed on its operation are unresolved issues.[92] The impact of new computing and database technologies will increase the reach of surveillance—with the coupling of surveillance cameras to fast, inexpensive computers capabilities such as facial recognition, real-time vehicle and person tracking, and behavior recognition programs that can identify street disturbances are realities. Widespread police access to real-time, computer-analyzed visual surveillance data will soon be commonplace. In addition to law enforcement-based surveillance, a great impact of surveillance will result from the widespread availability of new media technologies making social surveillance an activity that anyone can engage in.[93]

THE BRAVE NEW MEDIA WORLD

Today, the media can be used to influence people's attitudes about crime and make more crime-related information available to the police. Other uses can speed the processing of criminal cases. The technology of the media can be used to videotape police patrols, vehicle stops, and interrogations. And the technology is useful in the investigation, surveillance, and deterrence of crime. The administrative—mostly crime control—benefits associated with these uses follow quickly, and projects have consistently been evaluated as efficient and cost-effective. Increased social fears as well as technological advances that make the equipment more economical, more flexible, more capable, and less obtrusive are hastening wider use of media surveillance. However, there are concerns about potential social costs. If evidence of negative effects is found in future studies, the technological genie will be out of the bottle, and it will be difficult to curtail established practices.

Media-based anticrime efforts that do not include surveillance show no behavioral effects, and it appears doubtful that the media can by themselves deter criminal behavior—much as they alone cannot criminalize individuals. Surveillance programs do show deterrence effects, but their ability to deter crime without displacement and other worrisome social effects remains unproven. Media efforts to reduce victimization by teaching crime preventive behaviors have high recognition levels among the general public and have increased public knowledge and changed public attitudes about crime prevention, but they have not yet shown an ability to significantly change crime prevention behavior. Finally, programs designed to increase public cooperation by advertising crimes are effective in gathering information and in solving some types of crimes. Their effect on the overall crime rate is not known, but it is likely negligible.

With all of these caveats in mind, media technology is still an extremely useful tool, but social costs invariably accompany technological benefits. Costs include increased depersonalization of the criminal justice system; isolation of the police from the policed; increased citizen suspicion of surveillance; polarization of society due to the creation of affluent, technologically secured garrison communities; and possible decreased citizen support and legitimization of the criminal justice system. Finally, when news media convey the message that these efforts are the answer for reducing crime rates and when this is coupled with the entertainment message of crime being generated through individually based causes, the social construction of crime as a technological rather than a social problem becomes the logical result. The belief that we can engineer our way out of the crime problem through more equipment and manpower is bolstered. The collective lesson is that media-based programs are panaceas for the general crime problem. To the extent that the public believes this and policy makers act on it, resources for other approaches will be drained.

To solve crimes and deter criminals, governments must intervene in citizens' lives. The media and media technology provide a means to do so in new ways that are felt to be both more efficient and less obviously intrusive. In practice such applications cannot avoid opening up for view new areas of public life, of the criminal justice system, and of police–citizen interactions. In certain instances, such as in the use of patrol car cameras, which record police actions as much as citizen actions, this is seen as a positive course. In other instances, such as in the use of hidden police surveillance systems, the desirability of widely doing so is not so clear. Still, with proper oversight, the use of media and media technology in the criminal justice system can have both due process and crime control benefits. The media are a potentially positive but, it must be remembered, ultimately limited resource for criminal justice. The media should be an element of the total criminal justice policy picture, but media cannot be the mainstay of crime-and-justice policies. Ultimately, the media affects social attitudes and perceptions more than social behaviors so they are restrained to influencing policy support and public beliefs more than criminal acts. Connected to the question of how much of our criminal justice policy should be media based is the question of how many criminal justice policies are media generated. Chapter 9 looks at the broader relationship between the media and criminal justice policy.

SUMMARY

- The roots of media-based anticrime efforts are found in public service announcements, public communication campaigns, and pro-social media that established the possibility of using targeted content to influence people's knowledge, attitudes, and behaviors.

- Using the media to reduce crime and victimization has proved difficult due to unanticipated and counterproductive effects. The primary difficulty is the need to raise concern about crime and its consequences in the target audience without triggering negative effects from raising levels of fear.

- Media efforts aimed at offenders are based on deterrence and aim to get offenders to voluntarily reduce their offending.

- Media efforts aimed at victims are based on self-protective behaviors and aim to get potential crime victims to reduce their likelihood of being selected by an offender.

- Media efforts aimed at citizens are based on encouraging cooperation with law enforcement and aim to increase information and tips regarding crimes.

- Media technology, especially visual communications, has been increasingly adopted in the criminal justice system in video interrogations and lineups and visual presentation and records of arraignments, evidence, pleas, and trials.

- The capacity for digital manipulation of visual images has worked to undermine the credibility of pictures as evidence.

- Police surveillance of public spaces has expanded and camera systems are common in many U.S. communities. Concerns with these systems involve privacy, displacement of crime, and the impact of a surveillance effect on society.

- Media-based anticrime efforts do not appear to be able to reduce crime on their own. Camera surveillance projects show the greatest impact on actual offender behavior.

CLASS DISCUSSIONS

1. Discuss why media technology has been embraced as a solution for various criminal justice system tasks while some police officers oppose the installation of cameras in their patrol cars.

2. Discuss who should have access to the records and images produced by a government agency surveillance system and whether surveillance video should be released to news agencies, used in civil cases, or employed in infotainment programming.

CHAPTER 8

3. Discuss where and when surveillance cameras are acceptable and if it should matter if they are hidden or openly displayed. Discuss the phenomenon of a surveillance effect and whether people should be informed that they are within the view of a surveillance system.

4. Research computer-monitored surveillance systems and discuss the pros and cons of computer versus human monitors.

5. After noting the location and number of surveillance cameras seen over a 24-hour period, discuss what entities (government, business, or private) were operating the camera systems, whether the boundary of the surveilled areas could be determined, whether there were signs announcing the presence of the surveillance cameras, and whether the cameras were difficult or easy to spot. Discuss how individuals feel about being under involuntary surveillance.

6. Discuss a recent anticrime PSA in terms of its target audience, the problem its addresses, its use of fear, the behaviors it strives to encourage or discourage, and how effective it is perceived as.

SUGGESTED READINGS

Coleman, R. and McCahill, M. (2011). *Surveillance & crime*. London: Sage.

Goold, B. (2004). *CCTV and policing*. Oxford: Oxford University Press.

Norris, C., and Armstrong, G. (1999). *The Maximum surveillance society: The rise of CCTV*. Oxford, UK: Berg.

Norris, C., Moran, J., and Armstrong, G. (1998) (Eds.). *Surveillance, closed circuit television and social control*. London: Ashgate.

O'Keefe, G., Rosenbaum, D., Lavrakas, P., Reid, K., and Botta, R. (1996). *Taking a bite out of crime*. Thousand Oaks: Sage.

Smith, G. (2013). *Opening the black box: The everyday life of surveillance*. London: Routledge.

CHAPTER 9

The Media and Criminal Justice Policy

CHAPTER OBJECTIVES

After reading Chapter 9, you will

- Understand the link between media content and criminal justice policy
- Comprehend the policy effects of the backwards law
- Know about the media's crime-and-justice ecology
- Appreciate how immanent justice underlies media crime-and-justice portrayals
- Learn how technology has advanced as a crime-fighting tool
- Recognize how the public crime-and-justice agenda, beliefs about criminality, and attitudes toward policy are influenced by the media

SLAYING MAKE-BELIEVE MONSTERS

The cumulative result of the media's construction of crime, crime fighters, courts, corrections, and crime control are punitive criminal justice policies. When the dominant media portrait is of predatory offenders committing violent crimes in continuous battle with the criminal justice system, nonpunitive policies come across as naïve. You don't need crime-fighting heroes to battle wayward citizens who have made mistakes they regret. Nor do you rehabilitate innate predators. In that you very rarely find the regretful offender and usually find the innate predator, the ultimate policy push from the overall media social construction of crime and justice is seldom rehabilitative and more often punitive.[1] What remains to be clarified are the pathways through which media content influences criminal justice policy.

Herbert Packer's well known due process and crime control models serve as conceptual frames for understanding the criminal justice system, its goals, and the mass media's effects on the system.[2] Both models describe organizational case flows. Under the *due process* model, the criminal justice system is seen as an obstacle course in which the government must prove an accused person's guilt while conforming to strict procedural rules. The system's most important goal under this model is the protection of citizen rights and the prevention of arbitrary and capricious government action. The key determination in this model is legal guilt, which is decided at the end of a long and exacting process. In contrast, in the *crime control* model, the criminal justice system is perceived as an assembly line along which defendants should be processed as quickly and efficiently as possible. The primary goal of the system is to punish criminals and to deter crime. The key determination in this model is factual guilt, which is decided early in the process in accordance with the perceived strength of evidence and police judgment.

Beyond aiding in understanding the criminal justice system, these models are also useful for understanding the conflicting perceptions that exist regarding the mass media and their impact on crime-and-justice policy.[3] Conflicts arise because some view the media as mainly promoting a due process reality by ensuring that power is not exercised capriciously, while others view them as retarding due process protections by increasing the difficulty of finding impartial juries and conducting fair trials. Paradoxically, some also see the media as promoting crime control by educating the public about the functions of the justice system and by enhancing deterrence by publicizing punishment of criminals. Others see them as hindering crime control efforts by interfering with the efforts of law enforcement to investigate and prosecute crimes, by negatively reporting unethical but effective law enforcement practices, and by withholding information and evidence from the courts. Hence, even if people agree on the effects of the mass media on the criminal justice system, they may disagree as to whether these effects are good or bad. The same media effect—such as making it more difficult for the police to conduct evidence searches—can be seen by some observers as promoting due process and therefore good, while other observers see it as hindering crime control and therefore bad. Given these competing interpretations, the media can be seen as either enhancing or hindering the criminal justice system. The media do what they do, and their effects are seen as promoting (or interfering with) due process or crime control policies depending on the observer's point of view. Despite the fact that their effects can be variously interpreted, in general, the media is seen as forwarding the crime control model and disparaging the due process model. This imbalance is tied to two crime-and-justice tenets.

MEDIA CRIME-AND-JUSTICE TENETS

Two crime-and-justice tenets provide insight into the way criminal justice as a social issue is constructed. The first tenet is the "backwards law," which is associated with a particular crime-and-justice "ecology." The second tenet is the rule of **"immanent justice,"** which paradoxically is associated with an enhanced view of technological solutions to crime. The two media-constructed tenets have the police imbedded in a randomly violent environment where they battle predators more than keep the peace; the courts deal with psychotic offenders and conduct investigations more than dispense justice; corrections exist as a bizarre, primitive lost world of frequent brutality; constant surveillance of the public is the most prudent course, and the entire criminal justice system points unwaveringly toward the need for swift, sure, and increased punishment.[4] In this media-generated Darwinian crime-and-justice reality, survival of the violent emerges as the operative selection rule.

The Backwards Law

In nearly every subject category—crimes, criminals, crime fighters, attorneys, correctional officers, and inmates; the investigation of crimes and making of arrests; the processing and disposition of cases; and the experience of incarceration—the media construct and present a crime-and-justice world that is not found in reality. Whatever the truth about crime and the criminal justice system in America, the entertainment, news, and infotainment media seem determined to project the opposite. The wildly inaccurate and inevitably fragmentary images and facts found in the entertainment and infotainment media reflect this law most clearly. They provide a distorted reflection of crime within society and an equally distorted reflection of the criminal justice system's response to crime. Basic to this process is a front-end-loaded portrait that concentrates on crime fighting. The further past law enforcement and into the criminal justice system one looks, the fewer criminal justice activities are shown. The lack of system-wide information and the unreality of the narrow information that is available demonize criminality while mystifying the criminal justice system. The result is the exacerbation of the public's lack of understanding of crime and justice while constructing a topsy-turvy portrait of criminal justice reality.[5]

The backwards law also applies to crime-and-justice news content. First, the criminal justice system and its component parts are seldom the subject of news reports. The criminal justice system serves as a background setting for a news story more often than it appears as the subject. When the justice system is explicitly referred to, it is usually the courts that are portrayed, not as institutions but as backdrops to present information about individual cases. Seldom are broader system issues covered. For example, the broader policy issue of sentencing as a range of options incorporating fines, community supervision, and incarceration is not often discussed. Instead, references to sentencing are reported within stories about an individual receiving a sentence, most often prison. Non-incarceration sentencing options such as fines appear infrequently in news stories.[6] Alternate sentences, such as restitution or community service, almost never appear. Similarly, crime prevention stories are rare when compared to the number of stories about individual violent crimes—and when crime prevention does get covered, the coverage is usually negative. The end result is news that approaches criminal justice policy from the bottom up—that is, as the piecemeal, cumulative result of a focus on individual crimes and individuals rather than as a coherent system of justice.

This bottom-up perspective can be found in the way news stories are formatted, either as episodic or thematic.[7] The more common **episodic format** treats stories as discrete events: a crime is described and a resulting case is followed. The rarer **thematic format** highlights trends, persistent problems, or other systemic phenomena: a crime-

HO/UPPA/Photoshot

The "Viginia Tech masasacre" shooter killed 32 in a 2007 rampage. Episodic style coverage of such events drives media influence on criminal justice policy formation.

and-justice issue or a category of crimes is explored. Episodic formatted stories encourage viewers to place responsibility for social problems totally on individuals and to ignore possible societal forces—an individual committed a crime, why did he do it? Stories told in the thematic format take the opposite approach and effect—a set of problems have developed, what changed in society? The entertainment media reflects the same dichotomy, concentrating on events more than issues—the big heist, a murder spree, an investigation, a trial, a riot, and so on. By being episodic rather than thematic, the media reinforce the popular view that says crime is caused by individual choices and that punitive, harsh deterrent-based policies are the only effective response.[8]

The media therefore supply a large amount of information about specific crimes and convey the impression that criminals threaten the social order and its institutions with imminent collapse. Media provide less information to help the public comprehend the larger society-wide forces that underlie individual crimes and cases. Rare is the thematic interpretive analysis that places criminal justice information in historical, sociological, or political context. In the absence of system-wide information, the public is left to build its own picture of the effectiveness of current criminal justice policies and the desirability of newly offered ones.

Thus, most media evaluations of the criminal justice system are implicit rather than explicit, indirectly conveyed through countless episodic references to the ability or inability of the system to apprehend specific criminals, to convict and punish them when they are apprehended, and to return them to society reformed and deterred. Concerning the main components of the criminal justice system—the police, courts, and corrections— the media portray the police as doing a fair job, and the courts and the correctional system as doing poor jobs. When queried, the public ranks the system's components as slightly better in the same order—police being rated as good to fair, the courts as fair to poor, and corrections as poor.[9] The media's construction of the criminal justice system appears to lead the public to evaluate the overall system poorly while leading the same public to increase support for crime-and-justice policies so long as they are crime control and law enforcement oriented.

This paradox has been attributed to the public's view of street criminals as the most pressing crime image and to media depictions that show curable deficiencies in the justice system and personality defects in individuals as the main causes of apparently rampant crime.[10] Within this paradox, the faulty system frame has done the best in the media. Not surprisingly, researchers have found that most people who pay regular attention to the media support as their first policy choice criminal justice reforms that would toughen and strengthen the existing system.[11] This is true even though these same people place a large share of the blame for current crime levels on the existing criminal justice system. Despite the media presentation and public acceptance of the criminal justice system as ineffective, the media implicitly suggest that improving it, at least as a law enforcement and punitive system, is the best hope against the many violent crimes and predatory criminals that are portrayed.[12] From the backwards law emerges a recurrent picture of social reality that disparages social structure solutions while constructing a particular social structure regarding crime and justice. This constructed social reality incorporates a unique crime-and-justice ecology.

The Crime-and-Justice Environment in the Media

The social dynamic underlying the media image of crime—an image that has not substantively changed over the hundred-plus-year history of the modern media—is of a trisected society populated by predators, victims, and protectors. In the media vision of society, evil and cunning predator criminal wolves create general mayhem and prey on weak, defenseless—and often stupid—victim sheep (women, the elderly, the general public), while good crime-fighting heroic guard dogs (usually middle class, white, and male) intervene and protect the sheep in the name of retributive justice. Over the course of the last century, characters in this ecological landscape have darkened. Media criminals have become more animalistic, irrational, and predatory—as have media crime fighters—and media crimes more violent, random, senseless, and sensational. In parallel, media victims have become more innocent. Differences between the general public and criminals have widened. In a subtle shift, the earlier predatory but rational criminal wolves have become unpredictable, irrational mad dogs, while over the years the protective noble guard dogs have become wolf-like rogues and vigilantes for whom the law is an impediment to stopping crime. Heroes and villains have become more alike and less human, the former a demigod, the latter a demon. Today's media-constructed crime-and-justice ecology is populated with ideal offenders, victims, and heroes.[13] The **ideal offenders** are the outsiders, strangers, foreigners, aliens, and intruders who lack essential human qualities. Offenders have become generic others and as such can never be rehabilitated or resocialized.[14] The **ideal victim**, on the other hand, is the innocent, naive, trusting, obviously-in-need-of-protection true human. Children are the archetypal innocent victims and key symbols in the media's social construction of crime.[15] Finally, although capable of great violence similar to the ideal offender, the **ideal hero** displays the additional admirable qualities of morality, sacrifice, and strength. When these ideal types combine, memorial legislation can result, as shown in Box 9.1.[16]

Megan's Law provides an example of memorial criminal justice policy based on a media portrait of the "ideal victim," in this case an innocent child. The law memorializes Megan Kanka, a seven-year-old abduction, rape, and murder victim of a repeat sex offender. Megan's laws were passed nationwide to increase public access to information about registered sex offenders, especially their current place of residence. The various versions of Megan's Law usually require sex offender registration lists and community notification mechanisms. Although the effectiveness of these laws has been questioned (see Zgoba, Dalessandro, Veysey and Witt, 2008), they remain popular.

SOURCE: Zgoba, K., M. Dalessandro, B. Veysey, and P. Witt. 2008. *Megan's Law: Assessing the Practical and Monetary Efficacy.* Rockville, MD: National Institute of Justice/NCJRS. Downloaded Jan 15, 2010 from http:// www. ncjrs.gov/App/publications/ abstract.aspx?ID=247350

John Garofalo UPI Photo Service/Newscom

President Clinton signs legislation into National law known as "Megan's Law" requiring states to inform communities when convicted sex offenders move into their neighborhood.

By depicting this predatory violent social environment, the media project messages to the audience, both criminal and law-abiding, concerning whom to trust, whom to victimize, and how victims and criminals should act. The consistent message is that crime is caused by predatory individuals who are inherently different from the rest of us—more ruthless, greedy, violent, or psychotic. Combating these predators requires a special person, an equally tough, predatory, and most important, unfettered crime fighter. Criminality is an individual choice and other social, economic, or structural explanations are irrelevant and can be ignored. Limited to this simplistic, incomplete picture of crime as mostly individual, socially isolated acts, the public is shown that counterviolence is the most effective means of combating crime, that due process considerations hamper the police, and that, in most cases, the law works in the criminal's favor. The public is further instructed to fear others because criminals are not always easily recognized and often are rich, powerful, and in positions of trust.

This constructed social environment, combined with the emphasis on investigations and arrests—the front end of the criminal justice system—ultimately promotes pro-law enforcement and crime control policies. When the public relies on infotainment-formatted media and avoids media that present criminality as a complex social problem, punitive "quick fixes" are supported over preventive long-term approaches to crime.[17] Paradoxically, although the media frequently portray the criminal justice system unfavorably, the solutions they depict as being the most effective—harsher punishments and more law enforcement—entail expansion of the existing criminal justice system. Underlying this construction is a persistent, if often unstated, explanation of crime. The media consistently point to individual personality traits as the cause of crime and to violent interdiction as its solution. If one accepts the media's explanation of crime as being caused by predatory personality traits—by innate greed and violence—then the only valid approach to stopping crime is to hold individual offenders responsible for their past crimes and forcibly deter them from committing future ones. In the media's simplistic notion of crime, the most effective solution is dramatic, individual action that emphasizes violence and aggression, with a preference for weapons and sophisticated technology. By portraying criminality as innate and crime as an act of nature, bolstered by the idea of immanent justice, the logical response is found in revenge and punishment.

The Media Dynamic of Immanent Justice

Immanent justice is the belief that a divine higher power will intervene, and reveal and punish the guilty while protecting the innocent. The operation of immanent justice in the media becomes most clear in entertainment gunplay. Weapon accuracy and killing power are unequally held by the evil criminals and the good crime fighters, their aim apparently guided by the moral imperatives of right and wrong. Sinful, evil criminals miss or inflict benign flesh wounds while blessed, good crime fighters hit and kill. Similar to the medieval socially constructed reality that made trial by ordeal and by combat logical, the modern media reality relies on the moral superiority of the crime fighter to ultimately defeat criminality. Lessened as a social problem, criminality is reduced to an individual moral battle. The idea that criminals personify evil has deep historical roots.[18] A dangerous, immoral underclass in turn justifies the wide use of violence and punishment. Sin must be resisted and sinners punished.

An evil Nazi who is ultimately destroyed by the ark in the film *Raiders of the Lost Ark. Evil criminals and their ordained defeat are inherent in the portrayals of immanent justice found in crime-and-justice media.*

This good versus evil perspective on crime and justice is also reflected in the common media crime fighter who is motivated by personal injury and revenge; upholding the law is secondary to individual retribution. This media portrait ties into the overall media emphasis on personal individual actions as the source of criminality and as the appropriate response to crime and victimization. The associated media-constructed punitive crime-and-justice policies gain support from our basic cultural values of free will, individualism, and personal responsibility. The result is that an individualized, revenge-oriented justice dominates where, God willing, the good guys win against heavy odds. This media portrait of individualized justice supported by immanent intervention crowds out other constructions of crime and justice and nonpunitive policies. In this fashion, crime is further diminished as a social problem. Instead, it becomes a theological contest of good versus evil. This contest does have a role for technology though.

Technology Enhances Immanent Justice.   In contrast to their focus on individual factors as the cause of crime, the media do portray some collective responses to crime as effective, but only if they are technology-based. Immanent justice is often helped along by technology and gadgets. If God is not handy, then a good engineer or scientist (not a social scientist, though) will do. The crime problem can be effectively reduced through a technological engineering solution. In the media, the good guys are often helped by some smart guys. Within this portrait, it makes sense to ignore social and structural sources of conflict such as racism, sexism, and economic inequality and focus on solutions requiring more equipment, manpower, and resources. Engineering our way out of a problem may work well for true technological challenges, like reaching the moon. Unfortunately, for true social problems like crime, technology-based moon-shot solutions do not work.

Real-World Crime-and-Justice Problems

In the real world, social problems come bundled together—crime is found with poverty, unemployment, poor health, poor schools, high divorce rates, high out-of-wedlock pregnancy rates, community decay and deterioration, drug use, illiteracy, high school dropout rates, and so on. Communities and societies that experience one of these problems tend to experience most if not all of them together. Unfortunately, the media present crime as largely autonomous from other social problems and not as linked to them in any serious way. With its individually rooted causes, crime is constructed as an autonomous plague on society (see Box 9.2), its genesis not associated with other historical, social, or structural conditions. It follows that criminological theories that are individually focused gain more support from the media's construction of crime and justice than do group or culturally focused theories. Retribution and deterrence are trumpeted; rehabilitation and social reform are belittled.

The end product from a constructed backwards world of immanent justice, where policy is steered by divine intervention and derived from contests between good and evil individuals is, ironically, a preference for high-tech policies. Crime in the media is ultimately painted as a technological problem imbedded in a randomly violent, socially impersonal landscape that can only be tamed by more manpower and equipment. But does the public make the connection between the content they see and the policies they support? Do they even pay attention to the implicit policy messages?

CRIMINAL JUSTICE POLICY AND MEDIA RESEARCH

While the content of the media certainly tilts toward some policies and away from others, it is worthwhile to examine the research evidence of the media's ability to influence crime-and-justice policy. This section looks at the relationship between media and criminal justice policy, examining the pathways that connect them: the effects on crime's rank on the list of social problems, attitudes about the world as mean and dangerous, fear of crime, and counterproductive and anticipatory effects.

Crime on the Public Agenda

Can the media, by emphasizing or ignoring topics, influence the ranking of issues that are important to the public—that is, what the public thinks about

---

B o x   9.2   Minor Celebrity Crime = Major Media Attention

Amanda Bynes (drug paraphernalia, DUI), Shaun White (public intoxication), Wesley Snipes (tax evasion), George Michael (lewd act), Lil' Kim (perjury), Justin Bieber (pictured below), Hugh Grant (pictured below) (solicitation of prostitute), Winona Ryder (shoplifting), Britney Spears, Paris Hilton, Lindsay Lohan, Mel Gibson, Bruno Mars, and Reese Witherspoon (DUI, drug, and various traffic violations) are all celebrities arrested in recent years for nonviolent or victimless crimes. These crimes would be considered not newsworthy if committed by ordinary people. The large amount of coverage these arrests generated displays how socially less important crimes (crimes that have smaller effect in terms of harm to society and would have had little social impact except for being linked to someone famous) can have large newsworthiness and be of great value to the media. The focus on individuals and celebrities further reduces the perception of crime and justice as a broad, complex social problem to simplistic individual-level explanations and solutions.

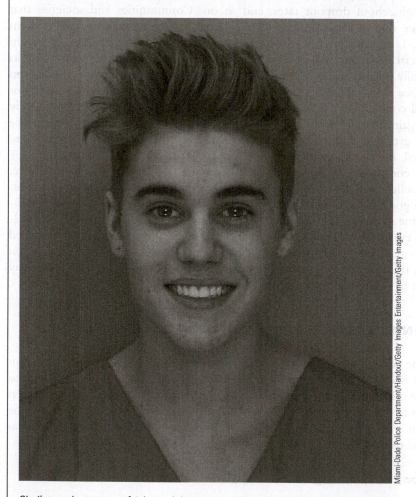

Miami-Dade Police Department/Handout/Getty Images Entertainment/Getty Images

Similar to the arrests of other celebrities, pop star Justin Bieber's recent arrest and resulting mug-shot for DUI and drag racing attracted immediate and immense international media attention.

Online USA/Hulton Archive/Getty Images

The Los Angeles Police Department booking photo of actor Hugh Grant arrested for soliciting sex.

rather than what the public thinks? The hypothesis is that people will tend to judge a social issue such as crime as significant to the extent that the media emphasize it. If true, in time the media will construct the **public agenda.**[19] When a correlation is looked for between media attention and public concern, a weak to moderate relationship is found.[20] Encouraged by this association, the agenda-setting research has concentrated on the media's effects on the public's ranking of issues with the idea that the issues that receive government attention are chosen from the public's list. An early assumption in agenda setting was that the media influence public policy through a linear process. Crime stories appear, crime as an issue increases in public importance, the public becomes alarmed, neighborhood and other public interest groups mobilize and rally for action, and crime-and-justice policymakers respond. Consistent evidence of such a linear process has not emerged from the research, however. The media's influence is seldom direct and is more often modified through multiple steps and social networks.

As the research now stands, a media effect on the public's agenda is generally acknowledged, but unless the effect also appears among policymakers, it is usually regarded as unimportant. Further complicating research, an opposite interaction between the media and criminal justice policy also is possible when policymakers influence what the media cover.[21] Not surprisingly, the research overall indicates that media effects are variable. Effects appear to increase with exposure (those who are exposed to the media content mirror the media ranking of issues more closely); are more significant the less direct experience people have with an issue; are more significant for newer, concrete issues than for older, abstract ones; diminish quickly; and are nonlinear, sometimes reciprocal, and highly interactive with other social and individual processes.[22] Specifically regarding crime and justice, the media emphasis on crime and associated claims about the nature of crime have been credited with raising the public's fear of being victimized and giving crime an inappropriately high ranking on the public agenda. It is felt that crime's high ranking also encourages moral crusades against specific crime issues, heightens public anxiety about crime, and pushes or blocks other serious social problems such as hunger or health care down or off the public agenda.

Beliefs and Attitudes about Crime

The second question is whether exposure to crime-and-justice claims in the media affect a person's beliefs and attitudes about crime—the claims about crime a person accepts as true, and the feelings about crime a person believes to be justified. George Gerbner and his colleagues investigated the association between watching large amounts of television and general perceptions about the world, with the idea that television creates a particularly pernicious social reality for its audience.[23] This process, first described as **worldview cultivation,** was felt to be directly related to the number of hours of television viewed. The researchers hypothesized that through exposure to television's content most everyone comes to have a similar media-constructed view of the world. Over time the repetitive themes and content of the mass media homogenize viewpoints and perspectives. People would come to think like the media and, consequently, to think alike. Prodded by critiques of their initial research,[24] Gerbner and his colleagues amended their initial hypothesis from one of "worldview cultivation," which stated that all media viewers would be affected, to one termed "mainstreaming." **Mainstreaming** posits that the media affect some viewers more than others regardless of exposure level. They now argue that the media are homogenizing society, influencing those heavy television consumers who are currently not in the mainstream to move toward it, while not affecting those already in the mainstream. The significance and extent of a media mainstreaming effect has yet to be determined. Effects on viewer beliefs about the world such as their estimates of the number of crimes in society are acknowledged; effects on the development of mean-world views and mainstreaming are weak and inconsistent and therefore still debated.[25]

One factor that has emerged as important in determining the impact of the media is the local environment of the media consumer. Local conditions and family context in which media information is obtained influence the acceptance or rejection of media-based claims about crime and justice.[26] For example, the relationship between exposure to media content and one's attitudes is expected to diminish when actual neighborhood crime levels are taken into account or if one lives in a violent household. If one's world truly is mean, the media will have less effect on one's view of the world. This conclusion is consistent with the general social construction proposition that media effects are most powerful for issues that are outside of your personal experiences or experienced reality. Media-based claims are expected to have less impact on beliefs about crime among those who have had direct neighborhood experience with crime and thereby have a powerful alternative source of information.

The crime-and-justice attitude that has been most often linked to the media is fear of criminal victimization. Fear-of-crime levels are socially important because they encourage support for punitive criminal justice policies and increased personal social isolation. Viewing television crime shows, for example, has been found to be related to fear of crime, perceived police effectiveness, opposition to gun control, and negative perceptions of sentencing, recidivism, parole, and probation.[27] As the most accessible and pervasive potential source of fear, the role of the media is therefore important—but that role is not clear.[28] Recent research has indicated that anger about crime may be more significant for punitive criminal justice policy support than personal fear of crime.[29] Currently, research suggests that media exposure to crime content is more strongly related to fear about distant, seldom-visited places than to fear about local, personal victimization. Not surprisingly, the public is more likely to accept fear-generating claims about places known only via the media than about directly experienced communities.[30] It also follows that media consumption is more strongly related to fear of general social violence than to fear of personal risk[31] and fear of urban areas more than fear of nonurban areas.[32] What does this research say about people's beliefs and attitudes about crime? At the least, heavy media consumers do share certain beliefs about high societal crime and victimization levels and live in a socially constructed world that is seen as more violent and dangerous—and feared—than the socially constructed world of those who consume less media. The most common effects are increased belief in the prevalence of crime, victimization, and violence, and increasingly cynical, distrustful social attitudes. The media provide the individual social construction "bricks" in the form of individual criminal events and associated crime-and-justice claims to build a crime-and-justice reality foundation. With attitudes about crime and justice as mortar, the public blends all of its media knowledge together with personal experiences into a final crime-and-justice social reality. The media's portrayal of crime and justice thus defines a broad public reality of crime. In that the media tend to construct a particular crime-and-justice reality for their consumers, the logical next question is whether the resulting beliefs and attitudes translate into support for specific crime-and-justice policies.

Crime-and-Justice Policies

Understanding the relationship between the media and the formation of criminal justice policies is important because media effects translate into how tax monies are spent and what actually happens to offenders and victims. Influence on crime-and-justice policy is the ultimate prize in the competition over the construction of crime-and-justice reality. Victorious, policy-influencing claims makers gain power, resources, and ownership of a core social issue (see Box 9.3). Recognizing this, they work diligently to garner media attention and favor. It is also important to distinguish the effect of the media on criminal justice policy formation from their effect on pre-existing popular crime-and-justice attitudes. To the extent that the media accurately reflect already established public attitudes, the media amplify public policy tendencies by simply reinforcing pre-existing punitive attitudes.[33] In this way, the media have a second route of influence on criminal justice policy, one by legitimizing and amplifying nascent punitive public attitudes, and the other by helping to create those attitudes.[34]

Researchers continue to explore the nature of the media–criminal justice policy relationship, and they have been able to report clear connections between the two. The results of the research have established that the media can directly affect what actors in the criminal justice system do without having to first change the public's attitudes or agenda. The idiosyncratic nature of the media–criminal justice policy relationship, however, makes predicting the direction and magnitude of media influence in specific situations difficult. The difficulty arises because the media may themselves be claims makers or serve as the megaphone for nonmedia claims makers, and because the media are as likely to affect criminal justice decision making indirectly as they are to directly influence the formation of crime-and-justice policy. As the models in Box 9.4 show, the media may actually be the cause of a criminal justice policy change (model A). Conversely, an external event may be the cause, while the media simply covers the event prior to the policy change, which would have occurred without media attention

---

B o x   9.3   Three   Strikes   and   You're   Out: A   Mediated   Criminal Justice Policy

---

In the Three Strikes and You're Out legislation, serious crime was redefined and part of the faulty criminal justice system was "fixed." In 1988, Diane Ballasiotes was abducted and stabbed to death in the state of Washington by a convicted rapist who had been released from prison. In reaction to this crime, a group called Friends of Diane formed to seek harsher penalties for sex crimes. This group eventually joined forces with another Washington state policy lobby group that was advocating for Three Strikes legislation. Despite their combined efforts, however, through 1992 there was little legislative or criminal justice professional interest in Three Strikes legislation in Washington. The proposed legislation was perceived as similar to a habitual offender law already on the books, and a petition drive to get three strikes on a statewide ballot failed. Although there was some media coverage, up to that time the Friends of Diane and the Three Strikes groups did not find a receptive social and media environment. As a result, they were unable to be successful claims makers and forward a new dominant construction of criminal justice policy.

In 1993, the Three Strikes group (renamed the Washington Citizens for Justice) allied with the National Rifle Association and succeeded in getting the proposition on the November ballot. This time, despite some opposition from elements of the criminal justice professional community, 77 percent of Washingtonians approved the Three Strikes law. The catalyst for this shift was a tragic "symbolic crime" in California. As the Washington vote approached, a young California girl, Polly Klaas, was abducted and murdered. Coupled to this crime, media coverage of the upcoming Three Strikes vote was extensive, and politicians and citizens across the nation and the political spectrum embraced the new policy as a crime panacea.

A number of social construction concepts clearly come into play in the Three Strikes saga. With the alliance of the NRA, Friends of Diane was able to become a much more powerful claims maker—the NRA was a pre-established group that the media would readily contact. Also, with the kidnapping and murder of Polly Klaas, the Three Strikes and You're Out claims makers had a tragic and powerful symbolic crime that they were able to use to reconstruct the crime problem. Symbolic crimes are crucial, as they ensure media access for claims makers while providing dramatic stories, visuals, and evidence of policies that must be implemented. In Three Strikes, the Polly Klaas murder became the symbolic event that focused the media's attention and lifted the new crime-defining legislation to become a new social reality. (For a recent review of the media role in the history of Three Strikes see Grimes, "The Social Construction of Social Problems".)

SOURCES: Callanan, V. 2005. *Feeding the Fear of Crime: Crime-Related Media and Support for Three Strikes*. New York: LFB Scholarly Publishing LLC; Gest, T. 2001. *Crime and Politics*, London, UK: Oxford University Press; Grimes, J. N. 2010. "The Social Construction of Social Problems: 'Three Strikes and You're Out' in the Mass Media." *Journal of Criminal Justice and Law Review* 2(1/2): 39—55; Shichor, D., and D. Sechrest. 1996. (Eds.) *Three Strikes and You're Out: Vengeance as Public Policy*. Thousand Oaks, CA: Sage.

(model B). Or the media's coverage of an external event and the event may both be influencing criminal justice policy (model C).

The available research indicates that among criminal justice officials, even more than among the public, the media significantly influence both policy development and support. Effects are multidirectional, and media content, the timing and presentation of the claims, and the characteristics and concerns of the general public, claims makers, and the criminal justice policy makers interact

---

B o x 9.4   Media–Criminal Justice Policy Relationship Models

A. Direct Media Influence

Media Coverage → Criminal Justice Policy Change

An investigative news report of ticket fixing leads to a new department policy regarding tickets.

B. No Media Influence External Event

External Event —┬— Criminal Justice Policy Change
                 └— Media Coverage

An external evaluation reveals that low-income defendants are less likely to be offered alternatives to jail sentences. The review and selection process is adjusted as part of a preplanned program refinement cycle at the same time as local media report on the existence of program bias.

C. Simultaneous Media Influence External Event

External Event ┬→ Media Coverage ┬→ Criminal Justice
               └─────────────────┴→ Policy Change

A prisoner on a furlough program commits a violent rape. As a result, the corrections department reviews and alters the furlough program. Due to media publicity of the rape, the program is also suspended for a number of months and more severe restrictions than would be otherwise considered are instituted.

---

to determine the media's influence on criminal justice policies.[35] Misinformation pervades the interplay between crime, politics, and public opinion, however, so as to create a comedy of errors in the formation of criminal justice policy.[36] In what has been called 'crime control theater', claims makers exploit misinformed public opinion with effects that range from broad, far-reaching policy crusades and criminal legislation to specific, narrow influences on decisions in individual cases.[37] The research difficulty is not that the media has insignificant policy effects, but in determining the form that significant effects will take. The task of sorting out the effects of the media from the effects of external events is obviously difficult. Compounding the difficulties, another set of unexpected effects arise from the novel manner in which the media relate to criminal justice policy. Three types appear: echo effects, counterproductive results, and anticipatory reactions.

A media coverage **echo effect** (discussed also in Chapter 6) refers to a tendency for officials to treat defendants in unpublicized cases harshly if the press has been demanding such treatment for defendants in publicized cases. For example, a study of the processing of criminal cases prior to, during, and following a highly publicized case involving the sexual abuse of toddlers at a private day care center demonstrated that an echo effect was in operation.[38] Initial analysis showed marked increases in the number of filings of cases involving child victimization following the publicized case and an increase in the sentences of defendants adjudicated guilty. The existence of echo effects portends an influence spillover from the coverage of newsworthy criminal cases onto unpublicized ones. Diffused but pervasive systemic media effects on a large number of unpublicized cases are likely.

The second unexpected result, **counterproductive effects,** occurs in situations where media attention results in unanticipated consequences, usually involving a crime reduction program. In this effect, some media-based anticrime campaigns have been found to have effects opposite to the campaign goals. For example, a massive multimedia Canadian anticrime campaign was found to actually result in fewer people taking personal anticrime measures.[39] This negative effect was credited to the campaign raising concern about crime to a fatalistic level among the target population, so that they stopped taking any precautions against crime.

A final unique effect is rare for other social research areas, but not uncommon for the media. **Anticipatory effects** seem to reverse the causal order of media attention and criminal justice policy change. It has been discovered that among criminal justice system officials, responses to the media can be either reactive or proactive—that is, they may react to what they have seen and heard in the media or act in anticipation of what they expect to find in the media. In the latter situations, the effect on policy occurs before any observable change in media content. The policy changes occur because criminal justice system officials respond in a proactive manner to anticipated media coverage, perhaps due to seeing negative media coverage of a criminal justice practice in a distant jurisdiction.[40] In these cases, even if the media pay no attention to an issue, an official still acts on the idea that attention might be forthcoming and initiates a new policy or fails to implement a requested policy, to avoid expected negative media attention. In the first instance, a successful policy change cancels the potential coverage, and in the second, the proactive non-policy change is in anticipation of coverage that might never have occurred. In either case, because the media influence policy without any tangible coverage, the task of determining and studying a media policy effect is daunting. The problem is similar to determining how many crimes were not committed as a result of the deterrent effect of a new punishment-based program. Not impossible, but more difficult than counting events that do occur.

Together, anticipatory, echo, and counterproductive effects underscore the idiosyncratic nature of the media–criminal justice policy construction relationship. The unpredictability makes it difficult to determine the direction and magnitude of influence or to specify the mechanism through which the media's influence is being exerted. They add a unique level of difficulty to deciphering the relationship of the media and the criminal justice system. Observed changes can be in anticipation of the media attention (as when prosecutors decide to increase DUI prosecutions to head off potential negative publicity), in anticipation of a policy being changed (as when prosecutors decide to pursue harsher sentences for drunk drivers due to the echo effect from a highly publicized DUI case), or due to a criminal justice policy change directly lobbied for by the media (as when DUI prosecutions increase due to an investigatory media series suggesting that lenient treatment for DUI offenders is common).

There is the real possibility of one effect occurring to prevent a second effect. In such a case, a pre-emptive decision to not change an established policy in favor of a new policy might occur so as to avoid the anticipated negative media coverage generated by the appearance and subsequent waning of an announcement effect of the (now rejected) new criminal justice policy. For example, a prosecutor sensitive to media dynamics may decide against launching a tougher but expensive new DUI policy to avoid the problem of future negative coverage of the apparent loss of initial prosecutorial effectiveness that will occur when the media-generated announcement effect wanes. At that point, the new DUI policy, cast as suddenly failing to maintain its initial successful deterrent impact, results in the prosecutor being called to task. Sensing this pitfall, the prosecutor might well decide to forgo this or other new policies. The recognition and delineation of the media's role in such a scenario would be Herculean. Indeed, based on the discussion thus far, confidently comprehending any policy effect of the media appears daunting, and it is perhaps surprising that knowledge has progressed as far as it has.

THE SOCIAL CONSTRUCTION OF CRIME-AND-JUSTICE POLICY

As stated earlier, the ultimate impact of social constructionism on criminal justice is found in its implication for criminal justice policy. For it is with our crime-and-justice policy decisions that we decide how we are going to collectively respond to crime, deal with offenders, and spend our taxes. The media's role is not praised. "We have a public dialogue that is segmented and reduced to sound bites, content that dulls an increasingly inattentive populace, and media that provides feedback via call-ins, Internet polls, and narrow constituencies."[41] Figure 9.1 lays out the relationship between the media, social constructionism, and criminal justice policy. As shown, the relationship between the media and their crime-and-justice content influences the social construction of crime-and-justice reality by supplying the narratives, symbolic crimes, and basic information needed to create factual and interpretative claims.[42] The media further provide the arena for the crime-and-justice social construction competition to be held, thereby favoring media-savvy claims makers. This in turn encourages a particular set of social attitudes and perceptions about crime and justice; predatory criminality and an overly lenient justice system are popular. The final and most important influence in this relationship chain is on criminal justice policies. How policies are presented and perceived determines whether they are supported or opposed and media-constructed crime waves are sometimes transformed into real-world criminal justice policies.[43]

The media are not the most important factor in the construction of crime-and-justice policy (real-world conditions and direct experiences are more

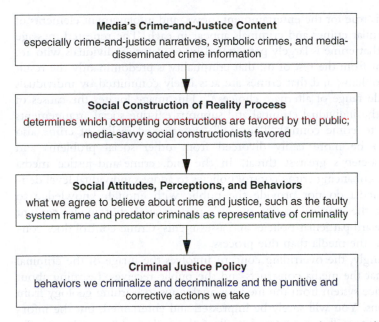

Media's Crime-and-Justice Content
especially crime-and-justice narratives, symbolic crimes, and media-disseminated crime information

Social Construction of Reality Process
determines which competing constructions are favored by the public; media-savvy social constructionists favored

Social Attitudes, Perceptions, and Behaviors
what we agree to believe about crime and justice, such as the faulty system frame and predator criminals as representative of criminality

Criminal Justice Policy
behaviors we criminalize and decriminalize and the punitive and corrective actions we take

F I G U R E 9.1   Media, Social Constructionism, and Criminal Justice Policy.

important) but the media's influence cannot be ignored.[44] The media are not often found to be direct causes of criminal justice policy shifts but they function as part of a larger social matrix that generates and preserves the dominant attitudes about crime and justice.[45] Beyond policy formation, the media also are important for the spread of criminal justice policies. A recent review of the literature on the diffusion of criminal justice policies reported that media attention was a significant factor in whether a criminal justice policy was adopted in other jurisdictions.[46] They remain influential because their content regarding social problems resonates strongly with the emotional framework of the public.[47] Perceptions of crime and justice appear to be intertwined with other social perceptions, and crime-related attitudes are not determined solely by one's perception of the crime problem. Instead, perceptions of crime and justice are part of a larger construction of the nature and health of society. And if perceptions of crime are intricately related to broader perceptions of the world, it is unrealistic to expect that they would change solely in accordance with media presentations of crime. That being said, if there is a general media effect on criminal justice policy, it is to increase punitiveness and surveillance as the first and sometimes only policy choices.[48] A punitive policy effect, however, need not be the default impact of the media; there is evidence that when media framing of capital punishment shifted from supportive to portraying capital punishment as flawed, an associated downward shift in public support for executions followed.[49]

For the most part though, the image of justice that most people find the most palatable and popular is the image that the media have historically projected. This is true for the entertainment, news, and infotainment elements of the media, as similar crimes and criminals appear in each. The repeated message in the media is that crime is largely perpetrated by predatory individuals who are basically different from the rest of us; that criminality is predominantly the result of individual problems; and that crimes are acts freely committed by individuals who have a wide range of alternate choices.[50] This image locates the causes of crime solely in the individual criminal and supports existing social arrangements and approaches to crime control. The media-constructed reality of crime also allows crime to be more easily divorced from other social problems and highlighted as society's greatest threat. In the end, crime-and-justice media advances system-enhancing crime control policies to address individual level deficiencies. The media do not provide the public with enough knowledge to directly evaluate the criminal justice system's performance, but media content steers people toward particular policies and assessments. Crime control does consistently better in the media than due process.

Not surprisingly, the overriding concern involves the image of the criminal justice system that the media constructs and the public receives. Learning about the criminal justice system from the media is analogous to learning geology from volcanic eruptions. You will surely be impressed and entertained, but the information you receive will not accurately reflect the real world, whether you're looking at volcanoes or at the criminal justice system. The media-constructed reality of predatory crimes, high-stakes trials, and violent riots contrasts starkly with the criminal justice system's daily reality of property crime, plea bargains, and order maintenance. The public is shown that the traditional criminal justice system is not effective and is simultaneously told that its improvement remains the best solution to crime. While critical pieces on criminal justice have increased in frequency and media exposés have led to the exoneration of some wrongly convicted persons, the tendency is to portray misconduct within a "bad apple" framework and to preserve the overall portrait of the police and the criminal justice system as the sole solution to crime.[51] These messages translate into support for order over law, punishment over rehabilitation and criminal-justice-based over non-criminal-justice-based policies.[52] This portrait has naturally led to concern. Criminologist David Altheide observes that: "The only response we seem to have is to wait and to prepare (get armed, lock doors, build walls, and avoid strangers and public places). This may be a good formula for cinema thrillers, but it is lousy for everyday life."[53] Fear and fatalistic acceptance of crime, mystification of the criminal justice system, myopic support for punitive criminal justice policies, and increased tolerance for illegal law enforcement practices all result.

How could the media portray crime and justice better? On the criminal justice system side, system impact statements have been recommended as required accompaniments for new crime-related legislation as counterbalances to the emotion driven waves that push through ill-conceived new legislation.[54] On the media side, the news media have the experience and a coverage model to adopt if they want to improve. The media provide comprehensive, contextual coverage for sporting events on a daily basis and sports coverage stands as a model for reporting on individual events, supplemented by statistics, trend analysis, forecasts, commentary, and discussion. Sporting events are consistently placed by the media in their larger social context (the world of sports) and constructed in a way that provides both historical understanding and current significance. Covering crime and justice like sports would provide the public with a counterweight to the distorted and currently unchallenged entertainment and infotainment constructions. In that manner, crime could be removed from the realm of the bizarre, grotesque, and sinister and placed in the social world of poverty, loss of community, alienation, group conflict, and psychological disorders.[55]

Sports, though, are covered in breadth and depth because there is strong public demand and interest. Lacking a similar incentive regarding criminal justice, there is no reason to expect the commercial media to direct their limited resources to delivering an expanded justice portrait. It's not that they cannot do it, but lacking a large enough market, they cannot afford to do it. In the social construction of crime and justice, we won't get what too few are willing to pay for. The crime-and-justice media that will be delivered will be that which can be produced profitably. The most profitable content follows entertainment narratives, formatting, and frames. Whether in news, infotainment, or entertainment, this profitable content carries imbedded messages about criminal justice polices and encourages public support for policies that will fix and enhance what some view as the "faulty" criminal justice system while discouraging support for other approaches. Some hold out hope that new social media can reverse this tendency.[56] The possibility of new media to the rescue is discussed in the ensuing chapter.

SUMMARY

- The backwards law says that in many respects the media portrait of crime and justice will be the opposite of what is true. This backwards portrait leads to a crime-and-justice ecology made up of wolf-like predatory offenders; heroic, protective crime fighters; and sheep-like victims. Crime control policies are advanced at the expense of due process model policies.

- The solution to crime constructed in the media is often aided by events that reflect a type of "immanent justice" in which fortuitous, seemingly divine intervention prevents criminals from prevailing and ensures that crime ultimately does not pay.

- Technology plays a central role in the media-constructed solution to crime. Equipment and surveillance are offered as core crime solution elements.

- Research on the relationship between media and criminal justice policy has focused on agenda setting, beliefs and attitudes about crime, and direct media effects on criminal justice policy formation. Relationships between media and policy have been reported in all three areas but consistent media effects are not reported.

- The relationship between the media and criminal justice policy is complex, hard to predict, and prone to unanticipated effects including news coverage echoes, anticipatory actions on the part of policy makers, and counterproductive consequences from media attention.

- Criminal justice policy development and debate would be better served if crime and justice was covered as thoroughly as sports. The snapshot episodic coverage of crime overwhelms media content that discusses criminal justice policy issues.

CLASS DISCUSSIONS

1. Discuss a local crime or criminal justice event that resulted in heavy media coverage and in calls for a change in a criminal justice policy. Discuss how the competing constructions of the issue were framed, whether the event became a symbolic crime, and whether a policy change followed or appears likely. Discuss which features of the crime or event made it more or less likely to generate a memorial criminal justice policy.

2. Discuss the use of immanent justice ideas in the social construction of terrorism by both terrorists and governments.

3. Discuss how criminal justice policy is debated and covered in the media noting how references to crime-and-justice events by politicians and other policy makers are couched and how different criminal justice policies are framed and socially constructed in the media by claims makers.

SUGGESTED READINGS

Altheide, D. (2002). *Creating fear: News and the construction of crisis*. Hawthorne: Aldine de Gruyter.

Beckett, K., and Sasson, T. (2000). *The politics of injustice*. Thousand Oaks: Pine Forge Press.

Callanan, V. (2005). *Feeding the fear of crime: Crime-related media and support for three strikes*. New York: LFB Scholarly Publishing LLC.

Gest, T. (2001). *Crime and politics*. London: Oxford University Press.

Shichor, D., and Sechrest, D. (1996) (Eds.). *Three strikes and you're out: Vengeance as public policy*. Thousand Oaks: Sage.

Silverman, J. (2012). *Crime, policy and the media: The shaping of criminal justice, 1989-2010*. New York: Routledge.

CHAPTER 10

New Media, Crime, and Justice

CHAPTER OBJECTIVES:

After reading Chapter 10, you will

- Appreciate the difference between legacy media and new media
- Recognize the social effects and concerns related to new media
- Have an overview of the ways new media, crime, and justice intersect
- Comprehend how new media broaden criminality and encourage performance crimes
- See how new media have been adopted by law enforcement, the courts, and corrections

NEW MEDIA, CRIME, AND JUSTICE

The quip "Everyone wants their fifteen gigabytes of fame" describes one way that new media have changed society.[1] Changes in society associated with new media dominate social experiences and today many people communicate and compete for attention through their media more often than in their face-to-face encounters with people. This change has had significant effects on crime and justice. The key characteristic of new media that underlies the social changes is that new media's content is composed of digital information that is quickly and easily shared among large audiences. It follows that the main difference between old and new media is not the quality of content found (the portraits of crime and justice for example are similar in legacy and new media products) but lies in the access to content, the distribution of content, and the creation of content that new media affords. In the legacy media world, media content was created and distributed by a distant media industry. With new media avenues, consumers are also distributors of others' content and producers of their own self-generated content.[2]

B o x 10.1   An Overview of Cybercrime

Cybercrime encompasses a broad range of behaviors that include old and new types of crime and has its historical roots in the culture of computer hacking, a skill that depending upon its application can be criminal or non-criminal in nature. A useful cybercrime typology offered by David Wall breaks cybercrime into four realms: trespass (hacking into restricted or private online sites); deception and theft (online piracy, fraud, and identity theft); pornography and obscenity (including prostitution and pedophilia); and violence (harassment, stalking, and terrorism).

Regarding specific cybercrimes, piracy is one of the most studied, with ongoing debate about whether it should be classified as a crime or not. Fraud and identity theft are two traditional crimes that have been significantly enhanced as cybercrimes through new media avenues. Their growth in new media has generated a new vocabulary with terms such as the coined word, "phishing" (using a false e-mail or other new media avenue to obtain personal information) entering common usage. Sex crimes are another area that has been significantly impacted by new media. In the present day a wide range of deviant and criminal sexual behaviors are enabled through the Internet and social media. New media has been credited with influencing general sexual social practices, encouraging sexual "performance" acts via sexting and webcams, and changing the nature and marketing of the illicit sex trade. Two particular characteristics of new media, anonymity and intimacy, have encouraged specific subcultures to develop around the crimes of hacking, terrorism, and pedophilia.

Theories of cybercrime are embryonic. Reflecting the broad range of crimes and behaviors that fall under the cybercrime umbrella, a single theory of cybercrime has not developed and criminological explanations incorporate a broad range of traditional theoretical explanations. Neutralization has been forwarded as a theoretical explanation for both piracy and child predation but routine activities theory, differential association (linked to the anonymity of the Internet), and control theories have also been forwarded as explanations. The criminal justice system response to cybercrime has been generally one of playing catch up. The assessment of law enforcement's ability to investigate and the judicial system to prosecute cybercrime is one of insufficient ability coupled with limited resources. Police officer perceptions of the problem have been driven more by media depictions of cybercrime than by crime or victimization data. With offenders often in one country and victims in another, traditional police departments remain unprepared to investigate or pursue cybercrimes.

The existence of new media, in particular social media, has resulted in broad cultural changes in how the public receives and processes information and understands and interacts with the world.[3] People today communicate more frequently but less often in face-to-face encounters than in the past. Our personal social networks are broader but shallower. More and more, how we define ourselves and how others define us are determined in the digital world of new media. In terms of knowledge about the world, enormous amounts of information and people are accessible and new media provide access to the personal diaries,

SOURCES:Brenner, S. 2007. "Cybercrime: Re-thinking Crime Control Strategies." In *Crime Online*. Yvonne Jewkes (Ed.), 12–28. Portland: Willan; DiMarco, H. 2003. "The Electronic Cloak; Secret Sexual Deviance in Cybersociety." In *Dot.coms: Crime, Deviance, and Identity on the Internet*. Yvonne Jewkes (Ed.), 53–67. Portland: Willan; Durkin, K and Bryant, C. 1999. "Propagandizing Pederasty: A Thematic Analysis of the On-Line Exculpatory Accounts of Unrepentant Pedophiles." *Deviant Behavior* 20: 103–127; Higgins, G. 2004. "Can Low Self-Control Help with the Understanding of the Software Piracy Problem?" *Deviant Behavior* 26: 1–24; Hollinger, R. and Lanza-Kaduce, L. 2006. "The Process of Criminalization: The Case of Computer Crime Laws." *Criminology* 26: 101–126; Holt, T. 2013. "Cybercrime" Oxford Bibliographies Online. Downloaded July 18, 2013 from http://www.oxfordbibliographies.com/view/document/obo-9780195396607/obo-9780195396607-0025.xml?rskey=thchdS&result=22&q=; Holt, T. and Bossler, A. 2009. "Examining the Applicability of Lifestyle-Routine Activities Theory for Cybercrime Victimization." *Deviant Behavior* 30: 1–25; Holt, T., and K. Blevins. 2007. "Examining Sex Work from the Client's Perspective: Assessing Johns Using Online Data." *Deviant Behavior* 28: 333–354; Ingram, J. and Hinduja, S. 2008. "Neutralizing Music Piracy: An Empirical Examination." *Deviant Behavior* 29: 334–366; Levy, S. 1984. Hackers: Heroes of the Computer Revolution. Garden City: Anchor Doubleday; Marsh, I. and Melville, G. 2009. Crime Justice and the Media. London: Routledge; Newman, G. and Clarke, R. 2003. Superhighway Robbery: Preventing E-Commerce Crime. Portland, OR: Willan; Sanjo. S. 2004. "An Analysis of Computer-Related Crime: Comparing Police Officer Perceptions with Empirical Data." *Security Journal* 17 (2): 55–71; Taylor, R., Fritsch, E., Liederbach, J., and Holt, T. 2011. Digital Crime and Digital Terrorism. Upper Saddle River: Prentice Hall; Wall, D. 2001. Crime and the Internet. NY: Routledge; Yar, M. 2007."Teenage Kicks or Virtual Villainy? Internet Piracy, Moral Entrepreneurship, and the Social Construction of a Crime Problem." *In Crime Online*. Yvonne Jewkes (Ed.), 95–108. Portland: Willan Publishing.

photo albums, and home movies of millions of people, most of it freely provided by the subjects. The early twenty-first century is an era of unprecedented self-surveillance where people voluntarily place themselves open to the voyeuristic gaze of others.[4] Lastly, multi-function new media devices have permanently altered the "media creation-individual consumption" relationship so that in the contemporary media world content consumption is a participatory activity. People no longer just consume media content, they also participate in how news stories are covered and entertainment is crafted.

The world of crime and criminal justice has not been immune to these changes. The most obvious is that new media allow the public to not only watch crime and justice but to participate in criminal justice.[5] Legacy media allowed us to look over the shoulder of criminals and crime fighters in the war on crime; new media allow us to directly join the battle. This chapter explores some of the ways that new media have altered how offenders, victims, and police react to crime; how crimes are committed and investigated; how the courts operate and process cases; and how sentenced prisoners behave and corrections operate. The administration of justice, the investigation of crimes, the prosecution and defense of the accused, and the administration of corrections have all changed.[6] New media provide platforms for crime-related content to influence perceptions and attitudes about crime and justice and in the process to entertain within an emergent "mediated reality." Within this mediated reality, the ability of traditional criminal justice agencies to maintain ownership of crime issues and events is more difficult than in the past. The social construction of crime and justice in new media is a more fluid, multi-directional process; multiple social constructions emerge and compete, each adopted by different audience segments.

New media in the form of the Internet and social media are accepted parts of the criminal justice system. Agencies throughout the justice system have incorporated the information sharing and distribution capabilities of new media in investigations and case processing. As these capabilities become a routine part of the administration of justice, the issuing of warrants, complaints, and discovery requests; the preservation and presentation of evidence; and the conducting of post-conviction motions and hearings will be commonly administered through new media mobile devices and on social media platforms.[7] As found for legacy media, though, new media are double-edged swords. On the negative side, new media means new ways to commit old crimes and opportunities to commit entirely new types of crimes. Cybercrime has become a leading criminal justice concern (see Box 10.1). New media also distribute false information as quickly as accurate information and extend the reach and impact of rumors.[8] The spread of unsubstantiated rumors through YouTube, Facebook, and online news outlets such as followed recent school shootings provide examples of this moral panic process.[9] In addition, direct effects on criminality have been noted with the new media generated phenomenon of "flash mobs" as one example and the development of "performance crime" by people willing to settle for infamy in place of fame as another.[10]

Between the benign impact of moving documents from paper to digital mode and obvious criminality linked to new media-based terrorism and the "dark web" (see Box 10.2), there are a set of middle ground issues and impacts that are yet to be determined as positive or negative. Issues under debate concerning social media include what constitutes criminality within social media, what is admissible as evidence obtained from social networking-generated information and virtual crime scenes; and what restrictions on new media access can be part of a criminal sentence?[11] A discussion of new media's effects on criminality is next, followed by reviews of their effect on each component of the criminal justice system: law enforcement, the courts, and corrections.

B o x   10.2   The Dark Web

The "dark web" (also known as the deep or invisible web) refers to a secretive online world described as beyond regular internet search engines and as anonymous, virtually untraceable, and global. The operation of the dark web relies on free software that enables online anonymity. In the dark web one finds an online black market for fake passports, guns, child pornography, and drugs. Gaining access requires downloading free software based on peer-to-peer file sharing which scrambles the location of users and dark web Web sites. With the cover of anonymity, the potential for criminality in the dark web is significant. A drug dealer was quoted: "I feel much safer online than doing transactions in the real world. Nowadays I almost strictly use the dark web for any drug transaction." Law enforcement has only recently begun to address these online markets. For example, in 2013 the FBI arrested the owner/organizer of "Silk Road," an anonymous Internet marketplace for illegal drugs and criminal activities. Like all media, the dark web is not totally pernicious. It has been cited as a positive means for communication between dissidents in totalitarian countries and was credited with having helped organizers behind the 2010 Arab Spring protests.

SOURCE: Goldberg, A. 2012. "The Dark Web: Guns and Drugs for Sale on the Internet's Secret Black Market." www.bbc.co.uk/news/business-16801382; Flitter, E. 2013. "FBI Shuts Alleged Online Drug Marketplace, Silk Road." http://www.reuters.com/article/2013/10/02/us-crime-silkroad-raid-idUSBRE9910TR20131002.

NEW MEDIA, CRIMINALITY, AND VICTIMIZATION

New media effects on criminality happen in five ways. First, new media provide new ways to commit old types of crime. Second, new media provide new types of crime to commit. Third, social media provide a new means to "perform" criminality as a social statement. Fourth, new media generate copycat crimes. Lastly, new media affects the behaviors of potential crime victims.

Old Crimes in New Ways

New media has provided a means for offenders to commit traditional crimes in new ways.[12] A prime example is provided by terrorism, which has been a means of displaying political violence for over 2,000 years. New media has altered both how acts of terror are committed and the strategic goals of terrorists.[13] The change in how terrorism is committed is shown by cyber-attacks that allow both state and non-state terrorist groups to attack governments, organizations, and individuals who have an online presence. New media effects on terrorism are linked to the reach of the content that social media provides. New media allow simultaneous global recruitment of new terrorists and dissemination of pro-paganda. Terrorist messages can be tailored for near and distant audiences, victims, enemies, and supporters. The regular online posting of videos of terrorism, the use of mobile phones to organize and carry out terrorism, and the numerous terrorist related Internet sites exemplify how the contemporary terrorist has embraced new media.[14] Lastly, a phenomena termed "**crime sourcing**" has emerged. Crime sourcing is described as taking a portion of a criminal act and outsourcing it to a crowd of either witting or unwitting helpers.[15] In crime-sourcing large numbers of strangers can be recruited to help commit a crime such as money laundering or computer hacking. One example is provided by an armored car robber who used a Craigslist ad to assemble similarly dressed decoys to cover his escape by leaving a large crowd of look-alike suspects behind at the robbery scene.[16]

Research on new media and traditional crime is not extensive, but long-standing property and white collar crimes such as theft and fraud have become international in nature through new media. Internet fraud and identity theft are forecast to be the most significant crime problem associated with new media as hackers, spies, organized crime, and terrorists as well as common criminals tap into new media to victimize people.[17] Social media and global networks have made it easier for identity thieves to obtain names, addresses, dates-of-birth, work and school locations, phone numbers, and additional personal information. Social media combined with mobile phones have provided mechanisms to arrange riots, gang fights, and shoplifting sprees in a new fashion. For example, recent riots in the United Kingdom were coordinated through social media when rioters used Facebook, Twitter, and BlackBerrys to disseminate information, coordinate rioting, and evade the police.[18] A number of Facebook users were subsequently jailed for using the site to incite violence. A final set of examples are provided by the two historically face-to-face offenses of bullying and stalking that have evolved with new media. "Cyber-bullying" has become recognized as a unique new form of social harassment with its own pernicious dynamics of anonymity, broad social exposure, and continuous threats that make social media based "peer-to-peer" bullying more harmful than the older face-to-face schoolyard version.[19] Along similar lines, social media have made stalking a distant, virtual experience where stalkers can follow from afar and digitally drop in and out of someone's life.[20] In addition to these longstanding criminal acts, criminals also utilize new media capabilities to select and maneuver their victims. This has emerged as a special concern regarding sexual predation.

A major public apprehension regarding new media and victimization involves the use of the Internet by sexual predators.[21] In 2009, for example, when MySpace removed 90,000 sex offenders from its site, more than 8,000 of them immediately reappeared on Facebook. Despite public concern and periodic moral panics, little actual research has been conducted on sexually predatory males, called "travelers" in the literature, who solicit children online, establish virtual relationships, and arrange meetings for sex.[22] The use of new media to reach victims is not limited to sexual crimes. Murderers have had their initial contacts with their homicide victims on social media and burglars have identified unoccupied homes from Internet- and social media-provided information.[23] In a limited law enforcement response, counterefforts by law enforcement include online undercover child sex stings where law enforcement agents place ads on social networking sites soliciting sexual encounters with children or child pornography and pose as either children or as parents looking to prostitute their children.[24] These efforts have produced popular infotainment programming in the genre of the "Dateline NBC: To Catch a Predator" series, which depicted a parade of males appearing at a home expecting to have sex with a child only to be arrested by waiting police. How effective these efforts are at deterrence is not known, but the fact that some offenders have been caught more than once by the same ploy is not encouraging. In addition to providing criminal predators' new means to acquire victims, new media also provide new types of crimes to commit.

New Media and New Crime

In addition to the morphing of old crimes, new media have generated entirely new types of crime. An example is provided by the social media–generated phenomenon of "flash mobs," which sometimes turn criminogenic. Coordinated via social media to appear as a seemingly spontaneous activity, flash mobs involve the convergence of a large number of strangers at an agreed upon time and place to perform some agreed upon behavior. Initially benign activities such as dancing or singing would seemingly spontaneously 'break out' among the assembled mob. However, riots and "flash mob" shoplifting and vandalism sprees have also been generated.[25] The online reaction to a movie provides a specific example. The film, *Project X* shows a wild house party arranged by a group of unsupervised teenage males. The imitation of the film led to copycat flash mob parties in the United Kingdom, the Netherlands, and the United States.[26]

The bizarre nature of life in the new media world confounds what constitutes crime. In new media, when a crime occurs is a debatable issue. As Box 10.3 relates, whether new–media–based activity qualifies as real-world criminality and when someone is the victim of a crime in virtual reality are unclear. Law enforcement agencies and the courts are still determining where the borders lie. While new crimes and new ways of committing old crimes continue to develop, currently the most obvious impact of new media on crime is through "performance crime", or crime purposely committed to gain attention in the new media reality world.

New Media and Performance Crime

Performance crime encompasses the spectacle of performing acts of crime and deviance in order to record, share, and upload them to the Internet.[27] Media-generated **performance crime** can be traced to the early twentieth century and the recording of torture and ritual humiliation of prisoners and hostages by governments and terrorist groups.[28] The photos of the abuse at the Iraq Abu Ghraib prison provide a recent example. The recent explosion of performance crime is linked to the celebrity culture of the early twentieth century. The emergence of "celebrated criminals" (people who because of their criminality became celebrities, the gangster Al Capone for example) and "criminal celebrities" (persons who were celebrities first and subsequently became linked to crime) through either serious crimes such as murder (football stars O. J. Simpson and Aaron Hernandez come to mind) or strings of comparatively minor offenses (Lindsay Lohan, Paris Hilton, or Justin Bieber) paved the way for criminality as a way to enhance fame.[29] Laying the foundation for the development of the celebrity criminal was the recognition that a famous criminal could be a valuable commodity. Their value continues today, as reflected in the bus tours that visit famous crime scenes and the continuous sale of artwork and other memorabilia

---

B o x 10.3   New Media, New Crimes

The Cannibal Police Officer A New York City police officer was convicted in 2013 for kidnapping conspiracy for discussing on an Internet site the kidnapping, rape, murder, and cannibalization of females. The question the case raised was: when does a virtual crime, contemplated in an Internet chat room, become criminality? The answer hinges on the distinction between fantasy and reality and when a perverse fantasy crosses into a culpable criminal plan. As described, the trial of the officer "highlighted some of the darkest corners of the Internet, where fetishists hide behind Web identities like Girlmeat Hunter." The crux of the case was the prosecutor's ability to convince a jury that the police officer was not simply role playing, but rather laying the groundwork for actually kidnapping, torturing and killing women he had targeted.

In a second case that shows the current fog over who is a victim of crime in new media settings, a woman in Japan was arrested for killing her virtual-reality husband. Divorced in a virtual online game, "Maple Story," the woman killed the online avatar of her ex-virtual-reality husband by hacking his computer. When he discovered that he was now digitally dead, the victim complained to the police, who arrested the woman on suspicion of illegally accessing a computer and manipulating electronic data. The woman did not plan any real-world revenge but was held criminally responsible for her actions within the game world.

SOURCES: 'Ugly Thoughts' Defense Fails; Officer Guilty in Cannibal Plot." Benjamin Weiser, N.Y. Times. March 13, 2013, Wed. A1, A20; "Woman Arrested for Killing Virtual Reality Husband." CNN.com/technology. Downloaded from: http://www.cnn.com/2008/TECH/ptech/10/23/avatar.murder.japan.ap/index.heml.

The New York Daily News and the New York Post on Tuesday, February 26, 2013 both use the same headline in their coverage of the trial of NYPD officer Gilberto Valle, accused of fantasizing about cannibalism.

---

associated with famous predators (for example, the Bonnie and Clyde death car can be viewed at a roadside museum in Nevada). However, as victims gained public and media interest, predatory criminality became the primary portrait of criminals, and punitive criminal justice policies gained public support, celebrated criminals fell into disfavor and were supplanted by the more benign celebrity criminal which dominates the world of crime fame today.[30]

Mass-produced performance crime is possible due to the shift from one-way media effects associated with legacy media to the new media dynamic where consumers are also producers of self-generated media content.[31] With this shift, the time process of self-promotion through criminality changed. With legacy media, the process most often followed this sequence: First one had a crime career, second came an arrest and punishment, and third their story was promoted and marketed. With new media, especially social media, the process is often that crime and promotion are simultaneous. As the examples in Box 10.4 demonstrate, new media encourages people to be seen and socially validated and YouTube's call to 'broadcast yourself' has resulted in a host of video postings of offenders voluntarily posting incriminating visual records of their crimes.

Today, popular attention to celebrated criminals continues to decline, but following criminal celebrities is on the rise.[32] Whereas until the late twentieth century, connection to criminality was a career killer for media personalities, criminal behavior by pre-existing celebrities is more accepted today.[33] The confluence of social acceptance of celebrity criminals, heavily covered media trials, and new media supported audience participation expectations have resulted in a significant surge in performance crime. The contemporary public expectation of entertaining crime-and-justice spectacles has increased the number of celebrity criminals, celebrity victims, and criminal performances by non–celebrities seeking attention.[34] The capability of new social media to rapidly elevate the visibility of previously unknown individuals means that anyone can become celebrated, at least for a while. The distinction between fame and infamy has blurred and the growth of performance crime has also encouraged an increase in new media generated copycat crime as criminal performances attract large audiences and trigger imitators.

New Media and Copycat Crime

The spread of the 2010 "Arab Spring" uprisings in the Middle East provide an example of a powerful contagion effect related to new media.[35] An earlier, more pernicious example comes from the cluster of Internet-posted beheadings of hostages displayed by various terror groups in the 1990s. The copycat effect related to new media that has generated the greatest debate, however, concerns digital video games, particularly those that portray crime and violence. There is a long and continuing debate about the impact of video games on video game players and the causal role that video games might play in the generation of violent behavior in society (discussed in Chapter 4). On one side, the association between game play and aggression has been repeatedly reported.[36] The view of this set of research is that adolescents who play violent video games show increases in aggression over time and that the effect of playing violent games is substantively different from the more benign effects from playing nonviolent video games. On the opposing side of the debate, critics argue that much of the research used to demonstrate a causal link ignores important factors such as the level of competitiveness within games and player characteristics. These factors are argued to be more important in the generation of violent behavior than

---

B o x 10.4   Performance Crime Examples

In addition to making available innumerable videos of news, trials, crimes, and criminal justice-related events, the popular Internet site YouTube, where people can post personal videos and view from among thousands of videos posted by others, has resulted in some unique performance crimes. Offenders have posted videos of themselves in the act of committing offenses, generating in some cases the evidence used for their arrest and conviction and in other cases launching a series of copycat crimes.

In one example, a woman appears in a YouTube video bragging about a bank robbery she had committed. In the seven-minute video she is pictured flashing cash and holding handwritten signs stating that she had robbed a bank and stolen a car. At one point the woman holds a large bundle of money up to the camera and then pauses to smoke what the subtitles call "a full bowl of weed." A copy of the video was entered as evidence after her arrest. A second example is "Smack Cam," the hitting of people while recording the assaults for later posting (also known as the "knockout game" or "happy slapping"). A unique feature of this type of performance criminality is the purposeful organization and recording of the crimes as they were committed. A live record of a performance crime usually requires a multi-person production crew of at least one person to commit the crime and another to record it – the equivalent of an actor and a cameraman. An extreme example from Australia involved eight teenagers who sexually assaulted a girl, filmed the assault, created DVDs, and sold them on-line for five dollars a copy. Before the distribution of the video was halted, the price of the DVD rose to sixty dollars a copy following publicity of the incident. A last example is provided by a Miami, Florida man who after shooting his wife, confessed on his Facebook page and posted a photo of her bloody body. His last Facebook status update read: "I'm going to prison or death sentence for killing my wife. Love you guys. Miss you guys. Take care. Facebook people you will see me in the news."

SOURCES: Locker, M. (2012, Dec 5 http://newsfeed.time.com/2012/12/05/women-brags-about-robbery-on-youtube; Yar, M. 2012. "Crime Media, and the Will-To-Representation." *Crime Media Culture* 8(3): 252; http://en.wikipedia.org/wiki/2006_Melbourne_teenage_DVD_controversy; http://www.news.com.au/breaking-news/werribee-dvd-assault-offered-for-sale-for-60/story-e6frfkp9-1111112438164; Ovalle, D and Ducassi, D. 2013, August 9. "Facebook Status: I Killed My Wife." *Miami Herald*, A1.

---

simple exposure to violent video games.[37] The conclusion of the opposing perspective is that the research findings reported thus far are not strong enough to warrant the marketing restrictions on video games that have been called for.[38]

In time, the details of the dynamics of video game effects and a consensus regarding them should emerge. Collectively, the research from both sides of the debate suggests that a significant interactive effect between game player and video game characteristics exists. Strong evidence of a direct causal video game role in the generation of criminality is not found with video games.[39] Still, they do not escape as free of influence. Gaming appears to interact with other prior risk factors to heighten predisposed criminogenic impulses. Current speculation is that video games play the role of catalytic rudders in the formation of crime, not directly causing it but shaping its appearance.[40] Regardless of the causal role for video games, there exist a number of examples of new media copycat crime

New media have made performance crimes more common. Shown are two fighting boys being filmed by other teenagers with their mobile phones.

Kuttig-People/Alamy

waves linked to video games and YouTube videos. Of course, crime needs victims and new media have also influenced the behavior of victims.

New Media and Criminal Victimization

The psychological impact of communicating through new media, the feeling of safety and personal contact that accompanies live, often visual communication, has changed how people sometimes assess social situations and risk. New media have led to faulty, and sometimes fatal risk assessments by some victims while becoming part of the victimization process for other crimes. In the first process, the psychological sense with new media that you are not alone because you are able to converse in real time with others and thus feel "safe," has led some eventual victims to ignore risks and individuals have walked into dangerous high-crime-risk situations.[41]

In the second process, the social need to share and a sense that a criminal act has become socially acceptable because its distribution on social media has a waiting audience adds an additional public humiliation layer to being a crime victim. Akin to cyber-bullying, a depressing set of examples currently exist where someone was victimized, often in a sexual assault, and their victimization was subsequently publicized in a secondary follow-on victimization involving public exposure and ridicule (see Box 10.5). A number of suicides by postcrime victimization victims exposed to additional social humiliation have occurred. In these cases, new media play an initial role as part of a performance crime that has been recorded by offenders. It is the distribution via new media platforms of the visual record of the initial victimization that adds additional harm in a perverse "shaming the victim" social process. In a less pernicious example, recent revelations of the hacking of crime victim's mobile phones and social media accounts by news media in the United Kingdom further demonstrates the emerging convoluted relationships that are developing between victims, offenders, the media, and the criminal justice systems in the new media era.[42]

In sum, regarding crime and victimization, new media have demonstrated the collective capability to create new ways to commit crime and reach victims. New media furthermore can encourage the performance and copying of crimes while extending the harm of being a victim of crime. Like all media, the effects of new media are not solely negative and offenders and predators are not the only ones to have tapped the potential of new media. The components of the criminal justice system have begun to embrace new media as a useful tool.

NEW MEDIA AND LAW ENFORCEMENT

Similar to offenders, law enforcement agencies have also learned to utilize new media. New media are emerging as a law enforcement resource for both proactive crime prevention and reactive crime response. Currently police agencies employ new media in their investigations of crimes, their identification and pursuit of suspects, their apprehension of offenders, and in their crime prevention efforts. Proactive applications are exemplified in digital efforts that are akin to prior legacy media victimization reduction efforts such as the McGruff the Crime Dog public service advertising campaigns (see Chapter 8). Contemporary agencies also post crime prevention and victimization reduction materials on departmental Web sites and distribute it through Facebook pages.[43] Employing new communication avenues like 'twitter-bots" (software automated Twitter feeds that automatically send messages to targeted subscribers such as residents in a particular neighborhood) highly focused information distribution of crime alerts has been tested. Information tailored to zip codes or individual streets and that describe police calls for service, give crime and fugitive alerts, and provide crime prevention tips have begun to be automated and married to social media distribution platforms. Seen as replacements for in-person neighborhood watch programs which depend on pamphlets, street signs, and telephone call trees to distribute messages, these efforts aim to raise community crime fighting to a digital level.[44] And as related

---

B o x 10.5   New Media and Secondary Victimization

A recent case in the United States demonstrates the concepts of performance crime, double victimization, and social media impact on case processing. The Steubenville, Ohio case involved two high school football players who were convicted of the rape of a classmate. Social media activities played multiple roles in the crime's aftermath. A video of the drunken unconscious victim being carried between parties was posted, messages were sent on social media aimed at covering up or minimizing the rape, and a social media campaign against the defendants and perceived supportive small town football culture was launched by an online hacker group. In the bizarre aftermath to the assault, the victim texted one of the defendants: "It's on YouTube. I'm not stupid. Stop texting me." In an apt summation of the new media generated trial circus that resulted, a *New York Times* headline read: "Case Already Tried across Social Media Heads to Courtroom." The Steubenville city authorities eventually felt the need to launch their own Web site called "Steubenville Facts" to counter misinformation.

Similar if less visible examples occurred in Canada and California. In Canada, following an alleged gang rape, a 17-year-old girl hung herself after more than a year of online bullying. Her mother posted a message online that four boys had assaulted her daughter and posted a photo of the act online, branding the teen a "slut" and launching an avalanche of harassment from her classmates. In the California incident, students shared photos of a girl being sexually assaulted in the days following the attack. The girl committed suicide eight days later and three teenage boys were arrested in the following months.

SOURCES: Goode, E. and Schweber, N. 2013, March 13. "Case Already Tried across Social Media Heads to Courtroom." A13, A16. *New York Times*; "Steubenville Facts" http://steubenvillefacts.squarespace.com/blog/2013/1/5/steubenville-facts Alpert, E. 2013, April 12. "Outrage in Canada after Teen Suicide, Alleged Gang Rape." *L.A. Times.* http://articles.latimes.com/2013/apr/12/world/la-fg-wn-alleged-gang-rape-canada-teen-suicide-20130412 Serna, J. 2013, April 12. "Lawyer Says Students Passed around Photos of Sexual Assault." *L.A. Times.* http://articles.latimes.com/2013/apr/12/local/la-me-ln-saratoga-sexual-assault-suicide-20130412

---

earlier, digital undercover police investigators have been assuming the online personas of children or pedophiles to proactively identify sexual offenders in new media sting operations for a number of years.

In reactive applications, law enforcement has embraced the ubiquitous surveillance provided by digital media for leads and evidence. A recent example is provided by the Boston Police Department, which tweeted the general public after the 2013 Marathon Bombings asking for leads and were rewarded with thousands of responses. Offender-posted online videos are another investigatory source that has been tapped by law enforcement. Associated with offender-provided 'performance crime' material, social media videos have supplied suspect identifications as well as incriminating visual evidence for criminal investigations (examples of new media content leading directly to suspect arrests are provided in Box 10.6).

While the police have tapped the Internet and social media as valuable sources of previously unavailable information and as a novel means to reach the public with crime control and public safety applications, the courts have explored the utility of new media for case processing, but with a wary eye on possible negative impacts on due process protections.

B o x 10.6	Busted by New Media

A quick search of the Internet will uncover numerous examples of suspects who have posted incriminating images of themselves after committing a crime or provided the information needed to track and locate them. A sample of these unintended "social media surrenders and confessions" include an example where a new media device allowed the police to quickly find their suspects. Using an application (or app) designed to help owners track the location of lost iPhones, police were able to find the stolen phone and with it burglary suspects. Home burglars had not only left a stolen iPhone on, but had not gone far with it. When police officers triggered the location app, the phone was revealed to be directly outside of the burglarized house. Expecting to find the phone thrown on the ground, the police instead found the suspects trying to dig their car out of the mud with a stolen shovel. In another case, a burglarized homeowner examined her computer after the break-in and noticed that the computer was logged into someone else's Facebook account. The person who logged on (speculated by the reporter to perhaps update his status to "feeling lucky today") had not logged off. His identification and arrest quickly followed. In another example, a teenage robber was identified and arrested after someone who had seen him commit the robbery also saw a YouTube video in which he appeared. In the final two examples, suspects who had stolen jewelry and another group who had broken into a business posted incriminating images of themselves on social media. The first suspects posted photos of themselves posing with the stolen jewelry; the second group posted photos of themselves holding up the thousands of dollars in cash and goods that had been stolen.

SOURCES: Stennett, D. 2012, Sept. 29. "Deputies Tap iPhone App, Find Burglary Suspects Stuck in Mud" Orlando Sentinel B1, B3.; Matyszczyk, C. 2009, Sept. 17. "Facebook Break Leads to Burglary Suspect" CNET News; "You tube video leads to arrest of teen robber" www.wdbo.com; "Teenage Thieves Post Pictures of Stolen Items on MySpace" http://www.wtsp.com/news/local/crime/story.aspx?storyid=44133; "Facebook Photos Lead Police To Suspects in Burglary" http://pittsburgh.cbslocal.com/2011/12/22/facebook-photos-lead-police-to-suspects-in-burglary/

NEW MEDIA AND THE COURTS

Judicial applications of new media's capabilities revolve around court administration issues. Document processing through new media communication platforms has sped the processing of cases and reduced court delay.[45] In Australia, for example, the courts have approved contact through a person's social media online profile as sufficient to satisfy legal notice, issuing of complaints, and delivery of court orders.[46] Worries about new media effects on judicial systems are generated from both high-public-interest cases that are heavily socially constructed in social media communications and in run-of-the-mill low visibility judicial proceedings where negative effects on the behaviors of trial participants have been noted. From these dual streams of high- and low-interest cases the shared concern over the undermining of the integrity of the judicial system through pernicious effects on attorneys and jurors, trial fairness, evidence, and verdicts emerged.[47]

Regarding the effects of new media on high-public-interest trials such as terrorist trials, the most important change occurred with the shift from observer to participant on the part of the public audience. The watershed event in this shift was the first cyber-trial, the 1996 O. J. Simpson murder trial. Simpson's trial was the first trial to be fully discussed, dissected, and socially constructed in new media cyberspace.[48] In its rendering as a crime-and-justice infotainment production, the trial was transformed from a criminal justice event to be simply observed by the public into the equivalent of a massive multi-player game experience.[49] Since the O. J. trial, the social construction of justice has been dominated by new media where the "audience as trial observer" has been replaced by the "audience as trial participant."[50] In this new media world, effects on attorney activities are a major concern.

New Media and Attorney Activities

In that "all the rules that the legal profession relies upon to instruct lawyer behavior were forged before the emergence of new media,"[51] the judiciary continues to struggle with defining inappropriate behavior and ethical boundaries regarding this emergent media realm. Existing rules for ethical attorney conduct were largely written to address phone conversations and audio recordings, not social media or the Internet, so it is not surprising that lawyers have drifted into difficulties. A short list includes attorneys who have been reprimanded for posting privileged and prejudicial material on YouTube and in social media, discovered to have misrepresented their reasons for extensions and case delay requests from social media postings, and brought to task for posting criticisms of judges, colleagues, and other individuals associated with ongoing cases. A particular area of concern regarding attorney behavior involves jury selection. Using new media search engines, the researching of jury pool member is quick and inexpensive and attorneys can obtain a wealth of information regarding potential juror socioeconomic status, religious affiliation, educational background, political leanings, and criminal backgrounds. The effect on the juror selection process has not been researched but concerns and unknown risks of jury tampering, professional responsibility, trial disruption, and privacy have been raised.[52]

Attorneys however cannot just ignore new media as the benefits outweigh the risks. Meeting effective counsel standards frequently requires attorneys to actively tap new media as a case resource. Thus, attorneys currently use online profiles, instant messaging, and online videos to gather information about clients, potential jurors, opposing counsel, judges, and witnesses.[53] Using social media as a research tool is now common and Internet searches are a standard pre-trial case preparation step.[54] Rules of proper attorney conduct have not been clearly delineated yet and seemingly benign actions such as "friending" someone on Facebook can be an inappropriate form of contact. It appears that an attorney can ask to be a "friend" on Facebook and not violate ethical codes as currently understood but cannot give false statements to gain "friend" status without raising a false representation issue. Other issues related to attorney use of new media include lawyer social media postings that might reveal client confidences (lawyers are advised to obtain informed consent prior to posting material even when based upon open court factual statements), advertising (advised to include a clear notice that identifies the content as advertising), and approaching an individual online who you are not representing ("friending" your adversaries is a particularly questionable practice).[55]

The primary legal issue comes down to pretexting or the practice of gaining information under false pretenses.[56] For example, the creation of a false online profile by an attorney would be a problem and can trigger computer fraud, cyber-bullying, and harassment charges. How information is obtained and whether informed consent is provided are crucial elements in determining ethical from non–ethical social media attorney behavior.[57] An attorney visit to a public Website, even if entry fees are required, would be viewed differently from making direct contact with an individual through that web site. Visits and information gathered that could be obtained by anyone willing to pay the entrance fee are not viewed as problems. Surreptitious contact to obtain information not available to the public raises flags though. The dilemma for lawyers is that failure to explore online presence of clients, victims, and witness may result in findings of "ineffective counsel" on appeal. Attorneys can neither ignore social media, nor blindly stumble around within them. An additional issue to be resolved is the use of new media content as evidence.

New Media as Evidence

The value of social-media-based evidence is that it can provide the best evidence of what an individual was thinking and doing at a specific time. Content obtained from social networking sites has both established and undercut alibis, mental health defenses, and punitive or lenient sentencing arguments; it has impeached testimony and eyewitness credibility; and proved strong community roots and positive reputations in support of bail and pre-trial release.[58] At the boundary of the courts and corrections, new media supplied content has resulted in increased bail amounts for defendants, revocation of supervised release sentences, and provided evidence for 'no contact' sentence provisions and their violation.[59]

Similar to other types of evidence, social-media-based evidence must be properly authenticated under the general rules of evidence. Yet, unlike other evidence, the ephemeral nature of online digital information requires that the preservation of digitally published evidence be conducted differently. There is nothing physical to be stored in an evidence locker. Preserving online profiles and Web pages requires discovery orders requiring that profiles be frozen and downloaded. Preservation of such evidence has become the norm and lawyers who advise their clients to erase Facebook pages and other social media content can trigger sanctions for evidence destruction. The conflict regarding new media content as evidence faced by the courts lies in the conflicting questions of when to preserve online profiles by issuing protective orders versus when to order their deletion to prevent eventual jurors from being exposed to inadmissible information.[60]

In addition, while it has been established that e-mails, tweets, materials posted on Facebook and other information from social media can be introduced as evidence, privacy issues related to this content remain unsettled. Early privacy laws arose in response to photographic technology with the privacy boundary set where one entered public. If you are out in public you can usually be photographed with or without your consent. With new media technology, it is ambiguous whether your online presence is public or not and new media mobile technologies simultaneously make it possible for virtually anything a person does in public (and often in private) to be videotaped, texted, or otherwise made part of a digital record.[61] When and how much of that information is private, who owns it, and who can acquire it is under dispute.[62] The successful use of mining new-media-supplied data for anti-terrorism efforts has, not surprisingly, led law enforcement agencies to see new media content as a valuable resource. An idea of the scope of the issue is given by requests related to just one new media source, the digital content of cell phones. Access to information contained in modern cell phones—the location of the phones and the content of phone communications—are constantly requested by law enforcement and contested in the courts. In 2011, cellphone carriers reported that they responded to 1.3 million government requests for text messages.[63] At this time, the levels of privacy afforded to new media vary by state, with some state courts ruling that the electronic contents of cell phones, for example, can be digitally searched if the phone is found on an arrested person and that the location and tracking information provided by mobile phones is not private.[64]

New Media and Jurors

In addition to attorney behavior and new media as evidence, a third judicial issue is the effect of new media on juror activities. By providing easy access to the outside world, social media and the Internet pose tremendous challenges to sealing off courtrooms from external influences. Social media are a direct challenge to a judges' traditional role as the courtroom information gatekeeper.[65] Juror social media activities have the potential to undermine the fundamental fairness of judicial trial proceedings and undermine public integrity for the judicial system. Misuse of social media by jurors has caused mistrials, resulted in juror dismissals, and triggered contempt findings against misbehaving jurors.[66] Specifically, jurors have looked up definitions of legal terms on Wikipedia, viewed crime scenes via Google Earth, updated their blogs and Facebook pages with remarks about proceedings, and "friended" criminal defendants, witnesses, lawyers, and each other during trials.[67]

Unfortunately, most of the available information on new-media-based juror misconduct is anecdotal and rigorous research is sparse. Available juror survey data reports that about 25 percent of jurors viewed reports on the Internet about their ongoing trial and about 10 percent had purposely searched the Internet during a trial to learn additional information.[68] When corrective steps are taken, the most common judicial countermeasure to such activities are bench instructions to the jury which are reinforced at various points in a trial. A recent pilot study provides mixed messages regarding the effectiveness of instructions. Suggesting their effectiveness, many jurors in the study reported that although jurors wanted to use the Internet and social media during trials, juror instructions from the bench not to do so were understood and effective.[69] On the other hand, a substantial minority of the jurors could not recall receiving instructions or thought Internet searches were permissible based on their interpretation of the instructions. In addition, a small proportion of jurors said they would be unable to refrain from Internet use for the duration of a trial even if ordered to do so.[70] Adding to the concerns, despite the indicators of a persistent level of new-media-based juror misconduct, many contemporary judges do not perceive new media use as a pressing threat to trial fairness and a substantial number of sitting judges apparently do not take special precautions.[71]

Irrespective of unsettled research questions, the working assumption in the courts today is that juror instructions are effective and mitigate the risks of juror misconduct through social media.[72] The fate of trial fairness in a new-media-saturated courtroom currently therefore rests upon the effectiveness of juror instructions. Assuming an impartial jury has been seated and pre-trial social media effects are neutral, fair trials are seen as the expected norm and the current appeals court posture is that mistrials are generally not warranted unless extrinsic prejudicial evidence has been shown to have been directly interjected into a trial. Appeals courts have therefore put the burden of proof for showing a prejudice effect from juror social media use on defendants.[73] In-trial dismissal of individual misbehaving jurors and curative instructions are usually seen as sufficient, but grievous violations have resulted in a small number of mistrials.[74] As new media becomes an inescapable, integral part of everyone's life, the judicial system may need to invoke less common, more intrusive steps, such as courthouse technology bans, contempt of court rulings, and requiring jurors to sign pre-trial pledges not to use social media. In the interim, the courts appear willing to rely on juror instructions to prevent misuse. In comparison, corrections have hardly needed to address new-media-generated issues. Following this book's idea of crime-and-justice media content being front-end-loaded with more content about crime and crime fighting, less about the courts, and little about corrections, the impact of new media follows a similar diminishing path. Historically reluctant to deal with legacy media, the impact of new media on corrections has also been limited.

NEW MEDIA AND CORRECTIONS

The impact of new media on corrections has largely focused on keeping inmates and new media separated. Aside from staff and administrative uses, there is little new media in correctional facilities and the general goal is to prevent inmates from gaining access to mobile phones and the Internet for security reasons. It is in association with sentencing determination that new media has most directly affected corrections. Information garnered from new media is often introduced at sentencing, usually as a means to argue for increased punishment. Prosecutors frequently use defendant postings and damaging Internet photos to cast doubt on defendant's character, to undermine claims of defendant remorse, and to counter arguments that the criminal behavior was an aberration.[75] In addition to being used to impact sentence punitiveness or leniency, new media also shows up as a condition of sentencing.

In the pursuit to better protect the public from new-media-based predation, restricted access to new media as a condition of a sentence has been pursued. Offenders utilizing new media to further harass their crime victims are one driver of this trend. For example, it was reported that offenders in the United Kingdom were posting taunting and terrorizing messages on Facebook to their crime victims and victim's families.[76] As a result, a call for the automatic loss of "cyber liberties" in addition to loss of civil liberties when found guilty of a serious crime has been lobbied for in the United Kingdom.[77] Such sentencing policy drives raise the question of whether bans on access to new media as part of a sentence are constitutional in the United States. The anti-ban argument is that new media access is a basic social practice related to free speech and freedom of association and that access bans would so severely limit employment opportunities as to constitute cruel and unusual punishment.[78]

Irrespective of the continuing debate, the banning of access to the Internet has become a more common condition of correctional sentences.[79] Appeals courts' rulings regarding these restrictions have noted that probation sentences are aimed at rehabilitation and therefore conditions must reasonably encourage law-abiding behavior and not simply be punitive. Blanket restrictions to large groups of offenders without a logical linkage to the sentenced crime have accordingly not been supported. The meaning of reasonable restrictions on Internet or computer access is what remains unclear. Regarding general computer access, the banning of computer use has usually been ruled as acceptable if the conviction crime involved computer usage in some fashion and was appropriate for preventing similar future crimes. As computer access is required for many jobs, blanket prohibitions on computer use have been less favorably viewed. Specific restrictions on elements of computer use such as e-mail access have also been upheld, if e-mail was a component of the conviction crime.[80] Thus, an offender convicted of e-mail-based fraud or stalking can be banned from all e-mail use as part of their probation.

Concerning Internet access, appeal cases to date have focused around child pornography. As with blanket bans on computer use, blanket bans on Internet access that include non-pornography related access to the Internet for e-mail, news, weather, work, and research seen as essential to modern life have been successfully challenged.[81] Deemed acceptable were focused restrictions which bar Internet access to specific types of sites and the installation of filtering software for the monitoring of offender computer activity as additional conditions of a sentence.

In sum, the acceptance of bans on new media use as a sentencing condition is determined by their relation to the offense and their impact on possible rehabilitation.[82] The monitoring and revocation of new-media-connected sentence conditions put additional burdens on correctional personnel and require an increased level of knowledge with new media and technology.[83] Correctional personnel who directly supervise offenders in the community will need to understand new media as both a source of offending and rehabilitation. Current research has not clarified the relationship between the criminogenic versus the treatment potential of new media. For example, a study of online communications between a small set of male juvenile delinquents in Singapore found that Facebook was one of their principal means of social interaction, supplanting in importance direct face-to-face contacts for many of these juveniles. This study suggests that in the new social media environment, even offenders in high supervision correctional rehabilitation programs will have access to persons who they would not be allowed to physically come in contact with. In much the same manner that television in the 1950s circumvented the nuclear family to socialize children, the nature of social media works to undermine correctional rehabilitation efforts by affording extended opportunities to offenders for unstructured and unsupervised interactions with delinquent peers. Keeping offenders apart and removing them from their communities may no longer be enough if the goal is to change their social networks. In the Singapore study, new media allowed the endorsement of delinquent acts by distant delinquents, increased pressure on separated delinquents to continue to display criminal gang group loyalty, and increased the difficulty for delinquents looking to rehabilitate themselves to create and maintain a social distance from their prior delinquent associates.[84] In a manner similar to the expanded reach of law enforcement, criminogenic influences are also given greater breath by new media. The social reality that new media have already brought to criminality, law enforcement, and the courts will have to be eventually addressed within the field of corrections.

NEW MEDIA AND THE FUTURE OF CRIME AND JUSTICE

A reality in which media-generated digital content interweaves with non-mediated face-to-face reality is developing and changing the way society functions.[85] As the mediated experience moves closer to a real world experience human interactions are more often conducted via "face-to-face-like" communications, less often in face-to-face contacts. In this evolution, new media bring new capabilities to the criminal justice system. They have proved helpful in investigations, case processing, and crime prevention but have also increased the capability of criminals to commit crime. These mediated criminal justice experiences are realistic, participatory, and entertaining and new media enable users to communicate with almost anyone, at any time, from anywhere. An individual today can experience crime and criminal justice via new media and come away with a sensation akin to actual experience.[86] In addition, contemporary social media are the first crime news source for many and combined with the images of surveillance cameras are powerful crime-and-justice social construction engines.

Stresses on the criminal justice system from the emergence of new media are unavoidable. First, new media are by their nature decentralized and multidirectional while the criminal justice system by nature is centralized and unidirectional. Information flows in all directions through new media while in criminal justice it tends to flow from law enforcement to courts to corrections. Furthermore, new media are intimate yet anonymous and information is loosely owned and widely distributed across blurry digital boundaries. In contrast, in the criminal justice system cases and information usually flow in one direction and the loosely coupled criminal justice agencies have separated budgets and independent ideologies. Criminal justice system agencies therefore tend to hold tight to their information, frequently demanding court orders before divulging anything. Even the form of legacy and new media content conflicts. New media content is multimedia, digital, holistic, emotional, and image-dominated, whereas the criminal justice system content is textual, linear, impersonal, and paper-based.[87] In the face of these basic differences, it is not a surprise that the introduction of new media created both issues and opportunities for the criminal justice system.[88] New media provide access to a new source of evidence and information and a means to reach citizens that no longer monitor traditional media while simultaneously undermining long held criminal justice habits.[89] The transition from one to the other will be slow and for some agencies painful. The most important policy-related concern of the transition from old to new media is the creation of a permanent crime-related moral panic.[90]

In these moral panics, new media will extend and sustain social crises over crime that previously would have been short lived. In an amplification effect that forwards the faulty system frame, extreme rare crimes will be highlighted and transformed into national moral panics as social media pick up, repeat, and loop crime stories. In the new media echo chamber, discussions of crime and justice will be constructed without objectivity and with statements of outrage replacing factual claims.[91] A pernicious dynamic has been noted in which predator criminals are emphasized in new media based discussions that lead to heightened fear among the participant-audience. To keep the audience involved and the sense of fear sustained, this panic must be extended beyond a fear of criminal predators to a fear of inaction and lack of punitiveness on the part of the criminal justice system.[92] To an increasing degree, the new media worldview is of a society-at-risk where constant and lethal dangers must be aggressively and punitively addressed in a never-ending crisis.[93] Ironically but not surprisingly, although both society and the criminal justice system are painted as failing, the solution forwarded in the new media is the reform and enhancement of the criminal justice system. Reform is seen as a ratcheting back on due process, enhancement as the ratcheting up of punishment. With the effects of new media gaining predominance, speculation as to where the reality of media, crime and justice might go is considered in Chapter 11.

SUMMARY

- The key difference between old and new media is not content but access to content, distribution of content, and creation of content.

- Cybercrime has become a leading criminal justice concern and new media provide new ways to commit old crimes and opportunities to commit entirely new types of crime.

- Performance crime encompasses the spectacle of people recording, sharing, and uploading acts of crime to social media. Performance crime has encouraged new-media-generated copycat crime.

- Law enforcement agencies have learned to utilize new media in their investigations of crimes, their identification and pursuit of suspects, their apprehension of offenders, and in their crime prevention efforts.

- Regarding the effects of new media on high-public-interest trials, the most important change has been the shift from the "audience as trial observer" to the "audience as trial participant".

- Attorney use of social media as a research tool is a standard pre-trial case preparation step. However, rules of proper attorney conduct have not been clearly delineated and seemingly benign actions such as "friending" someone on Facebook can be inappropriate.

- The impact of new media on corrections has largely focused on keeping inmates and new media separated.

- Restricting access to new media as a condition of sentencing has grown. It is less likely to be successfully challenged if a direct link between the criminal behavior and new media has been established.

- The nature of social media works to undermine correctional rehabilitation efforts by affording extended time and opportunities to offenders for unstructured and unsupervised social contacts.

- Transition from legacy to new media will continue to put stresses on the criminal justice system and a steady stream of moral panics over crime are expected for the foreseeable future.

CLASS DISCUSSIONS

1. Discuss how new media have influenced the structure and function of your interpersonal network, how you gather news, and how you assess criminal justice policies.

2. Discuss what new criminal justice policies might be needed to respond to the impacts of new media such as an increased number of moral panics on crime and justice.

3. Discuss how crime and terrorism has changed because of new media.

4. Discuss the phenomena of 'performance crime' and its relationship to media-oriented terrorism.

5. Discuss the pros and cons of new media influences on attorneys, jurors, and trials.

6. Discuss the fairness and effectiveness of including a ban on new media use as a sentence condition.

SUGGESTED READINGS

Quayle, E. & Taylor, M. (2003). *Child pornography: An Internet crime*. New York: Routledge.

Schmalleger, F. & Pittaro, M. (2009). *Crimes of the Internet*. Upper Saddle River: Pearson Prentice hall.

Taylor, R., Fritsch, E., Liederbach, J., & Holt, T. (2011). *Digital crime and digital terrorism*. Upper Saddle River: Prentice Hall.

Yar, M. (2006). *Cybercrime and society*. London: Sage.

Wall, D. (2001). *Crime and the Internet*. New York: Routledge.

CHAPTER 11

New Media, Crime, and Justice in the Twenty-first Century

CHAPTER OBJECTIVES

Chapter 11 provides

- A summary of what the reader has learned about crime, justice, and the media
- An overview of the relationship between media and crime and justice
- Two postulates that encapsulate the media crime-and-justice relationship
- A description and discussion of two alternative scenarios of the future of the media's role between the public and the criminal justice system
- A discussion of the likely impact of new media on crime and justice

CRIME-AND-JUSTICE MEDIA MESSAGES

By the late nineteenth century, early print-based media contained the same criminal stereotypes and causal explanations of crime found in today's media. Narratives of individually focused crime and retributive justice became common more than a hundred years ago. Composed of ever-multiplying outlets and new media technologies, today a pervasive multimedia Web constructs a distorted crime-and-justice portrait. The merging of news and entertainment media combined with the constant looping of crime-and-justice content means that the portraits of crime and justice in each will continue to be more alike than different. Infotainment media presentations will continue unabated and new media platforms will speed the distribution of this content and broaden its reach. Crime constitutes a constant, significant portion of the total media content; criminals are normally constructed as either predatory street criminals or dishonest businesspeople and professionals; and the criminal justice system is shown as an ineffective, often counterproductive means of dealing with crime. The crime-and-justice media messages conform to a backwards law and media persistently reverse the real world of crime and justice in their media-constructed world. As a basic rule of thumb, news, entertainment, and infotainment media take the least common crime or justice event and make it the most common crime or justice image. In this media-made reality, traditional criminal justice system personnel and standard practices suffer, but alternatives to the criminal justice system fare even worse.

The lack of realistic information in the media additionally mystifies and obscures criminality and the criminal justice system.[1] The media emphasize individual personality traits as the cause of crime and violent interdiction as its solution, showing a preference for crimes involving weapons and solutions involving violence and sophisticated technology. Media present criminality as an individual choice and imply that other social, economic, or structural explanations are irrelevant. The "crime fighter" and "war-on-crime" icons suggest to the public that crime must be fought rather than solved or prevented.[2] Media portraits further instruct the public to fear others, for the criminal is not easily recognizable and is often found among the rich, powerful, and seemingly trustworthy. These images tilt public perceptions toward law enforcement and crime control policies. The result is that although the criminal justice system is not shown favorably, the solutions to crime suggested by the media involve expansion of the existing criminal justice system through harsher punishments and more law enforcement. Increasing the punitiveness of the real criminal justice system appears to be the only reasonable policy course. And in a looping cycle, the actions of the real criminal justice system are evaluated by the public against the expectations and desires raised by the media-constructed criminal justice system.

The dominant crime-and-justice portrait shows people outside of the criminal justice system and unburdened by due process considerations to be the most effective crime fighters. At the same time, media bolster the existing criminal justice system as being the best policy course. This media-constructed, ineffective, last resort criminal justice system sits within a portrait of a stark social ecology filled with predatory criminals, violent crime fighters, and helpless victims.

The media's influence on criminality, independent of its effect on criminal justice, has not been adequately explored, and the specter of media-oriented terrorism is an issue of immediate concern.[3] The available evidence suggests, and most researchers agree, that the media do affect criminals and motivate terrorists. Aggregate crime rate studies further suggest that the media affect crime independently of their violent content and more by molding crime than by triggering it. In addition, the media likely have a copycat effect more on property crime than on violent crime. The more heavily a potential copycat criminal relies on the media for information about the world and the more predisposed the individual is to commit crime, the more likely a copycat effect is. Violence-prone children and individuals who have difficulty distinguishing fact from fantasy are particularly at risk for aping media violence. When sexual and violent content are yoked, hyper-masculine males are most influenced. When the news media sensationalize crimes and make celebrities of criminals, people seeking notoriety imitate those crimes, sometimes posting movies of them for all to watch. And when successful innovative crimes, in particular property crimes, are detailed, criminals emulate them.

On the other side of the media social construction equation are media-based anticrime efforts. These efforts appear to be an effective means of disseminating information and influencing attitudes, but their ability to significantly affect behavior has not been established. Although useful in specific areas, media-based anticrime programs are not likely to significantly reduce the overall crime rate. No program has empirically demonstrated a significant long-term and displacement-free effect on crime. Single-handedly, the media and media technology are as unable to deter criminal behavior as they are able to criminalize previously law-abiding individuals. The media should not be looked to as crime panaceas. Even so, media-based anticrime programs can have significant immediate effects and their careful utilization is warranted.

By constructing crime-and-justice reality, the media also subtly but significantly affect crime-and-justice policies. To varying degrees, media influence the agenda, perceptions, and policies of consumers with regard to crime and justice. These media effects interact with other factors, are not easy to discern, and are difficult to counteract. Perceptions of crime and justice are intertwined with other, broader perceptions of social conditions, and so it is not surprising that consistent relationships have not been found between the media and public attitudes or policies on crime and justice.

As reflected in Figure 11.1, the conflicting arguments of the media as a primary cause versus a negligible cause of crime, aggression, terrorism, and other unwanted behaviors not only posit differing causal relations between the media and behavior but imply vastly different public policies as well. The *primary cause models* argue that a significant, direct linear relationship exists between media content and consumer behavior. In these models, the media, independent of other factors, directly cause undesired social behaviors. If valid, these models indicate that strong intervention is necessary in the creation, content, and distribution of media.

The *negligible cause models* concede a statistical association between the media and some negative behaviors but argue that the connection is due not to a causal relationship but to persons predisposed to certain behaviors seeking out particular types of media and concurrently behaving in ways similar to the behavior displayed in the media. As the relationship is associative and not causal, if these models are correct, policies targeted at the media will have no effect on social behavior and the media can safely be ignored.

Neither of these models is felt to accurately describe the true media–social behavior relationship. As shown in Figure 11.2, the actual relationship is believed to be bidirectional and cyclical. In addition to people acting out their predispositions while seeking out supportive media and to media causing behavior to be modeled, the media play a role in the generation of people

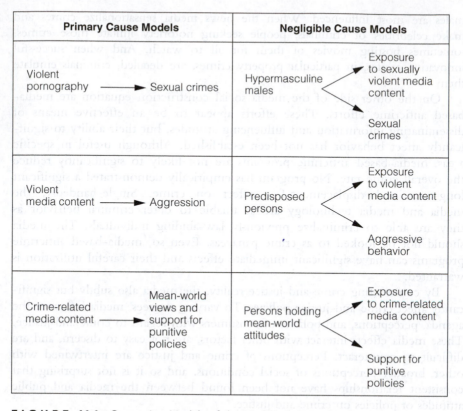

FIGURE 11.1 Competing Models of the Media's Relationship to Sex Crimes, Aggression, and Support for Punitive Criminal Justice Policies.

predisposed to crime. As the made-for-TV movie industry exemplifies, real-world crime sometimes results in the creation of criminogenic media. Providing live models and creating community and home environments that are more inured to and tolerant of crime results in more criminally predisposed individuals in society. New media broaden access to this criminogenic media content. Therefore, although the direct effect of media content on social behavior may not be large, the media's influence loops, recycles, and accumulates.[4]

Two Postulates of Media and Crime and Justice

Overall, the media are constant, occasionally subtle, and usually unpredictable crime-and-justice agents—beneficial if carefully used—but they are neither the magic cure nor the potent demon they are sometimes cast as. Media cannot be ignored but should not be seen as omnipotent. Where do we stand in terms of a

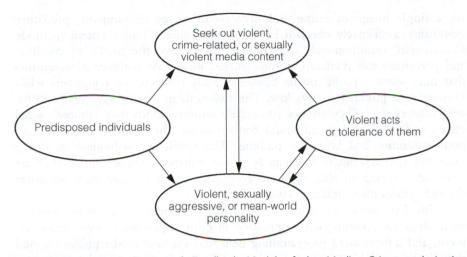

FIGURE 11.2 A Reciprocal Feedback Model of the Media, Crime, and Justice Relationship.

broad understanding of media and the social construction of a crime-and-justice reality? This question is addressed using two postulates of media, crime, and justice distilled from prior chapters. These postulates drive expectations about future media, crime, and justice interactions.

> *Postulate 1:* The media more often than not construct the criminal justice system and its people negatively and as ineffective. Yet the cumulative effect is support for more police, more prisons, and more money for the criminal justice system.

The media-constructed reality argues that the criminal justice system does not work well but remains the best hope against crime.

> *Postulate 2:* Media have increasingly blurred the line between news and entertainment, between fact and fiction, and between audience and producers. In the process, crime stories have become a mainstay of hybrid infotainment programs and new media content.

Led by the electronic visual media, the media have become more able and willing to portray events previously considered private and to expose and distribute new information previously considered cloistered. Spurred by competition and digitized for maximum dissemination, media present these events and information in formats to maximize audience participation and revenues. The result is that content that goes into and comes out of the media is processed through an infotainment lens.[5]

Together these postulates result in the continuing disparity between the media-constructed reality of crime and justice and the real-world reality of crime and justice. This disparity has developed because the media converge on a single image of crime and justice—an image of rampant, predatory criminality ineffectively checked by traditional criminal justice system methods. Commercial, organizational, and cultural forces drive the media to construct and perpetuate this predatory crime-centered image. As commercial enterprises that must show a profit, media businesses must compete for consumers while keeping their production costs low. This makes them socially aggressive and fiscally conservative. They are not particularly sensitive about their content's social effects and will copy any successful content ideas. The result is media that are both redundant and boundary pushing. The media are redundant in that a successful type of content will rapidly spawn imitations and spinoffs.[6] They are boundary pushing in that they are constantly trying to lure new audiences through provocative, titillating content.

This dual process of similar types of media vehicles trying to outcompete each other for consumers is emphasized in crime-and-justice news, entertainment, and infotainment programming delivered via new media platforms. And though the media have increased their capability to discover and deliver information about the world, they have also moved toward greater reliance on prepackaged information, stereotypes, and entertainment-style content that consumers can participate in creating. As a result, the public receives an image of crime and justice that is not only distorted but that basically supports only one anticrime policy. Enhanced crime control mechanisms are advanced at the expense of due process protections and social policies that do not rely on the criminal justice system. Guarding against the violent predator criminal becomes the main message and policy focus.

Long-established cultural forces come into play in the wide-scale social acceptance of the media-generated predator criminal icon. As a culture, depictions of predatory criminals both entertain and comfort us. They entertain because they frighten and provide glimpses of realities we are not likely to encounter. We look over the shoulder of the predator criminal as crimes are committed, join with the crime fighters as they investigate and pursue the predators, and participate in the trials that result. The predator criminal icon comforts because it relieves our conscience of personal responsibility for crime and violence by constructing crime as not connected to social inequities, racism, or poverty—things society could be held responsible for and might address. The media's maddened, greedy predators are criminals by their own will, or maybe God's will, but certainly not society's will. Such criminals can, therefore, be guiltlessly battled and eliminated. Together, the commercial, organizational, and cultural forces create a constructed reality that is resistant to alternative broader constructions of crime and justice. The media resist because they cannot commercially afford to seriously challenge the popular construction, and we resist as consumers because we are more comfortable partaking in a narrower, entertaining, and guilt-free constructed reality.

Expanded Public Access to Criminal Justice Procedures

Driven by the social effects of new media and running counter to the narrow construction of crime is the modern media's ability to expand our access to

AF Images/Iraqi State Television

This image made from video shows ex-Iraq dictator Saddam Hussein's guards placing a noose around the deposed leader's neck moments before his execution. New media have made it nearly impossible to have crime and justice events that do not become part of the the social construction of crime and justice reality.

previously hidden criminal justice realms and thus to expand our crime-and-justice reality. Phrases such as "government in the sunshine" and "freedom of information" reflect responses to a media-driven social trend toward more open public institutions and enhanced scrutiny of public officials. Two dominant social institutions, the media and the criminal justice system, play critical roles in this process, which can be understood as part of the general process of exposing more of the previously private backstage areas of society to the public.[7] In our hypermedia society, closed institutions and proceedings and secret information and sources are automatically viewed with suspicion and challenged.[8] Ironically, the criminal justice system and the mass media are among a handful of social institutions that resist full, open access and struggle to keep their realities closed. New media has made that goal nearly impossible and previously low-visibility criminal justice events are now revealed, more graphic news and entertainment programs are presented, the public's tolerance for surveillance has increased, judicial steps and interactions between the police and citizens are more often recorded. Media trials proliferate and there is increased acceptance of social media and entertainment formatting in crime and justice.

Mediated Reality

The critical issue is ultimately the media's role in the social construction of reality. Evidence is building that the media alter reality by affecting the ways in which the audience perceives, interprets, and behaves. The question is no longer whether the media have a substantial impact but rather how their impact will be felt. These effects cycle through the media in loops where content is extracted from one context or medium, is reframed, and reused, often resulting in new, ambiguous media realities. These looping effects are observed in both real events that are massively mediated, such as the 2013 Boston Marathon bombing, and in the created-for-media pseudo-events found in crime-and-justice reality shows. The ultimate effect these media-reality loops will have on crime and justice is unknown.

In addition, new media are evolving rapidly and the distinctions between media genres such as news and entertainment are disappearing.[9] The availability of video and new media technologies has expanded the genre of reality programming, which relies heavily on images of real crimes, criminal investigations, and criminal justice agency activities for its content fodder. What effect the common use of new media will have on the reporting of citizen crime, authority malfeasance, and other types of crime-and-justice events is unclear. Pictures invariably increase the newsworthiness of events and new media thrives on images, so perhaps the public debate will move from arguments about factual claims to interpretative ones as there more often will be images available to establish basic facts. If this is the case then fewer will argue about what crime happened and more will argue about why crime happens. In that way, there possibly will be the positive benefit from moving the criminal justice debate to discussions about alternate policies and beyond the current focus on how to best implement a single policy.

The impact of new social media and the development of interactive virtual media forever changes the relationship between media and users. The media experience has steadily moved closer to direct personal experience. It has also changed the way people interact with each other, with less direct, face-to-face conversation but more face-to-face-like communication via media technology. Individuals are more often physically in one place, psychologically in another. Today people interact less with those physically near them such as neighbors and more with distant people via mobile phones, home computers, and other "being there" technology. The full effects on the social construction of crime-and-justice reality will be significant. New media also provide new ways of committing old crimes such as consumer fraud and ways to commit new crimes such as murdering a virtual person. With increased interaction will come increased demands to be able to participate. If someone is having the experience of "being there," it is natural for them to expect to be able to participate in what they previously only watched. Audiences are increasingly encouraged to contribute to the conversation, vote on the verdict, determine the next step, and decide the final outcome.

An interactive participatory media has led to a hybrid reality in which a media-generated reality loops and interweaves with nonmediated reality. Many children today already spend more time in this media-constructed reality than in their directly experienced reality.[10] Across the United States a web of media-linked technology and products gives media reality enormous reach and impact. Unfortunately, we cannot have some of the media forces for social change without having other unwanted consequences.[11] We cannot use the media for fighting crime and processing criminal cases or providing media access to criminal justice proceedings without also changing the reality of the criminal justice system. Mixing and remixing media-constructed and real-world events harbingers a future where media constructions of other media constructions will dominate the social construction of reality process. Directly experienced reality will lose its preeminence to mediated knowledge and experience. Crime and justice will be understood and experienced in a mass media reality mixing bowl.

THE FUTURE OF CRIME-AND-JUSTICE REALITY

What might the future media crime–and–justice reality look like? Let's look at two possible scenarios. Both are driven by crime–and–justice media currently available and both rely on the visual image. One emphasizes crime–and–justice spectacle, the other emphasizes surveillance. While recent academic concern has tended to focus on surveillance, the spectacle of crime and justice is felt to be just as important. Crime-related spectacles have evolved so that the audience has changed from an onlooker to a participant. Spectacles are continuously generated in images of crimes and crime victims, investigations of crimes, searches for wanted fugitives, media trials, and final punishments.[12] New media venues and technologies enhance the plausibility of both of the following scenarios developing.

Participatory Spectacles

Violence would be a mainstay in the unrestrained infotainment of media participatory spectacles.

In the first scenario, a free-wheeling infotainment media dominates the culture in a new-media-technology-saturated journalism driven by intrusive voyeurism. In this world, the media push the boundaries of taste and decency without constraints. In such an environment, a host of crime-and-justice programs are possible. Live executions would be a natural, with the modern version of the gallows speech again prominent as YouTube 'last words' postings. Following the last meal and hours of life, imbedded retrospective segments of the condemned prisoner's life and crimes, behind-the-scenes interviews with the executioner and other participants, close-ups of the family of the condemned and victim's relatives at the moment of death, and of course the execution itself would all be compiled into dramatic, entertaining productions. A "Death Row Talk Show" with inmates, attorneys, victim families, and other commentators also has marketing possibilities. Numerous other reality TV programs would also be explored. "The Halfway House," a show based on the activities of various offenders in an urban community corrections home that has been fitted throughout with cameras, would show the lives of drug abusers, prostitutes, and other offenders on probation and living in a court-ordered group home. Driven by the drama of "caught-on-camera" rule breaking resulting in probation revocation and imprisonment, the show would allow audience input into who should be revoked and who given additional chances. "Hostage," a show where a traveling media production crew is alerted beforehand by a hostage taker or cohort, and provides camera coverage of hostage situations, could be another venue. Each episode would be edited and formatted into an hour-long production containing interviews with hostages and hostage takers, film of law enforcement efforts and conditions inside the hostage site, and entertaining background information on participants. The show would also provide telegenic negotiators to move the incident along to its conclusion. The list of possible infotainment shows based on the entertainmentized stories of persons caught up in crime and justice is endless. Graphic shocking media constructions and shows with titles like "Rape Victim," "Drug Dealer," "Pedophile," and so on would compete for audience shares.

Aggressive, proactive news will take off with news agencies staging their own sting operations aimed at offenders, politicians, police officers, and citizens. Catching people committing illegal acts will be a primary journalistic aim. Journalists will ride along not just with the police but with offenders, filming crimes as they happen and editing the material into entertaining news stories. In the criminal justice system, policy changes will be fast tracked and enacted without public debate due to massive media attention and the emotional impact of widely publicized symbolic tragic crimes. For the general public, expectations of privacy will be all but eliminated. Images taken through a bedroom window, for example, would be legally publishable as the courts rule that if couples don't want their sexual encounters filmed, they should not have relations near open windows. Similarly, conversations, files, and information obtained by any means can be utilized by the media as the courts advance the position that media possession of information in whatever form and however obtained is usable under the First Amendment. Prior arrests, personal activities, past marriages, romances, illnesses, and indiscretions great and small all become open to media scrutiny and public review. A new television reality show, "What's Your Neighbor Hiding?," that randomly picks families with solid reputations and investigates and broadcasts embarrassing details of their lives is a big hit. Harbingers of participatory spectacles are found in the host of performance crime postings on YouTube and the frantic paparazzi focus on criminal celebrities.

Self-Surveillance

In the second scenario, the commercial media operates under heavy restrictions, and their ability to cover, comment on, and portray crime-and-justice issues and cases is tightly restrained. At the same time, media technology is applied to its full capabilities in crime control efforts. Self-surveillance through social media would be encouraged and fully tapped by government agencies in crime control efforts. No digital data would be considered private or require search warrants to access. Combined, these two trends create a society where the watchdog function of the media is disabled while the surveillance and control capabilities of the media and media technology are maximized.

Regarding the elimination of the media's constitutionally mandated government watchdog function, criminal cases would be processed absent media coverage, and verdicts would be announced only after trials are concluded and sentences imposed. Filming and coverage of police operations, courtroom proceedings, and correctional facilities would not be allowed. Police chiefs, court officers, and correctional administrators could deny without explanation or appeal media access to their agency personnel, records, and meetings. Access to suspects and prisoners would never be granted.

Concerning the commercial media, all televisions would be equipped with sensors that identify viewers so that all "inappropriate" content can be automatically blocked. Other recording devices would be blocked from making copies of all but approved, prepaid materials. All print, visual, and audio entertainment media must be processed, reviewed, and approved by the new Federal Bureau of Media before marketing. Media programmers must prove "no harm" and provide evidence that content will not result in negative social effects on consumers before marketing approval is granted. Media liability is assumed by the courts for any copying by consumers of stunts, crimes, and other injury-causing behaviors contained in the media. Successful damage suits against the media need only show a similarity in the behavior shown in a media product to subsequent consumer behaviors resulting in harm or injury. To avoid paying compensation, media companies would have to prove that there is no significant relationship between their media content and consumer actions.

Alan Thornton/The Image Bank/Getty Images

The images of a street mugging captured by a CCTV camera exemplifies the surveillance scenario.

What we watch is no less important than who watches us and media-based anticrime efforts utilizing the full capabilities of social media and media technologies proliferate. Information about wanted suspects is continually run as crawl lines across the bottom of all TV programs. All print, visual, and audio media products are required to carry crime prevention public service announcements, re-enactments of unsolved crimes, and Most Wanted fugitive descriptions as part of their advertising allotment and to give these messages prominent times and placement to promote increased citizen surveillance. Most dramatic, all streets and public spaces in communities and the transportation links between them are under the continuous gaze of a national camera surveillance system. In addition, commercial and corporate camera security systems are tied into the overarching government camera matrix. Each of the millions of separate cameras analyzes its video output, automatically recognizing and flagging behaviors such as assaults, break-ins, fires, injuries, vandalism, speeding, reckless driving, loitering in shopping malls, and unauthorized work breaks in corporate areas. The video streams are linked to allow tracking of individual vehicles and persons from one location to another within a single city or from one city to another across the nation. Face recognition programs notify authorities when people are deemed "out-of-place" and when fugitives or terrorist suspects appear. They also allow retroactive searches for specific individuals and reconstruction of any individual's movements and actions that have occurred in a camera's field of view. Alibis and adherence to probation conditions are frequently checked using the video data files generated by the camera matrix. Augmenting the camera surveillance systems are Web and communication tracking software programs accessible by government agencies and private corporations. Although everyone is not watched all the time, it is now possible to determine where the majority of Americans are and what they were doing at any particular time and date.

Obviously neither the spectacle nor surveillance scenario is attractive. Fortunately neither is likely to come to full fruition, but the technology is already available.[13] Neither scenario contains outcomes that are technologically impossible to implement today. Because they are possible, if not plausible, it is vital that we understand how the media and crime and justice interact and plan for the type of media crime-and-justice relationship world we desire.

MEDIATED CRIMINAL JUSTICE

Half a century ago W. I. Thomas stated that "if actors define situations as real they are real in their consequences."[14] What it is like to live in a society; how its citizens feel about their government, authorities, and neighbors; and the daily social expectations of people are all strongly influenced by what people see, hear, read, and share about crime and justice. The social construction of crime and justice loops back to influence the entire social reality of a nation.

Therefore, despite being only one of many factors, the media cannot be ignored. Exactly how and to what extent the media cause long-term changes in social behavior remains undetermined, but it is clear that they play an important, but not autonomous role. The media are one engine in the crime-production and crime-perception process, working in combination with other engines. Ethnic violence, racial strife, oppressive living conditions, violent cultural history, economic disparities, family destruction, and interpersonal violence are all more important for crime levels than the media, but all are subject to exacerbation by the media. As with individuals, the media alone cannot criminalize a country—but once a country criminalizes its media through an emphasis on predatory and unrealistic portraits, a slow spiral of increased crime and tolerance for crime begins.[15] For modern societies, the media set the expectations and moral boundaries for crime, guide the public policies, and steer the social construction of crime-and-justice reality. In the twenty-first century, new media have come to play the lead role in this process.

Today media content distribution is a diffused, decentralized experience.[16] The decentralization of the creation and distribution of content when combined with interactivity lead to powerful social effects.[17] Due to the increasingly active role of audiences as co-producers of content, the traditionally separate domains of "media" (where content and information are made) and "society" (where content and information are consumed) are no longer separated.[18] The traditional research question of what are media effects on society is less relevant than the study of how a "mediated society" functions. New media has expanded access to crime-and-justice content while enhancing the entertainment value of criminal justice events and legacy media's role as the primary crime-and-justice gatekeeper is being rapidly supplanted.[19] In addition, a technological race between data swamping from the enormous amount of digital information produced daily by new media and the mining of this data for useful insights is occurring.[20] The contest between being overwhelmed by the mass of raw information versus the ability to make sense of this information will determine whether criminal justice remains an infotainment sideshow or becomes a considered, policy-driven entity. As the coverage and investigation of the 2013 Boston Marathon bombings (see Box 11.1) show, new media play roles in all aspects of crime and justice today from criminalization, crime planning, committing crimes, identifying suspects and victims, pursuing and capturing suspects, locating evidence, and communicating with the public. Contemporary crimes are extracted from one context, reused, reframed, and employed to create new, fully mediated realities of crime. Currently new media crime content cycles out to the media-sphere to return to society in alternate media forms and vehicles. Such looping of content is observed in both massively mediated real events such as the 2013 Boston Marathon bombings, and in the continuous created for media pseudo-events (think anything Kardashian) common in infotainment media.[21]

B o x   11.1   The Boston Marathon Bombing—A Multi-Mediated Event

The 2013 terrorist bombings at the finish line of the Boston Marathon serve as a harbinger of how crime-and-justice events will be mediated in the future. Due to the participatory and live nature of new media, the planning and committing of crimes; the identification of suspects, victims, and witnesses; the pursuit and apprehension of suspects; the collecting of evidence, and interaction with the public will all be conducted in a different fashion than in the past. Excerpts from newspaper stories on the bombings exemplify the developing multi-faceted relationship between crime, justice, and new media. The first excerpt, "Boston Suspects Are Seen as Self-Taught and Fueled by Web" discusses how the two suspects were recruited to terrorism through Internet sites.

> The portrait investigators have begun to piece together of the two brothers suspected of the bombings suggests that they may have learned to build bombs simply by logging onto the online English-language magazine of the affiliate of Al Qaeda in Yemen. Some of Dzhokhar Tsarnaev's statements suggested that the two brothers could represent the kind of emerging threat that federal authorities have long feared: angry and alienated young men, apparently self-trained and unaffiliated with any particular terrorist group, able to use the Internet to learn their craft. "The increasing signals are that these were individuals who were radicalized over a period of time—radicalized by Islamist fundamentalist terrorists, basically using Internet sources to gain not just the types of philosophical beliefs that radicalized them, but also learning components of how to do these sorts of things." When Dzhokhar Tsarnaev spoke to investigators he indicated that he and his brother had learned to make the pressure-cooker bombs that they used at the marathon from Inspire, the online Al Qaeda magazine. The magazine's first issue contained bomb-making instructions in articles with titles like "Make a Bomb in the Kitchen of Your Mom."

The second excerpt, "Manhunt's Turning Point Came in the Decision to Release Suspects' Images" describes the use of surveillance camera images and the level of public participation that followed the bombing to first identify the bombers and then to locate them.

(continued)

B o x   (Continued)

F.B.I. officials, who had been debating all week whether to go to the public, were ultimately convinced that they had to release the photographs because the investigation was stalling and bureau analysts had finally developed clear images of the suspects from hours of video footage. [An] official added: "We had these murderers on the loose, and we couldn't hold back, and we needed help finding them." The decision was one of the most crucial turning points in a remarkable crowd-sourcing manhunt … [and] resulted in the arrest of one of the men, it set in motion a violent string of events that lasted for 26 hours. Over that time, a police officer was killed; one of the suspects died, several officers sustained life-threatening injuries and one of the country's major cities was shut down.

The culling of social media for evidence and clues about the identity of the bombers was discussed in "Unraveling Boston Suspects' Online Lives, Link by Link."

It is America's first fully interactive national tragedy of the social media age. The Boston Marathon bombings quickly turned into an Internet mystery that sent a horde of amateur sleuths surging onto the Web in a search for clues to the suspects' identity. And once the search focused on Tamerlan and Dzhokhar Tsarnaev, the brothers' social media postings provided a rich vein of material to mine and sift.

There are more than a thousand messages on Dzhokhar's Twitter account in addition to a profile page on VKontakte, a popular Russian social networking site, and in Tamerlan's case, a list of favorite videos on YouTube and what appears to be an Amazon wish list belonging to him. These posts instantly became dots that people began trying to connect.

America has processed the Boston Marathon bombings in different ways from the terror attacks of 9/11—in part because the level of digital sophistication has grown so exponentially since then (in 2001, there was no YouTube, no Facebook, no Twitter). The social media droppings the Tsarnaev brothers left behind not only attest to their own immersion in the interactive, electronic world, but they have also provided plenty of digital data from which to extract patterns and possible meaning—fulfilling that need to try to make narrative sense of the tragic and the overwhelming.

Lastly, the new-media-linked manhunt was described in a fourth story, "News Media and Social Media Become Part of a Real-Time Manhunt Drama."

Last month, the show, "American's Most Wanted" was canceled after 25 years. On Friday, manhunt television drama was back, and it was playing on every news channel. The all-consuming search in Massachusetts for the suspects in Monday's Boston Marathon bombings gripped the nation with some of the most startling, and at times unnerving, news coverage in years. In the middle of it all were reporters, camera crews and ordinary citizens with cellphone cameras who were suddenly entwined with the story.

As thousands of police officers fanned out on Friday, the Massachusetts State Police asked local and national television networks to refrain from showing any live video of police movements, and for a time the Federal Aviation Administration restricted news helicopters from hovering above the area where one of the suspects was believed to be hiding. Members of the news media by and large complied. "We've only been showing the feeds that authorities are comfortable with," the CNN anchor told viewers. By then the first suspect was dead. The second suspect's face was omnipresent on news Web sites and television.

(continued)

**Box   11.1   The Boston Marathon Bombing—A Multi-Mediated
Event (Continued)**

*The tension also played out on Twitter, where seemingly every utterance from
the local police scanners was repeated, often without any context. On Friday night,
as word spread that the second suspect had been spotted, more than 250,000
people were simultaneously tuned to a Ustream rebroadcast of a scanner.*

*On Friday, network programming was pre-empted most of the day for live cov-
erage of the manhunt. As day turned to night, ABC, CBS and NBC scrapped their
prime-time schedules for news and refrained from taking commercial breaks. In
places where reporters could not tread because of police restrictions, local residents filled in some of the audio and video gaps. From their front stoops and
through their windows, they posted videos of an early-morning shootout and
photographs of a vehicle said to be involved in a police chase. The material was
quickly scooped up by local television stations and Twitter users. NBC's "Today"
show was able to interview two Watertown residents sheltering at home, thanks to
a Skype video connection. The residents showed images of bullet holes in their
walls, presumably from the shootout.*

Thus, in a single event, the marathon bombing features the following new media effects:
bombers who were Internet-fueled, a media-oriented terrorist bombing of a popular live
televised event, an attack aftermath which was media-saturated, a search for suspects
which was heavily involved with social media and public participation, a capture which
was broadcast live and unedited, and if it reaches a trial a prosecution that will produce
a media infotainment trial in the "evil stranger" narrative.

SOURCES: Cooper, M., Schmidt, M., and Schmitt, E. 2013, April 23. "Boston Suspects Are Seen as Self-Taught and
Fueled by Web" *The New York Times*.; Kakutani, M. 2013, April 24. "Unraveling Boston Suspects' Online Lives, Link
by Link" *The New York Times*.; Stelter, B. 2013, April 19. "News Media and Social Media Become Part of a Real-Time
Manhunt Drama." *The New York Times*.; Schmidt, M. and Schmitt, E. 2013, April 21. "Manhunt's Turning Point Came
in the Decision to Release Suspects' Images" *The New York Times*.

*Runners continue to run towards the finish line of the 2013 Boston Marathon as an
explosion erupts.*

In the same vein, the social effects of surveillance are difficult to predict. The uploading of surveillance images, for example, has triggered violent reprisals and been used to justify criminal assaults[22] and the conflicting roles that law enforcement agencies hold as sources of crime prevention education and as surreptitious surveillance and apprehension agents is not resolved.[23] How will the public balance trusting agencies funded to protect them with wariness toward those same agencies who are surreptitiously watching so as to arrest them? It follows that a social effect of increasing concern involves new-media-based surveillance and loss of privacy. A decline in privacy is intertwined with an increase in surveillance, so as surveillance has increased the loss of privacy has become a criminal justice issue. The impact that everyday surveillance and digital information that is instantly and widely available will have on law enforcement and on society is yet to be determined in the new media world of high visibility, constant surveillance, and little regulation.[24]

The marketing of camera surveillance systems to the public has emphasized their benefits and their benign effects on those not engaged in crime.[25] The mantra has been "If you're not doing anything wrong you have nothing to fear." Thus, belief in the protective watch of "Big Father" has replaced the fear of "Big Brother" in the twenty-first century where the many watch the few and the hidden watch the many. So it is that the voyeuristic public follows the lives of celebrities through social media while an enormous amount of aggregated visual and digital information posted by the surveilled is culled by government and business.

The first observable change in the new media society is the shift in focus on the part of criminal justice from the past to the future. Traditionally, the criminal justice system focused on reacting to past events where a crime occurred first and the system reacted by investigating, arresting, prosecuting, and punishing. New media has not only shortened the time frame between a crime and the distribution of news of the crime, but has shifted the point in time considered appropriate for criminal justice intervention. In the new media world, the justice system is increasingly involved in proactive precrime activities exemplified by surveillance and crime prevention aimed at victim target hardening, anticrime programs aimed at recognizing and reducing risk, and pre-emptive reverse stings and interventions.[26] No longer is a response to crime enough, criminal justice professionals and government policy makers are today held to a 'no-crime' standard. When a serious crime occurs the outcry is no longer just "what should we do next?" but includes the question "Why was this allowed to happen and who is at fault?"

Another significant general new media societal effect is on the news. New media age "news" has reduced the time lag between a crime and a crime report so that timely interpretation of crime occurs less often. The speed of the process makes thoughtful contextualization, explanation, and alternate policy consideration impossible. In their place are images and emotional reactions which are often delivered live, on-demand, and before events have concluded.[27] New media have ironically enormously increased access to large amounts of information and multiple worldviews while having the effect of decreasing the diversity of the content being accessed and the viewpoints considered.

In this new media reality, it must be emphasized that the single most significant social effect of media crime-and-justice content is not the direct generation of crime but an effect on criminal justice policies. The fear and loathing we feel toward criminals is tied to our media-generated image of criminality. We see more often live and unedited portraits about atypical occurrences, and we see them day after day. The media typically portray criminals as animalistic, vicious predators. The public debate is flooded with dire warnings and sensational crime stories imbedded in a burlesque media, which is dominated by the demands of the marketplace. This image translates into a more criminal society by influencing the way we react to all crime in America. We imprison at a much greater rate and make re-entry into law-abiding society, even for our nonviolent offenders, more difficult than other advanced but less crime-focused, less fear-driven nations.[28] The predator criminal image results in crime-and-justice policy being based on our worst-case criminals with a constant ratcheting up of punishments for all offenders.

YING QIANG/Xinhua /Landov

Related to crowd sourcing and other social media-based activities, flash mobs that result in property damage and other crimes have become more common due to the social impact of new media.

In its cumulative effect, media constructions provide both violent models to emulate and justification for a myopic, harshly punitive public policy reaction to all offenders.

What You Have Learned?

As the reader of this book you have learned to appreciate the role that the media play in contemporary crime and justice, especially in the formation of crime-and-justice policy. You have learned about the history and evolution of the media from print to visual to digital and interactive-based outlets and how this evolution shapes the information that the public receives about crime and criminal justice. You know that in the contemporary mediated world of crime and justice, images, speed, and flexible access are key and you understand that infotainment media values steer the selection, formatting, and delivery of crime-and-justice media content. In the new media crime-and-justice world, audiences pick from a vast store of media outlets and control what content they expose themselves to and when they consume it. You have also learned about social constructionism as a perspective to understand the various interactions between the media and crime and justice and can dissect competing social construction efforts, recognizing claims makers and their strategies to promote crime and justice constructions. You now know about symbolic crimes, frames, narratives, and ownership in social construction and can see the process play out as you use media.

Specifically regarding crime and justice, you have learned that the most common media portrait of criminality is that of a violent predator criminal who hunts innocent victims. You have learned that the most common explanation of crime found in the media relies on individual level characteristics—particularly defective personality traits such as greed or innate evilness. You have also learned that the media has the capacity to influence criminal behavior in some people but that there is no evidence of widespread criminalizing effects. You understand that the media more likely provides criminal models and techniques to individuals already engaged in criminal behavior or about to commit an offense. You now know that the media works on copycat crime as a rudder more than as a trigger. Along the same lines, you know that the media's role in terrorism is evolving in reaction to the Internet and social media and that media-oriented terrorism is expected to increase.

Concerning crime fighters, you know that armed civilians and elite rogue law enforcement officers are portrayed in the media as the most successful crime fighters. You understand how forensics and criminalistics have merged with infotainment to produce a "crime fighting scientist" hero that currently reigns in popularity. You further comprehend that the judicial system is shown in a backwards manner with rare events like trials and homicide cases dominating and common events like plea bargains and property cases rare. You know that trials selected for massive coverage parallel entertainment media story lines of sinful rich, power-abusing, or evil predatory defendants. You have a grasp of the historical tension between the courts and the media and the ongoing attempts to balance due process protections and media access to the courts. Concerning the portrait of the correctional system, you now perceive how corrections are constructed in a manner that focuses on negative events and images. You recognize the media "smug hack" icon that paints corrections as a set of failed institutions staffed by defective personnel. You know that the media image of these institutions has them filled with violent dangerous individuals who prey on heroic victimized inmates.

Most importantly, you understand that the media's greatest impact on crime and justice is in the area of public policy. You know that the use of the media in anticrime efforts has been increasing in both public service "ads" aimed at reducing crime and in enhanced surveillance based on improved media technology. You comprehend that the effect of these efforts on crime and society is yet to be determined but that public support ensures their increased use. Lastly, you know that media content lends support to punitive over preventive or rehabilitative criminal justice policies but that the exact relationship between media and criminal justice policy is convoluted, shifting, and not fully understood. You have gained an understanding of your new role as a participant in the social construction of crime and justice each time you post, tweet, like, friend, or blog about a crime, criminal, or victim.

In addition to these lessons, the most important message running through this book is that social construction is inescapable and that the media are powerful engines in the reality-construction process. Although not the sole or even the most powerful cause of crime, the media are tightly tied into the other crime-generating engines and their influence is recycled, enhanced, and compounded. New media have emerged as a particularly important social construction engine. The result has been a national character and crime-and-justice reality that is individualistic, materialistic, and often violent. American's popular media sets the stage for how we understand crime and the media construct the images that have become the taken-for-granted stories about crime and justice. But it is a social construction with a paradox: with new and old media providing a 24/7 window, there is now so much attention on crime that the end result has not been an advance in understanding, but an obfuscation of reality. An obscuring flood of media information about crime and justice flows in unabated looping circles. Hysteria reigns and a sensible, rational discussion of how crime might be dealt with seems impossible, even as we see more images and more messages, and spend more money trying to deal with the problem.[29]

Is there hope? A little. One observer suggests that online bloggers might serve as a check and balance mechanism on both the news media tendency to focus on rare violent crimes and to present unsubstantiated facts and interpretations about events and on the tendency of legislators to push through emotionally driven but ill-conceived laws.[30] The thought is that social media bloggers, by virtue of being outside the mainstream news media and political domains, but with the capability to directly reach the general public, can provide oversight to limit the thoughtless emotion of crime news and the myopic policymaking of politicians. It has been observed that blogs and Twitter already provide real-time, in-depth analysis of events and offer more detailed information than conventional media.[31] Online blogs have also provided outsider claims-makers with greater opportunity to have a voice in the social construction competition.[32]

Regardless of how society responds, from this base of knowledge you can personally observe and interact with crime-and-justice media from an informed position, recognizing when your personal social construction of reality is being influenced. You have learned to enjoy crime-and-justice media in a manner that will allow you to use what it offers in a more insightful and perceptive way. You are now prepared to move from an unconscious consumer of mediated crime-and-justice knowledge to an interactive author of your own socially constructed crime-and-justice reality.

SUMMARY

- Collectively, the media's crime-and-justice content construct a violent, predatory world and an ineffective criminal justice system. Despite this, enhancement of the system and aggressive personal security measures are seen as the best choices for dealing with crime.

- The line between fact and fiction, entertainment and news, is increasingly blurred. Infotainment media currently dominates the social construction of crime and justice.

- New media has expanded the access and speed with which crime-and-justice information circulates in society and a mediated crime-and-justice reality is today an important source of crime-and-justice knowledge for large numbers of people.

- Media and social forces are currently simultaneously forwarding two threatening scenarios: Unrestrained infotainment in which the media will expose and dramatize everything connected with crime and justice and extensive media-based anticrime efforts in which surveillance and commercial media are used to solve and prevent crime.

- Enhanced by the social effects and communication capabilities of new media, the social construction of crime and justice in the media will continue to obscure the social reality of crime and justice.

CLASS DISCUSSIONS

1. Discuss each of the two scenarios and the social forces and trends that encourage and discourage their development. Discuss how new media might affect each scenario's likelihood of becoming reality and which scenario is most disturbing personally. What steps would you support (increased censorship, for example) or what social conditions might you tolerate (more minor crime, for example) to prevent either scenario from becoming a reality?

2. Discuss how new media will change crime and justice, criminal justice procedures, criminal justice policies, and the public's relationship to the criminal justice system.

Glossary

abuse of power Media trials in which the defendant occupies a position of trust, prestige, or authority. The general rule is the higher the rank, the more media interest in the case.

announcement effect Media audience behavior changes in anticipation of a new criminal justice policy that has been heavily publicized in the media.

anticipatory effects Policy changes made when criminal justice officials respond in a proactive manner to anticipated local media, reversing the usual order wherein media attention to an issue causes criminal justice policy changes.

authority and control correctional films A pessimistic cinematic view of corrections against a backdrop of riots and escapes by offenders confined for less serious offenses; this genre is most significant for immortalizing the "smug hack" portrait of correctional officers.

backwards law The idea that media will present an image of criminality opposite that of crime-and-justice reality. In every subject category—crimes, criminals, crime fighters, attorneys, correctional officers, and inmates; the investigation of crimes and making of arrests; the processing and disposition of cases; and the experience of incarceration—the media construct and present a crime-and-justice world that is the opposite of the real world.

biological theories Theories of crime that hold that crime is the result of innate genetic differences or the constitutional nature of criminals.

business and professional criminals A media criminality frame in which criminals are characterized as shrewd, ruthless, often violent, ladies' men for whom crime is another form of work or business, similar to other careers but more exciting and rewarding.

CCTV (closed circuit television) A limited access video system and the most common media technology used in surveillance systems. The term CCTV has become a common acronym for public safety surveillance systems regardless of the underlying technology employed.

CSI effect The impact of criminalistics and forensic science media on expectations regarding evidence-gathering and the use and presentation of evidence in court proceedings. A CSI effect is hypothesized to unduly raise doubts about the strength of a case when forensic evidence and tests are absent and to unduly reduce doubts about case strength when such evidence is present.

civilian crime fighters Two groups of civilian crime fighters are popular in the media: private investigators (PIs), who occupy the boundary between civilians and police officers as independent law enforcement contractors, and personally motivated private citizens who take on solving crimes as a hobby or due to some personal connection with a victim.

claims makers The promoters, activists, professional experts, and spokespersons with a particular point of view who make specific claims about a social problem or condition.

commodification The for-profit packaging and marketing of crime information for popular consumption.

conversational reality Information people receive directly from people close to and similar to them, which is combined with personal experiences to make up the most influential social construction engine.

cops A media law enforcement frame that constructs the local police as aggressive, crime-fighting, take-no-prisoners, frontline soldiers in the war on crime.

copycat crime A crime inspired by an earlier, news-media-covered or entertainment-media-portrayed crime.

correctional horrors Negative correctional news stories often employing the death of an inmate as a symbol of the correctional system's failure; they are exemplified by corruption and misconduct exposés.

counterproductive effects Media-based anticrime campaigns that have effects opposite to the campaign goal of crime reduction.

crime sourcing Taking all or a portion of a crime and outsourcing it to a crowd of either witting or unwitting individuals using the capabilities of new media. In crime-sourcing large numbers of strangers can be anonymously recruited to help commit crimes such as money laundering and computer hacking.

criminogenic media Media content that is hypothesized as a cause or catalyst of crime.

diffusion of benefits Associated with surveillance systems, diffusion is a bonus benefit from the use of surveillance technology. Offenders are not aware of the boundaries of surveillance coverage and therefore reduce their offenses in adjacent nonsurveilled areas. See also *displacement of crime*.

displacement of crime Associated with the use of surveillance systems, displacement pushes crime into adjacent communities without surveillance systems. See also *diffusion of benefits*.

echo effect A spillover effect from media news coverage of a high-profile criminal case onto similarly charged but nonpublicized cases affecting their processing and dispositions.

episodic format The most common crime news format, in which a particular crime is described and a resulting case is followed. Episodic formatted stories encourage viewers to place responsibility on the individual and to ignore societal forces by focusing on the question: Why did this individual commit this crime? See also *thematic format*.

evil strangers Media trials composed of two subgroups: non-American suspects or psychotic killers. Non-American evil stranger media trials involve ethnic and minority advocates of various unpopular causes. Psychotic killer media trials focus on bizarre murder cases in which the defendant is portrayed as a maddened, predatory killer.

experienced reality Knowledge gained from one's directly experienced world; all of the events that have happened to you.

factual claims Statements that purport to describe the world and "what" happened; they are put forth as objective, true "facts" about the world.

frames Prepackaged constructions that include factual and interpretative claims and associated recommended policies. A frame is a fully developed social construction that allows the categorization, labeling, and conceptualization of real-world events that fit into a pre-existing frame.

freedom and release correctional films A cinematic view of corrections that emphasizes extreme violence, exemplified by prison action films. The ambiguity and confusion about the function and role of prisons in society is reflected in these films. The keepers are certifiably crazy or dehumanized, and the constructed correctional world reflects the comics more than any recognizable social reality.

G-men A media law enforcement frame that originated in the 1930s and focuses on effective, professional, federal "crime-busters."

gatekeeper An individual occupying a checkpoint in the crime news creation process where crimes are selected, molded, and passed on as candidate news stories about crime. Key gatekeepers in the crime news process are crime reporters and law enforcement public information officers.

generator crime The initial media-portrayed crime that serves as the crime model source for subsequent copycat crimes.

heroic inmates The dominant media construction of male prisoners, which employs the role-reversal of offenders being caught up in a corrupt criminal justice system and shown as victims and heroes.

ideal heroes Ideal heroes in the media display the admirable qualities of sacrifice, nobleness, and strength. Sometimes they are traditional by-the-book police officers, but frequently they are rogue officers or civilians.

ideal offenders The outsiders, strangers, foreigners, aliens, and intruders who are portrayed in the media as lacking essential humanity and the potential to be rehabilitated.

ideal victims The innocent, naïve, trusting, and protection-needing humans; children are the most ideal of the ideal victims in the media.

immanent justice Belief that a divine power will intervene and reveal the guilty while protecting the innocent. Similar to the medieval socially constructed reality that made trial by combat logical, the modern media reality relies on the moral superiority of the crime fighter to ultimately defeat criminality. In this battle criminality is reduced to an individual moral battle of good versus evil.

infotainment Media content that delivers information about the world in an entertainment format.

interactivity The ability of consumer actions and decisions to influence media story lines and content as the story lines and content are being created.

interpretative claims Statements that focus on the meanings of events and either offer an explanation of why the world is as described in associated factual claims or offer a course of action and public policy that needs to be followed.

lampooned police A popular media frame that satirizes law enforcement as foolish, slapstick police work.

legacy media Traditional types of media represented by print (newspapers, books, and magazines), sound (radio programming, phonograph records), and visual (films and television programming) media.

linkage Association of one social construction effort with another previously accepted construction so that the significance of the first construction is connected to the latter.

looping Reuse of media content in new contexts and media products.

mainstreaming The idea that the media affect some viewers more than others regardless of exposure level, influencing heavy television consumers who are currently not in the mainstream to move toward it, while not affecting those already in the mainstream. In total effect, the media are hypothesized to have a homogenizing influence on society.

manipulative model A model of news creation that has crime news selected not according to general public interest but according to the interests of news agencies' owners. The news media are argued to purposefully distort reality and use the news to shape public opinion to support the status quo.

market model A model of news creation that sees crime news as selected largely by public interest and journalists as objective reporters who accurately reproduce the world.

media–oriented terrorism A terrorist strategy where the primary goal of a terror campaign is to attract media attention. Terrorist acts are frequently carried out in a manner that maximizes media attention and are characterized by the selection of high-visibility targets and locations, graphic dramatic acts, pre-event contact with media outlets, and post-event videos, interviews, and other media accommodations.

media trials A regional or national crime or justice event in which the media co-opt the criminal justice system as a source of drama, entertainment, and profit. They involve the social construction of selected trials as info-tainment products that are commodified and mass marketed. Coverage is live whenever possible, pictures are preferred over text, and content is characterized by conjecture and sensationalism. See *abuse of power media trials*, *evil strangers media trials*, and *sinful rich media trials*.

media lineups A crime investigation step in which crime witnesses are shown a series of videotaped images selected for their similarity.

media mug books An investigation step in which a computer searches a pictorial data file for specific characteristics (for example, tattoo, bald, heavy, white, and male) and displays matching pictures.

mediated experience The comparative experience an individual has when he or she experiences an event via the media versus actually physically being at an event.

memorial criminal justice policy Link-ing a criminal justice policy and legislation to an individual by name (such as the Brady law and Amber Alerts); the person is usually the victim of a violent, deadly crime.

multimedia Web The interconnected and pervasive mix of contemporary media exemplified by the constant looping of media content.

narratives Recurring pre-established social roles, characters, and story lines found throughout crime-and-justice media. Narra-tives are usually associated with a single individual or crime rather than with general criminality or a criminal justice issue.

narrative persuasion The ability of storytelling-based media to affect consumers through transportation, engagement, and absorption in media content.

narrowcasting Marketing media content to small special interest self-selecting groups rather than to large, heterogeneous mass markets. Originally applied to television marketing with the introduction of cable

networks, today the principle is applicable to all media.

nature of confinement correctional films A cinematic view of corrections in which inmates are victims of injustice; a good man is either framed or accidentally impri-soned or pushed into crime by powerful societal forces. A recurrent message in this genre is the pervasive corruption of the correctional system and its administrators.

new media Digital interactive media exemplified by the Internet, electronic games, and smart phones. New media are character-ized by interactive social media and the looping of multimedia content. New media employ digital information that is easily shared and can take the form of print, sound, moving or still images and all of their combinations.

newsworthiness The value of an event or crime to a news agency and the criteria by which news producers choose which crimes are presented to the public as news about crime.

organizational model A model of news creation that has crime news filtered and presented to the public following an assembly-line process within law enforce-ment and news organizations. Crime news is argued to be stylized information that fits the organizational and production needs of news agencies.

on-demand Time and place access to media content is determined by the con-sumer rather than by the producer of the content.

ownership Identification of a social condi-tion with a particular set of claims makers who come to dominate the social construc-tion of that issue. Claims makers own an issue when they are sought out by the media and others for information regarding its nature and policy solutions.

performance crime Crime purposely committed to gain attention and attract an audience, performance crime is frequently created using social media to record, share, and distribute images of a crime as it is committed.

police procedurals A media law enforcement frame that concentrates on the dramatic backstage realities of police investigations. The crime fighters in these portraits normally rely heavily on team-work and criminalistics to solve crimes.

police reality programs Highly edited television productions in which viewers are invited to share a cop's point-of-view as a partner officer in voyeuristic ride-alongs.

political theories of crime Theories that assert that the political and economic structure of a society are the root causes of crime.

popular criminology The criminological ideas and explanation of crime that are popular with the general public and often have inferred counterparts in mass media content.

predatory criminality The most common portrait of criminality found in the media, which is characterized by criminals who are animalistic, irrational, innate predators committing violent and senseless crimes.

prejudicial publicity Dissemination by the media of either factual information that bears on the guilt of a defendant or emotional information without evidentiary relevance that simply arouses emotions against a defendant.

priming When people read, hear about, or witness a criminal event via the mass media, priming influences them to hold similar ideas and engage in related copycat acts.

private investigator (PI) Nongovernmental independent contractors of law enforcement and a major subset of media-portrayed crime fighters.

privileged conversation A constitutionally based argument to protect journalists from having to divulge unpublished story information or to identify their sources. It is argued that a privileged conversation protection is needed so that journalists can fulfill their constitutional function as watchdogs of government activities and guarantee future access to story information and sources.

proactive mechanisms Judicial measures such as closure, restrictive orders, and protective orders that are employed to counteract the production of news media publicity. The proactive approach to dealing with publicity directly clashes with the First Amendment protection of freedom of the press and has been vigorously resisted by the media.

prosocial television Programs of various types (animated, adventure, comedy, fantasy) that have the ability to elicit socially valued behaviors and attitudes from viewers. *Sesame Street* is a well-known example.

psychological theories of crime The idea that crime is caused by defective personality development.

psychotic super-male criminals A popular media frame of criminality in which criminals possess an evil, cunning intelligence and superior strength, endurance, and stealth. Crimes committed by media psychotic super-males are generally acts of twisted, lustful revenge or random acts of irrational violence.

public agenda The ranked list of social problems the public see as important and needing to be addressed.

public service announcements (PSAs) Information disseminated in the media in ad-style messages. Anticrime PSAs are a common means of getting crime prevention information to the public.

pursuit of justice correctional films A cinematic view of corrections where offenders are personally responsible for their actions and confinement is therefore justified. Although many of these films revolve around violence—riots, escapes, and assaults—individual offender rehabilitation is seen as possible.

rational choice theories of crime The idea that crime is a rational, free-will decision that individual will make when the gains from committing a crime outweigh the likelihood of punishment.

reactive mechanisms Judicial procedures used to counteract the effects of news media publicity, which include expanding the jury selection (the voir dire), granting trial continuances, granting changes of venue, sequestering jurors, and giving special instructions to the jury.

scripts Sets of well-rehearsed, highly associated concepts held in memory, often involving causes, goals, and actions that generate a set of cognitive directions that define situations and guide behavior. Once learned, a media-provided behavior script is hypothesized to be able to create behaviors similar to that observed in the media content.

shield laws Legislation to prevent the forced divulgence of sources and testimony from journalists.

sinful rich Media trials in which socially prominent defendants are involved in bizarre or sexually related crimes.

smug hack The dominant media portrayal of correctional officers as caricatures of brutality, incompetence, low intelligence, and indifference to human suffering.

smug hack corrections The dominant media construction of corrections that emphasizes physically brutal inmate discipline, corporal punishment and the infliction of pain, and the exploitation of inmates as a cheap source of labor and profit. Staff incompetence, corruption, and cruelty are common, ingrained, and unchallenged. Prisoners suffer systemic racial prejudice, homosexual rape, and between-prisoner assaults.

social constructionism A theoretical view that knowledge is socially created. Social constructionism focuses on human relationships and the way relationships affect how people perceive reality. Social constructionism studies the shared ideas, interpretations, and knowledge that groups of people agree to hold in common.

socially constructed reality The reality perceived as the "real" world by each individual. It is constructed from knowledge each individual gains from his or her experienced and symbolic realities mixed together. The resulting constructed reality is what we individually believe the world to be like.

sociological theories of crime The idea that criminal environments cause crime, and that people are criminals because of the people they associate with or share a neighborhood or culture with.

surveillance effect The psychological effect of believing that you might be under observation.

symbolic crimes that individual will make highlighted by claims makers as perfect examples to support a particular crime-and-justice construction.

symbolic reality Knowledge of the world gained from other people, institutions, and the media that is shared via symbols, language being the most common symbolic system to share knowledge. Art, music, and mathematics are others.

thematic format A crime news format that highlights criminal justice trends and persistent problems. Stories told in the thematic format explore crime and justice issues in terms of their causes and effects and focus on the question: A set of problems has developed, what changed in society? See *episodic format*.

true crime A media law enforcement infotainment frame wherein the audience looks over the criminal's (frequently a killer) or cop's shoulder as they either commit crime or pursue criminals and solve murders.

ultraviolence A media style popular since the 1960s that portrays violence using slow motion, detonating blood capsules, multiple camera views, and graphic visuals and special effects.

victims and heroic criminals The least common media criminality frame, it presents criminals as either victims of injustice or unrecognized good guys. This frame often supports sociological and political explanations of crime.

videotaped interrogations Videotaped interactions between police and suspects that provide visual evidence regarding the physical and mental condition of suspects, the voluntariness of their statements, their understanding of their rights, and the use of coercion and adherence to standard interrogation practices by the police.

white-collar crime A crime committed by a respectable person of high social status in the course of his or her occupation. White-collar crime overlaps with corporate and business crime and usually includes fraud, bribery, insider trading, embezzlement, computer crime, identity theft, and forgery.

worldview cultivation A media effect that hypothesizes that watching many hours of television will result in viewers holding general perceptions about the world as being a pernicious and dangerous place.

yellow journalism A term for a style of newspaper coverage first associated with U.S. newspapers in the 1890s that emphasized exaggeration, scandals, and sensationalism regarding crime and other topics.

Notes

Chapter 1

1. Except for discussions of media technology applications in criminal justice, media is considered herein in the narrow sense of popular culture, which includes all commercial media in all their forms that are marketed for popular consumption (Asimow and Mader, *Law and Popular Culture*, 4).

2. Marsh and Melville, "Crime, Justice and the Media," 1–10.

3. Rafter, "Crime, Film and Criminology," 417.

4. Altheide, *Creating Fear*, 128; Dowler, Fleming and Muzzatti, "Constructing Crime," 837–850.

5. Leishman and Mason, *Policing and the Media*, 144. Don Oberdorfer historically places the transition to a media-driven policy during the coverage of the Vietnam War: "The electronics revolution, which took the battlefield into the American living room via satellite, increased the power and velocity of fragments of experience, with no increase in the power or velocity of reasoned judgment. Instant analysis was often faulty analysis" (Oberdorfer, *TET!*, 322).

6. Griffin and Miller, "Child Abduction," 159–176.

7. Shichor and Sechrest, *Three Strikes and You're Out*, Grimes, "The Social Construction of Social Problems."

8. Although not identical, the policy influencing "symbolic crimes" referred to in this work are analogous to the "signal crimes" described by Innes ("Signal Crime").

9. Mathiesen, "Television, Public Space and Prison Population;" Curran, "Communications, Power and Social Order."

10. Surette, "Some Unpopular Thoughts about Popular Culture."

11. Adoni and Mane, "Media and the Social Construction of Reality."

12. This focus on violent predatory crime is tied to a historical interest in crime and justice as theater. Crime and justice has been a source for story lines since antiquity, and the media construct crime as predatory and as a frightening (and hence entertaining) phenomenon caused by individually based deficiencies (Ball, *The Promise of American Law*).

13. Manning, "Media Loops." This concept is related to the idea of intertextuality as decribed by Asimow and Mader (*Law and Popular Culture*, 15). An early criminal-justice-related example is provided by Wood ("The Third Degree," 469) regarding the "Third Degree" and its portrayal in news and crime fiction in the United Kingdom.

14. Wood, "The Third Degree."

15. Asimow and Mader, *Law and Popular Culture*, 15.

16. Stempel, Hargrove, and Stempel, "Media Use, Social Structure, and Belief;" Langer, "Legacy of Suspicion."

17. Dowler, Fleming and Muzzatti, *Constructing Crime*, 837–850.

18. Grodal, "Stories for Eye, Ear and Muscles," 129–155. Alternate histories of crime and media can be found in Carrabine, *Crime, Culture and the Media* and in Greer, *Crime and Media: A Reader*.

19. Gordon and Heath, "The News Business, Crime, and Fear," 227.

20. Papke, *Framing the Criminal*, 35.

21. Gorn, "The Wicked World."

22. Casey, "Common Misperceptions."

23. Stark, *Glued to the Set*, 237. For an historic overiew of the relationship between detective stories, public opinon and the law see Friedman and Rosen-Zvi, "Illegal Fictions."

24. For an overview see Nyberg, "Comic Books and Juvenile Delinquency;" Phillips and Strobe, *Comic Book Crime*.

25. Nyberg, "Comic Books and Juvenile Delinquency;" 61.

26. Since the 1960's "underground comics" have provided explicit sex and violence content (Westfahl "Bloodshed and Circuses").

27. Phillips and Strobe, *Comic Book Crime*.

28. DeFleur and Ball-Rokeach, *Theories of Mass Communication*, 84; Cheatwood, "Early Images of Crime and Criminal Justice."

29. Cheatwood, "Early Images of Crime and Criminal Justice."

30. Oliver and Marion, *Crime, History, and Hollywood*.

31. Armour, *Film*, xxi.

32. See Leishman and Mason, *Policing and the Media*, Chapter 4 for a history of police shows on British television.

33. Allen, Livingstone, and Reiner, "True Lies;" Boyd-Barett, Herrera, and Baumann, "Hollywood, the CIA, and the War on Terror;" Broe, "Class, Crime, and Film Noir."

34. See Leishman and Mason, *Policing and the Media*, Chapter 4 for a history of police shows on British television.

35. The social impact of television has been compared to the medieval Christian church's influence on European culture (Curran, "Communications, Power and Social Order," 210).

36. Stevens and Garcia, *Communication History*, 143.

37. If you are a typical American, for every ten years of your life you will spend one solid year (8,760 hours) looking at a television screen. In 1990, a Congressional Subcommittee on the Constitution stated: "The typical American child is exposed to an average of 27 hours of TV each week—as much as eleven hours a day for some children. That child will watch 8,000 murders and more than 100,000 acts of violence before finishing elementary school. By the age of 18, that same teenager will have witnessed 200,000 acts of violence on TV including 40,000 murders" (cited in Perlmutter, *Policing the Media*, 33).

38. Commenting in *The New York Times Magazine* (November 28, 1954, 56) television producer Gilbert Seldes states: "Television finds itself on the defensive, facing investigations and threats. Most of these arise from the part of the program schedule usually held as the industry's worst—its endless stream of crime shows, many of them available to children."

39. Dominick, "Crime and Law Enforcement in the Mass Media."

40. Lichter, Lichter, and Rothman describe early crime-and-justice television content as seeming to require "two shootouts with police, a beating, and a cold-blooded murder" (*Prime Time*, 282).

41. Cole, *The UCLA Television Violence Monitoring Report*; Gunter, Harrison and Wykes, *Violence on Television*.

42. Flew, *New Media: An Introduction*, 11; Lister, Dovey, Giddings, Grant and Kelly, *New Media: A Critical Introduction*. The 1991 trial of William Kennedy Smith was the first trial to be covered gavel-to-gavel on cable Court-TV television (now TruTV channel) (Fox, Van Sickel, and Steiger, *Tabloid Justice*.

43. Ling and Campbell, *The Reconstruction of Space and Time: Mobile Communication Practices*.

44. Lee, Peng, and Klein, "Will the Experience of Playing a Violent Role," 1022.

45. Grodal, *Stories for Eye, Ear and Muscles*, 129–155.

46. Reiner, "Media Made Criminality," 389.

47. Thompson, Young, and Burns, "Representing Gangs in the News," 427; see also Dowler, "Comparing American and Canadian Local Television Crime Stories," 589–590.

48. Gilliam and Iyengar, "Prime Suspects," 561. Yvonne Jewkes discusses twelve news values operating in the twenty-first century that result in crime news focusing on violent rare crimes (*Media and Crime*,

40–60). Robert Reiner summarizes the differences between crime news and crime as the over reporting of serious crime, especially murder and other violent crimes; the concentration on crimes that are solved; and coverage of offenders and victims who are disproportionately older and from a higher social class than their counterparts in reality (*The Politics of the Police*, 141).

49. Robinson, *Media Coverage of Crime and Criminal Justice.*

50. Drechsel, *News Making in the Trial Courts*, 35 citing Shaaber, *Some Forerunners of the Newspaper in England.*

51. Chibnall, *Chronicles of the Gallows*, 179–217; Flanders, *The Invention of Murder.*

52. Chibnall, *Chronicles of the Gallows*, 190.

53. See Chibnall, *The Production of Knowledge by Crime Reporters*, 75–97; Isaacs, *The Crime of Crime Reporting*, 312–320; and Sherizen, *Social Creation of Crime News.*

54. Hughes, *News and the Human Interest Story*, 23.

55. Drechsel, *News Making in the Trial Courts*, 53–54; Freedman, "Crimes which Startle and Horrify."

56. Drechsel, *News Making in the Trial Courts*, 68; Papke, *Framing the Criminal*, 54; Casey, *Common Misperceptions,*

57. Cohen and Young, *The Manufacture of News.*

58. Ibid., 17–18.

59. Cohen and Young, *The Manufacture of News*; Ericson, Baranek, and Chan, *Negotiating Control.*

60. Wisehart ("Newspapers and Criminal Justice") makes a similar point in 1922.

61. Ericson, Baranek, and Chan, *Representing Law and Order.*

62. Ericson, Baranek, and Chan, *Representing Law and Order*; Hall, Chritcher, Jefferson, Clarke, and Roberts, *The Social Production of News*, 335–367.

63. Martens and Cunningham-Niederer, *Media Magic, Mafia Mania*, 62; see also Pritchard, *Race, Homicide and Newspapers*, 500–507.

64. Drechsel, *News Making in the Trial Courts*, 12, 49, citing Sigal, *Reporters and Officials*, 4–5.

65. Gans, *Deciding What's News*, 284.

66. Mason, *Misinformation, Myth and Distortion*, 498; Franklin, *Local Journalism and Local Media.*

67. Lipschultz and Hilt, *Crime and Local Television News.*

68. Cohen and Young, *The Manufacture of News*, 22–23.

69. Lipschultz and Hilt, *Crime and Local Television News*; Roshier, *The Selection of Crime News in the Press*, 40–51.

70. Warr, *America's Perceptions of Crime and Punishment*, 14.

71. Jones, *The Press as Metropolitan Monitor*, 244.

72. Shoemaker, *Gatekeeping.*

73. Sherizen, *Social Creation of Crime News*, 203–224.

74. Ericson, Baranak and Chan, *Negotiating Control*; Chermak, *Police, Courts, and Corrections in the Media.*

75. Schlesinger, Tumber and Murdock, *The Media Politics of Crime and Criminal Justice*, 399.

76. Ericson, Baranek, and Chan, *Visualizing Deviance*; Ericson, Baranek, and Chan, *Negotiating Control*; Ericson, Baranek, and Chan, *Representing Law and Order*; Gordon and Heath, "The News Business, Crime, and Fear;" Roshier, *The Selection of Crime News in the Press*; Sherizen, *Social Creation of Crime News*, 212.

77. Chibnall, *The Production of Knowledge by Crime Reporters*; Tuchman, *Making News by Doing Work*, 110–131; Tuchman, *Making News: A Study in the Construction of Reality.*

78. Rhineberger-Dunn, "Comparing Large and Small Metropolitan Newspaper Coverage."

79. Although the depth of its impact is recent, infotainment has existed in some form since the seventeenth century. In the mid-1600s, for example, newspaper weeklies carried details of the more interesting crimes along with moral exhortations to their readers to avoid crime, sin, and evil. Early folk music in the form of crime ballads also established crimes and criminals as accepted sources of social entertainment and narrative. Hanging, public floggings, branding, and other punishments of the time were as much popular entertainment as criminal justice events

(Chibnall, *Chronicles of the Gallows*; Papke, *Framing the Criminal*).

80. Surette and Otto, "A Test of a Crime and Justice Infotainment Measure."

81. The growth of infotainment in television news has been traced to the year 1963, when network television news expanded from 15 to 30 minutes. Doris Graber ("The Infotainment Quotient," 483) quotes a memo from Reuven Frank, executive producer for NBC nightly news: "Every news story should, without any sacrifice of probity or responsibility, display the attributes of fiction, of drama. It should have structure and conflict, problem and denouncement, rising action and falling action, a beginning, a middle, and an end. These are not only the essentials of drama; they are the essentials of narrative."

82. Brants and Neijens, "The Infotainment of Politics," 150; Graber, "The Infotainment Quotient."

83. Cavender and Fishman, "Television Reality Crime Programs."

84. Goidal, Freeman, and Procopio, "The Impact of Television Viewing on Perceptions of Juvenile Crime," 119.

85. Fishman and Cavender, *Entertaining Crime*.

86. Cavender, "In the Shadow of Shadows."

87. Tunnel, "Reflections on Crime, Criminals, and Control."

88. Gaeta, "Catch and Release."

89. Chiou and Lopez, "The Reality of Reality Television."

90. Cavender, "In Search of Community on Reality TV;" Oliver, "Portrayals of Crime, Race, and Aggression."

91. Goidal, Freeman, and Procopio, "The Impact of Television Viewing on Perceptions of Juvenile Crime," 134.

92. Surette, "Media Trials."

93. Wasserman, "No Big Deal."

94. The Lizzie Borden schoolyard poem (anonymous, sometimes attributed to Mother Goose, a folk music version is available from The Chad Mitchell Trio):

    Lizzie Borden took an axe,
    and gave her mother forty whacks.
    And when she saw what she had done,
    she gave her father forty one.
    Close your door, lock and latch it,
    cause here comes Lizzie with her hatchet.

95. Valier, *Crime and Punishment in Contemporary Culture*.

96. Grodal, "Stories for Eye, Ear and Muscles," 129–155.

97. Manning, "Media Loops."

98. Reiner, "Media Made Criminality," labels the two competing views as subversive and hegemonic.

Chapter 2

1. Malcolm Gladwell in his book (*Blink*, 194–197) describes a similar socially constructed tragic encounter in which an unarmed man was shot to death by four New York City undercover police officers.

2. Lippmann, *Public Opinion*, 54.

3. The ideas included within a social construction of reality fall under the broad umbrella of the sociology of knowledge tradition. See also Foucault, *The Archaeology of Knowledge*.

4. Gergen, "Social Constructionist Inquiry."

5. An introduction to social constructionism applied to crime and other social issues can be found in Spector and Kitsuse, *Constructing Social Problems*.

6. Lindlof, "Media Audiences as Interpretive Communities."

7. Spector and Kitsuse, *Constructing Social Problems*, 6.

8. Maxson, Hennigan, and Sloane, *Factors That Influence Public Opinion of the Police*, 10.

9. It is assumed that you are not one of the few astronauts who have been to the moon and have experienced reality to draw upon for these questions.

10. Adoni and Mane, "Media and the Social Construction of Reality;" Sparks, *Television and the Drama of Crime*.

11. Rentschler, "Victims' Rights and the Struggle over Crime," 219–239.

12. Best, *Images of Issues*, 327.

13. As quoted in Sherwin, *When Law Goes Pop*, 142.

14. Joel Best describes a claim as an argument with four elements: that some condition exists; that it is troubling and ought to be addressed; that it has specific characteristics such as being common or increasing, has known causes or serious consequences, or

is a particular type of problem; and that a particular action should be taken to deal with it ("The Diffusion of Social Problems").

15. Thompson, Young, and Burns, "Representing Gangs in the News," 427–428.

16. Ferrel, "Criminalizing Popular Culture."

17. Sasson, *Crime Talk*, 13–17. See also Reiner, *The Politics of the Police*, 139. A cultural criminology-based collection of additional various ways of framing crime and justice issues is offered in Hayward and Presdee, *Framing Crime*. Boda and Szabo ("the Media and Attitudes towards Crime," 337) suggest that the media offer an additional 'cruel world' frame which portrays life as dangerous, unpredictable and filled with crime that can strike anyone at any time.

18. Sasson, *Crime Talk*, 14.

19. David Bruck as cited in Sasson, *Crime Talk*, 15.

20. As cited in Sasson, *Crime Talk*, 15.

21. Ibid., 16.

22. Sasson, *Crime Talk*, 16, quoting Thomas Elmendorf's testimony before the House Subcommittee on Communication.

23. Dardis, Baumgartner, Boydstun, De Boef and Shen, "Media Framing of Capital Punishment," 16–17.

24. In the broader research world, media narratives share many characteristics with "scripts" as developed by cognitive psychologists (see Schank and Abelson, *Scripts, Plans, Goals, and Understanding*). They also are related to the concepts of "motif" and "rhetorical idioms," both of which refer to recurring rhetorical elements and speech used to describe and culturally anchor social problems. Unlike narratives, these are brief common catchphrases and metaphors used to describe crime. Examples include these phrases: *epidemic, menace, scourge, crisis, blight, casualties, tip of the iceberg, war on drugs, crime, gangs,* or *terrorism* (Ibarra and Kitsuse, "Vernacular Constituents of Moral Discourse," 47). See also Best and Hutchinson, "The Gang Initiation Rite as a Motif in Contemporary Crime Discourse," 384.

25. Examples of popular crime-and-justice narratives are offered by Rafter (*Shots in the Mirror*, 141–146): (1) Mystery and detective narratives: basic pattern is of the search, most P.I. and cop films fall into this category; (2) Thrillers: unexpected violence, nail-biters, regular episodic scares; (3) Capers: complicated audacious heist planning, organization and member recruitment, and execution; (4) Justice violated/justice restored: many prison films, false accusations and unjust punishments; (5) Disguised westerns: heroic outsider reluctantly consents to clean up the town; (6) Revenge and vigilantes: lead figure is violated and retaliates; (7) Chronicles of criminal careers: biographies and fictional characters; (8) Action films: lacking developed plots, series of episode transitions with fights and explosions, violent spectacles, epic heroes.

26. Best and Hutchinson, "The Gang Initiation Rite as a Motif in Contemporary Crime Discourse," 388–389; and Sumser, *Morality and Social Order in Television Crime Drama*, 46.

27. Wardle, "It Could Happen to You," 515–533.

28. A similar concept is "signal crime" described by Innes ("Signal Crimes," 15–16) and again in Innes ("Signal Crimes and Signal Disorders," 335–355).

29. Yar, "Crime, Media, and the Will-to-Representation," 248.

30. Ibid., 249.

31. Mittell, "Wikis and Participatory Fandom," 37.

32. Kiousis, "Interactivity: A Concept Explication."

33. Collins, "Content Analysis of Gender Roles in Media," 296.

34. Grodal, "Stories for Eye, Ear, and Muscles."

35. Grochowski, "Running in Cyberspace."

36. Lindgren, "YouTube Gunmen?"

37. Flew, *New Media: An Introduction*; Lister, Dovey, Giddings, Grant, and Kelly, *New Media: A Critical Introduction*.

38. Ling and Campbell, *The Reconstruction of Space and Time*.

39. Delwiche and Henderson, "Introduction: What is Participatory Culture?" 6.

40. Rogers, *Diffusion of Innovations*, 215–216.

41. Flichy, "New Media History," 146.

42. Ibid.

43. Hayward and Presdee, *Framing Crime*; Maratea, "The E-Rise and Fall of Social Problems," 141–142.

44. Beale, "The News Media's Influence" 440.

45. Ibid., 464.

46. Maratea, "The E-Rise and Fall of Social Problems," 143–144.

47. Britto and Dabney, "Fair and Balanced?"

48. Maratea, "The E-Rise and Fall of Social Problems," 143–144.

49. Maratea, "The E-Rise and Fall of Social Problems," 139.

50. Rentschler, "Victims' Rights and the Struggle over Crime," 219–239.

51. Lydon, Bonds-Raacke and Cratty, "College Students Facebook Stalking;" Reyns, "A Situational Crime Prevention;" Wykes, "Constructing Crime," 158–174.

52. Ruddell and Decker, "Kids and Assault Weapons," 45–63.

53. Quinney in his 1970 book, *The Social Reality of Crime*, provides the first effort in applying social constructionism to crime. Jenkins in *Using Murder* in 1994 and Potter and Kappeler in *Constructing Crime* in 2006 provide updated examples.

54. Best, *Images of Issues*, 332.

55. Reinarman, "The Social Construction of an Alcohol Problem."

56. Grimes, "The Social Construction of Social Problems."

57. Kupchik and Bracy, "News Media on School Crime and Violence."

58. Rentschler, "Victims' Rights and the Struggle over Crime," 219–239.

Chapter 3

1. Frosdick and Marsh, *Football Hooliganism*. Kerr, *Rethinking Aggression and Violence in Sport*.

2. Westfahl, "Bloodshed and Circuses."

3. Bok, *Mayhem*.

4. Westfahl, "Bloodshed and Circuses."

5. Signorielli, N. Violence in the media," 2; Wright, "Violent Entertainment, Popular Culture, and Technological Change."

6. Stark, "Perry Mason Meets Sonny Crockett," 236.

7. Rafter, *Shots in the Mirror*; see also Leitch, *Crime Films*.

8. Escholz, Mallard, and Flynn, "Images of Prime Time Justice," 161–180. While not historically reported as the most common image of criminality, media portraits of minorities as offenders do raise concerns that racist and ethnic stereotypes are reinforced. See Bing, *Race, Crime, and the Media*; Hussain, "(Re)presenting: Muslims;" Mann and Zatz, *Images of Color Images of Crime*; Rome, *Black Demons*; and Shaheen, *Reel Bad Arabs* for discussions of media portraits of minority offenders.

9. Bailey and Hale, *Blood on Her Hands*; Bond-Maupin, "That Wasn't Even Me They Showed," 30–44; Cecil, "Dramatic Portrayals of Violent Women," 243.

10. Lynch, Stretesky, and Hammond found, for example, that regarding chemical crimes, a very small percentage of events are reported as news; those that are reported are likely to be cast as caused by an individual and the harm of the event downplayed ("Media Coverage of Chemical Crimes," 121–122).

11. Graber, *Crime News and the Public*. Travis Dixon and others further report that minorities are represented in news and entertainment in such a way as to encourage the perception of minorities as violent and criminal. See Dixon, "Crime News and Radicalized Beliefs," 106–125; Dixon, Azocar, and Casas, "The Portrayal of Race and Crime on Television Network News," 495–520; Dixon and Linz, "Overrepresentation and Underrepresentation of Victimization on Local Television News," 547–573; Dixon and Maddox, "Skin Tone, Crime News, and Social Reality Judgments," 1555–1570.

12. Curran, "Communications, Power, and Social Order," 227.

13. Bing, *Race, Crime, and the Media*; Bjornstrom, Kaufman, Person, and Slater, "Race and Ethnic Representations of Lawbreakers and Victims;" Leverentz, "Narratives of Crime and Criminals;" Westfahl, "Bloodshed and Circuses."

14. Chesney-Lind and Eliason, M. "From Invisible to Incorrigible;" Gurian, "Media Portrayals of Female Murder Offenders." Jewkes, *Media & Crime*, 127. Marsh and Melville, *Crime Justice and the Media*, 76–84.

15. Jewkes, "Much Ado About Nothing?"

16. Jewkes, *Media & Crime*, p. 253.

17. Kort-Butler, "Rotten Vile and Depraved!"

18. Miller ("Terrorism and Global Popular Culture") argues that electronic games make the war on terror an entertaining commodity and help military recruitment. See Ivory, Williams, Hatch, and Covucci, "Terrorism in Film Trailers" for a discussion of how the image of terrorists changed following the September 11, 2001, terrorist attacks.

19. Valverde, *Law and Order*. For example, Eric Hickey (*Serial Murderers and Their Victims*, 3) tracks the number of serial murder themed films: 2 (1920s), 3 (1930s), 3 (1940s), 4 (1950s), 12 (1960s), 20 (1970s), 23 (1980s), and 117 (1990s). Yvonne Jewkes (*Media and Crime*, 94–105) describes an analogous process in Britain concerning pedophiles.

20. Simpson, *Psycho Paths*.

21. Jenkins, *Moral Panic*. Rennison, *Intimate Partner Violence*, 1993–2001

22. For discussions of the culture that has developed around serial killers, see Ian Conrich, "Mass Media/Mass Murder;" Jarvis, *Monsters Inc.*, and Schechter, *The Serial Killer Files*, 369–402. For a discussion of the interplay of community and local media when both are faced with an active serial killer see Fisher, *Killer Among US*.

23. The popularity of violent predatory crime is also likely associated with a downward comparison effect. Downward comparison is a psychological process in which people feel better about their own situation when they see someone in a worse one. Therefore, a media image of violent urban crime would have a soothing effect on middle-class suburban Americans by holding up to them a crime-and-justice construction of reality that is more violent and dangerous than what they are experiencing. And, as this violent crime is shown as due to individual deficiencies like greed and innate evil, the apparently better-off-by-comparison rest of America can enjoy a guilt-free boost regarding their crime situation while being encouraged to purchase security products.

24. Chermak, *Victims in the News*; Mawby and Brown, "Newspaper Images of the Victim: A British Study;" Meyers, *News Coverage of Violence Against Women*; Pritchard and Hughes, "Patterns of Deviance in Crime News;" Reiner, Livingstone, and Allen, "From Law and Order to Lynch Mobs: Crime News since the Second World War;" Sorenson, Peterson-Manz, and Berk, "News Media Coverage and the Epidemiology of Homicide."

25. Boyle, *Media and Violence: Gendering the Debates*; Greer, *Crime and Media: A Reader*; Johnston, Hawkins, and Michner, "Homicide Reporting in Chicago Dailies;" Meyers, "News of Battering;" Meyers, *News Coverage of Violence Against Women*; Wilbanks, *Murder in Miami*.

26. Altheide, *Creating Fear*, 146. In a new research direction that explores the effect of media content on victims rather than their media depiction, a recent study reported a relationship between real world victims of crime, their psychological distress from victimization, and their amount of television exposure and gratifications sought from television. Minnebo, "The Relation between Psychological Distress, Television Exposure, and Television-viewing," 65–93.

27. Wardle, "It Could Happen to You," 515.

28. Rentschler, "Victims' Rights and the Struggle over Crime," 219–239.

29. Sumser, *Morality and Social Order*, 78.

30. Escholz, Mallard and Flynn, "Images of Prime Time Justice," 161–180; Cecil, "Dramatic Portrayals of Violent Women," 243–258; Sumser, *Morality and Social Order*, 141.

31. Chermak, *Victims in the News*; Meyers, *News Coverage of Violence Against Women*.

32. Chermak, *Victims in the News*, 107. Reiner, Livingstone, and Allen ("No More Happy Endings?," 118) found, however, that since World War II crime films have become more likely to show victims in a central role.

33. Lichter and Lichter, *Prime Time Crime*. Robert Reiner points out that, ironically, in relation to property crime risk, television has become safer than the real world ("Media Made Criminality," 391).

34. Wilson, Kunkel, Linz, Potter, Donnerstein, Smith, Blumenthal, and Gray, "Violence in Television Programming Overall."

35. Shelly and Ashkins, "Crime, Crime News, and Crime Views;" see also Dowler, "Comparing American and Canadian Local Television Crime Shows," 583; Duwe, "Body-Count Journalism;" Reiner, Livingstone, and Allen, "No More Happy Endings?" 114–115.

36. For a recent typology see Levi and Burrows, "Measuring the Impact of Fraud," 292–318.

37. Coleman, *The Criminal Elite*, 182.

38. Burns, "Media Portrayal of White-Collar Crime;" Levi, "Suite Revenge."

39. Ericson, Baranek, and Chan, *Representing Law and Order*; Levi, "Inside Information;" Levi, "The Media Construction of Financial White-Collar Crimes;" Stephenson- Burton, "Through the Looking-Glass;" and Tombs and Whyte, "Reporting Corporate Crime Out of Existence."

40. Levi, "The Media Construction of Financial White-Collar Crimes," 1052. Levi points out that commercial films such as *Wall Street* and *Catch Me If You Can* periodically construct white-collar criminality.

41. Lackey, "Visualizing White-Collar Crime."

42. Coleman, *The Criminal Elite*, 123–124.

43. Ponzi, Charles (1882–1949). The namesake and inventor of the "Ponzi" fraud scheme in which investors are lured into investing funds in a financial operation in the belief that they are buying into a high profit venture. The belief is generated by showing initial investors earning large profits on their money. These initial profits are created simply from the recycled money of later investors minus the money skimmed off for the operator of the Ponzi scheme. Eventually there are too few new investors to keep up the appearance of false profits and the scheme collapses.

44. Gans, *Deciding What's News*; Goff, *The Westray Mine Disaster*; Wright, Cullen, and Blankenship, *The Social Construction of Corporate Violence*.

45. Cavender and Mulcahy, "Trial by Fire: Media Constructions of Corporate Deviance."

46. Friedrichs, *Trusted Criminals*, 18; Benediktsson, "The Deviant Organization and the Bad Apple CEO."

47. Geis, *White-Collar and Corporate Crime*, 77.

48. Friedrichs, *Trusted Criminals*.

49. Friedrichs, *Trusted Criminals*, 18–19; Levi, "Measuring the Impact of Fraud in the UK," 295.

50. Levi, "White-Collar Crime in the News," 25.

51. Friedrichs, *Trusted Criminals*, 18–19.

52. Levi, "The Media Construction of Financial White-Collar Crimes," 1037. See also Levi and Pithouse, *White-Collar Crime and Its Victims*.

53. Benediktsson, "The Deviant Organization and the Bad Apple CEO."

54. Tombs, "Corporations and Health and Safety," 23.

55. Levi, "White-Collar Crime in the News," 25.

56. Lynch, Stretesky and Hammond, "Media Coverage of Chemical Crimes."

57. Ibid., 121–122.

58. Coleman, *The Criminal Elite*, 123.

59. Friedrichs, *Trusted Criminals*, 19. Relatively recent films that focused on white-collar criminality include *Erin Brockovich* (2000), *Catch Me If You Can* (2002), *Wall Street: Money Never Sleeps* (2010), and *Abritrage (2012)*. Perhaps signaling a new media focus on these crimes, a television program titled *White Collar* has survived since 2009. A countertrend to more realistic portrayals of economic crime is to imbed their depictions inside traditional action movies. This is exemplified by the film, *Tower Heist*, a 2011 comedy action film.

60. Lackey, "Visualizing White-Collar Crime: Generic Imagery in Popular Film;" Nichols, "White Collar Cinema;" Rafter, *Shots in the Mirror*.

61. Friedrichs, *Trusted Criminals*, 19.

62. Levi, "The Media Construction of Financial White-Collar Crimes," 1037.

63. Breit, "On the (Re)Construction of Corruption in the Media."

64. Rebovich and Kane, "An Eye for an Eye in the Electronic Age."

65. Fleming and Zyglidopoulos, *Charting Corporate Corruption*, 140.

66. Shipley and Cavender, "Murder and Mayhem at the Movies."

67. Rafter, "Crime, Film and Criminology," 415.

68. Kohm and Greenhill, "Pedophile Crime Films as Popular Criminology."

69. Rafter, *Shots in the Mirror*, 48.

70. Hesse, "Portrayal of Psychopathy in the Movies."

71. Rafter, "Crime, Film and Criminology," 403–420.

72. Ibid.

73. Lichter and Lichter, *Prime Time Crime*.

Chapter 4

1. Thomas, "The Psychology of Yellow Journalism," 491.

2. *Sourcebook of Criminal Justice Statistics— 2000*. "Table 2.42: Attitudes toward the Causes of Crime in the United States," and "Table 2.45: Respondents Perceptions about the Primary Cause of Gun Violence."

3. Sasson, *Crime Talk*, 161.

4. Sparks and Sparks list five theoretical groups: catharsis, priming, arousal, desensitization, and cultivation as potential violent media effect mechanisms ("Effects of Media Violence," 278–280). For a recent review of the media violence debate, see Boyle, *Media and Violence: Gendering the Debates*.

5. Reviews of this research are offered by Ferguson, "Media Violence: Miscast Causality," 446–447; Freedman, "Media Violence and Its Effect on Aggression;" Grimes, Anderson, and Bergen, *Media Violence and Aggression*; Gunter, "Media Violence: Is There a Case for Causality," 1061–1122; Huesmann, "The Impact of Electronic Media Violence," 6–13; Huesmann and Taylor, "The Role of Media Violence in Violent Behavior," 393–415; and Murray, "Media Violence: The Effects Are Both Real and Strong," 1212–1230.

6. Westfahl, "Bloodshed and Circuses" quoting Gentile, "Introduction, Media Violence and Children."

7. Westfahl, "Bloodshed and Circuses" quoting Freedman, "Media Violence and Its Effect on Aggression."

8. See, for example Heath, Bresolin, and Rinaldi, "Effects of Media Violence on Children;" and Wilson, Kunkel, Linz, Apotter, Donnerstein, Smith, Blumenthal, and Gray, "Violence in Television Programming Overall," 3–267.

9. Anderson, "The Production of Media Violence and Aggression Research," 1260–1279; Browne and Hamilton-Giachritsis, "The Influence of Violent Media on Children and Adolescents," 701–710; Pennell and Browne, "Film Violence and Young Offenders," 13–28.

10. Wilson and Herrnstein, *Crime and Human Behavior*, 343; Krahe et al, "Desensitization to Media Violence."

11. Huesmann and Taylor, "The Role of Media Violence," 394; Gunter, "Media Violence," 1110–1113.

12. Lee, Park, and Jin, "Narrative and InterActivity in Computer Games."

13. Yee "Motivations for Play." Of the reasons, escapism with immersion has been noted as the best predictor of problematic video game usage.

14. Reviews of positive effects from video game play are found in Adachi and Willoughby, "Do Video Games Promote Positive Youth Development;" Greitemeyer, "Effects of Prosocial Media on Social Behavior;" and Greitemeyer and Osswald, "Effects of Prosocial Video Games."

15. A general effect on risk taking behavior has been reported. Fischer, Peter et al, 2007, 2009 for example found that video racing games increases players' risk-taking inclinations (risk taking in a subsequent simulated road traffic situation and their risk-promoting cognitions, and attitudes toward reckless driving and sensation seeking).

16. Willoughby, Adachi, and Good, "A Longitudinal Study."

17. Fischer et al. "The Delinquent Media Effect," 202.

18. Fischer et al. "The Delinquent Media Effect," 203. Participants were left alone in the lab where pans and candy bars had been left. A paper sign stating that these items must not be taken was in front of the items. Theft was determined by counting the items before and after each player's session.

19. Fischer et al. "The Delinquent Media Effect," 204.

20. Bushman and Gibson "Violent Video Games," 30.

21. Bushman and Gibson "Violent Video Games."

22. Willoughby, Adachi, and Good, "A Longitudinal Study."

23. Moller and Krahe, "Exposure to Violent Video Games." See Wallenius and Punamaki ("Digital Game Violence and Direct Aggression," 286) for another multi-wave survey based self-report longitudinal study. They found that game violence effects were moderated by parent-child communication in interaction with sex and age but good parent–child communication did not protect an adolescent in the long run.

24. Willoughby, Adachi, and Good, "A Longitudinal Study."

25. Adachi and Willoughby ("The Effect of Video Game Competition," 259) found in their study that more competitive games produced greater levels of aggression behavior irrespective of the amount of violence in a game.

26. Ferguson, "Video Games and Youth Violence."

27. Ward, "Video Games and Crime."

28. DeLisi et al, "Violent Video Games, Delinquency, and Youth Violence," 138.

29. Ward, "Video Games and Adolescent Fighting."

30. Gentile and Bushman, "Reassessing Media Violence Effects;" Whitaker and Bushman, "A Review of the Effects of Violent Video Games."

31. Willoughby, Adachi, and Good "A Longitudinal Study," 1045.

32. Willoughby, Adachi, and Good "A Longitudinal Study," 1046.

33. Fishcer, Kastenmuller, and Greitemeyer. "Media Violence and the Self." 2010.

34. Lee, Peng, and Klein "Will the Experience of Playing a Violent Role."

35. The original 1961 reference was to television by Schramm, Lyle, and Parker, *Television in the Lives of Our Children.*

36. Gentile and Bushman, "Reassessing Media Violence Effects." For example, in the Gentile and Bushman (2012) study risk factors included: media violence exposure, physical victimization, gender,

hostile attribution bias, parental monitoring, and prior aggression.

37. Gentile and Bushman, "Reassessing Media Violence Effects," 138.

38. Coyne, "Does Media Violence Cause Violent Crime," 205–211; Savage, "Does Viewing Violent Media Really Cause Criminal Violence," 99–128; Savage, "The Role of Exposure to Media Violence in the Etiology of Violent Behavior," 1123–1136.

39. Heath, Wharton, Del Rosario, Cook, and Calder, "Impact of the Introduction of Television on Crime in the United States," 474.

40. Browne and Hamilton-Giachritsis, "The Influence of Violent Media on Children and Adolescents," 701–710; Coyne, "Does Media Violence Cause Violent Crime," 205–211; Huesman and Taylor, "The Role of Media Violence in Violent Behavior," 393–415; Savage, "Does Viewing Violent Media Really Cause Criminal Violence," 99–128; Savage, "The Role of Exposure to Media Violence in the Etiology of Violent Behavior," 1123–1136; Savage and Yancey, "The Effects of Media Violence Exposure on Criminal Aggression," 772–791.

41. Helfgott, *Criminal Behavior.*

42. Miller, *Introduction to Collective Behavior and Collective Action.*

43. Bleyer, *Main Currents in the History of American Journalism.* One of the earliest examples of media specifically created to generate crime were the how-to manuals for terrorism published by anarchist Johann Most in 1885. In his book, *Revolutionary War Science*, Most provided instructions on how to make nitroglycerin, dynamite, inflammable liquids, and poisons and advocated their use in antigovernment bombings and attacks. The 1886 Chicago Haymarket Square bombing is thought to have been a direct result (Papke, *Framing the Criminal,* 171–172.)

44. Hays, *President's Report to the Motion Picture Producers and Distributors' Association.*

45. Surette, "Pathways to Copycat Crime." One of the earliest uses of the word "copycat" in the context of an imitative crime in English is found in a minor story

in the British newspaper, *The Daily Telegraph*, April 1, 1961 (page A;16, column 6) which briefly describes a copycat murder.

46. Cook, Kendzierski, and Thomas, "The Implicit Assumptions of Television Research;" Canter, Sheehan, Alpers, and Mullen, "Media and Mass Homicides."

47. Gunter, "Media Violence: Is There a Case for Causality," 1066.

48. Surette, "Self-Reported Copycat Crime among a Population of Serious Violent Juvenile Offenders," 46; Surette, "Estimating the Prevalence of Copycat Crime." Surveys of self-reported copycat crime has included U.S. and non-U.S. offenders, youth and adults, males and females, and incarcerated and non-incarcerated subjects. A copycat effect has also been empirically established and generally accepted for suicides. For example a recent copycat suicide research in the tradition of Phillips finds that celebrity suicides are followed by significant increases in emergency room visits for suicide attempts and self-injury (see Jeong, Shin, Kim, Hong, Hwang, and Lee, "The Effects of Celebrity Suicide;" and Yang, Tsai, Yang, Shia, Fuh, Wang, Peng, and Huang, "Suicide and Media Reporting").

49. Curtis, "Gabriel Tarde," 142–157; Vine, "Gabriel Tarde." 292–304.

50. Tarde, *Penal Philosophy*, 340. Research on the diffusion of riots from large to small cities has supported Tarde's ideas while including the impact of modern mass media. See Myers, "The Diffusion of Collective Violence: Infectiousness, Susceptibility, and Mass Media Networks," 172–208.

51. Daniel Glazer's 1956 article re-introduced media as a concept worthy of study to criminology (Glaser, "Criminality Theories and Behavioral Images," 433–444). It was during the 1960's that the term "copycat crime" first began to appear in the media (Siegelberg, "What a Copycat").

52. Akers, *Social Learning and Social Structure*; Bandura, *Aggression: A Social Learning Analysis*.

53. Doley, Surette, and Ferguson, "Copycat Arson."

54. Berkowitz, "Some Effects of Thoughts on Anti- and Prosocial Influences of Media Events;" see also Berkowitz and Rogers, "A Priming Effect Analysis of Media Influences."

55. Dijksterhuis and Bargh, "The Perception-Behavior Expressway;" Roskos-Ewoldsen, Roskos-Ewoldsen, and Carpentier, "Media Priming: A Synthesis."

56. Jo and Berkowitz, "A Priming Effect Analysis of Media Influences," 46.

57. Huesmann, "The Role of Social Information Processing and Cognitive Schema," 73–109.

58. Claxton, "Joining the Intentional Dance;" Goldman, "Imitation, Mind Reading and Simulation;" Huesmann, "Psychological Process Promoting the Relation," 131.

59. Huesmann, "Psychological Process Promoting the Relation," 130.

60. Mazur, "Bomb Threats and the Mass Media."

61. Gunter, "Media Violence: Is There a Case for Causality," 1097.

62. Shrum, "Media Consumption and Perceptions of Social Reality," 69–95; Petty, Priester, and Brinol, "Mass Media Attitude Change," 155–198.

63. Green and Brock, "The Role of Transportation," 701–721.

64. Slater and Rouner, "Entertainment-education and Elaboration Likelihood," 173–191.

65. Ibid., 185.

66. This first path is based on the theory of reasoned action, which assumes that people consider the implications of their actions (Petty et al., 2002). In a central route to persuasion, a person is actively involved in evaluating information, scrutinizes all relevant information, and extensively applies prior knowledge (Petty et al., 2002).

67. When the potential copycat offender is not motivated to closely search the media for crime information than the second path, heuristic peripheral cognitive processing is employed. In this path,

only readily available information is accessed and used. The second path is therefore taken when motivation to develop a reasoned action is not significant and behavior is spontaneous. In this path, behavior can result from a relatively automatic process that requires little conscious thought. Path 2 is more common than path 1 because a heuristic sufficiency principle operates for most people (See Shrum, "Media Consumption and Perceptions of Social Reality").

68. The narrative persuasion path is derived from research on the ability of media narratives to influence attitudes and behaviors and from entertainment-education research on the utility of using entertainment media to invoke social change. As most people utilize the media as a source of entertainment, this path is speculated as the one most involved in copycat crime via media-supplied narratives (Strange, "How Fictional Tales Wag Real-World Beliefs"). The majority of copycat offenders, even those who eventually travel paths 1 or 2, will first travel the narrative persuasion path.

69. Green and Brock, "The Role of Transportation."

70. Brock, Strange, and Green, "Power beyond reckoning."

71. Green, Garst, Brock, and Chung, "Fact versus fiction labeling."

72. Polichak and Gerrig, "Get Up and Win!"

73. Slater and Rouner, "Entertainment-education and Elaboration Likelihood."

74. Surette, "Estimating the Prevalence of Copycat Crime;" Surette, "Pathways to Copycat Crime."

75. Surette, "Estimating the Prevalence of Copycat Crime."

76. Bandura, *Self-Efficacy in Changing Societies.*

77. Bandura, *Aggression.*

78. Bandura, *Aggression*, citing Claster, "Comparison of Risk Perception."

79. Surette, "Self-Reported Copycat Crime among a Population of Serious Violent Juvenile Offenders." In addition, few differences have been found between juvenile offenders and nonoffenders in media consumption and use. See also

Bandura, *Aggression: A Social Learning Analysis* and Hagell and Newburn, *Young Offenders and the Media.*

80. Bandura, *Aggression.*

81. Bandura, *Aggression.*

82. Akers, *Social Learning and Social Structure.*

83. Sacco, *When Crime Waves.*

84. Surette, "Pathways to Copycat Crime."

85. Akers, *Social Learning and Social Structure*; Rogers, *Diffusion of Innovations.*

86. Meloy and Mohandie, "Investigating the Role of Screen Violence;" Myers, Eggleston, and Smoak, "A Media Violence-Inspired Juvenile;" and Rogers, *Diffusion of Innovations.*

87. Bandura, *Aggression.*

88. Akers, *Social Learning and Social Structure.*

89. Rogers, *Diffusion of Innovations.*

90. Akers, *Social Learning and Social Structure.*

91. Mazur, *Learning and Behavior*, 297, citing Dowrick and Raeburn, "Self-Modeling."

92. Akers, *Social Learning and Social Structure.*

93. Akers, *Social Learning and Social Structure*; Bandura, *Aggression*; Rogers, 2003

94. Mundorf and Laird, "Social and Psychological effects;" Rogers, *Diffusion of Innovations.*

95. Akers, *Social Learning and Social Structure*; Haridakis, "Viewer Characteristics, Exposure to Television Violence."

96. Akers, *Social Learning and Social Structure.*

97. Rogers, *Diffusion of Innovations.*

98. Haridakis, "Viewer Characteristics, Exposure to Television Violence."

99. Bandura and Walters, *Social Learning and Personality Development*; Mazur, *Learning and Behavior.*

100. Fisher, "The Spread of Violent Crime."

101. Akers, *Social Learning and Social Structure.*

102. Sadistic fantasy, often supplemented by various media content (print, films, video games, Internet sites, pornography), has been reported as a precursor to juvenile sexual homicides (see Bailey, "Fast Forward to Violence," 6; and Meyers, *Juvenile Sexual Homicide*, 163–164) and a media role in the killing of children by strangers (see Wilson, "Stranger Child-Murder," 49–59).

103. Pease and Love, "The Copycat Crime Phenomenon;" Surette, "Estimating the

Prevalence of Copycat Crime." In a seminal study of copycat crime in the 1960s, researchers Melvin Heller and Samuel Polsky (*Studies in Violence and Television*, 151–152) stated: "A significant number of our subjects, already embarked on a criminal career, consciously recall and relate having imitated techniques of crimes. For such men, detailed portrayals of criminal techniques must be viewed as a learning process."

104. A copycat effect has been extended to police practices and the spread of 'the third degree' from the United States to the United Kingdom in the twentieth century. See Wood, "The Third Degree," 472.

105. Al-Marashi, "Iraq's Hostage Crisis;" Borowitx, "Packaged Death;" Gupta and Mundra, "Suicide Bombing as a Strategic Weapon;" Holden, "The Contagiousness of Aircraft Hijacking;" Pape, "The Strategic Logic of Suicide Terrorism."

106. As cited in Alexander, "Terrorism and the Media," 161.

107. For a specific example of the complicated relationship between the media and terrorism, see Hayes, "Political Violence, Irish Republicanism and the British Media."

108. Surette, Hansen and Noble, "Measuring Media Oriented Terrorism;" Tuman, *Communicating Terror*; and Weimann and Winn, *The Theater of Terror: Mass Media and International Terrorism*, 47.

109. Tuman, *Communicating Terror*.

110. Poland, *Understanding Terrorism*, 47; and Weimann and Winn, *The Theater of Terror*.

111. Weimann and Winn, *The Theater of Terror*, 57.

112. Surette, Hansen, and Noble, "Measuring Media Oriented Terrorism." See Paletz and Schmid, *Terrorism and the Media* for an overview.

113. Livingstone, *The War Against Terrorism*, 62.

114. Schmid and de Graaf, *Violence as Communication*; and Weimann and Winn, *The Theater of Terror*.

115. Chermak and Gruenewald, "The Media's Coverage of Domestic Terrorism," 428–461.

116. Holden, "The Contagiousness of Aircraft Hijacking," 874–904.

117. Matusitz, *Terrorism and Communication*.

118. Surette, Hansen and Noble, "Measuring Media Oriented Terrorism," 363.

119. Nacos, *Mass-Mediated Terrorism*; Ross, "Deconstructing the Terrorism-News Media Relationship," 215–225.

120. Anderson, "An Update on the Effects of Playing Violent Video Games," 113–122; Anderson, Gentile and Buckley, *Violent Video Game Effects on Children and Adolescents: Theory, Research, and Public Policy*; Sherry, "The Effects of Violent Video Games on Aggression," 409–432; Whitaker and Bushman, "A Review of the Effects of Violent Video Games," 1033–1051.

121. Rogers, *The Diffusion of Innovations*, 215–216.

122. Parks and Robers, *Making MOOsic*, 517–537; Rogers, 207.

123. Fox, Sickel and Steiger, *Tabloid Justice*, 100; Valier, *Crime and Punishment in Contemporary Culture*, 91–110.

124. Courtwright, *Violent Land*. A wry comment on the level of violence in pre-mass media society in the United States is provided by the *Salt Lake Desert News* in the 1860s: "The place is rapidly becoming civilized. Several men having been killed there already" (as cited in Ambrose, *Nothing Like It in the World*, 337).

Chapter 5

1. Wilson, *Cop Knowledge*.

2. Gorelick, "Join Our War."

3. Rafter, *Shots in the Mirror*.

4. Inciardi and Dee, "From the Keystone Cops to Miami Vice."

5. Reiner, "Keystone to Kojak."

6. Stark, "Perry Mason Meets Sonny Crockett," 239.

7. Scharrer, "More Than "Just the Facts?"

8. Hays, *President's Report to the Motion Picture Producers and Distributors' Association*. See also Blumer, *The Movies and Conduct*; Blumer, and Hauser, *Movies, Delinquency, and Crime*; Charter, *Motion Pictures and Youth: A Summary*; Dale, *Children's Attendance at Motion Pictures*; Holaday and Stoddard, *Getting Ideas from the Movies*; Peterson and Thurstone, *Motion Pictures*

and the *Social Attitudes of Children*; and Shuttleworth and May, *The Social Conduct and Attitudes of Movie Fans*. For a summary of the Payne Fund studies, see Chapter 2 in Lowery, and DeFleur, *Milestones in Mass Communication Research*.

9. Ibid., 118.

10. *Dirty Harry*, 1971. *Director Don Siegel*, Warner Brothers.

11. The discussion on cop narratives draws on ideas from Wilson, *Cop Knowledge*. In a similar vein, Reiner (*The Politics of the Police*, 150–152) offers twelve ideal type models of law enforcement stories found in the media. See also Nichols-Pethick, *TV Cops*.

12. Rabe-Hemp, "Female Forces;" see also Hale, "Keeping Women in Their Place," 159–179 for an analysis of the portrait of policewomen in commercial films from 1972 –1996.

13. Wilson, *Cop Knowledge*, 134.

14. Wilson, *Cop Knowledge*, 134; and Eschholz, Mallard, and Flynn, "Images of Prime Time Justice."

15. Brown and Benedict, "Perceptions of the Police;" Mawby, "Completing the 'Half-Formed Picture'? Media Images of Policing." See also Lawrence, *The Politics of Force*, 15; Payne, *Brutal Cops, News Coverage*, 1–10.

16. *Bad Boys* (1993) by Inner Circle, Atlantic Records.

17. Donovan, "Armed with the Power of Television."

18. Doyle, *Arresting Images*.

19. Kooistra, Mahoney, and Westervelt, "The World of Crime According to COPS," Table 2: Index Crimes on "COPS" and in the UCR (1994), 148.

20. Kooistra, Mahoney, and Westervelt, "The World of Crime According to COPS," 153.

21. Cavender, "In the Shadow of Shadow."

22. Sherwin, *When Law Goes Pop*, 184–185.

23. Doyle, "Cops: Television Policing as Policing Reality."

24. Hallett and Powell, "Backstage with COPS."

25. Littlefield ("Historicizing CSI") links the recent social construction of a "CSI Effect" historically back to American

scientific detective fiction of the early twentieth century.

26. Houck, "CSI: Reality;" Wise, "Providing the CSI Treatment."

27. Cole and Dioso-Villa, "CSI and Its Effects."

28. Patry, Stinson, and Smith, "CSI Effect: Is Popular Television Transforming Canadian Society?"

29. Hays and Levett, "Community Members' Perceptions of the CSI Effect."

30. Durnal, "Crime Scene Investigation;" Robbers, *Blinded by Science*, 88.

31. Cavender and Deutsch, "CSI and Moral Authority," 67–81; Tyler, "Viewing CSI and the Threshold of Guilt," 1073.

32. Houck, "CSI: Reality."

33. For example Hayes-Smith and Levett ("Jury's Still Out," 43) report some support for a pro-defense effect and Smith, Stinson and Patry ("Fact or Fiction," 7) report results that support a pro-prosecution bias.

34. Maricopa County, "The CSI Effect and Its Real-Life Impact;" Tyler, "Viewing CSI and the Threshold of Guilt," 1054.

35. Hays and Levett, "Community Members' Perceptions of the CSI Effect;" Wise, "Providing the CSI Treatment."

36. Dutelle, *The CSI Effect and Your Department*, 113–114; Robbers, *Blinded by Science*, 92.

37. Gillis, "New Crime Shows Educate Criminals."

38. Cavender and Deutsch, "CSI and Moral Authority," 77; Durnal, "Crime Scene Investigation;" Tyler, "Viewing CSI and the Threshold of Guilt," 1068–1073; Roane, "The CSI Effect," 48. Podlas ("The CSI Effect," 463) points out that "the few times a CSI effect has found its way into a criminal trial, it was the prosecution who attempted to exploit its mythology to obtain a conviction."

39. Holmgren and Fordham, "The CSI Effect and the Canadian and the Australian Jury;" Mancini, "The CSI Effect Reconsiders;" Schweitzer and Saks, "The CSI Effect."

40. Podlas, "The CSI Effect," 429–465; Shelton, "*The CSI Effect: Does It Really*

Exist?;" Tyler, "Viewing CSI and the Threshold of Guilt," 1050–1085.

41. Shelton, "The CSI Effect: Does It Really Exist?," 5. Podlas ("The CSI Effect") reports similar lack of effects on verdicts.

42. Baskin and Sommers, "Crime-Show viewing Habit;" Schweitzer and Saks, "The CSI Effect."

43. Hays and Levett, "Community Members' Perceptions of the CSI Effect."

44. Schweitzer and Saks, "The CSI Effect;" Smith, Stinson and Patry, "Fact or Fiction?," 7.

45. Hayes-Smith and Levett, "Jury's Still Out."

46. Robbers, "Blinded by Science," 87.

47. Mopas, *Examining the CSI Effect Through an ANT Lens*, 110–117; Podlas, "The CSI Effect," 442.

48. Perlmutter, *Policing the Media*.

49. Lenz, *Changing Images of Law*.

50. Scharrer, "More Than 'Just the Facts'?"

51. Lichter and Lichter, *Prime Time Crime*. Reiner, Livingstone, and Allen ("No More Happy Endings?," 115–116) found a decline in civilian heroes in films over the latter half of the twentieth century.

52. The Chevalier C. Auguste Dupin, an American amateur detective living in France, appeared in three stories: "The Murders in the Rue Morgue," "The Mystery of Marie Roget," and "The Purloined Letter." He is described in the *Oxford Companion to Crime and Mystery Writing* (Herbert, *Oxford Companion to Crime and Mystery Writing*, 126): "Dupin is an isolated figure. Well aware of his intellectual superiority, Dupin is particularly contemptuous of the unimaginative methods of the police."

53. Leishman and Mason, *Policing and the Media*, 70, 74. Lenz (*Changing Images of Law*) has put forth the notion that recent media reflects a transition in society away from conservative crime control policies and Dorikx, van den Bulck and Parmentier ("The Police as Societal Moral Agents") argue that in at least four fictional police shows police officers act in a trustworthy, respectful and neutral manner, generally follow fair procedures while sometime breaking the rules, however in contexts which strengthens their role as positive moral agents.

54. Price, Merrill, and Clause, "The Depiction of Guns on Prime Time Television."

55. Reiner, "Media Made Criminality," 392.

Chapter 6

1. Sherwin, *When Law Goes Pop*, ix.

2. Robinson (*Justice Blind?*, 133) characterizes the content of the media as constructing due process protections as if they were a cause of crime in the United States.

3. Tyler, "Viewing CSI and the Threshold of Guilt," 1074.

4. Rafter, "American Criminal Trial Films," 9.

5. Asimow and Mader, *Law and Popular Culture*, Chapter 2; Stark, "Perry Mason Meets Sonny Crockett;" Surette, "Media Trials."

6. Asimow and Mader, *Law and Popular Culture*.

7. Stark, "Perry Mason Meets Sonny Crockett," 275.

8. Lichter and Lichter, *Prime Time Crime*; Rafter, "American Criminal Trial Films," 9.

9. Greenfield and Osborn, "Film Lawyers;" Stark, "Perry Mason Meets Sonny Crockett."

10. Lenz, *Changing Images of Law*.

11. Rafter, *Shots in the Mirror*.

12. Bailey, Pollock, and Schroeder, "The Best Defense."

13. Carpenter, Lacy, and Fico, *Network News Coverage of High-Profile Crime*, 901–916.

14. Fox, Sickel, and Steiger (*Tabloid Justice*) discuss the impact of media trials under their related tabloid justice concept.

15. Friedman, "Front Page."

16. Media trials have emerged as a twenty-first-century global phenomenon and have posed concerns for authoritarian countries with emerging mass media such as China (Chen and Zhang, "Trial by Media").

17. Fox, Sickel, and Steiger, *Tabloid Justice.*

18. Banner, "Trials and Other Entertainment;" Friedman, "Front Page;" Mathiesen, *Prison on Trial*, 66–67.

19. Friedman, "Front Page."

20. Carpenter, Lacy, and Fico, *Network News Coverage of High-Profile Crime*, 901–916; Valier, *Crime and Punishment in Contemporary Culture*. Andie Tucher ("Framing the Criminal," 908) cites an 1836 New York trial of a teenage clerk for the murder of a prostitute as the first media circus trial in America due to extensive coverage in the New York penny press.

21. The impact of celebrity status on case outcomes has not been a subject of much research. In a recent study that employed a "Celebrities Worshiper scale," verdicts rendered by mock jurors were examined. High scorers on the scale were found to be less likely to find movie stars guilty but overall for all the mock jurors in the study a movie star was more likely to be convicted (Wong, Goodboy, Murtagh, Hackney, and McCutcheon, "Are Celebrities Charged with Murder," 633.

22. Barber, *News Cameras in the Courtroom*, 112–114; Carpenter, Lacy, and Fico, *Network News Coverage of High-Profile Crime*, 901–916; Nasheri, *Crime and Justice in the Age of CourtTV.*

23. Banner, "Trials and Other Entertainment."

24. Ibid.

25. Ibid., 1290.

26. Fox, Sickel, and Steiger, *Tabloid Justice.*

27. Hariman, "Performing the Laws: Popular Trials and Social Knowledge," 23.

28. Friedman, "Front Page."

29. Surette, "Media Trials." Friedman ("Front Page") offers a more expansive media trial typology of "political, corruption and fraud," "was justice done?" (unfair or erroneous case processing), "tabloid" (lurid events), "celebrity" (crime secondary to fame of people involved), "whodunit" (murder mysteries), "soap opera" (love triangles), "worm in the bud" (sleazy underside of prominent society exposed), "who would have thought" (human monster trials), and "moral panic" (witch hunts) trials.

30. David Papke (*Framing the Criminal*, 22) reports that similar themes existed in the 1830s. Popular pamphlets portrayed crime within two long-standing themes—the rogue (a semi-hero who commits property fraud) and the fiend (a diabolical, frenzied villain). This period saw the creation of a new theme—the fiendish rogue. An example from the early part of the twentieth century is the 1913 Leo Frank case involving the strangulation of a 14-year-old female factory worker in Georgia. As was common in such cases, coverage was heavily biased against the defendant. An Atlanta paper was typical: "Our little girl—ours by the Eternal God!—has been pursued to a hideous death and bloody grave by this filthy, perverted Jew of New York." The commutation of Frank's sentence from death to life imprisonment led to Georgia's governor being driven out of office. A year after his conviction, Frank was taken from a prison farm by a band of men, driven 125 miles to the scene of the murder, and lynched.

31. Like many things in life, it appears that being rich and famous and accused of a crime is double-edged. Access to a top-notch defense assures that your case will follow strict due process procedures and that every step in the criminal justice process will be exercised. It wasn't the race card that helped O. J. Simpson in his criminal trial, it was the money card. The rich can depend on a strong, aggressive defense. The poor are much more likely to plea bargain and be adjudicated guilty. However, if you are rich and famous and are found guilty, you are likely to receive a stern sentence. Judges and the state do not want to appear to be favoring rich guilty defendants. Contrary to usual sentencing practices, this appears to be especially true for female defendants of late. Leona Helmsley, Patty Hearst, and Martha Stewart all received jail time as first offenders. In sum, money and fame help you avoid guilty verdicts, but if you are found guilty, you are more likely to be made an example.

32. Sherwin, *When Law Goes Pop.*

33. Surette, "21st Century Crime and Justice."

34. Drucker, "The Televised Mediated Trial."

35. Surette, "Media Echoes."

36. Loften, *Justice and the Press*, 138; Wisehart ("Newspapers and Criminal Justice") makes the earliest historical references to echolike effects from media coverage in 1922.

37. Kaplan and Skolnick, *Criminal Justice*, 467–468.

38. Surette, "Media Echoes."

39. *Estes v. Texas*, 381 U.S. 532, at 570 (1965).

40. Altheide and Snow, *Media Worlds in the Postjournalism Era*.

41. Marcus, "The Media in the Courtroom," 276.

42. 62 A.B.A. Rep, 1134–1135 (1937) cited by Kirtley, "A Leap Not Supported by History."

43. In a case important in Texas due to Estes's political associations, Texas financier Billie Sol Estes was accused of a salad-oil swindle. Cameramen crowded into a tiny courtroom and seriously disrupted the proceedings. After the trial, which was televised despite his objection, Estes appealed his conviction, arguing that the presence of television cameras denied him a fair trial. The Supreme Court agreed and reversed the decision. It would reverse *Estes* sixteen years later in *Chandler v. Florida*.

44. *Estes v. Texas*, at 538 and 544.

45. Florida policeman Noel Chandler was tried and convicted with another police officer for a series of burglaries. The case received a large amount of regional media attention and was televised over Chandler's objection as part of a Florida pilot program for televising judicial proceedings. The Supreme Court held that if other constitutional due process guarantees are met, a state could provide for television coverage of a criminal trial over the objection of defendants.

46. "Public Confidence in Selected Institutions, 1973–1996," Table 2.9.

47. Synodinou, "The Media Coverage of Court Proceedings in Europe;" Kinlay, "Televised Court Proceedings;" Marsh and Melville, *Crime Justice and the Media*, 140–145.

48. Adkins, "The Unblinking Eye;" Cameras in our Federal Courts;" "Federal Pilot Program."

49. "Cameras in our Federal Courts."

50. Examples include the 1992 Los Angeles riots following the not guilty verdict for the police officers involved in the Rodney King beating; the 1980 Miami riots following the acquittal of police officers charged in the beating death of black motorist Edward McDuffie; and the 1993 acquittal of police officer William Lozano in the shooting death of a black motorcyclist.

51. *United States v. Burr*, cited in Marcus, "The Media in the Courtroom," 237.

52. Butler, "Capital Pretrial Publicity;" Daftary-Kapur, Dumas, and Penrod, "Jury Decision-Making Biases;" Ruva and LeVasseur, "Behind Closed Doors;" Ruva, Guenther and Yarbrough, "Positive and Negative Pretrial Publicity;" Ruva and McEvoy, "Negative and Positive Pretrial Pubicity." Concerns over negative effects of pretrial publicity may extend to the broader public also as a recent survey of Quebec, Canada residents found strong support for restrictions on media reporting of court proceedings (Fusco and Sabourin, "Public Opinion on Media").

53. *United States v. Burr*, 25 F. Case 49, 49. (1807).

54. "Trial by Media," U.S. Press.

55. For an overview and discussion of the research and issues associated with pretrial publicity and fair trials, see Bruschke and Loges, *Free Press vs. Fair Trials*. They note a discrepancy between laboratory research, which generally concludes that pretrial publicity biases trials, and field research, which reports that such effects are not common and occur only when the publicity is excessive and includes persuasive information and when trial evidence is inconclusive.

56. Bruschke and Loges (*Free Press vs. Fair Trials*, 137) argue that combinations of reactive judicial remedies appear to be effective and that pretrial publicity will only bias a trial outcome in rare circumstances. See also Daftary-Kapur, Dumas, and Penrod, "Jury Decision-Making Biases."

57. Tyler, *Viewing CSI and the Threshold of Guilt*, 1062.

58. There may also be less public support for press access to courts than in the past. A Canadian-based survey found that nearly 80 percent of respondents supported access and reporting restrictions on the media (Fusco and Sabourin, "Public Opinion on Media").

59. Reporters Committee for Freedom of the Press, "Number of States with Shield Law Climbs to 40" Downloaded June 18, 2013 from http://www.rcfp.org/browse -media-law-resources/news-media-law/ news-media-law-summer-2011/number -states-shield-law-climbs.

60. Kirtley, "Shield Laws and Reporter's Privilege," 164.

61. Dalglish, *Protecting Reporters Who Protect Sources*, 30–32; Fargo, *Analyzing Federal Shield Law Proposals*, 35–82.

62. Kirtley, "Shield Laws and Reporter's Privilege," 170.

63. See Docter, "Blogging and Journalism;" Laptosky, "Protecting the Cloak and Dagger;" Rich, "New Media and the News Media;" Turner, "Protecting Citizen Journalists;" Ugland, "The New Abridged Reporter's Privilege;" and Wischnowski, "Bloggers with Shields" for discussions.

64. Kinlay, "Televised Court Proceedings."

65. Laptosky, "Protecting the Cloak and Dagger;" Turner, "Protecting Citizen Journalists;" Ugland, "The New Abridged Reporter's Privilege."

66. Sherwin, *When Law Goes Pop*, 219.

67. An outgrowth of the dominance of visuals discussed by Valverde (*Law and Order*, Chapter 9) is the legal dilemma involved in the release or withholding of "gruesome pictures" from crime scenes.

68. Sherwin, *When Law Goes Pop*, 34–35. Amy Fisher, the 17-year-old "Long Island Lolita" who shot the wife of her 38-year-old boyfriend Joey Buttafuoco, in 1992, became a tabloid legend. She was released from prison in 1999.

69. Fox, Sickel, and Steiger, *Tabloid Justice*.

70. Wheeler, "Symposium Examines Courts and the New Media."

71. Lenz, *Changing Images of Law*.

72. Fox, Sickel, and Steiger, *Tabloid Justice*, 188, 201.

Chapter 7

1. Freeman, *Popular Culture and Corrections*, 208; Kieby, "Prison Life Through a Lens," 22–23; Levenson, "Inside Information: Prisons and the Media," 14–15.

2. Graber, *Crime News and the Public*; and Roberts and Stalans, *Public Opinion, Crime, and Criminal Justice*.

3. Marsh, "A Comparative Analysis of Crime Coverage in Newspapers," 76.

4. Freeman, *Popular Culture and Corrections*. 47

5. The most successful television show based on corrections was the HBO cable program *Oz*, which ran from 1997 to 2003.

6. Mason, "The Screen Machine," 279–280; O'Sullivan, "Representations of Prison in Nineties Hollywood Cinema," 317–334; Schauer, "Masculinity Incarcerated," 28–42; and Wilson and O'Sullivan, *Images of Incarceration*. Bennett ("The Good, the Bad and the Ugly," 97–115) presents a unique take on the prison film study by exploring how prison films have depicted the relationship between the media, crime, and punishment.

7. Cheatwood, "Prison Movies;" and Freeman, "Public Perception and Corrections."

8. Rafter, *Shots in the Mirror*, 127.

9. Cheatwood, "Prison Movies." For a critique of Cheatwood's typology, see Mason, "The Screen Machine," 284–288.

10. Mason, "Prison Decayed," 607.

11. Ibid., 621.

12. For a discussion of British television programs about corrections, see Jewkes, "Creating A Stir?;" Marsh and Melville, *Crime Justice and the Media*; Mason, "Watching the Invisible;" and Wilson and O'Sullivan, *Images of Incarceration*.

13. Mason, *Captured by the Media*; Mason, "Lies, Distortion and What Doesn't Work," 251–267; Russell, "Tabloid Tactics," 32–33.

14. Chermak "Police Courts and Corrections in the Media," 96.

15. Doyle and Ericson, "Breaking into Prison." See also Lotz, *Crime and the American Press*.

16. Andrew Hochstetler ("Reporting of Executions in U.S. Newspapers," 8) provides evidence that the backwards law of media content extends to coverage of death row so that the more sensational cases receive the most coverage. A small body of research has also examined the portrait of capital punishment in films. See Garland, *The Culture of Control*; Greer, "Delivering Death," 84–102; Harding, "Celluloid Death," 1167–1179; Sarat, "Death Row, Aisle Seat," 1–3; and Sarat, *When the State Kills*.

17. This was found to be true for the 1970s by Jacobs and Brooks, "The Mass Media and

Prison News;" and for the 1990s by Doyle and Ericson, "Breaking into Prison," 157–158.

18. Mason, "Misinformation, Myth and Distortion," 481–496; Sussman, "Media on Prisons."

19. One counterbalance to this is the coverage that efforts to free wrongly convicted inmates will periodically garner. See www.InnocenceProject.org. When they do result in a prisoner's release the accompanying news coverage contributes to the general negative view of corrections, as well as the police and courts. In these cases, by portraying them as locking up the wrong people.

20. Chermak, *Victims in the News.*

21. Campbell, "Journalists Should Demand Prison Access," 34.

22. Doyle and Ericson, "Breaking into Prison," 167.

23. Ibid., 183.

24. Ibid., 183–184.

25. An exception to this pattern of negative, sexually-focused coverage is reported for the coverage of the imprisonment of Martha Stewart. See Cecil, "Doing Time in Camp Cupcake," 142–160.

26. Freeman, *Popular Culture and Corrections,* 114–115.

27. Bennett, "The Good, the Bad and the Ugly," 112; Drake, "The 'Dangerous Other';" Mason, "Prison Decayed," 616.

28. Ciasullo, "Containing Deviant Desire," 195–223.

29. Britton, *At Work in the Iron Cage;* Ciasullo, "Containing Deviant Desire," 197; Clowers, "Dykes, Gangs, and Danger," 28.

30. Clowers, "Dykes, Gangs, and Danger," 28.

31. Cecil, "Looking Beyond Caged Heat," 321; Cecil, "Dramatic Portrayals of Violent Women," 243–258.

32. Cecil, "Looking Beyond Caged Heat," 321; Freeman, *Popular Culture and Corrections,* 46.

33. Cecil, "Looking Beyond Caged Heat," 322.

34. Freeman, *Popular Culture and Corrections,* 46. See also Wilson and O'Sullivan, *Images of Incarceration.*

35. Mason, "Prison Decayed," 616.

36. Davis, *Are Prisons Obselete?,* cited by Mason, "Prison Decayed," 616.

37. Ross, "Debunking the Myths of American Corrections," 412.

38. Robinson, *Media Coverage of Crime and Criminal Justice,* 225–240.

39. Cheliotis, "The Ambivalent Consequences of Visibility;" Drake, "The 'Dangerous Other';" Mathiesen, "Television, Public Space and Prison Population," 39; Welsh, Fleming and Dowler, "Constructing Crime and Justice on Film."

40. Bennett, "The Good, the Bad and the Ugly," 99.

41. Ibid., 112.

42. Mason, "Prison Decayed," 609; Mathiesen, *Prisons on Trial;* Zaner, "The Screen Test," 64. See also Getty, "Media Wise," 126–131.

Chapter 8

1. Research on media effects on public attitudes began in the 1930s with a set of research projects collectively called the Payne Fund studies. Among other findings, this early research reported that films such as *Birth of a Nation*—a sympathetic and romantic portrayal of the creation of the Ku Klux Klan—could generate unfavorable attitudes toward blacks among viewers. Although the effects eventually wore off, they were found to persist for a significant period of time (up to eight months).

2. Greitemeyer, "Effects of Prosocial Media;" National Institute of Mental Health, *Television and Behavior,* 90.

3. Engle, "Celebrity Diplomacy."

4. Lindesmith, *The Addict and the Law.*

5. Other movies in which illegal drugs are shown positively include *The Forty Year Old Virgin, Harold and Kumar Go to White Castle,* and *Dazed and Confused.*

6. American Association of Advertising Agencies, *What We've Learned about Advertising.*

7. Black, *Changing Attitudes toward Drug Use;* and O'Keefe, Rosenbaum, Lavrakas, Reid, and Botta, *Taking a Bite Out of Crime.*

8. Surette, "Methodological Problems in Determining Media Effects on Criminal Justice."

9. Weinstein, "Cross-Hazard Consistencies."

10. See O'Keefe and Reid, "Media Public Information Campaigns and Criminal Justice Policy;" and O'Keefe, Rosenbaum, Lavrakas, Reid, and Botta, *Taking a Bite Out of Crime*.

11. Rosenbaum, Lurigio, and Lavrakas, *Crime Stoppers*, 110.

12. Rosenbaum, Lurigio, and Lavrakas, "Enhancing Citizen Participation and Solving Serious Crime," 417.

13. An assessment of a Florida program's "crime of the week" and "most wanted" cases for the first two years of operation revealed that the types of crime portrayed most often were violent crimes; nonviolent crimes were rarely portrayed, and homicides were the single most popular crime shown. On the whole, the program portrayed criminality as an attribute of a young, violent, dangerous class of criminals composed mostly of minorities. Crime was portrayed as largely stranger-to-stranger, injurious, or fatal encounters in which handguns had a dominant role. See Surette, "The Mass Media and Criminal Investigations." Yvonne Jewkes (*Media and Crime*, 155–161) found that in the United Kingdom nearly all of the crimes shown on *Crimewatch UK* conform to news values of predatory violence, particularly against women and children.

14. Pfuhl, "Crimestoppers," 519.

15. Lavrakas, Rosenbaum, and Lurigio, "Media Cooperation with Police."

16. Rheingold, Campbell, Self-Brown, de Arellano, Resnick, and Kilpatrick, "Prevention of Child Sexual Abuse," 352–363; Santa and Cochran, "Does the Impact of Anti-Drinking and Driving," 109–129.

17. Adkins, "The Unblinking Eye Turns to Appellate Law;" Lambert, "Television Courtroom Broadcasting Research."

18. Surette and Terry, "Videotaped Misdemeanor First Appearances."

19. Marx, "Electric Eye in the Sky," 228.

20. Surette and Terry, "Video in the Misdemeanor Court."

21. Grant, "The Videotaping of Police Interrogations in Canada."

22. Patton, "Caught," 125, quoted by Graham in "Toward the Fifth Utility?," 89.

23. Loftus and Goold, "Covert Surveillance and the Invisibilities of Policing."

24. The looping of media content does move some surveillance images into newscasts so that the more entertaining and newsworthy scenes are shown to a mass audience.

25. Coleman and McCahill, *Surveillance & Crime*; Simon, "The Return of Panopticism." Three academic journals have recently produced issues focused upon the growth of surveillance in crime control efforts: *Surveillance and Society*, vol. 4(3), 2007; *Theoretical Criminology*, vol. 15 (3), 2011; and *Criminology and Criminal Justice*, vol. 12(3), 2012. Brief introductions and overviews regarding law enforcement considerations linked with creating public space police surveillance camera systems can be found in Clancey, *Considerations for Establishing a Public Space CCTV Network*; McLean and Worden, *Public Surveillance Cameras: A Synopsis*; and Ratcliffe, *Video Surveillance of Public Places*.

26. The effectiveness of CCTV systems for reducing terrorist acts has been called into question however. See Fussey, "Observing Potentiality in the Global City," 171–192.

27. Little research has been conducted on the impact of police surveillance cameras on social behavior. One example is Mazerolle, Hurley, and Chamlin, "Social Behavior in Public Space."

28. Norris, McCahill, and Wood ("The Growth of CCTV," 110) credit the first large scale open public space CCTV system as opening in England in 1985.

29. Zedner, "Pre-Crime and Post-Criminology?"

30. Barnard-Wills, "E-Safety Education;" Barnard-Wills and Wells, "Surveillance, Technology and the Everyday;" Haines and Wells, "Persecution or Protection?"

31. Haggerty and Gozso, "Seeing Beyond the Ruins," 169–187.

32. Williams, "Effective CCTV and the Challenge," 97–107.

33. Gill and Loveday, "What Do Offenders Think about CCTV?," 17–25. See also Allard, Wortley, and Stewart, "The Effect of CCTV on Prisoner Misbehavior," 404–422.

34. Hier, Greenberg, Walby, and Lett, "Media, Communication and the

Establishment," 734; Sutton and Wilson, "Open-Street CCTV in Australia," 310–322; Webster, "The Evolving Diffusion, Regulation and Governance," 230–250.

35. Bloss, "Escalating U.S. Police Surveillance after 9/11;" Coleman and McCahill, *Surveillance & Crime.*

36. Penfold-Mounce, *Celebrity Culture and Crime.* Strutin, "Social Networking Evidence in a Self-Surveillance Society." Coleman, R. and M. McCahill. 2011. *Surveillance & Crime.*

37. User contracts setting terms of service and technology options set by social networking providers currently set the standards of online privacy and what is considered acceptable criminal behaviors (Strutin, 2011). The basis of much policy and judicial decisions regarding new media and privacy is based on a 1986 law, the Electronic Communications Privacy Act of 1986 (ECPA). The act prohibits ISP employees from disclosing contents of electronic communications with exceptions when there is good faith belief that disclosure would prevent death or serious physical injury, waivers of privacy, and law enforcement warrants.

38. Warren and Brandeis, "The Right to Privacy," 195: "Recent inventions and business methods call attention to the next step which must be taken for the protection of the person, and for securing to the individual what Judge Cooley calls the right 'to be let alone.' Instantaneous photographs and newspaper enterprise have invaded the sacred precincts of private and domestic life; and numerous mechanical devices threaten to make good the prediction that 'what is whispered in the closet shall be proclaimed from the house-tops.'"

39. In a symbiotic criminal justice policy parallel development, while the United States works to mirror the United Kingdom in terms of public space camera surveillance systems, Britain has followed the U.S. lead on enacting punitive criminal justice sentencing policies (Silverman, *Crime, Policy and the Media,* 19).

40. Fussey ("Beyond Liberty, Beyond Security," 121) estimates one camera for every 14 Britons. See also Norris and Armstrong, *The Maximum Surveillance Society,* 39, quoting a 1997 assessment offered in an article in the British newspaper *The Econo-*

mist: "Britain is leading the world in CCTV technology and its use. Precise figures are not available, but it appears that Britain now has more electronic eyes per head of population than any other country in the world, one-party states included ("The All-Seeing Eye,"52). See also Sheldon, "Camera Surveillance within the UK."

41. Chris Horne ("The Case for: CCTV Should Be Introduced") states that one of the first systems was installed in 1961 in Cumbernauld, England. Norris and Armstrong (*The Maximum Surveillance Society,* 18) state that the first systems were launched in English retail stores in 1967. Chris Williams ("Police Surveillance and the Emergence of CCTV in the 1960s," 14) places the first police use of a CCTV system in Liverpool, England, in 1964.

42. Borg, "The Structure of Social Monitoring in the Process of Social Control," 287–288.

43. Sheldon, "Camera Surveillance within the UK," 194. Prior estimates by Wardell ("4.2 Million Cameras Keep Eye on British") had placed the total as high as 4.2 million.

44. Newburn and Hayman, *Policing, Surveillance and Social Control.* Of course, the traditional criminal justice system's inability to deal with crime is a mainstay of the entertainment media's content.

45. Goold, *CCTV and Policing,* 34–35.

46. Marx, *Undercover;* Fussey, "Observing Potentiality in the Global City," 173; Hier, Greenberg, Walby, and Lett, "Media, Communication and the Establishment," 734.

47. Norris, McCahill, and Wood, "The Growth of CCTV," 110–135.

48. Graham, "The Eyes Have It."

49. Barnard-Wills and Wells, "Surveillance, Technology and the Everyday."

50. Fussey, "Beyond Liberty, Beyond Security," 120–135.

51. "The All-Seeing Eye," 52.

52. Bloss, "Escalating U.S. Police Surveillance after 9/11," 213.

53. Marx, *Undercover.*

54. Short and Ditton, *Does Closed Circuit Television Prevent Crime?* and "Seen and Now Heard."

55. Welsh and Farrington, "Evidence-Based Crime Prevention," 21.

56. Ratcliffe, Taniguchi, and Taylor, "The Crime Reduction Effects of Public CCTV Cameras;" Welsh and Farrington, "Public Area CCTV and Crime Prevention."

57. Sheldon, "Camera Surveillance within the UK," 199. See also Park, Oh, and Paek, "Measuring the Crime Displacement."

58. For research reviews see Gill, *CCTV*; Gill and Spriggs, Assessing the Impact of CCTV; Goold, *CCTV and Policing*; La Vigne, Lowry, Markman, and Dwyer, *Evaluating the Use of Public Surveillance Cameras;* Welsh and Farrington, "Crime Prevention Effects of Closed Circuit Television;" and Welsh and Farrington, "Public Area CCTV and Crime Prevention."

59. Piza, Caplan, and Kennedy, "Analyzing the Influence of Micro-Level Factors."

60. Caplan, Kennedy, and Petrossian, "Police-Monitored CCTV Cameras in Newark;" Piza, Caplan, and Kennedy, "Analyzing the Influence of Micro-Level Factors;" Shah and Braithwaite, "Spread Too Thin."

61. Bromby, "To be Taken at Face Value?" Davies and Thasen, "Closed-Circuit Television: How Effective."

62. Brown, *CCTV in Town Centres*; Burrows, Sheldon, "Camera Surveillance within the UK."

63. Agustina and Cavell, "The Impact of CCTV on Fundamental Rights."

64. For a general discussion of CCTV related issues see Lyon, *Theorizing the Panopticon and Beyond*. For a alternate discussion of surveillance that examines surveillance as part of a therapeutic treatment program and not as a negative control mechanism see Moore, "The Benevolent Watch."

65. Surette, "The Thinking Eye," 152.

66. Williams, "Effective CCTV," 104. See also Lomell, "Targeting the Unwanted," 3472–3561; Smith, "Behind the Screens," 376–395.

67. Surette, "CCTV and Citizen Guardianship Suppression," 100–125; Zedner, "Pre-Crime and Post-Criminology?"

68. Hentschel, "Making (In)Visible," 300.

69. Coleman and McCahill, *Surveillance & Crime.*

70. Bowers and Johnson, "Measuring the Geographical Displacement."

71. Brown, *CCTV in Town Centres*; Burrows, "Closed Circuit Television and Crime on the London Underground;" and Welsh and Farrington, "Crime Prevention Effects of Closed Circuit Television."

72. Tilley, "Understanding Car Parks, Crime and CCTV."

73. Park, Oh, and Paek, ("Measuring the Crime Displacement") reported in 2012 that in one South Korea city significant crime reduction occurred after a CCTV system was installed without evidence of displacement.

74. The Supreme Court's legal reasoning is summarized in *United States v. Knotts* 368 U.S. 276, 281–82 (1983): "A person traveling in an automobile on public thoroughfares has no reasonable expectation of privacy in his movements from one place to another. When [an individual] traveled over the public streets he voluntarily conveyed to anyone who wanted to look the fact that he was traveling over particular roads in a particular direction, and the fact of his final destination when he exited from public roads onto private property."

75. "A Primer on Body-Worn Cameras for law enforcement."

76. Grant and Williams, "The Importance of Perceiving Social Contents."

77. Willaims, "Effective CCTV and the Challenge."

78. Sechrest, Liquori, and Perry, "Using Video Technology in Police Patrol."

79. Jefferis, Kaminski, Holmes, and Hanley, "The Effect of a Videotaped Arrest on Public Perceptions of Police Use of Force," 381; Weitzer, "Incidents of Police Misconduct and Public Opinion."

80. Parrish, "Police and the Media," 25.

81. Hentschel, "Making (In)Visible," 294.

82. "Americans OK with Video Scrutiny," CBS News Poll.

83. Barnard-Wills, "E-Safety Education;" Barnard-Wills and Wells, "Surveillance, Technology and the Everyday;" Haines and Wells, "Persecution or Protection?"

84. Barnard-Wills and Wells, "Surveillance, Technology and the Everyday;" Haines and Wells, "Persecution or Protection?;" Surette, "The Thinking Eye."

85. Agustina and Cavell, "The Impact of CCTV on Fundamental Rights;" Keval and Sasse, "Not the Usual Suspects;" Scott-Brown and Cronin, "Detect the Unexpected;" Surette, "The Thinking Eye."

86. Coleman and McCahill, *Surveillance & Crime.*

87. Ibid.

88. Allard, Wortley, and Stewart, "The Effect of CCTV on Prisoner Misbehavior," 404–422; Newburn and Hayman, *Policing, Surveillance and Social Control.*

89. Young, *The Exclusive Society*, 192.

90. Barnard-Wills and Wells, "Surveillance, Technology and the Everyday."

91. Fussey, "Observing Potentiality in the Global City," 171–192.

92. Agustina and Cavell, "The Impact of CCTV on Fundamental Rights;" Coleman and McCahill, *Surveillance & Crime.*

93. Surette, "The Thinking Eye," 152.

Chapter 9

1. Beale, "The News Media's Influence on Criminal Justice Policy."

2. See Packer, *The Limits of the Criminal Sanction.*

3. Tajgman, "From Estes to Chandler," 509.

4. Altheide, "The Mass Media, Crime and Terrorism," 982–997; Hron, "Torture Goes Pop!," 22–30.

5. Mason, "Misinformation, Myth and Distortion," 491.

6. Roberts and Doob, "News Media Influences on Public Views on Sentencing," citing Canadian Sentencing Commission, *Sentencing in the Media.*

7. Iyengar, *Is Anyone Responsible?*

8. Beale, "The News Media's Influence on Criminal Justice Policy;" Cheliotis, "The Ambivalent Consequences of Visibility;" Drake, "The 'Dangerous Other' in Maximum-Security Prisons."

9. Graber, *Crime News and the Public.*

10. Beckett and Sasson, *The Politics of Injustice.*

11. Barrile, "Television and Attitudes about Crime;" Graber, *Crime News and the Public*, 73; and Sasson, *Crime Talk.*

12. Cheliotis, "The Ambivalent Consequences of Visibility;" Drake, "The 'Dangerous Other' in Maximum-Security Prisons."

13. Christie, "The Ideal Victim."

14. Drake, "The 'Dangerous Other' in Maximum-Security Prisons."

15. Altheide, *Creating Fear*, 146.

16. Thompson ("From Sounds bites to Sound Policy" 785, note 58) offers a short list of contemporary memorial legislation associated with the single state of New York: Sean's Law (2000, DUIs), Stephanie's Law, (2003, stalking), Leaf-Brandi Woods Law (2006, vehicular homicide), Cynthia's Law (2006, assault on child), Todeschini Laws (2006, motor vehicle reckless fleeing).

17. Sotirovic, "Affective and Cognitive Processes as Mediators of Media Influences on Crime-Policy Preferences," 311.

18. Rennie, *The Search for Criminal Man.*

19. McCombs, *Setting the Agenda.*

20. Lasorsa and Wanta, "Effects of Personal, Interpersonal and Media Experiences on Issue Saliences;" and Protess, Cook, Doppelt, Ettema, Gordon, Leff, and Miller, *The Journalism of Outrage.*

21. Jones and Wolfe, "Public Policy and the Mass Media;" Silverman, *Crime, Policy and the Media.*

22. Rogers and Dearing, "Agenda-Setting Research."

23. Gerbner, Gross, Morgan, and Signorielli, "Growing Up with Television;" and Morgan and Shanahan, "Two Decades of Cultivation Research."

24. See, for example, Hirsch, "The 'Scary World,'" and "On Not Learning from One's Own Mistakes."

25. Grabe and Drew, "Crime Cultivations," 167; Hetsroni and Tukachinsky, "Television-World Estimates, Real-World Estimates," 134.

26. Banks, "Spaces of (In)Security," 169–187; Chermak, McGarrell, and Gruenewald, "Media Coverage of Police."

27. Dowler, "Media Consumption and Public Attitudes toward Crime and Justice," 116; Thompson, "From Sounds Bites to Sound Policy" 786–787. Valerie Callanan (*Feeding the Fear of Crime*), for example, found that in California heavy consumers of crime-related media are more fearful of

crime, more likely to believe crime is increasing, more likely to rate crime seriously, more likely to believe the world is "just," less likely to support rehabilitation, and much more likely to support three strikes sentencing.

28. Callanan, "Media Consumption, Perceptions of Crime Risk and Fear of Crime;" Chadee and Ditton, "Fear of Crime and the Media," 322–332; Kohm, Waid-Lindberg, Weinrath, Shelly & Dobbs, "The Impact of Media on Fear of Crime."

29. Hartnagel and Templeton, "Emotions about Crime;" Thompson, "From Sounds Bites to Sound Policy" 784–786.

30. Heath and Petraitis, "Television Viewing and Fear of Crime." Specific media effects are discussed by Weitzer and Kubrin ("Breaking News," 516–518).

31. Sparks and Ogles, "The Difference Between Fear of Victimization and the Probability of Being Victimized."

32. See Ditton, Chadee, Farrall, Gilchrist, and Bannister, "From Imitation to Intimidation," 595–610; Eschholz, Chiricos, and Gertz, "Television and Fear of Crime;" and Lane and Meeker, "Ethnicity, Information Sources, and Fear of Crime."

33. Mason, "Misinformation, Myth and Distortion," 491.

34. Cheliotis, "The Ambivalent Consequences of Visibility;" Drake, "The 'Dangerous Other' in Maximum-Security Prisons."

35. Gillespie, McLaughlin, Adams, and Symmonds, *Media and the Shaping of Public Knowledge*; Thompson, "From Sounds Bites to Sound Policy."

36. Green, "Public Opinion versus Public Judgment," 132; Allen, "There Must Be Some Way of Dealing with Kids," 5.

37. Green, "Public Opinion versus Public Judgment," 141; Griffin and Miller, "Child Abduction, AMBER Alert, and Crime Control Theater," 159–175.

38. Surette, "Media Echoes."

39. Sacco and Silverman, "Selling Crime Prevention."

40. For example, Snell, Bailey, Carona, and Mebane ("School Crime Policy Changes," 208) report that highly publicized school crimes impact school policy

decisions to install metal detectors and video cameras in distant states.

41. Green, "Public Opinion versus Public Judgment," 141; Thompson," From Sounds Bites to Sound Policy."

42. Raney and Bryant ("Moral Judgment and Crime Drama," 402–415) argue that crime dramas contain implied pro and con statements about justice policies. The greater the enjoyment of the drama, the more likely an effect on judgments and support of those justice policy statements will appear.

43. Thompson, "From Sounds Bites to Sound Policy," 797, 807.

44. Pfeiffer, Windzio, and Kleimann, "Media Use and Its Impacts," 259–285.

45. Boda and Szabo, "The Media and Attitudes towards Crime."

46. Bergin, "How and Why Do Criminal Justice Public Policies Spread."

47. Green, "Public Opinion versus Public Judgment," 144.

48. Altheide, "The Mass Media, Crime and Terrorism," 982–997; Fussey, "Beyond Liberty, Beyond Security," 124; Goidel, Freeman, and Procopio, "The Impact of Television Viewing on Perceptions of Juvenile Crime," 119–139; Ruddell and Decker, "Kids and Assault Weapons," 45–63.

49. Dardis, Baumgartner, Boydstun, De Boef, and Shen, "Media Framing of Capital Punishment," 15–16.

50. Mason, "Prison Decayed," 607–626; Mason, "Misinformation, Myth and Distortion," 491.

51. Reiner, "Media Made Criminality," 403.

52. Kupchik and Bracy, "The News Media on School Crime and Violence," 152. This is not to claim that alternate constructions of justice are non-existent in the media. Commercial films for example have been credited with offering two competing portrayals of justice by Welsh, Fleming and Dowler ("Constructing Crime and Justice on Film"), both as a punitive retributive system and as a restorative justice system and crime as both an individual problems and as a social problem.

53. Altheide, *Creating Fear*, 137.

54. Thompson, "From Sounds Bites to Sound Policy," 819.

55. Bennett, *News*, 96.

56. Thompson, "From Sounds Bites to Sound Policy," 819–820.

Chapter 10

1. Yar, "Crime, Media, and the Will-To-Representation," 250.

2. Ibid., 248.

3. "New Media and the Courts," 17.

4. Strutin, "Social Networking Evidence in a Self-Surveillance Society."

5. Surette, "21st Century Crime and Justice."

6. Strutin, "Social Media and the Vanishing Points."

7. Ibid., 233.

8. As the number of fake Web sites that appeared for the Boston bombers attests. See Kakutani, "Unraveling Boston Suspects Online Lives;" Stelter, "News Media and Social Media."

9. Lindgren 2011.

10. Yar, "Crime, Media, and the Will-To-Representation," 251.

11. Strutin, "Social Media and the Vanishing Points," 238–239. This is not to say that traditional media has suddenly become irrelevant. For example, recent research reports that community policing contacts with the public remain dominated not by department Web sites but by the information disseminated through traditional news outlets in print, ratio, and television (Kingshott, "Effective Police Management of the Media"). Legacy media will remain in play and at this time provide a substantial amount of the information that is circulated through new media outlets.

12. Grabosky, "Virtual Criminality;" Surette, "21st Century Crime and Justice."

13. Weimann, *Terror on the Internet*.

14. Musa, "Socio-Economic Incentives, New Media;" Surette, Hansen, and Nobel, *Measuring Media Oriented Terrorism*.

15. Goodman, "From Crowdsourcing to Crime-Sourcing."

16. The bank robber posted an ad on Craigslist that instructed persons interested in a road-maintenance job to show up wearing a yellow vest, safety goggles, respirator mask and blue shirt at a location and time that an armored car was to be delivering cash to a local bank. The robber, wearing the same outfit, overpowered the driver and made his escape leaving the police with numerous robbery suspects to deal with. See www.dshack.net/2011/10/crime-sourcing-craigslisting-unwitting-decoys-for-a-bank-robbery.html

17. Taylor, Fritsch, Liederbach, and Holt. *Digital Crime and Digital Terrorism*, 312–325.

18. Yar, "Crime, Media, and the Will-To-Representation," 254.

19. Hinduja and Patchin, *Bullying Beyond the Schoolyard*; Turan, Polat, Karapirli, Uysal and Turan, "The New Violence Type of the Era."

20. Brown, "(S)talking in Cyberspace;" Lyndon, Bonds-Raacke and Cratty, "College Students Facebook Stalking;" Reyns, "A Situational Crime Prevention Approach to Cyberstalking;"

21. Barnard-Wills, "E-safety Education;" Taylor, Fritsch, Liederbach, and Holt, *Digital Crime and Digital Terrorism*, Chapter 7.

22. Delong, Durkin, and Hindersmarck, "An Exploratory Analysis of the Cognitive Distortions." One study has examined the effect of viewing Internet child pornography on stress levels and cynicism by law enforcement investigators, see Perez, Jones, Englert, and Sachau, "Secondary Traumatic Stress and Burnout."

23. Examples include: "Three men have been accused of raping children they met using a mobile app designed for flirting between adults. The men are accused of posing as teenagers in a forum for 13 to 17-year-olds. Company employed a machine-learning technology—called the creepinator" to monitor for inappropriate content (Perlroth, "After Rapes Involving Children"). Two men charged with the murder of an Indiana women used her cellphone to update her Facebook status to hide the crime. "Police: Suspects sent 19-year-old's final Facebook post after killing her" http://www.theindychannel.com/news/local-news/police-suspects-sent-19-year-olds-final-facebook-post-after

-killing-her. Posted 6/13/2013. "Hoover police capture two suspected Facebook bandits;" "Two Men Used Facebook to Target and Burglarize Victims to Find Any Who Were Away."

24. Quayle and Taylor, *Child Pornography*.

25. Al-Lami, Hoskins, and O'Loughlin, "Mobilization and Violence in the New Media Ecology." Examples include a 2010 flash mob in Philadelphia in which hundreds of teenagers converged downtown brawling, assaulting pedestrians, and vandalizing property (Weiss, "FBI to Monitor Social Media to Fight 'Flash Mobs'").

26. Owns and Murphey, "Growing Number of 'Project X' Party Copycat;" "34 Arrests after Project X;" "They Did Everything You See in the Movie."

27. Yar, "Crime, Media, and the Will-To-Representation," 246.

28. Yar, "Crime, Media, and the Will-To-Representation."

29. Penfold-Mounce, *Celebrity Culture and Crime*.

30. Ibid.

31. Yar, "Crime, Media, and the Will-To-Representation," 248.

32. Penfold-Mounce, *Celebrity Culture and Crime*.

33. Ibid., 151. Even when caught up in serious crime, celebrities can minimize negative effects via acts of penance, public declarations of innocence or reduced culpability, or taking on the role of victim and rejecting the role of offender (this role reversal can be by claiming their victimization by the media, the justice system, the police, societal racism or sexism, or their accusers).

34. Penfold-Mounce, *Celebrity Culture and Crime*, 160–161.

35. Schillinger, "Social Media and the Arab Spring;" Taylor, "Arab Spring Really Was Social Media Revolution."

36. Bushman and Gibson "Violent Video Games Cause an Increase;" Kwan, Wei, and Julian, "Will the Experience of Playing a Violent Role."

37. Willoughby, Adachi, and Good, "A Longitudinal Study of the Association," 1045–1046.

38. Ward, "Video Games and Crime."

39. Surette and Maze, "Video Game Play and Copycat Crime."

40. Surette, "Cause or Catalyst."

41. Goodman, "Mystery Deepens." Goodman describes a U.S. woman murdered on her first trip outside the country as a tech-savvy young mother who had booked her trip to Turkey on her iPad, previewed her visit via digital photos with her virtual friends, and stayed in constant contact with friends and relatives through Skype and instant messages. Friends said it was as if she had never left.

42. Gilmour and McGloughlin, "In Crisis: Press, Rights and Privacy."

43. Barnard-Wills, "E-Safety Education."

44. Balogh, "Hyper-Connected," 12–15.

45. Strutin, "Social Media and the Vanishing Points."

46. Ibid., 252.

47. Eve and Zuckerman, "Ensuring an Impartial Jury;" Wheeler, "Symposium Examines Courts and the New Media."

48. Trial followers sent e-mails, joined online news groups and chat rooms, and created dedicated Web sites. Greek, "O.J. and the Internet," 66. See also Ferrell, "Slash and Frame," 47.

49. Greek, "O.J. and the Internet," 76.

50. Arrigo, "Media Madness as Crime in the Making."

51. Strutin, "Social Media and the Vanishing Points," 264.

52. Johnson, "Voir Dire: To Google or Not to Google."

53. Strutin, "Social Media and the Vanishing Points."

54. Eve and Zuckerman, "Ensuring an Impartial Jury," 8.

55. Gunnarsson, "Friending your Enemies."

56. Strutin, "Social Media and the Vanishing Points."

57. Ground rules that have been suggested are that neither attorneys, nor their agents, should e-mail nor post comments on Web sites that jurors are known to frequent. Requests for access to juror's private online sites and attempts to view a private page should be preceded by an electronic

message requesting access and providing potential jurors (and others) with enough information to make a decision to grant access with informed consent. In addition, like any improper communication and influence, any discovered bias on the part of a juror should be reported to the court (Johnson, "Voir Dire: To Google or Not to Google").

58. Silverman, *Crime, Policy and the Media*, 120; Strutin, 2009.

59. Strutin, "Social Networking Evidence in a Self-Surveillance Society."

60. Ibid., 258.

61. "Law School Hosts Panel on Social Media as Evidence," 2010.

62. Two appeal cases relate to new media content, access, and privacy. In *Quon v. Arch Wireless*. 529 F. 3d 892 (2008) police officer Quon worked for Ontario, California's police department which provided mobile pagers through Arch Wireless. City policy stated that they had the right to audit messages sent through the pagers, which the vender said would be treated as e-mails. Having gone over his mobile limit, Quon's messages were audited, and he was disciplined for sexually explicit content. The appeals court held that reviewing transcripts was reasonable because "it was an efficient and expedient way to determine whether Quon's overages were the result of work-related messaging or personal use" and the audits were not "excessively intrusive." In the second case involving a divorce (*White v. White*. 344 N.J. Super. 211. 781 A.2d 85 (2001)), a wife accessed her husband's e-mails on a family home computer and introduced them as evidence into divorce proceedings. The court ruled that since the e-mails were accessed on a home computer which was not password-protected; their retrieval was not a privacy violation. A key factor of the decision was the lack of a password, conceived as the functional equivalent of a physical lock by the court. Its absence was interpreted as an acceptance on the part of the husband of a reduced expectation of privacy.

63. Sengupta, "Courts Divided Over Searches of Cellphones."

64. Ibid.

65. Hannafor-Agor, Rottman, and Waters. "Juror and Jury Use of New Media," 1.

66. Nuss, "Death Row Inmate Gets New Trial after Juror Tweet." Schwartz ("As Jurors Turn to Web, Mistrials Are Popping Up") discusses a Florida drug case trial in which nine jurors were researching the case online in direct violation of judge instructions and specifically looking for evidence that had been excluded from the trial. In a different case, a juror was kicked off a jury after using Facebook to ask friends if they thought the defendants were guilty or not (Patrick, "Juror Axed for Verdict Poll on Net"). See also Greenwood, "Woman Juror Faces Jail after Facebook Chat."

67. Grow, "As Jurors Go Online;" Eve and Zuckerman, "Ensuring an Impartial Jury," 13, 15.

68. Thomas, "Are Juries Fair?" 43.

69. Hannafor-Agor, Rottman, and Waters, "Juror and Jury Use of New Media." Juror misconduct that was reported was not usually related to new media but was in the form of premature discussions among jurors and external discussions with family and friends about cases.

70. Ibid.

71. Dunn (*Jurors' Use of Social Media*) reported that a survey of 508 federal district judges revealed that most 94 percent reported no social media use problems.

72. Galli, "Litigation Considerations Involving Social Media."

73. Eve and Zuckerman, "Ensuring an Impartial Jury."

74. Galli ("Litigation Considerations Involving Social Media") lists 5 cases where mistrials were granted due to prejudicial evidence from new media being introduced to a jury.

75. Tucker, "Social Networking Puts the Bite."

76. Handley, "How Prisoners Harass Their Victims Using Facebook."

77. Ibid.

78. Kravets, "U.S. Courts Split on Internet Bans."

79. Strutin, "No-Computer Sentencing."

80. Ibid.
81. Ibid.
82. Ibid.
83. Taylor, Fritsch, Liederbach and Holt, *Digital Crime and Digital Terrorism*, 314.
84. Sun, Yoke, Hian, Shobha, and Iccha, "Managing Peer Relationships Online."
85. Rushkoff, "Media: It's the Real Thing."
86. Eve and Zuckerman, "Ensuring an Impartial Jury," 4.
87. "New Media and the Courts," 19–20.
88. Silverman, *Crime, Policy and the Media*. The difference between old and new media is more a difference in degree than kind. Legacy users can self-select by changing the channel or skipping articles in papers. Both Internet and political talk radio have an interactive format ... but new media broaden these capabilities and users can express their opinions in a less cumbersome and more instantaneous process (old—write a letter to the editor, new—post an anonymous comment]. New media provides more options in media formats: Web sites offer audio and video clips as well as print articles. And access to more resources, including vast archive systems (Beale, "The News Media's Influence on Criminal Justice Policy," 439.
89. Silverman, *Crime, Policy and the Media*, 135.
90. Grodal, "Video Games and the Pleasures of Control."
91. Fox, "Incurable Sex Offenders, Lousy Judges," 164–166.
92. Ibid., 171–173.
93. Ibid., 169.

Chapter 11

1. Sotirovic, "Affective and Cognitive Processes as Mediators of Media Influences on Crime-Policy Preferences," 313.
2. Gorelick, "Join Our War," 429.
3. Surette, Hansen, and Nobel, *Measuring Media Oriented Terrorism*.
4. Manning, "Media Loops."
5. Penfold, "The Star's Image, Victimization and Celebrity Culture," 289.
6. For example, the success of the reality show *Survivor* resulted in a spate of copycat reality shows.

7. Mathiesen, "The Eagle and the Sun."
8. The challenging of closed institutions has spurred the creation of new media entities focused on releasing guarded information such as WikiLeaks. WikiLeaks describes itself on its home Web site as "a not-for-profit media organisation. Our goal is to bring important news and information to the public. We provide an innovative, secure and anonymous way for sources to leak information to our journalists (our electronic drop box). One of our most important activities is to publish original source material alongside our news stories so readers and historians alike can see evidence of the truth" (http://wikileaks.org).
9. Grabe and Drew, "Crime Cultivations," 167.
10. Rushkoff, "Media: It's the Real Thing."
11. Meyrowitz, *No Sense of Place*, 319.
12. Valier, *Crime and Punishment in Contemporary Culture*. 149–150.
13. Richmond, "Can You Find Me Now," 283–319; Valier, *Crime and Punishment in Contemporary Culture*, 149.
14. Thomas, *Social Behavior and Personality*, 81.
15. Rapping, *Law and Justice as Seen on TV*.
16. Mittell, "Wikis and Participatory Fandom," 37.
17. Kiousis, "Interactivity: A Concept Explication."
18. Lindgren, 2011, "YouTube Gunman?"
19. Surette, "21st Century Crime and Justice."
20. Silverman, *Crime, Policy and the Media*, 139.
21. Grabe and Drew, "Crime Cultivations," 51.
22. Al-Lami, Hoskins, and O'Loughlin, "Mobilization and Violence in the New Media Ecology."
23. Barnard-Wills, "E-Safety Education."
24. Barnard-Wills and Wells. "Surveillance, Technology and the Everyday."
25. Ibid.
26. Zedner, "Pre-Crime and Post-Criminology?"
27. Maratea, "The E-Rise and Fall of Social Problems," 141–142. The change has been noticed by criminal justice practitioners who report that they feel that they have lost control over how case information is presented in the media

and their media image. Huey and Broll
("All It Takes is One TV Show to Ruin
It") report that police officers they surveyed attributed their loss of information
and image control to the expansion of
crime news and pressure on reporters to
cater to the public's insatiable appetite
for crime-and-justice stories.

28. Altheide, *Creating Fear*.

29. Poyntz, "Homey I Shot the Kids," 8.

30. Thompson, "From Sounds Bites to Sound
Policy."

31. Ibid., 819–820.

32. Maratea, "The E-Rise and Fall of Social
Problems," 139.

References

Adachi, P. and T. Willoughby. 2010. "The Effect of Violent Video Games on Aggression: Is It More Than Just the Violence?" *Aggression and Violent Behavior* 16: 55–63.

Adachi, P. and T. Willoughby. 2011. "The Effect of Video Game Competition and Violence on Aggressive Behavior: Which Characteristic Has the Greatest Influence?" *Psychology of Violence* 1(4): 259–274.

Adachi, P. and T. Willoughby. 2012. "Do Video Games Promote Positive Youth Development?" *Journal of Adolescent Research* 28(2): 155–165.

Adkins, M. 2010. "The Unblinking Eye Turns to Appellate Law: Cameras in Trial Courtrooms and Their Effect on Appellate Law." *Journal of Technology Law & Policy* 15(1): 65–83.

Adoni, H. and S. Mane. 1984. "Media and the Social Construction of Reality." *Communication Research* 11(3): 323–340.

Agustina, J. and G. Cavell. 2011. "The Impact of CCTV on Fundamental Rights and Crime Prevention Strategies: The Case of the Catalan Control Commission of Video Surveillance Devices." *Computer Law & Security Review* 27: 168–174.

Akers, R. L. 1998. *Social Learning and Social Structure: A General Theory of Crime and Deviance*. Athens, GA: Northeastern University Press.

Akers, R. L. Asimow, M., and S. Mader. 2004. *Law and Popular Culture*. New York: Peter Lang.

Alexander, Y. 1979. "Terrorism and the Media: Some Considerations." In *Terrorism: Theory and Practice*, eds. Y. Alexander, D. Carlton, and P. Wilkinson, 159–174. Boulder, CO: Westview Press.

Al-Lami, M., A. Hoskins, and B. O'Loughtin. 2012. "Mobilization and Violence in the New Media Ecology: The Dua Khalil Aswad and Camilia Shehata Cases." *Critical Studies on Terrorism* 5(2): 237–256.

Allard, T., R. Wortley, and A. Stewart. 2008. "The Effect of CCTV on Prisoner Misbehavior." *The Prison Journal* 88(3): 404–422.

Allen, J., S. Livingstone, and R. Reiner. 1998. "True Lies: Changing Images of Crime in British Postwar Cinema." *European Journal of Communication* 13(1): 53–75.

Allen, R. 2002. "There Must Be Some Way of Dealing with Kids: Young Offenders, Public Attitudes and Policy Change." *Youth Justice* 2(1): 3–13.

Al-Marashi, I. 2004. "Iraq's Hostage Crisis: Kidnappings, Mass Media and the Iraqi Insurgency." *Middle East Review of International Affairs* 8(4): 1–11.

Altheide, D. 2002. *Creating Fear*. Hawthorne, New York: Aldine de Gruyter.

Altheide, D. 2006. "The Mass Media, Crime and Terrorism." *Journal of International Criminal Justice* 4: 982–997.

Altheide, D. and R. Snow. 1991. *Media Worlds in the Postjournalism Era*. Hawthorne, New York: Aldine de Gruyter.

Ambrose, S. 2000. *Nothing Like It in the World*. New York: Simon & Schuster.

American Association of Advertising Agencies. 1990. *What We've Learned about Advertising from the Media-Advertising Partnership for a Drug-Free America*. New York: Author.

"Americans OK with Video Scrutiny." 2002. New York: CBS News Poll (April 21).

Anderson, C., D. Gentile, and K. Buckley. 2007. *Violent Video Game Effects on Children and Adolescents: Theory, Research, and Public Policy*. New York: Oxford University Press.

Anderson, C. 2004. "An Update on the Effects of Playing Violent Video Games." *Journal of Adolescence* 27(1): 113–122.

Anderson, J. 2008. "The Production of Media Violence and Aggression Research: A Cultural Analysis." *American Behavioral Scientist* 51(8): 1260–1279.

A Primer on Body-Worn Cameras for Law Enforcement. 2012, September. Washington, DC: National Institute of Justice.

Arendt, S. 2007. "Teens Kill Child While Acting out Mortal Kombat." *Wired* Downloaded from http://www.wired.com/gamelife/2007/12/drunk-teens-kil

Armour, R. 1980. *Film*. Westport, CT: Greenwood Press.

Arrigo, B. 1996. "Media Madness as Crime in the Making: On O. J. Simpson, Consumerism, and Hyyperreality.: In *Representing O. J.: Murder Criminal Justice and Mass Culture*, ed. G. Barak, 123–135. Albany, New York: Harrow and Heston.

Asimow, M. and S. Mader. 2004. *Law and Popular Culture*. New York: Peter Lang.

Balogh, C. 2012, June 7–13. "Hyper-Connected." *Orlando Weekly*, 12–15. Orlando, Fl.

Bailey, S., A. Carona, and D. Mebane. 2002. "School Crime Policy Changes: The Impact of Recent Highly-Publicized School Crimes." *American Journal of Criminal Justice* 26(2): 280–285.

Bailey, F. and D. Hale. 2004. *Blood on Her Hands: Women Who Murder*. Belmont, CA: Wadsworth.

Bailey, F., J. M. Pollock, and S. Schroeder. 1998. "The Best Defense: Images of Female Attorneys in Popular Films." In *Popular Culture, Crime and Justice*, eds. F. Bailey and D. Hale, 180–195. Belmont, CA: Wadsworth.

Bailey, S. M. 1993. "Fast Forward to Violence." *Criminal Justice Matters* 11: 1, 6–7.

Ball, M. 1981. *The Promise of American Law*. Athens, GA: University of Georgia Press.

Bandura, A. 1973. *Aggression: A Social Learning Analysis*. Englewood Cliffs, NJ: Prentice-Hall.

Bandura, A. 1995. *Self-Efficacy in Changing Societies*. Cambridge, UK: Cambridge University Press.

Bandura, A. and R. Walters. 1963. *Social Learning and Personality Development*. New York: Holt, Rinehart, and Winston.

Banks, M. 2005. "Spaces of (In)Security: Media and Fear of Crime in a Local Context." *Crime Media Culture* 1(2): 169–187.

Barber, S. 1987. *News Cameras in the Courtroom*. Norwood, NJ: Ablex.

Banner, S. 2011. "Trials and Other Entertainment." *Saint Louis University School of Law* 55(4): 1285–1292.

Barnard-Wills, D. 2012. "E-Safety Education: Young People, Surveillance and Responsibility." *Criminology & Criminal Justice* 12(3): 239–255.

Barnard-Wills, D. and H. Wells. 2012. "Surveillance, Technology and the Everyday." *Criminology & Criminal Justice* 12(3): 227–237.

Barrile, L. 1984. "Television and Attitudes about Crime: Do Heavy Viewers Distort Criminality and Support Retributive Justice?" In *Justice and the Media*, ed. R. Surette, 141–158. Springfield, IL: Thomas.

Baskin, D. and I. Sommers. 2010. "Crime-Show Viewing Habits and Public Attitudes Toward Forensic Evidence: The "CSI Effect" Revisited." *The Justice System Journal* 31(1): 97–113.

Batchelor, B. 2012, Dec 12. "Social Media and Youth Culture (Overview)." *Pop Culture Universe: Icons, Idols, Ideas*. ABC-CLIO 21012. http://popculture.abc-clio.com/Topics/Display/1513619

Beale, S. 2006. "The News Media's Influence on Criminal Justice Policy: How Market-Driven News Promotes Punitiveness." *William & Mary Law Review* 48: 397–481.

Beckett, K. and T. Sasson. 2000. *The Politics of Injustice: Crime and Punishment in America*. Thousand Oaks, CA: Pine Forge Press.

Benediktsson, M. 2010. "The Deviant Organization and the Bad Apple CEO: Ideology and Accountability in Media Coverage of Corporate Scandals." *Social Forces* 88(5): 2189–2216.

Bennet, W. L. 1996. *News: The Politics of Illusion*. New York: Longman.

Bennett, J. 2006. "The Good, the Bad and the Ugly: The Media in Prison Films." *The Howard Journal 45*(2): 97–115.

Berger, J. 2009. "Giuliani Criticizes Terror Trials in New York." *The New York Times*, November 16. Downloaded January 26, 2010 from http://www.nytimes.com/.

Bergin, T. 2011. "How and Why Do Criminal Justice Public Policies Spread throughout U.S. States: A Critical Review of the Diffusion Literature." *Criminal Justice Policy Review 22*(4): 403–421.

Berkowitz, L. 1984. "Some Effects of Thoughts on Anti- and Prosocial Influences of Media Events: A Cognitive-Neoassociation Analysis." *Psychological Bulletin 95*: 410–417.

Berkowitz, L. and K. Rogers. 1986. "A Priming Effect Analysis of Media Influences." In *Perspectives on Media Effects*, eds. J. Bryant and D. Zillman, 57–81. Hillsdale, NJ: Erlbaum.

Best, J. 1991. *Images of Issues: Typifying Contemporary Social Problems*. New York: Aldine de Gruyter.

Best, J. 2001. "The Diffusion of Social Problems." In *How Claims Spread: Cross-National Diffusion of Social Problems*, ed. J. Best, 1–18. New York: Aldine de Gruyter.

Best, J., and M. Hutchinson. 1996. "The Gang Initiation Rite as a Motif in Contemporary Crime Discourse." *Justice Quarterly 13*: 383–404.

Bing, R. 2010. *Race, Crime, and the Media*. New York: McGraw Hill.

Black, G. 1988. *Changing Attitudes toward Drug Use: Executive Summary and Statistical Report*. Rochester, New York: Partnership for a Drug-Free America.

Bleyer, W. 1927. *Main Currents in the History of American Journalism*. Boston: Houghton Mifflin.

Bloss, W. 2007. "Escalating U.S. Police Surveillance after 9/11: An Examination of Causes and Effects." *Surveillance and Society 4*(3): 208–228.

Blumer, H. 1933. *The Movies and Conduct*. New York: Macmillan.

Blumer, H. and P. Hauser. 1933. *Movies, Delinquency, and Crime*. New York: Macmillan.

Bond-Maupin, L. 1998. "'That Wasn't Even Me They Showed': Women as Criminals on America's Most Wanted. " *Violence Against Women 4*(1): 30–44.

Borg, M. 1997. "The Structure of Social Monitoring in the Process of Social Control." *Deviant Behavior 18*: 273–293.

Bjornstrom, E., R. Kaufman, R. Peterson, and M. Slater. 2010. "Race and Ethnic Representations of Lawbreakers and Victims in Crime News: A National Study of Television Coverage." *Social Problems 57*(2): 269–293.

Boda, Z. and G. Szabo. 2011. "The Media and Attitudes towards Crime and the Justice System: A Qualitative Approach." *European Journal of Criminology 8*(4): 329–342.

Borowitz, A. 1983. "Packaged Death: Forerunners of the Tylenol Poisonings." *American Bar Association Journal 69*(3): 282–286.

Bortner, M. A. 1984. "Media Images and Public Attitudes toward Crime and Justice." In *Justice and the Media*, ed. R. Surette, 15–30. Springfield, IL: Thomas.

Bowers, K. and S. Johnson. 2003. "Measuring the Geographical Displacement and Diffusion of Benefit Effects of Crime Prevention Activity." *Quantitative Criminology 19*(3): 275–301.

Boyd-Barett, O., Herrera, D. and Baumann, J. 2012. "Hollywoood, the CIA and the 'War on Terror.'" In *Media and Terrorism Global Perspectives*, eds. D. Freedman and D. Thussu, 116–133. Thousand Oaks, CA: Sage.

Boyle. K. 2005. *Media and Violence: Gendering the Debates*. Thousand Oaks, CA: Sage.

Brants, K. and P. Neijens. 1998. "The Infotainment of Politics." *Political Communication 15*: 149–164.

"Britain Is 'Surveillance Society.'" BBC News. Downloaded Jan 13, 2010 from http://news.bbc.co.uk/2/hi/ uk_news/6108496.stm

Breit, E. 2010. "On the (Re)Construction of Corruption in the Media: A Critical Discursive Approach." *Journal of Business Ethics 92*(4): 619–635.

Britto, S. and D. Dabney. 2010. "'Fair and Balanced?' Justice Issues on Political Talk Shows." *American Journal of Criminal Justice 35*(4), 198–218.

Britton, D. M. 2003. *At Work in the Iron Cage: The Prison as Gendered Organization*. New York: New York University Press.

Brock, T., J. Strange, and M. Green. 2002. "Power Beyond Reckoning: An Introduction to Narrative Impact." In *Narrative Impact*, eds. M. Green, J. Strange, and T. Brock, 1–15. Mahwah, NJ: Lawrence Erlbaum Associates.

Broe, D. 2003. "Class, Crime, and Film Noir." *Social Justice 30*(1): 22–41.

Bromby, M. 2002. "To Be Taken at Face Value: Computerized Identification." *Information & Communication Technology Law 11*(1): 63–73.

Brown, B. 1995. *CCTV in Town Centres: Three Case Studies. Police Research Group Crime Detection and Prevention Series*, paper no. 68. London: Home Office Police Department.

Brown, B. and W.R. Benedict. 2002. "Perceptions of the Police." *Policing 25*(3): 543–580.

Brown, S. 2010. "(S)Talking in Cyberspace: Virtuality, Crime and Law." In *Crime and Media: A Reader*, ed. C. Greer, 539–550. London, UK: Routledge.

Browne, K. and C. Hamilton-Giachritsis. 2005. "The Influence of Violent Media on Children and Adolescents: A Public-health Approach." *Lancet 365*: 701–710.

Bruschke, J. and W. Loges. 2004. *Free Press vs. Fair Trials*. Mahwah, NJ: Erlbaum.

Burns, R. 2007. "Media Portrayal of White-Collar Crime." In *Encyclopedia of White-Collar Crime*, eds., J. Gerber and E. Jensen, 182–184. Westport, CT: Greenwood Press.

Burrows, J. 1980. "Closed Circuit Television and Crime on the London Underground." In *Designing Out Crime*, eds. R. Clarke and P. Mayhew, 75–83. London: H. M. Stationery Office for Home Office Research Unit.

Bushman, B. and B. Gibson. 2011. "Violent Video Games Cause an Increase in Aggression long after the Game Has Been Turned Off." *Social Psychological and Personality Science 2*(1): 29–32.

Butler, B. 2012. "Capital Pretrial Publicity as a Symbolic Public Execution: A Case Report." *Journal of Forensic Psychology Practice 12*(3): 259–169.

Callanan, V. 2005. *Feeding the Fear of Crime: Crime-Related Media and Support for Three Strikes*. New York: LFB Scholarly Publishing LLC.

Callanan, V. 2012. "Media Consumption, Perceptions of Crime Risk and Fear of Crime: Examining Race/Ethnic Differences." *Sociological Perspectives 55*(1): 93–115.

"Cameras in Our Federal Courts—The Time Has Come." 2010, Feb. 21. *Judicature*, Editorial downloaded from https://www.ajs.org/judicature-journal/editorial/cameras-in-our-federal-courts/.

Campbell, J. 2007. "Journalists Should Demand Prison Access." *Quill 95*(4): 34.

Canadian Sentencing Commission. 1988. *Sentencing in the Media: A Content Analysis of English Speaking Newspapers in Canada*. Research Reports of the Canadian Sentencing Commission. Ottawa, Canada: Department of Justice.

Canter, C., P. Sheehan, P. Alpers, and P. Mullen. 1999. "Media and Mass Homicides." *Archives of Suicide Research 5*: 283–290.

Caplan, J., L. Kennedy, and G. Petrossian. 2011. "Police-Monitored CCTV Cameras in Newark, NJ: A Quasi-Experimental Test of Crime Deterrence." *Journal of Experimental Criminology 7*: 255–274.

Carpenter, S., S. Lacy, and F. Fico. 2006. "Network News Coverage of High-Profile Crime during 2004: A Study of Source Use and Reporter Context." *Journalism and Mass Communication Quarterly 83*(4): 901–916.

Carrabine, E. 2008. *Crime, Culture and the Media*. Cambridge, UK: Polity Press.

Casey, C. A. 2011. "Common Misperceptions: The Press and Victorian Views of Crime." *Journal of Interdisciplinary History 41*(3): 367–391.

Cavalli, E. 2007. "Chinese Teen Burns Classmate, Blames World of Warcraft." *Wired*. http://www.wired.com/gamelife/2007/12/chinese-teen-bu/

Cavender, G. 1998. "In the Shadow of Shadows: Television Reality Crime Programming." In *Entertaining Crime: Television Reality Programs*, ed. M. Fishman and G. Cavender, 79–94. New York: Aldine de Gruyter.

Cavender, G. 2004. "In Search of Community on Reality TV." In *Understanding Reality*, eds. S. Homes and D. Jermyn, 154–172. New York: Routledge.

Cavender, G. and M. Fishman. 1998. "Television Reality Crime Programs: Context and History." In *Entertaining Crime: Television Reality Programs*, eds. M. Fishman and G. Cavender, 3–15. New York: Aldine De Gruyter.

Cavender, G. and A. Mulcahy. 1998. "Trial by Fire: Media Constructions of Corporate Deviance." *Justice Quarterly 15*: 697–717.

Cavender, G. and S. Deutsch. 2007. "CSI and Moral Authority: The Police and Science." *Crime Media Culture 31*(1): 67–81.

Cecil, D. 2007. "Doing Time in Camp Cupcake: Lessons Learned from Newspaper Accounts of Martha Stewart's Incarceration." *Journal of Criminal Justice and Popular Culture 14*(2): 142–160.

Cecil, D. 2007. "Dramatic Portrayals of Violent Women: Female Offenders on Prime Time Crime Dramas." *Journal of Criminal Justice and Popular Culture 14*(3): 243–258.

Cecil, D. 2007. "Looking beyond Caged Heat: Media Images of Women in Prison." *Feminist Criminology 2*(4): 304–326.

Chadee, D. and J. Ditton. 2005. "Fear of Crime and the Media: Assessing the Lack of Relationship." *Crime, Media, Culture 1*(3): 322–332.

Chandler v. Florida, 101 S. Ct. 1981.

Charter, W. 1933. *Motion Pictures and Youth: A Summary*. New York: Macmillan.

Cheatwood, D. 1998. "Prison Movies: Films about Adult, Male, Civilian Prisons; 1929–1995." In *Popular Culture, Crime, and Justice*, eds. F. Bailey and D. Hale, 209–231. Belmont, CA: Wadsworth.

Cheatwood, D. 2001. "Early Images of Crime and Criminal Justice: Commercial Radio from 1929 to 1962." Paper presented at the American Society of Criminology, Atlanta, GA.

Cheliotis, L. 2010. "The Ambivalent Consequences of Visibility: Crime and Prisons in the Mass Media." *Crime, Media, Culture, 6*(2): 169–184.

Chen, K and X. Zhang. 2011. "Trial by Media: Overcorrection of the Inadequacy of the Right to Free Speech in Contemporary China." *Critical Arts-South-North Cultural and Media Studies 25*(1): 46–57.

Chermak, S. 1995. *Victims in the News*. Boulder, CO: Westview Press.

Chermak, S. 1998. "Police, Courts, and Corrections in the Media." In *Popular Culture, Crime and Justice*, eds. F. Bailey and D. Hale, 87–99. Belmont, CA: Wadsworth.

Chermak, S. and J. Gruenewald. 2006. "The Media's Coverage of Domestic Terrorism." *Justice Quarterly 23*(4): 428–461.

Chermak, S., E. McGarrell, and J. Gruenewald. 2005. "Media Coverage of Police Misconduct and Attitudes toward Police." *Policing 29*(2): 261–281.

Chesney-Lind, M. and M. Eliason. 2006. "From Invisible to Incorrigible: The Demonization of Marginalized Women and Girls." *Crime, Media, Culture 2*(1): 29–47.

Chibnall, S. 1980. "Chronicles of the Gallows: The Social History of Crime Reporting." In *The Sociology of Journalism and the Press*, ed. H. Christian, 179–217. Lanham, MD: Rowman & Littlefield.

Chibnall, S. 1981. "The Production of Knowledge by Crime Reporters." In *The Manufacture of News*, eds. S. Cohen and J. Young, 75–97. Thousand Oaks, CA: Sage.

Chiou, L. and Lopez, M. 2010. "The Reality of Reality Television: Does Reality TV Influence Local Crime Rates?" *Economics Letters 108*(3): 330–333.

Christie, N. 1986. "The Ideal Victim." In *From Crime Policy to Victim Policy: Reorienting the Justice System*, ed. E. A. Fattah, 17–30. New York: St. Martin's Press.

Ciasullo, A. 2008. "Containing Deviant Desire: Lesbianism, Heterosexuality and the Women-in-Prison Narrative." *Journal of Popular Culture 41*(2): 195–223.

Clancey, G. 2009. "Considerations for Establishing a Public Space CCTV Network." *Research in Practice, No. 08*. Australia: Australian Institute of Criminology.

Claster, D. 1967. "Comparison of Risk Perception between Delinquents and Nondelinquents." *Journal of Criminal Law, Criminology and Police Science 58*, 80–86.

Claxton, G. 2005. "Joining the Intentional Dance." In *Perspectives on Imitation: From Neuroscience to Social Science*. Vol. 2 , eds.

S. Hurley and N. Chater, 193–196. Cambridge, MA: MIT Press.

Clowers, M. 2001. "Dykes, Gangs, and Danger: Debunking Popular Myths about Maximum Security Life." *Journal of Criminal Justice and Popular Culture 9*(1): 22–30.

Cohen, S. and J. Young. 1981. *The Manufacture of News*. Thousand Oaks, CA: Sage.

Cole, J. 1996. *The UCLA Television Violence Monitoring Report*. Los Angeles: UCLA Center for Communication Policy.

Cole, S. and R. Dioso-Villa. 2007. "CSI and Its Effects: Media, Juries, and the Burden of Proof." *New England Law Review 41*(3): 435–469.

Coleman, J. 2006. *The Criminal Elite*. New York: Worth Publishers.

Collins, R. L. 2011. "Content Analysis of Gender Roles in Media: Where Are We Now and Where Should We Go?" *Sex Roles 64*, 290–298.

Conrich, I. 2003. "Mass Media/Mass Murder: Serial Killer Cinema and the Modern Violated Body." In *Criminal Visions: Media Representations of Crime and Justice*, ed. P. Mason, 156–171. Devon, UK: Willan.

Cook, T., D. Kendzierski, and S. Thomas. 1983. "The Implicit Assumptions of Television Research: An Analysis of the 1982 NIMH Report on Television and Behavior." *Public Opinion Quarterly 47*: 161–201.

Courtwright, D. 1996. *Violent Land: Single Men and Social Disorder from the Frontier to the Inner City*. Cambridge: Harvard University Press.

Coyne, S. 2007. "Does Media Violence Cause Violent Crime?" *European Journal of Criminal Policy Research 13*: 205–211.

Curran, J. 1982. "Communications, Power and Social Order." In *Culture, Society and the Media*, eds. M, Gurevitch, T. Bennett, J. Curran, and J. Woollacott, 202–235. London: Methuen.

Curtis, J. 1953. "Gabriel Tarde." In *Social Theorists*, ed. C. Mihanovich, 142–157. Milwaukee, WI: Bruce Publishing.

Daftary-Kapur, T., R. Dumas, and S. Penrod. 2010. "Jury Decision-Making Biases and Methods to Counter Them." *Legal and Criminological Psychology 15*(1): 133–154.

Dale, E. 1935. *Children's Attendance at Motion Pictures*. New York: Macmillan.

Dalglish, L. 2005. "Protecting Reporters Who Protect Sources. *Nieman Reports 59*(2): 30–32.

Dardis, F., F. Baumgartner, A. Boydstun, S. De Boef, and F. Shen. 2008. "Media Framing of Capital Punishment and Its Impact on Individuals' Cognitive Responses." *Mass Communication and Society 11*: 115–140.

Davies, G. and S. Thasen. 2000. "Closed-Circuit Television: How Effective an Identification Aid?" *British Journal of Psychology 91*: 411–426.

Davis, A. 2003. *Are Prisons Obsolete?* London: Open Media.

DeFleur, M. and S. Ball-Rokeach. 1975. *Theories of Mass Communication*. New York: McKay.

Dijksterhuis, A. and J. Bargh. 2001. "The Perception–Behavior Expressway: Automatic Effects of Social Perception on Social Behavior." In *Advances in Experimental Social Psychology 30*, ed. M. Zanna, 1–40. New York: Academic Press.

DeLisi, M., M. Vaughn, D. Gentile, C. Anderson, and J. Shook. 2012. "Violent Video Games, Delinquency, and Youth Violence: New Evidence." *Youth Violence and Juvenile Justice 11*(2): 132–142.

Delong, R., K. Durkin, and S. Hundersmarck. 2010. "An Exploratory Analysis of the Cognitive Distortions of a Sample of Men Arrested in Internet Sex Stings." *Journal of Sexual Aggression 16*(1): 59–70.

Delwiche, A. and J. Henderson. 2013. "Introduction: What is Participatory Culture?" In *The Participatory Cultures Handbook*, eds. L. Lieurouw and S. Livingstone, 3–9. New York: Routledge.

DeTardo-Bora, K. 2009. "Criminal Justice 'Hollywood Style': How Women in Criminal Justice Professions Are Depicted in Prime-Time Crime Dramas." *Women & Criminal Justice 19*(2): 153–168.

Dirikx, A., J. van den Bulck, and S. Parmentier. 2012. "The Police as Societal Moral Agents: Procedural Justice and the Analysis of Police Fiction." *Journal of Broadcasting & Electronic Media 56*(1): 38–54.

Ditton, J., D. Chadee, S. Farrall, E. Gilchrist, and J. Bannister. 2004. "From Imitation to

Intimidation." *British Journal of Criminology* 44(4): 595–610.

Dixon, R. and K. Maddox. 2005. "Skin Tone, Crime News, and Social Reality Judgments: Priming the Stereotype of the Dark and Dangerous Black Criminal." *Journal of Applied Social Psychology 38*: 1555–1570.

Dixon, T., C. Azocar, and M. Casas. 2003. "The Portrayal of Race and Crime on Television Network News." *Journal of Broadcasting and Electronic Media 47*: 495–520.

Dixon, T. 2008. "Crime News and Radicalized Beliefs: Understanding the Relationship Between Local News Viewing and Perceptions of African Americans and Crime." *Journal of Communication 58*: 106–125.

Dixon, T. and D. Linz. 2000. "Overrepresentation and Underrepresentation of Victimization on Local Television News." *Communication Research 27*: 547–573.

Docter, S. 2010. "Blogging and Journalism: Extending Shield Law Protection to New Media Forms." *Journal of Broadcasting & Electronic Media, 54*(4): 588–602.

Doley, R., R. Surette, and C. Ferguson. Forthcoming. "Copycat Arson: Bridging Two Research Areas." *Criminal Justice and Behavior.*

Dominick, J. 1978. "Crime and Law Enforcement in the Mass Media." In *Deviance and Mass Media*, ed. C. Winick, 105–128. Thousand Oaks, CA: Sage.

Donovan, P. 1998. "Armed with the Power of Television: Reality Crime Programming and the Reconstruction of Law and Order in the United States." In *Entertaining Crime*, eds. M. Fishman and G. Cavender, 117–140. New York: Aldine de Gruyter.

Dowler, K. 2003. "Media Consumption and Public Attitudes toward Crime and Justice: The Relationship Between Fear of Crime, Punitive Attitudes, and Perceived Police Effectiveness." *Journal of Criminal Justice and Popular Culture 10*(2): 109–126.

Dowler, K. 2004. "Comparing American and Canadian Local Television Crime Stories: A Content Analysis" *Canadian Journal of Criminology and Criminal Justice 46*(5): 573–596.

Dowler, K., T. Fleming, and S. Muzzatti. 2006. "Constructing Crime: Media Crime and Popular Culture." *Canadian Journal of Criminology and Criminal Justice 48*(6): 837–850.

Dowrick, J and J. Raeburn. 1995. "Self-Modeling: Rapid Skill Training for Children with Physical Disabilities." *Journal of Developmental and Physical Disabilities 7*: 25–37.

Doyle, A. 1998. "Cops: Television Policing as Policing Reality." In *Entertaining Crime*, eds. M. Fishman and G. Cavender, 95–116. New York: Aldine de Gruyter.

Doyle, A. 2003. *Arresting Images: Crime and Policing in Front of the Television Camera.* Toronto: University of Toronto Press.

Doyle, A. and R. Ericson. 1996. "Breaking into Prison: News Sources and Correctional Institutions." *Canadian Journal of Criminology 38*: 155–190.

Drake, D. 2011. "The 'Dangerous Other' in Maximum-Security Prisons." *Criminology & Criminal Justice 11*(4): 367–383.

Drechsel, R. 1983. *News Making in the Trial Courts.* White Plains, New York: Longman.

Drucker, S. 1989. "The Televised Mediated Trial: Formal and Substantive Characteristics." *Communication Quarterly 37*: 305–318.

Duffy, S. 2002. *Closing the Net: How They Cracked the Case,* CNN, October 25, Posted: 8:28 AM EDT downloaded from //archives.cnn.com/2002/US/South/10/24/sniper.case.cracked/index.html

Dunn, M. 2011. *Jurors' Use of Social Media during Trials and Deliberations.* Washington, DC: Federal Judicial Center.

Durnal, E. 2010. "Crime Scene Investigation (as seen on TV)." *Forensic Science International 199*: 1–5.

Dutelle, A. 2006. "The CSI Effect and Your Department." *Law & Order 54*(5): 113–114.

Duwe, G. 2000. "Body-Count Journalism: The Presentation of Mass Murder in the News Media." *Homicide Studies 4*(4): 364–399.

Engle, K. 2012. "Celebrity Diplomacy and Global Citizenship." *Celebrity Studies 3*(1): 116–122.

Ericson, R., P. Baranek, and J. Chan. 1987. *Visualizing Deviance.* Toronto: University of Toronto Press.

Ericson, R., P. Baranek, and J. Chan. 1989. *Negotiating Control: A Study of News Sources.* Toronto: University of Toronto Press.

Ericson, R., P. Baranek, and J. Chan. 1991. *Representing Law and Order: Crime, Law, and Justice in the News Media.* Toronto: University of Toronto Press.

Eschholz, S., T. Chiricos, and M. Gertz. 2003. "Television and Fear of Crime: Program Types, Audience Traits and the Mediating Effect of Perceived Neighborhood Racial Composition." *Social Problems* 50(3): 395–415.

Escholz, S., M. Mallard, and S. Flynn. 2004. "Images of Prime Time Justice: A Content Analysis of NYPD Blue and Law & Order.*" Journal of Criminal Justice and Popular Culture* 10(3): 161–180.

Estes v. Texas, 381 U.S. (1965).

Eve, A. and M. Zuckerman. 2012. "Ensuring an Impartial Jury in the Age of Social Media." *Duke Law and Technology Review* 1: 1–29.

Fargo, A. L. 2006. "Analyzing Federal Shield Law Proposals: What Congress Can Learn from the States." *Communication Law and Policy* 11(1): 35–82.

"Federal Pilot Program Puts Cameras in Northern District Courts." 2012. *Illinois Bar Journal* 100(2): 74–75.

Ferguson, C. J. 2002. "Media Violence: Miscast Causality." *American Psychologist* 57: 446–47.

Ferguson, C. J. 2011. "Video Games and Youth Violence: A Prospective Analysis in Adolescents." *Journal of Youth and Adolescence* 40(4): 377–391.

Ferrell, J. 1996. "Slash and Frame." In *Representing O. J.: Murder Criminal Justice and Mass Culture*, ed. G. Barak, 46–50. Albany, New York: Harrow and Heston.

Ferrel, J. 1998. "Criminalizing Popular Culture." In *Popular Culture, Crime, and Justice*, eds. F. Bailey and D. Hale, 71–83. Belmont, CA: Wadsworth.

Fisher, J. 1997. *Killer Among Us: Public Reactions to Serial Murder.* Westport, CT: Praeger.

Fischer, J., N. Aydin, A. Kastenmuller, D. Frey, and P. Fischer. 2012. "The Delinquent Media Effect: Delinquency-Reinforcing Video Games Increase Players Attitudinal and Behavioral Inclination toward Delinquent Behavior." *Psychology of Popular Media Culture* 3: 201–205.

Fischer, P., A. Kastenmuller, and T. Greitemeyer. 2010. "Media Violence and the Self: The Impact of Personalized Gaming Characters in Aggressive Video Games on Aggressive Behavior." *Journal of Experimental Social Psychology* 46: 192–195.

Fischer, P., J. Kubitzki, S. Guter, and D. Frey. 2007. "Virtual Driving and Risk Taking: Do Racing Games Increase Risk-Taking Cognitions, Affect, and Behaviors?" *Journal of Experimental Psychology: Applied* 13: 22–31.

Fischer, P., T. Morton, A. Kastenmuller, T. Postmes, D. Frey, J. Kubitzki, J. Odenwalder. 2009. "The Racing-Game Effect: Why Do Video Racing Games Increase Risk-Taking Inclinations?" *Personality and Social Psychology Bulletin* 35(10): 1395–1409.

Fisher, C. 1980. "The Spread of Violent Crime from City to Countryside, 1955 to 1975." *Rural Sociology* 45(3): 416–434.

Fishman, M. and G. Cavender. 1998. *Entertaining Crime: Television Reality Programs.* New York: Aldine de Gruyter.

Flanders, J. 2011. *The Invention of Murder.* London, UK: HarperCollins.

Flew, T. 2002. *New Media: An Introduction*, South Melbourne, Australia: Oxford University Press.

Flichy, P. 2008. "New Media History." In *The Handbook of New Media*, eds. L. Lieurouw and S. Livingstonre, 136–150. Thousand Oaks, CA: Sage.

Foucault, M. 1972. *The Archaeology of Knowledge.* London: Tavistock Press.

Fox, K. 2013. "Incurable Sex Offenders, Lousy Judges & the Media: Moral Panic Sustenance in the Age of New Media." *American Journal of Criminal Justice* 38: 160–181.

Fox, R., R. van Sickel, and T. Steiger. 2007. *Tabloid Justice.* Bolder, CO: Lynne Rienner Pub.

Franklin, B. 2006. *Local Journalism and Local Media: Making the Local News.* London: Routledge.

Fleming, P. and S. Zyglidopoulos. 2009. *Charting Corporate Corruption.* Northampton, MA: Edward Elgar Pub.

Freedman, E. 2011. "Crime Which Startle and Horrify: Gender, Age and the Racialization of Sexual Violence in White American Newspapers, 1870–1900." *Journal of the History of Sexuality 20*(3): 465–497.

Freedman, J. 2002. *Media Violence and Its Effect on Aggression: Assessing the Scientific Evidence.* Toronto: University of Toronto Press.

Freeman, R. 1998. "Public Perception and Corrections: Correctional Officers as Smug Hacks." In *Popular Culture, Crime, and Justice*, eds. F. Bailey and D. Hale, 196–208. Belmont, CA: Wadsworth.

Freeman, R. 2000. *Popular Culture and Corrections.* Lanham, MD: American Correctional Association.

Friedman, L. and I. Rosen-Zvi. 2001. "Illegal Fictions: Mystery Novels and the Popular Image of Crime." *UCLA Law Review 48*: 1411–1433.

Friedman, L. 2011. "Front Page: Notes on the Nature and Significance of Headline Trials." *Saint Louis University School of Law 55*(4): 1243–1283.

Friedrichs, D. 2004. *Trusted Criminals: White Collar Crime in Contemporary Society.* Belmont, CA: Thomson.

Frosdick, S. and P. March. 2013. *Football Hooliganism.* New York: Routledge.

Fusco, N. and M. Sabourin. 2012. "Public Opinion on Media Presence in the Courthouse." *International Journal of Law & Psychiatry 35*(1): 35–42.

Fussey, P. 2007. "Observing Potentiality in the Global City." *International Criminal Justice Review 17*(3): 171–192.

Fussey, P. 2008. "Beyond Liberty, Beyond Security: The Politics of Public Surveillance." *British Politics 3*: 120–135.

Gaeta, T. 2010. "Catch and Release: Procedural Unfairness on Primetime Television and the Perceived Legitimacy of the Law." *Journal of Criminal Law & Criminology 100*(2): 523–553.

Galli, N., C. Olszyk, and J. Wilhelm. 2010. "Litigation Considerations Involving Social Media." *Pennsylvania Bar Association Quarterly 81*: 59–75.

Gans, H. 1979. *Deciding What's News.* New York: Pantheon.

Garian, E. 2011. "Media Portrayals of Female Murder Offenders." *Prison Service Journal (194)*: 12–18.

Garland, D. 2001. *The Culture of Control.* Oxford, UK: Oxford University Press.

Geis, G. 2007. *White-Collar and Corporate Crime.* Upper Saddle River, NJ: Pearson Prentice-Hall.

Gentile, D. 2003. *Media Violence and Children: A Complete Guide for Parents and Professionals.* Westport, CN: Praeger.

Gentile, D. and B. Bushman. 2012. "Reassessing Media Violence Effects Using a Risk and Resilience Approach to Understanding Aggression." *Psychology of Popular Media Culture 1*(3):138–151.

Gerber, J. and E. Jensen. 2007. *Encyclopedia of White-Collar Crime.* Westport CT: Greenwood Press.

Gerbner, G., L. Gross, M. Morgan, and N. Signorielli. 1994. "Growing Up with Television: The Cultivation Perspective." In *Media Effects*, eds. B. Jennings and D. Zillman, 17–41. Hillsdale, NJ: Erlbaum.

Gergen, K. 1985. "Social Constructionist Inquiry: Context and Implications." In *The Social Construction of the Person*, eds. K. Gergen and K. Davis, 3–18. New York: Springer-Verlag.

Gerstein, J. 2009. *New York Terrorist Trial Raises Stakes.* November 13, Downloaded January 23, 2010 from http://www.politico.com/new/stories/1109/29486.html.

Getty, C. 2001. "Media Wise." *Corrections Today 63*(7): 126–131.

Gill, M. 2003. *CCTV.* Leicester, UK: Perpetuity Press.

Gill, M. and K. Loveday. 2003. "What Do Offenders Think about CCTV?" *Crime Prevention and Community Safety 5*(3): 17–25.

Gill, M. and A. Spriggs. 2005. *Assessing the Impact of CCTV.* Home Office Research Study 292. London: Home Office Research, Development and Statistics Directorate.

Gillespie, M., E. McLaughlin, S. Adams, and A. Symmonds. 2003. *Media and the Shaping of Public Knowledge and Attitudes towards Crime and Punishment.* London: Esmee Fairbairn Foundation. Downloaded April 6, 2010 from http://www.Rethinking.org.uk/latest/pdf/briefing4.pdf.

Gilliam, F. and S. Iyengar. 2000. "Prime Suspects: The Influence of Local Television News on the Viewing Public." *American Journal of Political Science* 44(3): 560–573.

Gillis, C. 2005 (November 7) "New Crime Shows Educate Criminals." *Maclean's Magazine*. Downloaded from www.thecanadianencyclopedia.com/index.cfm?PgNm=TCE&Params=M1ARTM0012851

Gilmour, A. and T. McGloughlin. 2011. "In Crisis: Press, Rights and Privacy." *Criminal Justice Matters* 85(1): 1.

Gladwell, M. 2005. *Blink*. New York: Little, Brown.

Glaser, D. 1956. "Criminality Theories and Behavioral Images." *American Journal of Sociology* 61(5): 433–444.

Goff, C. 2001. "The Westray Mine Disaster: Media Coverage of a Corporate Crime in Canada." In *Contemporary Issues in Crime and Criminal Justice*, eds. H. N. Potell and D. Schichor, 195–217. Upper Saddle River, NJ: Prentice-Hall.

Goidel, R., C. Freeman, and S. Procopio. 2006. "The Impact of Television Viewing on Perceptions of Juvenile Crime." *Journal of Broadcasting and Electronic Media*, 50(1): 119–139.

Goldman, A. 2005. "Imitation, Mind Reading, and Simulation." In *Perspectives on Imitation: From Neuroscience to Social Science*. Vol. 2, *Imitation*, Human Development, and Culture, eds. S. Hurley and N. Chater, 79–94. Cambridge, MA: MIT Press.

Goold, B. 2004. *CCTV and Policing*. Oxford, UK: Oxford University Press.

Gordon, M. and L. Heath. 1981. "The News Business, Crime, and Fear." In *Reactions to Crime*, ed. D. Lewis, 227–247. Thousand Oaks, CA: Sage.

Gorelick, S. 1989. "Join Our War: The Construction of Ideology in a Newspaper Crimefighting Campaign." *Crime and Delinquency* 35: 421–436.

Gorn, E. 1992. "The Wicked World: The National Police Gazette and Gilded-Age America." *Media Studies Journal* 6:3–4.

Goodman, D. 2013, Feb. 8. "Mystery Deepens as Staten Island Woman's Body Is Returned from Turkey." *The New York Times:* A21.

Goodman, M. 2011, September 29. "From Crowdsourcing to Crime-Sourcing: The Rise of Distributed Criminality." Downloaded from radar.oreilly.com/2011/09/crime-sourcing.html.

Grabe, M. and D. Drew. 2007. "Crime Cultivations: Comparisons across Media Genres and Channels." *Journal of Broadcasting and Electronic Media* 51(1): 147–171.

Grabe, M. and D. Drew. 2007. "Crime Cultivations: Comparisons across Media Genres and Channels." *Journal of Broadcasting and Electronic Media* 51: 147–171.

Grabosky, P. 2001. "Virtual Criminality: Old Wine in New Bottles?" *Social and Legal Studies* 10: 243–249.

Graham, S. 1998. "Toward a Fifth Utility? On the Extension and Normalization of Public CCTV." In *Surveillance, Closed Circuit Television and Social Control*, eds. C. Norris, J. Moran, and G. Armstrong, 89–112. Aldershot, UK: Ashgate.

Graber, D. 1980. *Crime News and the Public*. New York: Praeger. Graber, D. 1994. "The Infotainment Quotient in Routine Television News: A Director's Perspective." *Discourse and Society 5*: 483–509.

Graham, S. 1999. "The Eyes Have It—CCTV as the 'Fifth Utility.'" *Town and Country Planning* 68: 312–315.

Grant, A. 1990. "The Videotaping of Police Interrogations in Canada." In *The Media and Criminal Justice Policy*, ed. R. Surette, 265–276. Springfield, IL: Thomas.

Grant, D. and D. Williams. 2011. "The Importance of Perceiving Social Contexts When Predicting Crime and Antisocial Behavior in CCTV Images." *Legal and Criminological Psychology* 16: 307–322.

Greek, C. 1996. "O. J. and the Internet: The First Cybertrial." In *Representing O. J.: Murder, Criminal Justice and Mass Culture*, ed. G. Barak, 64–77. Albany, New York: Harrow and Heston.

Green, M., J. Garst, T. Brock, and S. Chung. 2006. "Fact versus Fiction Labeling: Persuasion Parity Despite Heightened Scrutiny of Fact." *Media Psychology*, 8: 267–285.

Green, D. 2005. "Public Opinion versus Public Judgment about Crime." *British Journal of Criminology* 46: 131–154.

Green, M. and T. Brock. 2000. "The Role of Transportation in the Persuasiveness of Public Narratives. *Journal of Personality and Social Psychology* 79(3): 701–721.

Greenfield, S. and G. Osborn. 2003. "Film Lawyers: above and beyond the Law." In *Criminal Visions: Media Representations of Crime and Justice*, ed. P. Mason, 238–253. Devon, UK: W. H. A.

Greenwood, C. 2011, June 15. "Woman Juror Faces Jail after Facebook Chat." *Mail Online*.

Greitemeyer, T. 2001. "Effects of Prosocial Media on Social Behavior: When and Why Does Media Exposure Affect Helping and Aggression?" *Current Directions in Psychological Science* 20: 251–255.

Greer, C. 2003. *Sex Crime and the Media*. Cullompton, UK: Willan.

Greer, C. 2006. "Delivering Death: Capital Punishment, Botched Executions and the American News Media." In *Captured by the Media: Prison Discourse in Popular Culture*, ed. P. Mason, 84–102. Cullompton, UK: Willan.

Greer, C. 2009. *Crime and Media: A Reader*. London, UK: Routledge.

Greitemeyer, T. and S. Osswald. 2010. "Effects of Prosocial Video Games on Prosocial Behavior." *Journal of Personality and Social Psychology* 98: 211–221.

Grey, S. and D. Carvajal. 2007. "Secret Prisons in 2 Countries Held Qaeda Suspects, Report Says." *The New York Times*. June 8: A12. Downloaded January 19, 2010 from http://proquest.umi.com/.

Griffin, T. 2010. "An Empirical Examination of Amber Alert 'Successes.'" *Journal of Criminal Justice* 38(5): 1053–1062.

Griffin, T., and M. Miller. 2008. "Child Abduction, AMBER Alert, and Crime Control Theater." *Criminal Justice Review* 33(2): 159–176.

Grimes, J. N. 2010. "The Social Construction of Social Problems: 'Three Strikes and You're Out' in the Mass Media." *Journal of Criminal Justice and Law Review* 2(1/2): 39–55.

Grimes, T., J. Anderson, and L. Bergen. 2008. *Media Violence and Aggression: Science and Ideology*. Thousand Oaks, CA: Sage.

Grochowski, T. 2006. "Running in Cyberspace." *Television and New Media* 7(4): 361–382.

Grodal, T. 2003. "Stories for Eye, Ear and Muscles." In *The Video Game Theory Reader*, eds. M. Wolf and B. Perron, 129–155. New York: Routledge.

Grodal, T. 2003. "Video Games and the Pleasures of Control." In *Media Entertainment*, eds. D. Zillmann and P. Vorderer, 197–212. Mahwah, NJ: Erlbaum.

Grodal, T. 2003a. "Video Games and the Pleasures of Control." In *Media Entertainment*, eds. D. Zillman and P. Vorderer, 197–212. Mahwah, NJ: Erlbaum.

Grodal, T. 2003b. "Stories for Eye, Ear, and Muscles." In *The Video Game Theory Reader*, eds. M. Wolf and B. Perron, 129–155. New York: Routledge.

Grow, B. 2010, Dec 8. "As Jurors Go Online, U.S. Trials Go Off Track." Dec. 8, Reuters.com

Gunnarsson, H. 2011. "Friending Your Enemies, Tweeting Your Trials: Using Social Media Ethically." *Illinois Bar Journal* 99: 500–504.

Gunter, B. 2008. "Media Violence: Is There a Case for Causality?" *American Behavioral Scientist* 51(8): 1061–1122.

Gupta, D. and M. Kusam. 2005. "Suicide Bombing as a Strategic Weapon: An Empirical Investigation of HAMAS and Islamic Jihad." *Terrorism and Political Violence* 17: 573–598.

Hagell, A. and T. Newburn. 1994. *Young Offenders and the Media: Viewing Habits and Preferences*. London: Policy Studies Institute.

Haggerty, K. and A. Gozso. 2005. "Seeing beyond the Ruins: Surveillance as a Response to Terrorist Threats." *Canadian Journal of Sociology* 30(2): 169–187.

Haines, A. and H. Wells. 2012. "Persecution or Protection? Understanding the Differential Public Response to Two Road-Based Surveillance Systems." *Criminology & Criminal Justice* 12(3): 257–273.

Hale, D. 1998. "Keeping Women in Their Place: An Analysis of Policewomen in Video, 1972–1996. In *Popular Culture, Crime and Justice.*, eds. F. Bailey and D. Hale, 159–179. Belmont, CA: Wadsworth.

Hall, S., C. Chritcher, T. Jefferson, J. Clarke, and B. Roberts. 1981. "The Social

Production of News: Mugging in the Media." In *The Manufacture of News*, eds. S. Cohen and J. Young, 335–367. Thousand Oaks, CA: Sage.

Hallett, M. and D. Powell. 1995. "Backstage with COPS: The Dramaturgical Reification of Police Subculture in American Crime Infotainment." *American Journal of Police 14*(1): 101–129.

Hamm, M. 2008. "Prisoner Radicalization: Assessing the Threat in U.S. Correctional Institutions." *NIJ Journal 261: 14–19*. Washington, DC: National Institute of Justice.

Handley, M. 2010. February 18. "How Prisoners Harass Their Victims Using Facebook." *Time*.

Hannaford-Agor, P., D. Rottman, and N. Waters. 2012. "Juror and Jury Use of New Media: A Baseline Exploration." *Perspectives on State Court Leadership*. Washington, DC: Bureau of Justice Assistance.

Harding R. 1996. "Celluloid Death: Cinematic Depictions of Capital Punishment." *University of San Francisco Law Review 30*(4): 1167–1179.

Haridakis, P. 2002. "Viewer Characteristics, Exposure to Television Violence, and Aggression." *Media Psychology 4*(4): 323–352.

Hariman, R. 1990. "Performing the Laws: Popular Trials and Social Knowledge." In *Popular Trials: Rhetoric, Mass Media, and the Law*, ed. R. Hariman, 17–30. Tuscaloosa: University of Alabama Press.

Hartnagel, T. and L. Templeton. 2012. "Emotions about Crime and Attitudes to Punishment." *Punishment & Society 14*(2): 452–474.

Hayes, M. 2003. "Political Violence, Irish Republicanism and the British Media: Semantics, Symbosis and the State." In *Criminal Visions: Media Representations of Crime and Justice*, ed. P. Mason, 133–155. Devon, UK: Willan.

Hayes, R. and L. Levett. 2012. "Community Members' Perceptions of the CSI Effect." *American Journal of Criminal Justice 38*(2): 216–235.

Hays, W. H. 1932. *President's Report to the Motion Picture Producers and Distributors' Association*. Washington, DC: U.S. Government Printing Office.

Hays-Smith, R. and L. Levett. 2011. Jury's Still Out: How Television and Crime Show Viewing Influence Jurors' Evaluations of Evidence." *Applied Psychology in Criminal Justice 7*: 29–46.

Hayward, K. and M. Presdee. (eds). 2010. *Framing Crime: Cultural Criminology and the Image*. New York: Routledge.

Heath, L., L. Bresolin, and R. Rinaldi. 1969. "Effects of Media Violence on Children: A Review of the Literature." *Archives of General Psychiatry 46*: 376–379.

Heath, L. and J. Petraitis. 1987. "Television Viewing and Fear of Crime: Where Is the Mean World?" *Basic and Applied Social Psychology 8*: 97–123.

Helfgott, J. 2008. *Criminal Behavior: Theories, Typologies, and Criminal Justice*. Thousand Oaks, CA: Sage.

Heller, M. and S. Polsky. 1976. *Studies in Violence and Television*. New York: American Broadcasting Company.

Hennigan, K., L. Heath, J. D. Wharton, M. Del Rosario, T. Cook, and B. Calder. 1982. "Impact of the Introduction of Television on Crime in the United States." *Journal of Personality and Social Psychology 42*: 461–477.

Hentschel, C. 2007. "Making (In)Visible: CCTV, Living Cameras, and Their Objects in a Post-Apartheid Metropolis, *International Criminal Justice Review 17*(4): 289–303.

Herbert, R. 1999. *Oxford Companion to Crime and Mystery Writing*. Oxford, UK: Oxford University Press.

Hersh, S. 2004. *Chain of Command: The Road from 9/11 to Abu Ghraib*. New York: Harper Collins.

Hesse, M. 2009. "Portrayal of Psychopathy in the Movies." *International Review of Psychiatry 21*(3): 207–212.

Hetsroni, A. and R. Tukachinsky. 2006. "Television-world Estimates, Real-world Estimates, and Television Viewing: A New Scheme for Cultivation." *Journal of Communication 56*: 133–156.

Hickey, E. 2004. *Serial Murderers and Their Victims*. Belmont, CA: Wadsworth.

Hier, S., J. Greenberg, K. Walby, and D. Lett. 2007. "Media, Communication and the Establishment of Public Camera

Surveillance Programmes in Canada." *Media, Culture and Society* 29(5): 727–751.

Hinduja, S. and J. Patchin. 2009. *Bullying beyond the Schoolyard: Preventing and Responding to Cyberbullying.* Thousand Oaks, CA: Corwin.

Hirsch, P. 1980. "The 'Scary World' of the Nonviewer and Other Anomalies." *Communications Research* 7: 403–456.

Hirsch, P. 1981. "On Not Learning from One's Own Mistakes: A Reanalysis of Gerbner et al.'s Findings on Cultivation Analysis, Part II." *Communications Research* 8: 3–37.

Hochstetler, A. 2001. "Reporting of Executions in U.S. Newspapers." *Journal of Crime and Justice* 24(1): 1–11.

Holaday, P. and G. Stoddard. 1933. *Getting Ideas from the Movies.* New York: Macmillan.

Holden, R. 1986. "The Contagiousness of Aircraft Hijacking." *American Journal of Sociology* 91(4): 874–904.

Holmgren, J. and J. Fordham. 2011. "The CSI Effect and the Canadian and the Australian Jury." *Journal of Forensic Sciences* 56: 63–71.

Horne, C. 1996. "The Case for: CCTV Should Be Introduced." *International Journal of Risk, Security and Crime Prevention* 1(4): 317–326.

Houck, M. 2006. "CSI: Reality." *Scientific American, 295*: 84–89.

Hron, M. 2008. "Torture Goes Pop!" *Peace Review* 20(1): 22–30.

Huesmann, L. R. 1986. "Psychological Process Promoting the Relation between Exposure to Media Violence and Aggressive Behavior by the Viewer." *Journal of Social Issues* 42(3): 125–139.

Huesmann, L. R. 2007. "The Impact of Electronic Media Violence: Scientific Theory and Research." *Journal of Adolescent Health* 41: 6–13.

Huesmann, L. R. 1998. "The Role of Social Information Processing and Cognitive Schema in the Acquisition and Maintenance of Habitual Aggressive Behavior." In *Human Aggression*, eds. R. Geen and E. Donnerstein, 73–109. New York: Academic Press.

Huesmann, L. R. and L. Taylor. 2006. "The Role of Media Violence in Violent Behavior." *Annual Review Public Health* 27: 393–415.

Huesmann, L. R., J. Moise-Titus, C. Podolski, and L. Eron. 2003. "Longitudinal Relations between Children's Exposure to TV Violence and Their Aggressive and Violent Behavior in Young Adulthood: 1977–1992." *Developmental Psychology* 39(1): 201–221.

Huey, L. and R. Broll. 2012. "All It Takes Is One TV Show to Ruin It: A Police Perspective on Police–Media Relations in the Era of Expanding Prime Time Crime Markets." *Policing & Society* 22(4): 384–396.

Hughes, H. 1940. *News and the Human Interest Story.* Chicago: University of Chicago Press.

Hunter, D., R. Lobato, M. Richardson, and J. Thomas. 2012. *Amateur Media: Social, Cultural and Legal Perspectives.* New York: Routledge.

Hunter, S. 1988. "Terrorists in Prison: Security Concerns and Management Strategies." *Corrections Today* 50(4): 30, 32, 34.

Hussain, A. 2010. "(Re)Presenting Muslims on North American Television." *Contemporary Islam* 4: 55–75.

Ibarra, P. and J. Kitsuse. 1993. "Vernacular Constituents of Moral Discourse: An Interactionist Proposal for the Study of Social Problems." In *Reconsidering Social Construction*, eds. J. Holstein and G. Miller, 25–58. New York: Aldine de Gruyter.

Inciardi, J. and J. Dee. 1987. "From the Keystone Cops to Miami Vice: Images of Policing in American Popular Culture." *Journal of Popular Culture* 21: 84–102.

Innes, M. 2003. "'Signal Crimes': Detective Work, Mass Media and Constructing Collective Memory." In *Criminal Visions: Media Representations of Crime and Justice*, ed. P. Mason, 13–32. Cullompton, UK: Willan.

Innes, M. 2004. "Signal Crimes and Signal Disorders: Notes on Deviance as Communicative Action." *British Journal of Sociology* 55(3): 335–355.

Isaacs, N. 1961. "The Crime of Crime Reporting." *Crime and Delinquency* 7: 312–320.

Ivory, J., A. Williams, J. Hatch, and D. Covucci. 2007. "Terrorism in Film Trailers: Demographics, Portrayals, Violence, and Changes in Content after September 11, 2001." Paper presented in August at Association for Education in Journalism and Mass Communication, Washington, DC

Iyengar, S. 1991. *Is Anyone Responsible? How Television Frames Political Issues.* Chicago: University of Chicago Press.

Jacobs, J. and H. Brooks. 1983. "The Mass Media and Prison News." In *New Perspectives on Prisons and Imprisonment*, ed. James B. Jacobs, 106–115. Ithaca, New York: Cornell University Press.

Jarvis, B. 2007. "Monsters Inc.: Serial Killers and Consumer Culture." *Crime, Media, Culture 3*: 326–344.

Jefferis, E., R. Kaminski, S. Holmes, and D. Hanley. 1997. "The Effect of a Videotaped Arrest on Public Perceptions of Police Use of Force." *Journal of Criminal Justice 25*(5): 381–395.

Jenkins, P. 1994. *Using Murder: The Social Construction of Serial Murder.* Hawthorne, New York: Aldine De Gruyter.

Jeong, J., S. Shin, H, Kim, Y. Hong, S. Hwang, and E. Lee. 2012. "The Effects of Celebrity Suicide on Copycat Suicide Attempt: A Multi-Center Observational Study." *Social Psychiatry and Psychiatric Epidemiology 47*(4): 957–965.

Jenkins, P. 1998. *Moral Panic: Changing Concepts of the Child Molester in Modern America.* New Haven, CT: Yale University Press.

Jewkes, Y. 2004. *Media and Crime.* London, UK: Sage.

Jewkes, Y. 2006. "Creating a Stir? Prisons, Popular Media and the Power to Reform." In *Captured by the Media: Prison Discourse in Popular Culture*, ed. P. Mason, 137–153. Cullompton, UK: Willan Publishing.

Jewkes, Y. 2010. "Much Ado about Nothing? Representation and Realities of Online Soliciting of Children." *Journal of Sexual Aggression 16*(1): 5–18.

Jewkes, Y. 2011. *Media & Crime.* Los Angeles, CA: Sage.

Jo, E., and L. Berkowitz. 1994. "A Priming Effect Analysis of Media Influences: An Update." In *Media Effects Advances in Theory and Research*, eds. J. Bryant and D. Zillman. Hillsdale, NJ: Erlbaum.

Johnson, J. 2008. "Voir Dire: To Google or Not to Google." *American Bar Newsletter 5*(1): 1–4.

Johnson, J., P. Cohen, E. Smailes, S. Kasen, and J. Brook. 2002. "Television Viewing and Aggressive Behavior during Adolescence and Adulthood." *Science 295*: 2468–2471.

Johnston, J., D. Hawkins, and A. Michner. 1994. "Homicide Reporting in Chicago Dailies." *Journalism Quarterly 71*: 860–872.

Jones, D. and M. Wolfe. 2010. "Public Policy and the Mass Media: An Information Processing Approach." In *Public Policy and Mass Media: The Interplay of Mass Communication and Political Decision Making*, eds. S. Koch-Baumgarter and L. Voltmer, 17–43. London: Routledge.

Jones, E. T. 1976. "The Press as Metropolitan Monitor." *Public Opinion Quarterly 40*: 239–244.

Jose, R. and G. Galdon. 2011. "The Impact of CCTV on Fundamental Rights and Crime Prevention Strategies: The Case of the Catalan Control Commission of Video Surveillance Devices." *Computer Law and Security Review 27*(2): 169–174.

Kakutani, M. 2013., April 23. "Unraveling Boston Suspects' Online Lives, Link by Link." Apr. 23, *The New York Times.*

Kaplan, J. and J. Skolnick. 1982. *Criminal Justice.* Mineola, New York: Foundation Press.

Karpf, J. 2013. "The Cost of Convenience: The Extent of the Reasonable Expectation of Privacy in the Internet Age." University of Central Florida Honors Thesis, Department of Legal Studies.

Kerr, J. 2013. *Rethinking Aggression and Violence in Sport.* New York: Routledge.

Keval, H. and M. Sasse. 2010. "'Not the Usual Suspects': A Study of Factors Reducing the Effectiveness of CCTV." *Security Journal 23*: 134–154.

Kieby, D. 2003. "Prison Life through a Lens." *Prison Service News 215*: 22–23.

Kingshott, B. 2011. "Effective Police Management of the Media." *Criminal Justice Studies 24*(3): 241–253.

Kinlay, A. 2010. "Televised Court Proceedings: The Relationship between the Media, Punitive Public Perceptions and Populist Policy." *Flinders Journal of History & Politics 27*: 71–85.

Kiousis, S. 2002. "Interactivity: A Concept Explication." *New Media and Society 4*(3): 355–383.

Kirtley, J. 1990. "Shield Laws and Reporter's Privilege—A National Assessment." In *The Media and Criminal Justice Policy*, ed. R. Surette, 163–176. Springfield, IL: Thomas.

Kirtley, J. 1995. "A Leap Not Supported by History: The Continuing Story of Cameras in the Federal Courts." *Government Information Quarterly 12*: 367–389.

Kohm, S. and P. Greenhill. 2011. "Pedophile Crime Films as Popular Criminology: A Problem of Justice?" *Theoretical Criminology 15*(2): 195–215.

Kohm, S., C. Waid-Lindberg, M. Weinrath, T. Shelley, and R. Dobbs. 2012. "The Impact of Media on Fear of Crime among University Students: A Cross-National Comparison." *Canadian Journal of Criminology & Criminal Justice 54*(1): 67–100.

Kooistra, P., J. Mahoney, and S. Westervelt. 1998. "The World of Crime According to Cops." In *Entertaining Crime: Television Reality Programs*, eds. M. Fishman and G. Cavender, 141–158. New York: Aldine de Gruyter.

Kort-Butler, L.A. 2012. "Rotten, Vile, and Depraved! Depictions of Criminality in Superhero Cartoons." *Deviant Behavior 33*(7): 566–581.

Krahe, B., I. Moller, L. Huesmann, L. Kirwil, J. Felber, and A. Berger. 2001. "Desensitization to Media Violence: Links with Habitual Media Violence Exposure, Aggressive Cognitions, and Aggressive Behavior." *Journal of Personality and Social Psychology 100*(4): 630–646.

Kravets, D. 2010, January 12. "U.S. Courts Split on Internet Bans." Wired.com November 8, 2013.

Kupchik, A. and N. Bracy. 2009. "The News Media on School Crime and Violence: Constructing Dangerousness and Fueling Fear." *Youth Violence and Juvenile Justice 7*: 136–155.

Kwan M., P. Wei and K. Julian. 2010. "Will the Experience of Playing a Violent Role in a Video Game Influence People's Judgments of Violent Crimes?" *Computers in Human Behaviors 26*: 1019–1023.

Lackey, C. 2001. "Visualizing White-Collar Crime Generic Imagery in Popular Film." *Visual Sociology 16*(2): 75–93.

Lambert, P. 2011. "Television Courtroom Broadcasting Research: the Problem, the Challenge and Eye Tracking." *Communications Law: Journal of Computer, Media & Telecommunications Law 16*(2): 52–59.

Laptosky, J. 2010. "Protecting the Cloak and Dagger with an Illusory Shield: How the Proposed Free Flow of Information Act Falls Short." *Federal Communications Law Journal 62*(2): 403–434.

Lasker, A. 2012. "Cameras Come to Illinois Trial Courts." *Illinois Bar Journal 100*(3): 126–127.

Lane, J. and J. Meeker. 2003. "Ethnicity, Information Sources, and Fear of Crime." *Deviant Behavior 24*: 1–26.

Langer, G. 2004. *Legacy of Suspicion*. New York : ABC News Poll, July.

Lasorsa, D. and W. Wanta. 1990. "Effects of Personal, Interpersonal and Media Experiences on Issue Saliences." *Journalism Quarterly 67*: 804–813.

Latanya, A. C. and N. Abeles. 2009. "Ethics, Prisoner Interrogation, National Security, and the Media." *Psychological Services 6*(1): 11–21.

La Vigne, N., S. Lowry, J. Markman, and A. Dwyer. 2011. *Evaluating the Use of Public Surveillance Cameras for Crime Control and Prevention*. Washington, DC: Urban Institute Justice Policy Center, COPS Dept. of Justice.

Lavrakas, P., D. Rosenbaum, and A. Lurigio. 1990. "Media Cooperation with Police: The Case of Crime Stoppers." In *Media and Criminal Justice Policy*, ed. R. Surette, 225–242. Springfield, IL: Thomas.

Lawrence, R. 2000. *The Politics of Force: Media and the Construction of Police Brutality*. Berkeley, CA: University of California Press.

"Law School Hosts Panel on Social Media as Evidence." 2010, Feb 5. University of California Davis School of Law.

Lee, J., N. Park, and S. Jin. 2006. "Narrative and Interactivity in Computer Games." In *Playing Video Games: Motives, Responses and Consequence*, eds. P. Vorderer and J. Bryant, 259–274. Mahwah, NJ: Lawrence Erlbaum Associates.

Lee, K. M., W. Peng, and J. Klein. (2010). "Will the Experience of Playing a Violent Role in a Video Game Influence People's Judgments of Violent Crimes?" *Computers in Human Behaviors 26*: 1019–1023.

Leishman, F. and P. Mason. 2003. *Policing and the Media: Facts, Fictions, and Factions*. Devon, UK: Willan.

Leitch, T., 2002. *Crime Films*. Cambridge, UK: Cambridge University Press.

Lenz, T. 2003. *Changing Images of Law in Film and Television Crime Stories*. New York: Peter Lang.

Levenson, J. 2001. "Inside Information: Prisons and the Media." *Criminal Justice Matters 43*: 14–15.

Leverentz, A. 2012. "Narratives of Crime and Criminals: How Places Socially Construct the Crime Problem." *Sociological Forum 27*(2): 348–371.

Levi, M. 2001. "White-Collar Crime in the News." *Criminal Justice Matters 43*: 24–25.

Levi, M. 2006. "The Media Construction of Financial White-Collar Crimes." *British Journal of Criminology 46*: 1037–1057.

Levi, M. 2009. "Suite Revenge: The Shaping of Folk Devils and Moral Panics about White-Collar Crime." *British Journal of Criminology 49*(1): 48–67.

Levi, M., and A. Pithouse. 2006. *White Collar Crime and Its Victims: The Social and Media Construction of Business Fraud*. Oxford: Clarendon Press.

Levi, M. and J. Burrows. 2008. "Measuring the Impact of Fraud in the UK." *British Journal of Criminology 48*: 292–318.

Lichter, L. S. and S. R. Lichter. 1983. *Prime Time Crime*. Washington, DC: Media Institute.

Lichter, S. R., L. S. Lichter, and S. Rothman. 1994. *Prime Time*. Washington, DC: Regnery.

Lindesmith, A. 1965. *The Addict and the Law*. Bloomington: Indiana University Press.

Lindgren, S. 2011. "YouTube Gunman? Mapping Participatory Media Discourse on School Shooting Videos." *Media, Culture & Society 33*(1), 123–136.

Lindlof, T. 1988. "Media Audiences as Interpretive Communities." In *Communication Yearbook 11*, ed. J. Anderson, 81–107. Newbury Park, CA: Sage.

Ling, R. and S. Campbell. 2010. *The Reconstruction of Space and Time: Mobile Communication Practices*. Piscataway, NJ: Transaction Press.

Lippmann, W. 1922. *Public Opinion*. New York: Macmillan.

Lipschultz, J. and M. Hilt. 2002. *Crime and Local Television News: Dramatic, Breaking, and Live from the Scene*. Mahwah, NJ: Erlbaum.

Lister, M., J. Dovey, S. Giddings, I. Grant, and K. Kelly. 2003. *New Media: A Critical Introduction*, New York: Routledge.

Littlefield, M. 2011. "Historicizing CSI and Its Effect(s): The Real and the Representational in American Scientific Detective Fiction and Print News Media, 1902–1935." *Crime, Media, Culture 7*(2): 133–148.

Livingstone, N. 1982. *The War against Terrorism*. Lexington, MA: Heath.

Locker, M. 2012., Dec 5. "Women Brags about Robbery on YouTube." Dec. 5, http://newsfeed.time.com/2012/12/05/women-brags-about-robbery-on-youtube

Loften, J. 1966. *Justice and the Press*. Boston, MA: Beacon Press.

Loftus, B. and Goold, B. 2012. "Covert Surveillance and the Invisibilities of Policing." *Theoretical Criminology 15*(3): 275–288.

Lomell, H. 2004. "Targeting the Unwanted: Video Surveillance and Categorical Exclusion in Oslo, Norway?" *Surveillance and Society 2*(2/3): 3472–3561.

Lotz, R. 1991. *Crime and the American Press*. New York: Praeger.

Lowery, S. and M. De Fleur. 1983. *Milestones in Mass Communication Research*. White Plains, New York: Longman.

Lynch, M., P. Stretesky, and P. Hammond. 2000. "Media Coverage of Chemical Crimes, Hillsborough County, Florida, 1987–97." *British Journal of Criminology 40*: 112–126.

Lyndon, A., J. Bonds-Raacke, and A. Cratty. 2011. "College Students' Facebook Stalking of Ex-Partners." *Cyberpsychology, Behavior, and Social Networking 14*(12): 711–716.

Lyon D. 2006. *Theorizing the Panopticon and Beyond*. Cullompton, UK: Willan.

Mancini, D. 2011. "The CSI Effect Reconsiders: Is it Moderated by Need for Cognition?" *North American Journal of Psychology 13*(1): 155–174.

Mann, C. and M. Zatz. 2002. *Images of Color Images of Crime: Readings*. Los Angeles, CA: Roxbury Publishing.

Manning, P. 1998. "Media Loops." In *Popular Culture, Crime and Justice*, eds. F. Bailey and D. Hale, 25–39. Belmont, CA: Wadsworth.

Maratea, R. 2008. "The E-Rise and Fall of Social Problems: The Blogosphere as a Public Arena." *Social Problems* 55(1): 139–160.

Marcus, P. 1982. "The Media in the Court-room: Attending, Reporting, Televising Criminal Cases." *Indiana Law Journal* (Spring): 235–287.

Maricopa County. 2005. *The CSI Effect and its Real-Life Impact on Justice: A Study by the Maricopa County Attorney's Office.* www .maricopacountyattorney.org/Press/PDF/ CSIReport.pdf.

Marsh, H. 1991. "A Comparative Analysis of Crime Coverage in Newspapers in the United States and Other Countries from 1960 to 1989: A Review of the Literature." *Journal of Criminal Justice* 19:67–80.

Marsh, I. and G. Melville. 2009. *Crime, Justice, Media.* London: Routledge.

Martens, F. and M. Cunningham-Niederer. 1985. "Media Magic, Mafia Mania." *Federal Probation* 49(2): 60–68.

Marx, G. 1988. *Undercover: Police Surveillance in America.* Berkeley: University of California Press.

Marx, G. 1996. "Electric Eye in the Sky: Some Reflections on the New Surveillance and Popular Culture." In *Computers, Surveillance, and Privacy,* eds. D. Lyon and E. Zureik, 193–233. Minneapolis: University of Minnesota Press.

Mason, P. 2000. "Watching the Invisible: Televisual Portrayal of the British Prison 1980–1990." *International Journal of the Sociology of Law* 28: 33–44.

Mason, P. 2003. "The Screen Machine: Cinematic Representations of Prison." In *Criminal Visions: Media Representations of Crime and Justice,* ed. P. Mason, 278–297. Devon, UK: Willan.

Mason, P. 2006. *Captured by the Media; Prison Discourse in Popular Culture.* Cullompton, UK: Willan.

Mason, P. 2006. "Prison Decayed: Cinematic Penal Discourse and Populism 1995–2005." *Social Semiotics* 16(4): 607–626.

Mason, P. 2006. "Lies, Distortion and What Doesn't Work: Monitoring Prison Stories in the British Media." *Crime, Media Culture* 2(3): 251–267.

Mason, P. 2007. "Misinformation, Myth and Distortion: How the Press Construct Imprisonment in Britain." *Journalism Studies* 8(3): 481–496.

Mathiesen, T. 1987. "The Eagle and the Sun: On Panoptical Systems and Mass Media in Modern Society." In *Transcarceration: Essays in the Sociology of Social Control,* eds. J. Lowman, R. Menzies, and T. S. Palys, 59–76. Brookfield, VT: Gower.

Mathiesen, T. 1990. *Prison on Trial: A Critical Assessment.* Belmont, CA: Sage.

Mathiesen, T. 2000. *Prisons on Trial.* Winchester, UK: Waterside Press.

Mathiesen, T. 2001. "Television, Public Space and Prison Population." *Punishment and Society* 3(1): 35–42.

Mawby, R. 2003. "Completing the 'Half-Formed Picture'? Media Images of Policing." In *Criminal Visions: Media Representations of Crime and Justice,* ed. P. Mason, 214–237. Devon, UK: Willan.

Mawby, R. and J. Brown. 1984. "Newspaper Images of the Victim: A British Study." *Victimology* 9(1): 82–94.

Maxson, C., K. Hennigan, and D. Sloane. 2003. *Factors That Influence Public Opinion of the Police.* Washington, DC: National Institute of Justice.

Matyszczyk, C. 2009., Sept. 17. "Facebook Break Leads to Burglary Suspect." Sept. 17, CNET News.

Mazerolle, L., D. Hurley and M. Chamlin. 2002. *Social Behavior in Public Space: An Analysis of Behavioral Adaptations to CCTV.* Security Journal 15: 59–75.

Mazur, A. 1982. "Bomb Threats and the Mass Media: Evidence for a Theory of Suggestion." *American Sociological Review* 47: 407–411.

Mazur, J. 2006. *Learning and Behavior.* Upper Saddle River, NJ: Pearson/Prentice Hall.

McLean, S. and R. Worden. 2010. *Public Surveillance Cameras: A Synopsis.* Albany, New York: John F. Finn Institute for Public Safety.

McCombs, M. 2004. *Setting the Agenda: The Mass Media and Public Opinion.* Cambridge, UK: Polity Press.

Meloy, J. and K. Mohandie. 2001. "Investigating the Role of Screen Violence in Specific Homicide Cases." *Journal of Forensic Science* 46(5): 1113–1118.

Meyers, M. 1994. "News of Battering." *Journal of Communication 44*: 47–63.

Meyers, M. 1996. *News Coverage of Violence against Women*. Thousand Oaks, CA: Sage.

Meyers, W. 2002. *Juvenile Sexual Homicide*. New York: Academic Press.

Meyrowitz, J. 1985. *No Sense of Place*. New York: Oxford University Press.

Miller, D. L. (2000). *Introduction to Collective Behavior and Collective Action*. Prospect Heights, IL: Waveland Press.

Miller, T. 2012. "Terrorism and Global Popular Culture." In *Media and Terrorism Global Perspectives*, eds. D. Freedman and D. Thussu, 97–115. Thousand Oaks, CA: Sage.

Miller, M., T. Griffin, S. Clinkinbeard, and R. Thomas. 2009. "The Psychology of AMBER Alert: Unresolved Issues and Implications." *Social Science Journal 42*: 111–123.

Minnebo, J. 2006. "The Relation between Psychological Distress, Television Exposure, and Television-Viewing Motives in Crime Victims." *Media Psychology 8*(2): 65–93.

Mittell, J. 2013. "Wikis and Participatory Fandom." In *The Participatory Cultures Handbook*, eds. L. Lieurouw and S. Livingstone, 35–42. New York: Routledge.

Moore, D. 2011. "The Benevolent Watch: Therapeutic Surveillance in Drug Treatment Court." *Theoretical Criminology 15*(3): 253–268.

Mopas, M. 2007. "Examining the CSI Effect through an ANT Lens." *Crime, Media, Culture 31*(1): 110–117.

Morgan, M. and J. Shanahan. 1997. "Two Decades of Cultivation Research: An Appraisal and Meta-Analysis." *Communication Yearbook 20*: 1–45.

Mundorf, N. and K. Laird. 2002. "Social and Psychological Effects of Information Technologies and Other Interactive Media." In *Media Effects: Advances in Theory and Research*, eds. J. Bryant and D. Zillmann, 583–602. Mahwah, NJ: Lawrence Erlbaum Associates.

Murray, J. 2008. "Media Violence: The Effects are Both Real and Strong." *American Behavioral Scientist 51*(8): 1212–1230.

Musa, A. 2012. "Socio-Economic Incentives, New Media and the Boko Haram Campaign of Violence in Northern Nigeria." *Journal of African Media Studies 4*(1): 111–124.

Myers, D. 2000. "The Diffusion of Collective Violence: Infectiousness, Susceptibility, and Mass Media Networks." *American Journal of Sociology. 106*(1): 173–208.

Myers, W., C. Eggleston, and P. Smoak. 2003. "A Media Violence-Inspired Juvenile Sexual Homicide Offender 13 Years Later." *Journal of Forensic Science, 48*(6) 1–6.

Nacos, B. 2007. *Mass-Mediated Terrorism*. Lanham, MD: Rowan and Littlefield.

Nasheri, H. 2002. *Crime and Justice in the Age of Court TV*. New York: LFB Scholarly Publishing LLC.

National Institute of Mental Health. 1982. *Television and Behavior: Ten Years of Scientific Progress and Implications for the Eighties*. Vol. *1*. Summary Report. Rockville, MD: U.S. Government Printing Service.

Newburn, T. 1994. *Young Offenders and the Media: Viewing Habits and Preferences*. London: Policy Studies Institute.

Newburn, T. and S. Hayman. 2002. *Policing, Surveillance and Social Control: CCTV and Police Monitoring of Suspects*. Portland, UK: Willan.

"New Media and the Courts." 2010. Conference of Court Public Information Officers. www.ccpio.org

Nichols, L. 1999. "White-Collar Cinema: Changing Representations of Upper World Deviance in Popular Films." *Perspectives on Social Problems 11*: 61–84.

Nichols-Pethick, J. 2012. *TV Cops: The Contemporary American Television Police Drama*. New York: Routledge.

Norris, C. and G. Armstrong. 1999. *The Maximum Surveillance Society: The Rise of CCTV*. Oxford, UK: Berg.

Norris, C., M. McCahill, and D. Wood. 2004. "The Growth of CCTV: A Global Perspective on the International Diffusion of Video Surveillance in Publicly Accessible Space." *Surveillance and Society 2*(2/3): 110–135.

Nuss, J. 2011, December 8. *"Death Row Inmate Gets New Trial after Juror Tweet."* http://Usatoday30.usatoday.com/tech/news/story/2011-12-08/juror-tweet-death-row/51741370/1 September 17, 2013

Nyberg, A. 1998. "Comic Books and Juvenile Delinquency: A Historical Perspective." In *Popular Culture, Crime, and Justice*, eds. F. Bailey and D. Hale, 71–70. Belmont, CA: Wadsworth.

Oberdorfer, D. 1977. *TET!* Baltimore, MD: Johns Hopkins University Press.

O'Keefe, G. and K. Reid. 1990. "Media Public Information Campaigns and Criminal Justice Policy: Beyond McGruff." In *Media and Criminal Justice Policy*, ed. R. Surette, 209–224. Springfield, IL: Thomas.

O'Keefe, G., D. Rosenbaum, P. Lavrakas, K. Reid, and R. Botta. 1996. *Taking a Bite Out of Crime*. Thousand Oaks, CA: Sage.

Oliver, M. 1994. "Portrayals of Crime, Race, and Aggression in Reality Based Police Shows: A Content Analysis." *Journal of Broadcasting & Electronic Media 38*: 179–192.

Oliver, W. and N. Marion. 2013. *Crime, History, and Hollywood*. Durham, NC: Carolina Academic Press.

O'Sullivan, S. 2001. "Representations of Prison in Nineties Hollywood Cinema: From Con Air to the Shawshank Redemption." *Howard Journal of Criminal Justice 40*(4): 317–334.

Ovalle, D. and D. Ducassi. 2013., August 9. "Facebook Status: I Killed My Wife." Aug. 9, A1. *Miami Herald*, A1.

Owns, R. and C. Murphey. 2012, March 17. "Growing Number of "Project X' Party Copycats Lead to Arrests Nationwide." http:abcnews.go.com/US/.

Packer, H. 1968. *The Limits of the Criminal Sanction*. Stanford, CA: Stanford University Press.

Paletz, D. and A. Schmid. 1992. *Terrorism and the Media*. Newbury Park, CA: Sage.

Pape, R. 2003. "The Strategic Logic of Suicide Terrorism." *American Political Science Review 97*: 1–19.

Papke, D. 1987. *Framing the Criminal*. Hamden, CT: Archon Books.

Park, H., G. Oh, and S. Paek. 2012. "Measuring the Crime Displacement and Diffusion of Benefit Effects of Open-Street CCTV in South Korea." *International Journal of Law, Crime and Justice 4*: 179–191.

Parks, M. R. and L. D. Roberts. 1998. "Making MOOsic: The Development of Personal Relationships Online and a Comparison to Their Off-line Counterparts." *Journal of Social and Personal Relationships 15*(4): 517–537.

Parrish, P. 1993. "Police and the Media." *FBI Law Enforcement Bulletin 62*(9): 24–25.

Patrick, G. 2008, November 24. "Juror Axed for Verdict Poll on Net." www.thesun.co.uk/sol/homepage/news/article1963544.ece.

Patry, M., V. Stinson, and S. Smith. 2008. "CSI Effect: Is Popular Television Transforming Canadian Society?" In *Communications in Questions: Canadian Perspectives on Controversial Issues in Communication Studies*, eds. J. Greenberg and C. Elliott, 291–310. Ontario: Thompson Nelson.

Patton, P. 1995. "Caught." *Wired* (January): 125–130.

Payne, G. 2007. "Brutal Cops, News Coverage, and Public Perceptions of Law Enforcement: An Experimental Investigation of Reality Construction." *Journal of Humanities and Social Sciences 1*(2): 1–10.

Pease, S. and C. Love. 1984. "The Copycat Crime Phenomenon." In *Justice and the Media*, ed. R. Surette, 199–211. Springfield, IL: Thomas.

Penfold, R. 2004. "The Star's Image, Victimization and Celebrity Culture." *Punishment and Society 6*(3): 289–302.

Penfold-Mounce, R. 2009. *Celebrity Culture and Crime*. London, UK: Palgrave.

Pennell, A. and K. Browne. 1998. "Film Violence and Young Offenders." *Aggression and Violent Behvaior 4*(1): 13–28.

Perez, L., J. Jones, D. Englert, and D. Sachau. 2010. "Secondary Traumatic Stress and Burnout among Law Enforcement Investigators Exposed to Disturbing Media Images." *Journal of Police & Criminal Psychology 25*(2): 113–124.

Perlmutter, D. 2000. *Policing the Media: Street Cops and Public Perceptions of Law Enforcement*. Thousand Oaks, CA: Sage.

Perlroth, N. 2012, June 12. "After Rapes Involving Children, Skout, a Flirting App, Bans Minors." *The New York Times Online*.

Peterson, R. and L. L. Thurstone. 1933. *Motion Pictures and the Social Attitudes of Children*. New York: Macmillan.

Petty, R., J. Priester, and P. Brinol. 2002. "Mass Media Attitude Change: Implications of the

Elaboration Likelihood Model of Persuasion." In *Media Effects: Advances in Theory and Research*, eds. J. Bryant and D. Zillmann, 155–198. Mahwah, NJ: Erlbaum Publishers.

Pfeiffer, C., M. Windzio, and M. Kleimann. 2005. "Media Use and Its Impacts on Crime Perception, Sentencing Attitudes and Crime Policy." *European Journal of Criminology* 2(3): 259–285.

Pfuhl, E. 1992. "Crimestoppers: The Legitimation of Snitching." *Justice Quarterly* 9(3): 505–528.

Phillips, N. and S. Strobi. 2013. *Comic Book Crime: Truth, Justice, and the American Way*. New York: New York University Press.

Piza, E., J. Caplan and L. Kennedy. 2013. "Analyzing the Influence of Micro-Level Factors on CCTV Camera Effect." *Journal of Quantitative Criminology*. Published online May 31 DOI 10.1007/s10940-013-9202-5.

Podlas, K. 2006. "The CSI Effect: Exposing the Media Myth." *Media and Entertainment Law Journal 16*: 429–465.

Poland, J. 1988. *Understanding Terrorism*. Englewood Cliffs, NJ: Prentice Hall.

Polichak, J. and R. Gerrig. 2002. "Get Up and Win! Participatory Responses to Narrative." In *Narrative Impact*, eds, M. Green, J. Strange, and T. Brock, 71–95. Mahwah, NJ: Lawrence Erlbaum Associates.

Pontell, H. and G. Geis, 2010, "How to Effectively Get Crooks like Bernie Madoff in Dutch," *American Society of Criminology* 9(3): 475–481.

Potter G. and V. Kappeler. 2006. *Constructing Crime*. Prospects Heights, IL: Waveland.

Powell, A. 2009. "Wendy's Vandalism Prank on West Bank Leads to Arrest of Texas Teenager." *New Orleans Metro Crime and Court News*. http://www.nola.com/crime/index.ssf/2009/09/jpso_announces_arrest_in_broke.html

Poyntz, S. 1997. "Homey, I Shot the Kids: Hollywood and the War on Drugs." *Emergency Librarian 25*(2): 3–9.

Price, J., E. Merrill, and M. Clause. 1992. "The Depiction of Guns on Prime Time Television." *Journal of School Health 62*(1): 15–19.

Priest, D. 2005. "CIA Holds Terror Suspects in Secret Prisons." *The Washington Post*, Wednesday, Nov. 2. Downloaded January 20, 2010 from http://www.washingtonpost.com/.

Pritchard, D. 1985. "Race, Homicide and Newspapers." *Journalism Quarterly 62*: 500–507.

Pritchard, D. and K. Hughes. 1997. "Patterns of Deviance in Crime News." *Journal of Communication 47*(3): 49–67.

Protess, D., F. Cook, J. Doppelt, J. Ettema, M. Gordon, D. Leff, and P. Miller. 1991. *The Journalism of Outrage: Investigative Reporting and Agenda Building in America*. New York: Guilford Press.

"Public Confidence in Selected Institutions, 1973–1996." 1996. *Sourcebook of Criminal Justice Statistics 1995*, Table 2.9. Washington, DC: Bureau of Justice Statistics.

Quayle, E. and M. Taylor. 2003. *Child Pornography: An Internet Crime*. New York: Routledge.

Quinney, R. 1970. *The Social Reality of Crime*. Boston: Little, Brown and Co.

Rabe-Hemp, C. 2011. "Female Forces: Beauty, Brains, and a Badge." *Feminist Criminology* 6(2): 132–155.

Rafter, N. 2000. *Shots in the Mirror: Crime Films and Society*. Oxford, UK: Oxford University Press.

Rafter, N. 2001. "American Criminal Trial Films: An Overview of Their Development, 1930–2000." *Journal of Law and Society 28*(1): 9–24.

Rafter, N. 2007. "Crime, Film and Criminology: Recent Sex-Crime Movies." *Theoretical Criminology 11*(3): 403–420.

Raney, A. and J. Bryant. 2002. "Moral Judgment and Crime Drama: An Integrated Theory of Enjoyment." *Journal of Communication 52*(2): 402–415.

Rapping, E. 2003. *Law and Justice as Seen on TV*. New York: New York University Press.

Ratcliffe, J. 2006. *Video Surveillance of Public Places*. Response Guide No. 4. Washington, DC: Office of Community Oriented Policing. http://www.ocpa-oh.org/Security%20Technology/Video%20Surveillance%20-%20COPS.pdf

Rebovich, D. and J. Kane. 2002. "An Eye for an Eye in the Electronic Age: Gauging Public Attitude toward White Collar Crime and Punishment." *Journal of Economic Crime Management* 1(2): 1–19.

Reinarman, C. 1988. "The Social Construction of an Alcohol Problem: The Case of Mothers against Drunk Drivers and Social Control in the 1980s." *Theory and Society* 17: 91–120.

Reiner, R. 1981. "Keystone to Kojak: the Hollywood Cop." In *Cinema, Politics and Society in America*, eds. P. Davies and B. Neve, 196–220. New York: St.Martin's Press.

Reiner, R. 2000. *The Politics of the Police.* Oxford, UK: Oxford University Press.

Reiner, R. 2002. "Media Made Criminality: The Representation of Crime in the Mass Media." In *The Oxford Handbook of Criminology*, eds. M. Maguire, R. Morgan, and R. Reiner, 376–416. Oxford, UK: Oxford University Press.

Reiner, R., S. Livingstone, and J. Allen. 2000. "No More Happy Endings?" In *Crime, Risk and Insecurity*, eds. T. Hope and R. Sparks, 107–125. London: Routledge.

Reiner, R., S. Livingstone, and J. Allen. 2003. "From Law and Order to Lynch Mobs: Crime News since the Second World War." In *Criminal Visions: Media Representations of Crime and Justice*, ed. P. Mason, 13–32. Devon, UK: Willan.

Rennie, Y. 1978. *The Search for Criminal Man.* New York: Lexington Books.

Rennison, M. 2003. *Intimate Partner Violence, 1993–2001.* Washington DC: U.S. Dept. of Justice.

Rentschler, C. 2007. "Victims' Rights and the Struggle over Crime in the Media." *Canadian Journal of Communication* 32(2): 219–239.

Reporters Committee for Freedom of the Press. (nd). "Number of states with shield law climbs to 40" Downloaded June 18, 2013 from http://www.rcfp.org/browse-media-law-resources/news-media-law/news-media-law-summer-2011/number-states-shield-law-climbs.

Reyns, B. 2010. "A Situational Crime Prevention Approach to Cyberstalking Victimization." *Crime Prevention and Community Safety* 12(2): 99–118.

Rheingold, A., C. Campbell, S. Self-Brown, M. de Arellano, H. Resnick, and D. Kilpatrick. 2007. "Prevention of Child Sexual Abuse: Evaluation of a Community Media Campaign." *Child Maltreatment* 12(4): 352–363.

Rhineberger-Dunn, G. M. 2011. "Comparing Large and Small Metropolitan Newspaper Coverage of Delinquency with Arrest Data: Differential Coverage or More of the Same." *Criminal Justice Studies* 24(3): 269–290.

Rich, J. 2012. "New Media and the News Media: Too Much Media, *Llc v. Hale* and the Reporter's Privilege in the Digital Age." *Loyola of Los Angeles Law Review* 45(3): 963–983.

Richmond, D. 2007. "Can You Find Me Now: Tracking the Limits on Government Access to Cellular GPS Location Data. *Communication Law Conspectus* 16(1): 283–319.

Roane, K. 2005, April. "The CSI Effect." *U.S. News & World Report* 138(15): 48–54.

Robbers, M. 2008. "Blinded by Science: The Social Construction of Reality in Forensic Television Shows and Its Effect on Criminal Jury Trials." *Criminal Justice Policy Review* 19(1): 84–102.

Roberts, J. and A. Doob. 1990. "News Media Influences on Public Views on Sentencing." *Law and Human Behavior* 14(5): 451–468.

Roberts, J. and L. Stalans. 1997. *Public Opinion, Crime and Criminal Justice.* Boulder CO: Westview Press.

Robinson, M. 2005. *Justice Blind?* Upper Saddle River, NJ: Pearson Prentice-Hall.

Robinson, M. 2011. *Media Coverage of Crime and Criminal Justice.* Durham, NC: Carolina Academic Press.

Rogers, E. 2003. *Diffusion of Innovations.* New York: Free Press.

Rogers, E. and J. Dearing. 1988. "Agenda-Setting Research: Where Has It Been, Where Is It Going?" In *Communication Yearbook 11*, ed. J. A. Anderson, 555–594. Thousand Oaks, CA: Sage.

Rome, D. 2004. *Black Demons: The Media's Depiction of the African American Male Criminal Stereotype.* Westport, CT: Praeger.

Rosenbaum, D., A. Lurigio, and P. Lavrakas. 1986. *Crime Stoppers: A National Evaluation of Program Operations and Effects*. Evanston, IL: Center for Urban Affairs and Policy Research, Northwestern University.

Rosenbaum, D., A. Lurigio, and P. Lavrakas. 1989. "Enhancing Citizen Participation and Solving Serious Crime: A National Evaluation of Crime Stoppers Programs." *Crime and Delinquency 35*: 401–420.

Roshier, B. 1981. "The Selection of Crime News in the Press." In *The Manufacture of News*, eds. S. Cohen and J. Young, 40–51. Thousand Oaks, CA: Sage.

Roskos-Ewoldsen, D., B. Roskos-Ewoldsen, R. Francesca, and D. Carpentier. 2002. "Media Priming: A Synthesis." In *Media Effects: Advances in Theory and Research*, eds. B. Jennings and D. Zillmann, 97–120. Mahwah, NJ: Erlbaum.

Ross, J. 2007. "Deconstructing the Terrorism–News Media Relationship." *Crime, Media Culture 3*: 215–225.

Ross, J. I. 2012. "Debunking the Myths of American Corrections: An Exploratory Analysis." *Critical Criminology 20*: 409–427.

Ruddell, R. and S. Decker. 2005. "Kids and Assault Weapons; Social Problem or Social Construction?" *Criminal Justice Review 30*(1): 45–63.

Rushkoff, D. 1994. "Media: It's the Real Thing." *NPQ* (Summer): 4–15.

Russell, L. 2005. "Tabloid Tactics: Pushing Prison Reduction." *Criminal Justice Matters 59*: 32–33.

Ruva, C. and C. McEvoy. 2008. "Negative and Positive Pretrial Publicity Affect Juror Memory and Decision Making." *Journal of Experimental Psychology: Applied 14*(3): 226–235.

Ruva, C. and M. LeVasseur. 2012. "Behind Closed Doors: The Effect of Pretrial Publicity on Jury Deliberations." *Psychology Crime & Law 18*(5): 431–452.

Ruva, C., C. Guenther, and A. Yarbrough. 2011. "Positive and Negative Pretrial Publicity: the Roles of Impression Formation, Emotion, and Pre Decisional Distortion." *Criminal Justice and Behavior 38*(5): 511–534.

Sacco, V. and R. Silverman. 1981. "Selling Crime Prevention: The Evaluation of a Mass Media Campaign." *Canadian Journal of Criminology 23*: 191–201.

Sacco, V. 2005. *When Crime Waves*. Thousand Oaks, CA: Sage.

Sacco, V. and Kennedy, B. 1996. *The Criminal Event: An Introduction to Criminology*. Belmont, CA: Wadsworth.

Santa, A., and B. Cochran. 2008. "Does the Impact of Anti-Drinking and Driving Public Service Announcements Differ Based on Message Type and Viewer Characteristics?" *Journal of Drug Education 38*(2): 109–129.

Sarat, A. 2000. "Death Row, Aisle Seat." *The American Prospect 11*(7): 1–3.

Sarat, A. 2002. *When the State Kills: Capital Punishment and the American Condition*. Princeton, NJ: Princeton University Press.

Sasson, T. 1995. *Crime Talk*. Hawthorne, New York: Aldine de Gruyter.

Savage, J. 2004. "Does Viewing Violent Media Really Cause Criminal Violence? A Methodological Review." *Aggression and Violent Behavior 10*: 99–128.

Savage, J. 2008. "The Role of Exposure to Media Violence in the Etiology of Violent Behavior." *American Behavioral Scientist 51*(8): 1123–1136.

Savage, J. and C. Yancey. 2008. "The Effects of Media Violence Exposure on Criminal Aggression: A Meta-Analysis." *Criminal Justice and Behavior 35*(6): 772–791.

Schank, R. and R. Abelson. 1977. *Scripts, Plans, Goals, and Understanding*. Mahwah, NJ: Erlbaum.

Scharrer, E. 2012. "More Than 'Just the Facts'?: Portrayals of Masculinity in Police and Detective Programs Over Time." *Howard Journal of Communications 23*(1): 88–109.

Schauer, T. 2004. "Masculinity Incarcerated: Insurrectionary Speech and Masculinity." *Journal for Crime, Conflict and Media Culture 1*(3): 28–42.

Schechter, H. 2003. *The Serial Killer Files*. New York: Ballantine.

Schillinger, R. 2011, Sept. 20. "Social Media and the Arab Spring: What Have We Learned?" Sept. 20, http://www.huffing tonpost.com/raymond-schillinger/arab-spring-social-media_b_970165.html

Schlesinger, P., H. Tumber, and G. Murdock. 1991. "The Media Politics of Crime and Criminal Justice." *British Journal of Sociology 42*: 397–420.

Schultz, P. 2012. "Trial by Tweet? Social Media Innovation or Degradation? The Future and Challenge of Change for Courts." *Journal of Judicial Administration 22*(1): 29–36.

Schmid, A. and J. de Graaf. 1982. *Violence as Communication*. Thousand Oaks, CA.: Sage.

Schramm, W., J. Lyle, and E. B. Parker. 1961. *Television in the Lives of Our Children*. Stanford, CA: Stanford University Press.

Schwartz, J. 2009. "As Jurors Turn to Google and Twitter, Mistrials Are Popping Up." *The New York Times, Wed.*, March 18: A1, A18.

Schweitzer, N. and M. Saks. 2007. "The CSI Effect: Popular Fiction about Forensic Science Affects the Public's Expectations about Real Forensic Science." *Jurimetrics 47*: 357–364.

Scott-Brown, K. and P. Cronin. 2008. "Detect the Unexpected: A Science for Surveillance." *Policing 31*(3): 395–414.

Sechrest, D., W. Liquori, and J. Perry. 1990. "Using Video Technology in Police Patrol." In *The Media and Criminal Justice Policy*, ed. R. Surette, 255–264. Springfield, IL: Thomas.

Self, R. 2007. "Stewart, Martha." In *Encyclopedia of White-Collar Crime*, eds. J. Gerber and E. Jenson, 270–271. Westport, CT: Greenwood Press.

Sengupta, S. 2010., November 25. "Courts Divided Over Searches of Cellphones." *The New York Times*.

Shaaber, M. 1929. *Some Forerunners of the Newspaper in England*. Philadelphia: University of Pennsylvania Press.

Shah, R. and J. Braithwaite. 2012. "Spread Too Thin: Analyzing the Effectiveness of the Chicago Camera Network on Crime." *Police Practice and Research 1*: 1–13.

Shaheen, J. 2001. *Reel Bad Arabs*. New York: Olive Branch Press.

Shelly, J. and C. Ashkins. 1981. "Crime, Crime News, and Crime Views." *Public Opinion Quarterly 45*: 492–506.

Sheldon, B. 2011. "Camera Surveillance within the UK: Enhancing Public Safety or a Social Threat." *International Review of Law, Computers & Technology 25*(3): 193–203.

Shelton, D. 2006. "The CSI Effect: Does It Really Exist?" *National Institute of Justice Journal 259*: 1–6.

Sherizen, S. 1978. "Social Creation of Crime News." In *Deviance and Mass Media*, ed. C. Winick, 203–224. Thousand Oaks, CA: Sage.

Sherry, J. L. 2001. "The Effects of Violent Video Games on Aggression: A Meta Analysis." *Human Communication Research 27*(33): 409–432.

Sherwin, R. 2000. *When Law Goes Pop: The Vanishing Line between Law and Popular Culture*. Chicago, IL: University of Chicago Press.

Shichor, D. and D. Sechrest. 1996. *Three Strikes and You're Out: Vengeance as Public Policy*. Thousand Oaks, CA: Sage.

Shipley, W. and G. Cavender. 2001. "Murder and Mayhem at the Movies." *Journal of Criminal Justice and Popular Culture 9*(1): 1–14.

Shoemaker, P. 1991. *Gatekeeping*, Thousand Oaks, CA: Sage.

Short, E. and J. Ditton. 1996. *Does Closed Circuit Television Prevent Crime?* Monograph of The Scottish Office Central Research Unit, Edinburgh, Scotland.

Shrum L. J. 2002. "Media Consumption and Perceptions of Social Reality: Effects and Underlying Processes." In *Media Effects: Advances in Theory and Research*, eds. J. Bryant Jennings and D. Zillmann, Dolf, 69–95. Mahwah, NJ: Erlbaum.

Shuttleworth, F. and M. May. 1933. *The Social Conduct and Attitudes of Movie Fans*. New York: Macmillan.

Siegelberg, B. 2011, August 12. *"What a Copycat: Why Do We Call Imitators 'Cats'? Why Not Monkeys?"* Downloaded September 30, 2011 from www.slate.com/articles/news_and_politics/explainer/2011/08/what_a_copycat.html

Sigal, L. 1973. *Reporters and Officials*. Lexington, MA: Heath.

Signorielli, N. 2005. *Violence in the Media: A Reference Handbook*. Santa Barbara, CA: ABC-CLIO.

Silverman, J. 2012. *Crime, Policy and the Media: The Shaping of Criminal Justice, 1989–2010.* London, UK: Routledge.

Simon, B. 2005. "The Return of Panopticism: Supervision, Subjection and the New Surveillance." *Surveillance & Society* 3(1): 1–20.

Simpson, P. 2000. *Psycho Paths: Tracking the Serial Killer through Contemporary American Film and Fiction.* Carbondale, IL: Southern Illinois University Press.

Slater, M. and D. Rouner. 2002. "Entertainment-Education and Elaboration Likelihood: Understanding the Processing of Narrative Persuasion." *Communication Theory* 12(2): 173–191.

Smith, D. 2004. "Behind the Screens: Examining Construction of Deviance and Information Practices among CCTV Control Rook Operators in the UK." *Surveillance Society* 2(2/3): 376–395.

Smith, S., V. Stinson, and M. Patry. 2011. "Fact or Fiction? The Myth and Reality of the CSI Effect." *Court Review* 47: 4–7.

Snell, C., C. Bailey, A. Carona, and D. Mebane. 2002. "School Crime Policy Changes: The Impact of Recent Highly-Publicized School Crimes." *American Journal of Criminal Justice* 26(2): 269–285.

Snider, L. 2008. "Corporate Economic Crimes." In *Corporate and White-Collar Crime*, eds. J. Minkes and L. Minkes, 39–60. Los Angeles, CA: Sage.

Sorenson, S., J. Peterson-Manz, and R. Berk. 1998. "News Media Coverage and the Epidemiology of Homicide." *American Journal of Public Health* 88(10): 1510–1514.

Sotirovic, M. 2001. "Affective and Cognitive Processes as Mediators of Media Influences on Crime-Policy Preferences." *Mass Communication & Society* 4(3): 311–329.

Sparks, G. and C. Sparks. 2002. "Effects of Media Violence." In *Media Effects: Advances in Theory and Research*, ed. J. Bryant and D. Zillman, 269–285. Mahwah, NJ: Erlbaum.

Sparks, G. and R. Ogles. 1990. "The Difference between Fear of Victimization and the Probability of Being Victimized: Implications for Cultivation." *Journal of Broadcasting and Electronic Media* 34(3): 351–358.

Sparks, R. 1992. *Television and the Drama of Crime.* Buckingham, UK: Open University Press.

Spector, M. and J. Kitsuse. 1987. *Constructing Social Problems.* Hawthorne, New York: Aldine de Gruyter.

Stark, S. 1987. "Perry Mason Meets Sonny Crockett: The History of Lawyers and the Police as Television Heroes." *University of Miami Law Review* 42: 229–283.

Stark, S. 1997. *Glued to the Set.* New York: Dell.

Stelter, B. 2013, April 19. "News Media and Social Media Become Part of a Real-Time Manhunt Drama." *The New York Times.*

Stempel, C., T. Hargrove, and G. Stempel. 2007. "Media Use, Social Structure, and Belief in 9/11 Conspiracy Theories." *Journalism & Mass Communication Quarterly* 84: 353–372.

Stennett, D. 2012, September 29. "Deputies Tap iPhone App, Find Burglary Suspects Stuck in Mud," *Orlando Sentinel*, B1, B3.

Stephenson-Burton, A. 1995. "Through the Looking-Glass: Public Images of White Collar Crime." In *Crime and the Media*, eds. D. Kidd-Hewitt and R. Osborne, 131–163. London: Pluto.

Stevens, J. and H. Garcia. 1980. *Communication History.* Thousand Oaks, CA: Sage.

Sumser, J. 1996. *Morality and Social Order in Television Crime Drama.* Jefferson, NC: McFarland.

Strange, J. 2002. "How Fictional Tales Wag Real-World Beliefs." In *Narrative Impact*, eds. M. Green, J. Strange, and T. Brock, 263–286. Mahwah, NJ: Lawrence Erlbaum Associates.

Strutin, K. 2005. "No-Computer Sentencing; Bans on Internet Use as Punishment Are Under Scrutiny; Rehabilitation or Restriction; Greater than Necessary." *New York Law Journal 236*: 1–5.

Strutin, K. 2009. "Social Networking Evidence in a Self-Surveillance Society." *New York Law Journal 241*: 1–5.

Strutin, K. 2011. "Social Media and the Vanishing Points of Ethical and Constitutional Boundaries." *Pace Law Review 31*: 228–288.

Sun, S., H. Yoke, C. Hian, V. Shobha, and B. Iccha. 2013. "Managing Peer

Relationships Online—Investigating the Use of Facebook by Juvenile Delinquents and Youths-At-Risk." *Computers in Human Behavior* 29: 8–15.

Surette, R. 1986. "The Mass Media and Criminal Investigations: Crime Stoppers in Dade County, Florida." *Journal of Justice Issues* 1(1): 21–38.

Surette, R. 1989. "Media Trials." *Journal of Criminal Justice* 17: 293–308.

Surette, R. 1992. "Methodological Problems in Determining Media Effects on Criminal Justice: A Review and Suggestions for the Future." *Criminal Justice Policy Review* 6(4): 291–310.

Surette, R. 1998. "Some Unpopular Thoughts about Popular Culture." In *Popular Culture, Crime and Justice*, ed. F. Bailey and D. Hale, xiv–xxiv. Belmont, CA: Wadsworth.

Surette, R. 1999. "Media Echoes: Systemic Effects of News Coverage." *Justice Quarterly* 16: 601–631.

Surette, R. 2002. "Self Reported Copycat Crime among a Population of Serious Violent Juvenile Offenders." *Crime and Delinquency* 48(1): 46–69.

Surette, R. 2005. "The Thinking Eye: Pros and Cons of Second Generation CCTV Surveillance Systems." *Policing* 28(1) 152–173.

Surette, R. 2006. "CCTV and Citizen Guardianship Suppression: A Questionable Proposition." *Police Quarterly* 9(1): 100–125.

Surette, R. 2012, December 12. "21st Century Crime and Justice, New Media, and Maximizing Audience Participation." *Pop Culture Universe: Icons, Idols, Ideas*. ABC-CLIO. Web.

Surette, R. Forthcoming. Estimating the Prevalence of Copycat Crime: A Research Note. *Criminal Justice Policy Review*.

Surette, R. 2013. "Cause or Catalyst: The Interaction of Real World and Media Crime Models." *American Journal of Criminal Justice* 38(3): 392–409.

Surette, R. 2013. "Pathways to Copycat Crime." In *Criminal Psychology*, ed. J. Helfgott, 251–273. Santa Barbara, CA: Praeger.

Surette, R. and A. Maze. 2013. *Video Game Play and Copycat Crime:' An Exploratory Analysis of Inmate's Perspectives*. Presented at the American Society of Criminology Annual Meeting, November, Atlanta, Georgia.

Surette, R. and C. Otto. 2002. "A Test of a Crime and Justice Infotainment Measure." *Journal of Criminal Justice* 30(5): 443–453.

Surette, R. and C. Terry. 1984. "Videotaped Misdemeanor First Appearances: Fairness from the Defendant's Perspective." In *Justice and the Media*, ed. R. Surette, 305–320. Springfield, IL: Thomas.

Surette, R. and C. Terry. 1985. "Video in the Misdemeanor Court: The South Florida Experience." *Judicature* 69(1): 13–19.

Surette, R., K. Hansen, and G. Noble. 2009. "Measuring Media Oriented Terrorism." *Journal of Criminal Justice* 37: 360–370.

Sussman, P. 2002. "Media on Prisons: Censorship and Stereotypes." In *Invisible Punishment: The Collateral Consequences of Mass Imprisonment*, eds. M. Mauer and M. Chesney-Lind, 258–278. New York: The New York Press.

Sutton, A. and D. Wilson. 2004. "Open-Street CCTV in Australia: Politics and Expansion." *Surveillance and Society* 2(2/3): 310–322.

Synodinou, T. 2010. "The Media Coverage of Court Proceedings in Europe: Striking a Balance between Freedom of Expression and Fair Process." *Computer Law & Security* 28(2): 208–219.

Tajgman, D. 1981. "From Estes to Chandler: The Distinction between Television and Newspaper Trial Coverage." *Communication/Entertainment Law Journal* 3: 503–541.

Tarde, G. 1912. *Penal Philosophy*. Translated R. Howell (1912 by Little, Brown, and Co.). Reprinted 1968. Montclair, NJ: Patterson Smith.

Taylor, K. 2011, Sept. *"Arab Spring Really Was Social Media Revolution."* http://www.tgdaily.com/software-features/58426-arab-spring-really-was-social-media-revolution#QS3aL0qE3GAvw482.99

Taylor, R., E. Fritsch, J. Liederbach, and T. Holt. 2011. *Digital Crime and Digital Terrorism*. Upper Saddle River, NJ: Prentice Hall.

"The All-Seeing Eye." 1997. *The Economist* 342: 79–99 (January 11).

"They Did Everything You See in the Movie': Partying Teenagers Wreck $500,000 Home in Copycat of Hit Film Project X." 2012, March 13. http://www.dailymail.co.uk/news/article-2114450/Teenagers-accused-wrecking-500-000-home-copycat-hit-film-Project-X.html#ixzz2bmNnC7nN

"34 Arrests after Project X Harem Viral Party Degenerates into a Riot." 2013, August 12. http://www.dutchnews.nl/news/archives/2012/09/25_arrests_after_project_x_har.php

Thomas, C. 2010. "Are Juries Fair?" *Ministry of Justice Research Series 1/10*. London, UK: Ministry of Justice.

Thomas, W. I. 1908. "The Psychology of Yellow Journalism." *American Magazine* 65: 491–496.

Thomas, W. I. 1951. *Social Behavior and Personality*. Chicago: University of Chicago Press.

Thompson, A. 2010. "From Sound Bites to Sound Policy: Reclaiming the High Ground in Criminal Justice Policy-Making." *Fordham Urban Law Journal* 38(3): 774–820.

Thompson, C., R. Young, and R. Burns. 2000. "Representing Gangs in the News: Media Constructions of Criminal Gangs." *Sociological Spectrum* 20: 409–432.

Tilley, N. 1993. "Understanding Car Parks, Crime and CCTV: Evaluation Lessons from Safer Cities." *Police Research Group Crime Detection and Prevention Series*, paper no. 42. London: Home Office.

Tombs, S. 2008. "Corporations and Health and Safety." In *Corporate and White-Collar Crime*, eds. J. Minkes and L. Minkes, 18–38. Los Angeles, CA: Sage.

Tombs, S. and Whyte, D. 2001. "Reporting Corporate Crime Out of Existence." *Criminal Justice Matters* 43: 22–23.

"Trial by Media." 1984. *U.S. Press 10* (30):4.

Tucher, A. 1999–2000. "Framing the Criminal: Trade Secrets of the Crime Reporter." *New York Law School Review* 6(3–4): 905–913.

Tuchman, G. 1973. "Making News by Doing Work." *American Journal of Sociology* 79: 110–131.

Tuchman, G. 1978. *Making News: A Study in the Construction of Reality*. New York: Free Press.

Tucker, E. 2008, July, 22. *"Social Networking Puts the Bite on Defendants."* The Associated Press.

Tuman, J. 2003. *Communicating Terror: The Rhetorical Dimensions of Terrorism*. Thousand Oaks, CA: Sage.

Tunnel, K. 1998. "Reflections on Crime, Criminals, and Control in News-magazine Television Programs." In *Popular Culture, Crime, and Justice*, eds. F. Bailey and D. Hale, 111–122. Belmont, CA: Wadsworth.

Turan, N., O. Polat, M. Karapirli, C. Uysal, and S. Turan. 2011. "The New Violence Type of the Era: Cyber Bullying Among University Students: Violence Among University Students." *Neurology, Psychiatry, and Brain Research* 17(1): 21–26.

Turner, S. B. 2012. "Protecting Citizen Journalists: Why Congress Should Adopt a Broad Federal Shield Law." *Yale Law & Policy Review* 30(2): 503–519.

Tyler, T. 2006. "Viewing CSI and the Threshold of Guilt: Managing Truth and Justice in Reality and Fiction." *Yale Law Journal* 115(5): 1050–1085.

United States v. Burr, 25F, Cas 49 (C.C.D. Va. 1807) No. 14692g.

Ugland, E. 2010. "The New Abridged Reporter's Privilege: Policies, Principles, and Pathological Perspectives." *Ohio State Law Journal* 71(1): 1–70.

Useem, B. and O. Clayton. 2009. "Radicalization of U.S. Prisoners." *Criminology and Public Policy* 8(3): 561–592.

Valier, C. 2004. *Crime and Punishment in Contemporary Culture*. New York: Routledge.

Valverde, M. 2006. *Law and Order: Images, Meanings, Myths*. New Brunswick, NJ: Rutgers University Press.

"Video Game 'Sparked Hammer Murder.'" 2004. CNN.com. Downloaded from http://www.cnn.com/2004/WORLD/europe/07/29/uk.manhunt/

Vine, M. 1973. "Gabriel Tarde." In *Pioneers in Criminology*, ed. H. Mannheim, 292–304. Montclair, NJ: Patterson Smith.

Vogt, E. 2007. *Terrorists in Prison: The Challenge Facing Corrections*. Inside Homeland Security. Downloaded January 26, 2010 from http://www.nicic.org/Library/022793

Wallenius, M. and P. Raija-Leena. 2008. "Digital Game Violence and Direct Aggression in Adolescence: A Longitudinal Study of the Roles of Sex, Age, and Parent–Child Communication." *Journal of Applied Development Psychology 29*: 286–294.

Ward, M. 2010. "Video Games and Adolescent Fighting." *Journal of Law and Economics 53*(3): 611–628.

Ward, M. 2011. "Video Games and Crime." *Contemporary Economic Policy 29*(2): 261–273.

Wardell, J. 2004. "4.2 Million Cameras Keep Eye on British." *Orlando Sentinel* (August 15): B2.

Wardle, C. 2006. "'It Could Happen to You': The Move towards 'Personal' and 'Societal' Narratives in Newspaper Coverage of Child Murder, 1993–2000." *Journalism Studies 7*(4): 515–533.

Warr, M. 1991. "America's Perceptions of Crime and Punishment." In *Criminology: A Contemporary Handbook*, ed. J. F. Sheley. Belmont, CA: Wadsworth.

Warren, S. D. and L. D. Brandeis. 1890. "The Right to Privacy." *Harvard Law Review 4*(5): 193–220.

Wasserman, E. 1995. "No Big Deal: O. J. Just Another 'Trial of the Century.'" *Miami Herald* (July 18): 1A, 10A.

Webster, C. 2004. "The Evolving Diffusion, Regulation and Governance of Closed Circuit Television in the UK." *Surveillance and Society 2*(2/3): 230–250.

Weimann, G. 2006. *Terror on the Internet: The New Arena, the New Challenges.* Washington, DC: U.S. Institute of Peace Press.

Weimann, G. and C. Winn. 1994. *The Theater of Terror: Mass Media and International Terrorism.* White Plains, New York: Longman.

Weinstein, N. 1987. "Cross-Hazard Consistencies: Conclusions about Self-Protective Behaviour." In *Taking Care: Understanding and Encouraging Self-Protective Behavior*, ed. N. Weinstein, 325–336. New York: Cambridge University Press.

Weinstein, S. 1995, January 26. "The O. J. Simpson Murder Trial: Live Coverage of Trial Gives TV Ratings a 30% Boost." Jan. 26, L.A. Times. downloaded from: http://articles.latimes.com/1995-01-26/news/mn-24704_1_o-j-simpson-trial

Weiser, G. 2009. "Secret C.I.A. Jails an Issue in Terror Case." *The New York Times*, July 2: A 20. Downloaded January 25, 2010 from http://proquest.umi.com/.

Weiss, D, 2010., March 25. *FBI to Monitor Social Media to Fight 'Flash Mobs' of Roving Teens.* Mar. 25, ABA Journal online.

Weitzer, R. and C. Kubrin. 2004. "Breaking News: How Local TV News and Real-World Conditions Affect Fear of Crime." *Justice Quarterly 21*(3): 497–520.

Weitzer, R. 2002. "Incidents of Police Misconduct and Public Opinion." *Journal of Criminal Justice 30*: 397–408.

Welsh, A., T. Fleming, and K. Dowler. 2011. "Constructing Crime and Justice on Film; Meaning and Message in Cinema." *Contemporary Justice Review 14*(4): 457–476.

Welsh, B. and D. Farrington. 2002. *Crime Prevention Effects of Closed Circuit Television: A Systematic Review.* Home Office Research Study 252. London: Home Office.

Welsh, B. and D. Farrington. 2004. "Evidence-Based Crime Prevention: The Effectiveness of CCTV." *Crime Prevention and Community Safety 6*: 21–33.

Welsh, B. and D. Farrington. 2009. "Public Area CCTV and Crime Prevention: An Updated Systematic Review and Meta-Analysis." *Justice Quarterly 26*(4): 716–745.

Westfahl, G. 2013. "Bloodshed and Circuses: The Changing Nature of Violence as Entertainment." *Pop Culture Universe: Icons, Idols, Ideas.* Santa Barbara, CA: ABC-CLIO.

Wheeler, R. 2011. "Symposium Examines Courts and the New Media." *Judicature 94*(5): 239–241.

Whitaker, J. and B. Bushman. 2009. "A Review of the Effects of Violent Video Games on Children and Adolescents." *Washington & Lee Law Review, Summer 66*: 1033–1051.

Wilbanks, W. 1984. *Murder in Miami: An Analysis of Homicide Patterns and Trends in Dade County (Miami) Florida, 1917–1983.* New York: University Press of America.

Williams, C. 2003. "Police Surveillance and the Emergence of CCTV in the 1960s." In *CCTV*, ed. M. Gill, 9–22. Leicester, UK: Perpetuity.

Williams, D. 2007. "Effective CCTV and the Challenge of Constructing Legitimate Suspicion Using Remote Visual Images." *Journal of Investigative Psychology and Offender Profiling 4*: 97–107.

Williams, K. and C. Johnstone. 2000. "The Politics of the Selective Gaze: Closed Circuit Television and the Policing of Public Space." *Crime, Law and Social Change 34*: 183–210.

Willoughby, T., P. Adachi, and M. Good. 2012. "A Longitudinal Study of the Association between Violent Video Games Play and Aggression among Adolescents." *Developmental Psychology 48* (4): 1044–1057.

Wilson, B., D. Kunkel, D. Linz, J. Potter, E. Donnerstein, S. Smith, E. Blumenthal, and T. Gray. 1997. "Violence in Television Programming Overall: University of California, Santa Barbara Study, Part I.: In *National Television Violence Study: Vol. 1.* Newbury Park, CA: Sage.

Wilson, C. 2000. *Cop Knowledge*. Chicago, IL: University of Chicago Press.

Wilson, P. 1987. "'Stranger' Child-Murder: Issues Relating to Causes and Controls." *International Journal of Offender Therapy and Comparative Criminology 31*: 49–9.

Wilson, D. and S. O'Sullivan. 2004. *Images of Incarceration: Representations of Prison in Film and Television Drama*. Winchester, UK: Waterside Press.

Wilson, J. Q. and R. Herrnstein. 1985. *Crime and Human Behavior*. New York: Simon & Schuster.

Wischnowski, B. J. 2011. "Bloggers with Shields: Reconciling the Blogosphere's Intrinsic Editorial Process with Traditional Concepts of Media Accountability." *Iowa Law Review 97*(1): 327–346.

Wise. J. 2010. "Providing the CSI Treatment: Criminal Justice Practitioners and the CSI Effect." *Current Issues in Criminal Justice 21*(3): 383–399.

Wisehart, M. K. [1922] 1968. "Newspapers and Criminal Justice." In *Criminal Justice in Cleveland*, eds. R. Pound and F. Frankfurter, 515–555. Montclair, NJ: Patterson Smith.

"Woman Arrested for Killing Virtual Reality Husband." 2008. CNN.com/ technology.

Downloaded from http://www.cnn .com/2008/TECH/ptech/10/23/avatar .murder.japan.ap/index.html.

Wong, M., A. Goodboy, M. Murtagh, A. Hackney, and L. McCutcheon. 2010. "Are Celebrities Charged with Murder Likely to be Acquitted?" *North American Journal of Psychology 12*(3): 625–636.

Wood, J. 2010. "The Third Degree: Press Reporting, Crime Fiction and Police Powers in 1920s Britain." *Twentieth Century British History 21*(4): 464–485.

Wright, J., F. Cullen, and M. Blankenship. 1995. "The Social Construction of Corporate Violence: Media Coverage of the Imperial Food Products Fire." *Crime & Delinquency 41*: 20–6.

Wright, K. 2013. "Violent Entertainment, Popular Culture, and Technological Change: From the Arena to YouTube." *Pop Culture Universe: Icons, Idols, Ideas.* Santa Barbara, CA: ABC-CLIO.

Wykes, M. 2007. "Constructing Crime: Culture, Stalking, Celebrity and Cyber." *Crime, Media, Culture 3*(2): 158–174.

Yang, A., S. Tsai, C. Yang, B. Shia, J. Fuh, S. Wang, C. Peng, and N. Huang. 2012. "Suicide and Media Reporting: A Longitudinal and Spatial Analysis." *Social Psychiatry and Psychiatric Epidemiology 48*(3): 427–435.

Yar, M. 2012. "Crime, Media, and the Will-to-Representation: Reconsidering Relationships in the New Media Age." *Crime, Media, Culture 8*(3): 245–260.

Yee, N. 2006. "Motivations for Play in Online Games." *Cyberpsychology & Behavior 9*(6): 772–775.

Young, J. 1999. *The Exclusive Society*. Thousand Oaks, CA: Sage.

Zaner, L. 1989. "The Screen Test: Has Hollywood Hurt Corrections' Image?" *Corrections Today 51*: 64–66, 94, 95, 98.

Zedner, L. 2007. "Pre-Crime and Post-Criminology?" *Theoretical Criminology 11*(2): 261–281.

Zgoba, K., M. Dalessandro, B. Veysey, and P. Witt. 2008. *Megan's Law: Assessing the Practical and Monetary Efficacy*. Rockville, MD: National Institute of Justice/ NCJRS. Downloaded Jan 15, 2010 from http://www.ncjrs.gov/App/publications/ abstract.aspx?ID=247350

Index

Page numbers in bold denote pages where the terms are defined; followed by "b" indicates a boxed item; followed by "f" indicates figures; followed by "t" indicates tables.